CHRIST AND THE SPIRIT

CHRIST
AND THE
SPIRIT

SPIRIT-CHRISTOLOGY IN
TRINITARIAN PERSPECTIVE

RALPH DEL COLLE

New York   Oxford
OXFORD UNIVERSITY PRESS
1994

Oxford University Press

Oxford New York Toronto
Delhi Bombay Calcutta Madras Karachi
Kuala Lumpur Singapore Hong Kong Tokyo
Nairobi Dar es Salaam Cape Town
Melbourne Auckland Madrid

and associated companies in
Berlin Ibadan

Copyright © 1994 by Ralph Del Colle
Published by Oxford University Press, Inc.
200 Madison Avenue, New York, New York 10016

Oxford is a registered trademark of Oxford University Press, Inc.

Library of Congress Cataloging-in-Publication Data
Del Colle, Ralph.
Christ and the Spirit : Spirit-christology in trinitarian
perspective / Ralph Del Colle.
p. cm. Includes bibliographical references and index
ISBN 0-19-507776-8
1. Jesus Christ—Person and offices. 2. Holy Spirit.
3. Trinity. I. Title
BT205.D45 1994
232'.8—dc20 92-47399

1 3 5 7 9 8 6 4 2

Printed in the United States of America
on acid-free paper

To the memory of my father,
Alfred Del Colle (1919–1987),
and for my mother,
Flavia Del Colle,
with love and gratitude

Preface

This work was motivated by interests of both mind and heart. What began many years ago as a journey of the heart into the experimental and experiential dimensions of Christian faith eventually led to the theological quest for understanding. Dogmatic coherence was the focus of that quest and likewise provides the framework for this book. Theology and praxis, speculation and devotion nicely balance the life and work of the theologian, and to discover that has been the reward of this particular effort.

The Christian experience of God is one with contours that are shaped by what Irenaeus imaged as the "two hands of God." Christ and the Spirit are God's way into the depths of the human condition, the divine grip, so to speak, upon our fragile and tenuous reality. To know this, to realize that one is in the grasp of divine knowing, is the beginning of all Christian theology. My attempt in the following pages is to come to terms with that in the realm of a christology that realizes its dynamism must proceed from a robust pneumatology.

Spirit-christology has enjoyed a renaissance in recent theological efforts. As this study portrays, it may proceed in a number of directions. Two of those choices may broadly be identified as either a trinitarian or post-trinitarian trajectory. I prefer the former and argue so, but as I hope the reader will appreciate, the discussion itself is rich and worth the debate. It is often in conversation with those with whom one disagrees that the full potential for theological clarification takes place.

I am grateful for those who have had an influence upon my theological musings and maturation. Christopher Morse of Union Theological Seminary in New York has been a friend and advisor. It was the excitement and challenge of that institution and his willingness to probe the classical tradition from Aquinas to Barth for its contemporary relevance that whetted my appetite to keep that conversation going. A seminar with Paul van Buren and discussions since contributed greatly to my understanding of the possibilities for interreligious dialogue, especially Christian-Jewish dialogue.

Geoffrey Wainwright, now of the Duke University Divinity School, has been a guide in more ways then he realizes. A taste for ecumenism, Eastern Orthodoxy, and the praise of God as a source for theology were his invaluable gifts to me as well as the encouragement to explore the theological riches of my own Roman Catholic tradition. Finally, my wife, Lee Coppernoll, has been a true companion and friend, making the years of teaching and trying to complete doctoral studies pass within the day-to-day reality of exchange that is our human need for one another. Having met at Union Theological Seminary as young divinity students, she and I have experienced the blessing of traveling together a path that mindful of John Wesley's exhortation, the inspiration for her Methodist tradition, can only be had if we "adventure ourselves with [Christ]" (from his Covenant Service, Directions for Renewing Our Covenant With God, 1780).

Miami Shores, Fla.   R. D.
Pentecost 1993

Contents

CHRIST AND THE SPIRIT

Introduction

Amid the renaissance of christologies proposed by Roman Catholic theologians since the Second Vatican Council there has been an important substream that we may identify as Spirit-christology. Spirit, Spirit-orientated, pneumatological or pneumatologically orientated christologies have all been mentioned as serious options for theological reflection and construction. As an alternative christological model, Spirit-christology can be proposed as a substitute for traditional Logos-christology; but for the most part, with only slight exception, Catholic theologians have envisaged Spirit-christology as a complement to Logos-christology, hoping to enhance the older model with a much needed pneumatological element.[1] This concern for pneumatology stems from a perceived neglect (in the history of Western theology especially) of the person and work of the Holy Spirit. To be a successful theological model, spirit-christology presupposes a robust pneumatology. Once having recognized this fact, however, the theologian must face a number of important dogmatic issues that logically lead into the mystery of the trinity. A brief conspectus is in order.

Spirit-christology focuses theological reflection on the role of the Holy Spirit in christology proper. It seeks to understand both "who Christ is" and "what Christ has done" from the perspective of the third article of the creed: "I believe in the Holy Spirit, the Lord and Giver of Life." Spirit-christology addresses directly the charge that something is lacking in the church's understanding and faith if in theory and praxis the basic christological confession is not informed by pneumatology. In the realm of religious experience this points directly to the experience of the Holy Spirit as well as of God and of Christ. Confessionally this means that the third article cannot simply be an addendum to the centrality of the second article in testimony to God's saving gospel. Rather, the evangel is truly the work of God only "in the Holy Spirit."

Thus far there is nothing really new in this contention. Except for the teaching of the Pneumatomachians ("fighters against the Spirit") and the Macedonians of the fourth century, no one has really denied the soteriological necessity for the deity of the Holy Spirit and the place of pneumatology in the overall Christian confession.[2] Nor has reference to the Holy Spirit, especially in regard to ecclesiology and the Christian life, been entirely neglected. What is new and distinctive in Spirit-christology is that, on the level of theological construction and doctrinal intepretation, it proposes that the relationship between Jesus and God and the role of Christ in redemption cannot be fully understood unless there is an explicitly pneumatological dimension. In other words, the relationship between Jesus and the Spirit is as important to conveying the truth of the christological mystery with its soteriological consequences as that of Jesus and the Word. The latter without the former leads to a truncated christology and (according to the claims of some of the theologians we shall examine) one that is seriously lacking in trinitarian perspective. At its strongest, the advocates of Spirit-christology argue that anything less than a mutual reciprocity between christology and pneumatology in the articulation of what Christians mean by God, revelation, and redemption results in a diminution of the full deposit of the faith.

But what exactly is involved in this new model of christological hermeneutics and doctrinal construction? The answer can be quite broad and includes a wide spectrum of Spirit-christologies. The model may refer to the most comprehensive form of Spirit-christology—namely, that which posits Spirit as the divine element in the person of Christ. The Spirit then may be either a substitution for or identical with the divine Logos. In the former case, the displacement of Logos-christology can be understood as a proposal to reach an alternative metaphysical understanding of the operation of divinity in Jesus, one that abandons the Chalcedonian notion of one person in two natures in preference for a christology of "inspiration." In the latter case, the identity between Spirit and Logos works to revise the concept of Logos from a pre-existent divine person or mediator or that of a cosmic principle of reason or order to emphasize a more functional notion of Logos as God's activity in the world. Although taken up by at least one Catholic theologian,[3] this version of Spirit-christology does not appeal to the majority of Catholic theologians who have advocated this new christological model.

The model of Spirit-christology that more commonly informs the proposals of Catholic theologians is one that seeks to articulate the relationship between the "person" of the Holy Spirit and that of the Son in the incarnation and the work of redemption. By introducing the word "person" I presume a certain fidelity to the traditional trinitarian confession of one God in three persons. I do not at this stage mean to define or foreclose *what* is meant by the word "person" except to say that it presupposes both the unity and non-identity in God of (in the traditional language) the Father, the Son, and the Holy Spirit—e.g., the Father is God but is not the Son, and likewise for the other persons. It also does not presume *how* the "persons" are one and yet distinct; whether, for example, the distinction is predicated on the origin of the persons (as in Greek theology) or on their opposition of relations (as in Latin theology). What I do suggest is that this model of Spirit-christology, the one to which I shall devote the bulk of this study, is one that attempts to inform christology with an equally important and central pneumatology, while at the same time preserving the integrity of the doctrine of the trinity. Also, as I hope to demonstrate, this new christological model not only preserves the integrity of the aforesaid doctrine but quite profoundly enriches trinitarian faith and thus our understanding of the Christian knowledge of God.

Spirit-christology, nevertheless, for all the possibilities just suggested, is not a precisely definable christological construction. As one enters into its arena it seems various theological problems begin to multiply. When traditional dogmatic treatises were divided into tracts that separated the existence and attributes of God from the triunity of God and likewise dealt separately with the person and work of Christ and the means of sanctification through grace, the church, and the sacraments, definitions could be arrived at with precision and clarity. In the case of Spirit-christology, however, a number of these rubrics are combined into one investigation wherein the scholastic concern to make precise distinctions is sorely tested. One illustration will be sufficient, and it will form a substantial part of this study: If Spirit-christology implies that the Holy Spirit is active in the incarnation and in the work of redemption that is accomplished through the paschal mystery (remembering liturgically that the paschal season concludes with Pentecost), how does one distinguish the temporal missions of the Son and the Spirit (for the Son and the Spirit are both sent by the Father—Jn 3:17; 14:26), and furthermore, how does this distinction relate to the intra-trinitarian distinctions between the persons? Logically, Spirit-christology must be related to some theory of trinitarian construction where the unity and distinction of the divine persons has been thoroughly formulated.

Additional challenges arise from the plurality of approaches to both Spirit-christology (even if we confine ourselves to the less revisionary type) and trinitarian doctrine. In regard to the latter I have already noted how Greek and Latin theologians have traditionally differed in their trinitarian theologies and doctrines, especially in regard to the procession of the Holy Spirit (the *filioque* or monopatrism!). Such plurality is not confined to the different theologies of the Eastern and Western churches. It also surfaces in Western scholasticism. Thomas Aquinas and Bonaventure could not agree on whether the Augustinian notion of the Holy Spirit as the mutual love of the Father and the Son is sufficiently able to distinguish the Holy Spirit as a person. In addition, the confessional divisions in the Western church that resulted from the Reformation complicate matters, although the dogma of the trinity was not the direct object of doctrinal reform by the evangelical churches. Finally, the passage of the churches into the milieu of secular modernity and post-modernity raises other issues, which, if nothing else, have made competing methodologies the norm for theological discussion if not the dominating concern of many theologians.[4]

I note the above complications only to suggest what cannot be accomplished in the following pages. This is not an investigation into the history of Christian doctrine relevant to the appearance of Spirit-christology or even into the wide spectrum of Spirit-christologies today. Rather, it is an inquiry into significant dogmatic themes that Spirit-christology must address relevant to its necessary contextualization within trinitarian theology and its intensification of this basic Christian mystery. The selection of theologians is based on relevance to the issues. What now remains is a more specific delineation of these dogmatic questions.

As already intimated, the most prominent area for dogmatic inquiry is that suggested by the title of the model itself, Spirit-christology. Included is reference to Christ and the Spirit, respectively in orthodox doctrine the second and third persons of the trinity. The focus, however, one might say tends toward one of the persons more than the other. Christology and not pneumatology is the primary locus for reflection. Reference to Spirit is meant as a modifier to christology, evoking a certain type of christology. But what of pneumatology? Does this mean that pneumatology, in fact, never does get to stand on its own? Will it always be tied to, or worse yet (in the minds of some) subordinated to, christology? What is the relationship between christology and pneumatology, considered especially in light of the perceived neglect of pneumatology in the West? This will entail some dialogue with Orthodox theology and its severe criticisms of the Western church in this regard. It will be argued that such criticisms should be openly and respectfully listened to in the West but that a solution will proceed in a direction that does not entirely abandon the Western tradition of trinitarian theology. This is due not simply to the peculiar character of this tradition since Augustine, but also to the nature of pneumatology as a theology of the Holy Spirit. Here we will have to speak of the person of the Holy Spirit in trinitarian perspective. These questions and interests will be the subject of our first chapter.

The second and third chapters will direct our inquiry into a slightly different direction, but one necessary for the proposal of Spirit-christology as a cogent dogmatic construction. Here our investigation will be specific to the Roman Catholic tradition, especially its tradition of speculative trinitarian theology. We will ask the crucial dogmatic question to which Spirit-christology must eventually address itself—namely, how in the relationship between the Son and the Spirit is the distinction of persons maintained and the prospect of the model not compromised? Although the inquiry will be focused on this question, the path to it will be somewhat indirect. We will contend with the peculiar nature of Catholic theology in its modern neo-scholastic form—i.e., roughly from Vatican I to Vatican II. The issues will revolve around the emergence of a fully developed pneumatology as the condition for Spirit-christologies (even if not so named). Therefore, neo-scholastic concepts such as the nature of trinitarian missions, the propriety of trinitarian persons, and types of causality inherent in trinitarian grace will be examined. To accomplish this I in large measure work with the analysis and suggestions of David Coffey in his seminal article, "The Gift of the Holy Spirit," which served for me as both a primer and a guide into the nuances of neo-scholastic theologies of grace and the trinity.[5] This effort is intended to demonstrate the compatibility of Spirit-christology with the traditional Latin paradigm, not however with some significant debatable revisions. In Chapter 4 we will examine Coffey's own constructive proposals in detail, which in my judgment bespeak a mature Spirit-christology in trinitarian perspective, one which (as he admits) pushes beyond the boundaries of neo-scholasticism.

Chapter 5 will attempt to regroup our efforts in contemporary perspective. There we shall test this model, as it emerges and departs from the neo-scholastic tradition. Specifically, we will take up issues in related christologies that we would expect the specifically Catholic model to be able to address. These will include issues raised by christologies of presence, non-orthodox Spirit-christologies and the results of New Testament scholarship on the relationship between Christ and the Spirit.

Finally, we will examine the productivity of the model of Spirit-christology we are recommending. Specifically, by introducing three issues on the agenda of contemporary theology we will be able to test the model as to whether it sheds light on them from a dogmatic perspective. These will include the contextualization of Christian faith relevant to culture and human experience, the emancipatory concerns of social justice, and the question of religious pluralism and interreligious dialogue. This will also afford us the opportunity to return to the Catholic setting.

We recognize that, since the Second Vatican Council, neo-scholasticism is no longer the dominant theological methodology for Roman Catholic theologians. Therefore, we will also seek to discover how the legacy of that tradition in making precise distinctions will serve us well in evaluating Spirit-christology in the light of other contemporary Catholic theologies, which I describe as non-scholastic and post-scholastic. Our purpose will be to employ the criteria gleaned from the previous chapters on the relationship between Spirit-christology and trinitarian theology (with its key question on the nature of identity and distinction between Christ and the Spirit) so that we might critically assess the model of Spirit-christology in trinitarian perspective from the viewpoint of different methods of theological discourse. This will afford us enough material to conclude with some specific dogmatic judgments on the prospects of Spirit-christology. Overall, this study will advance a notion of Spirit-christology along with its dogmatic warrants that will substantiate the claim that this model of christological and pneumatological inquiry enhances the theological task of "faith seeking understanding" as one that truly is a "trinitarian faith seeking understanding."

Notes

1. The various titles listed have been proposed respectively by Philip Rosato, Joseph Wong, Yves Congar, and Walter Kasper. As the others will be referred to again, I quote only Joseph H. P. Wong, whose intention is representative: "By a 'Spirit-orientated Christology' I do not intend a Spirit Christology in place of Logos Christology." *Logos-Symbol in the Christology of Karl Rahner* (Rome: Las, 1984), p. 244, n.109. For him the alternation in terminology between 'Spirit-orientated christology' and "Spirit-christology" bespeaks this difference; the latter would substitute for Logos-christology. While appreciating his point and agreeing with his theological intent, I shall use "Spirit-christology" for the sake of brevity.

2. For a brief description of these two groups and their orthodox opponents in the Cappadocians, see J.N.D. Kelly, *Early Christian Doctrines* (San Francisco: Harper & Row, 1978), pp. 258–263.

3. See James Mackey: *The Christian Experience of God as Trinity* (London: SCM, 1983), pp. 241–251; *Jesus the Man and the Myth: A Contemporary Christology* (New York: Paulist, 1979); *Modern Theology: A Sense of Direction* (New York: Oxford, 1987), pp. 63–95, 128–130; *New Testament Theology in Dialogue: Christology and Ministry*, with James D. G. Dunn (Philadelphia: Westminster, 1987), pp. 81–102.

4. David Tracy being perhaps the most notable example of this. See especially: *Blessed Rage for Order: The New Pluralism in Theology* (New York: Seabury, 1975), *The Analogical Imagination: Christian Theology and the Culture of Pluralism* (New York: Crossroad, 1981); *Plurality And Ambiguity: Hermeneutics, Religion, Hope* (San Francisco: Harper & Row, 1987).

5. *The Irish Theological Quarterly*, 38 (1971), 202–223.

1

"The Two Hands of God:" Pneumatological Christology in the Orthodox Tradition

The Irenaean title of this chapter intentionally suggests that the work of God in the world is best understood when both the Son and the Spirit are given their proper due. The neglect of one or the other attentuates the divine economy in the faith of the church and allows Christian praxis to fall into one of two extremes: either to claim an identity without relevance or to be relevant without an identity. These two unnecessary options, decried by Jürgen Moltmann in another context,[1] are especially applicable when christology is devoid of pneumatology or pneumatology is no longer anchored in christology. If the confession of faith in Christ is the source of Christian identity, surely discernment of the Spirit guides and empowers Christian witness. Both faith and discernment are human actions, and Christ and the Spirit communicate the reality of divine grace. The relationship between these two sets is not the subject of our inquiry, but if it is difficult to imagine authentic faith without timely discernment or vice versa, then one must be equally cautious in theological reflection and doctrinal construction not to absent one of the divine hands from the other. That will be the focus of our investigation in this chapter. To put it in dogmatic language, can one do christology without pneumatology and pneumatology without christology?

Of course, the answer to the above question is yes. It has been done, and for quite some time; but at what price? To answer these questions we will begin with criticism—specifically, that criticism directed at Western and especially Roman Catholic theology by our Orthodox colleagues. Here we will try to identify the problem and then view the alternative as proposed out of the context of their own theological heritage. Only later (three chapters to be specific) will we able to pose the question whether the Orthodox model can be grafted onto the *Roman* Catholic theological tree with its own long and revered tradition of Latin patrology and scholasticism. For the moment we simply turn to the critique and its implications for Spirit-christology.

The Orthodox Criticism of Western Pneumatology

We begin by directing our attention to pneumatology rather than christology. The Orthodox Churches of the East have often reproached the Western tradition of

Catholic Christianity for neglecting to give proper attention to the third person of the Blessed Trinity. In the many different aspects of pneumatology, whether it be the liturgical life of the church, spirituality, creedal confession, or formal theology, the East has long charged that in the West the Holy Spirit has been confined to the margins of its ecclesial life and thought, or when acknowledged has been subordinated to the Son. The *Filioque* is the dogmatic symbol of this (and for some, its cause), and at its worst, one hears accusations of trinitarian christomonism, ecclesial juridicism and theological rationalism.[2] Such accusations are in my judgment overdrawn, but they do point to a certain neglect of pneumatology that many Catholic theologians are themselves not hesitant to voice. Behind these general (although harsh) criticisms are some very specific dogmatic claims that are of interest. The most salient concerns the Western conceptualization of the hypostatic being of the Holy Spirit within the trinity. For this, we turn to one of the most trenchant of Orthodox critics, Vladimir Lossky.[3]

In its most succinct terms Lossky's criticism of the Latin trinitarian model—i.e., one based on the *filioque*—is that it compromises the full equality of the third person. This needs to be explicated against the background of Orthodox theology, but first an accounting of the consequences of this charge for Christian praxis demonstrates what is at stake. Two areas are of primary practical concern. In each of the traditions these areas can be quite divergent. First is the nature of spirituality or the doctrine of sanctification.

Lossky contends that in the West spirituality and liturgy often lose their trinitarian focus. There is an excessive christocentricity, which proffers a very different goal for the Christian *in via*. Take, for example, his critique of the following expressions of life in the Spirit according to his interpretation of the Western tradition. Lossky raises the question that if the Holy Spirit's origin as a divine hypostasis within the eternal trinity is not independent of the Son, is it not true that in the path of mystical union the Holy Spirit would function only as a way to Christ? The soul of the Christian, according to this reading of Western spirituality, is to be mystically united to Christ through the medium of the Holy Spirit, this being the goal of Christian mystagogy.[4] This is not entirely true for all the Western mystical traditions—e.g., the apophatism of many English and Rhineland mystics of the late Middle Ages—but it is true that for many in the West the spiritual relationship of the believer to God is one that, as Lossky puts it, "has as its object the person of Christ, who reveals to us the divine nature."[5] Here it could be argued that the focus is not really trinitarian but binitarian, one that alternates between God and Christ. The liturgical expression of this can be seen in the "adoration of Christ's humanity," one of the most popular forms of Western piety.[6] From the *imitatio Christi* to the adoration of the Sacred Heart of Jesus and the Blessed Sacrament and the many Protestant Jesucentric pietisms the humanity of the incarnate Son seems to be more accessible to Western believers than the transcendent trinity. This emphasis mystically, spiritually, and liturgically eventually leads to the eschatological goal of the Christian life in the beatific vision whose object is the divine essence itself. In Lossky's view this combines the christocentric focus in the divine economy with an essentialist focus in the divine immanency—i.e., one that posits a knowable entity as the nature of the divine being. What is the problem?

According to the above presentation the trinitarian character of the Christian life is compromised in a manner that is alien to the Orthodox churches. In the final analysis this is not just a matter of diverse theological styles, liturgical rites, or pious practices. What is at stake theologically is our understanding in faith of the Christian revelation of God as trinity. In contrast to the christologically dominated orientation of the Western church, Lossky argues that at the forefront of Christian experience is the distinct hypostatic being of each of the trinitarian persons. Thus, in the areas noted Orthodoxy emphasizes the priority of the trinitarian persons over the divine nature, which it is argued allows for a greater prominence given to the Holy Spirit than is usually the case in the West. The mystical path, therefore, is envisaged as a union not with the incarnate Son but as a "union with God in His energies," which is a participation in the divine nature by grace.[7] This is effected by the Holy Spirit, the giver of grace. We will need to turn shortly to the subtle distinctions made by Orthodox theologians concerning the divine essence, the energies, and the hypostases so that we might fully appreciate this statement. The key point to note, however, is that the believer's relationship with the divine is consciously directed to the entire trinity. As Lossky perceives it, this presents quite a different picture as well for the eschatological goal of the Christian life than what the notion of the beatific vision implies:

> The goal of Orthodox spirituality, the blessedness of the Kingdom of Heaven, is not the vision of the essence, but, above all, a participation in the divine life of the Holy Trinity; the deified state of the co-heirs of the divine nature, gods created after the uncreated God, possessing by grace all that the Holy Trinity possesses by nature.[8]

The consequences for liturgy and doxology are also significant. Christ is the risen one, "who is is adored, always with the Father and the Holy Spirit, never separated from the Trinity."[9] Therefore, Orthodox iconography does not lend itself to images of the Savior's suffering, or to the anatomical variations of christological piety—e.g., the precious blood, the five wounds, the sacred heart, etc.—so common in Roman Catholic christological devotion. Rather, it tends to focus on the glorified and victorious Christ, even when it comes to images of the cross.[10]

Second, the ecclesiologies of the two traditions also vary. When Lossky considers the consciousness of the church from the perspective of Christian anthropology he again contrasts the Roman and Byzantine perspectives. For the former he critically elaborates on the notion that the church is "the complement of the glorified humanity of Christ, . . . a continuation of the Incarnation," so to speak.[11] If this be true, then the consciousness of the community would be directed only to the person of the Son, all other human persons within the church being absorbed into that of the God-human, he being a sort of supra-person. The shortcomings of this position are evident from both anthropological and theological perspectives. On the anthropological level diversity within the church is obscured. If the consciousness of the community is focused only on the one hypostasis of the Son of God, the tendency is toward uniformity within the church and justification for the charge by Lossky of excessive juridicism in Roman Catholicism. Theologically, in a trinitarian context, "the dispensation of the Holy Spirit, the Pentecostal aspect of the Church," is relegated to an ancillary function vis-à-vis that of Christ.[12]

Catholic theologians are not entirely blind to these dangers, especially when the ecclesiological model of the church as the mystical body of Christ is pushed to an extreme. Dominican theologian Yves Congar cautions that it can imply an ecclesio- logical monophysitism. This issue can also be raised in the light of modern papal encyclicals wherein Christ is presented as the head of the church and the Holy Spirit as its soul.[13] What place is then left for the "souls" or "persons" of its members? More accurately, however, Lossky identifies the problem as the exclusion of "poly- hypostasity" in the understanding of the church as the *communio sanctorum*.[14] The issue is not whether the divine nature absorbs the human nature of Christ (the monophysite heresy), now extended to the church as his body (except in the sense that the human element of the church is completely discounted, clearly a theological rarity), but whether the persons who are members of the church are given their full due as participants in its life by virtue of the universal anointing of the Holy Spirit. In Lossky's ecclesiology there is not simply one hypostasis, that of the glorified Christ, that is the subject of the consciousness of the church. The notion that all the members of the church are "contained as particles of His [Christ's] unique Person" and that this constitutes the church recalls for Lossky "the image of Uranus devouring his children."[15] Rather, the church is constituted by many human hypostases united in Christ's name but nevertheless with their diversity affirmed and sanctified by the Holy Spirit. Again, one could easily argue the accuracy of Lossky's presentation of the Catholic position, but the theological point is well taken especially in the interests of pneumatology.

Greek Trinitarian Theology Relative to the Latin Tradition

Preliminary Definitions

The use of the term "hypostasis" for "person" is significant. It is derived from Greek patrology, where the term designates the personal reality of God and is not quite the equivalent of the Latin *persona*, which actually translated the Greek *prosopon*. Its definition, or the difficulty of defining it, is quite important for Lossky. First of all, it is a nonconceptual term. By that Lossky means that secular philosophy cannot on the basis of reason alone provide an accurate definable understanding of its meaning as used by the Greek Fathers. It is really only understood along with its companion word *ousia* within the context of the trinitarian formula "one ousia, three hypostases." The two terms "coincide without being completely identical."[16] On the one hand, hypostasis is a synonym for ousia, for all three hypostases are the same as the divine ousia—what Lossky identifies as the "superessence" of God. On the other hand, the three hypostases are irreducible to the ousia and to one another. While a hypostasis possesses all the same attributes and negations that can be attributed to the divine essence, nevertheless it is not simply this essence except in the sense that all three hypostases are the "triunity" of God's being. Relative to one another, the hypostases are absolute in their difference as well as in their similarities. Fond of quoting St. Maximus the Confessor that "God is identically a monad and a triad,"[17] Lossky insists that the one (the ousia) and the three (the hypostases) are not arithmetical significations but ones that transcend any opposition between them insofar as the Christian confession maintains that the one equals the three and the three equal the one—God is both a "unitrinity" and a "triunity."[18] Therefore, the term "hypostasis" cannot be conceptually defined over against ousia, but simply functions as a sign "pointing out the radically personal character of Christian revelation."[19]

Conceptuality is transcended by a dialectic of affirmation and nonopposed negation. In other words, the affirmation by divine revelation of three hypostases in God is not opposed to the "negation" involved in knowledge of the mystery of God who is unknowable in the divine essence. This renders a profound apophatic structure to the trinitarian understanding of God as one who is beyond all affirmation and negation and who even transcends the opposition between "the transcendent and the immanent."[20] Indeed, it is this structure that allows the dogma of the trinity its full scope, effectively barring an essentialist doctrine of God—i.e., being able to define God as to what God is, since the divine essence remains in complete darkness to the human intellect. Positive statements about divinity are limited to the manifestation of God as trinity, which Lossky argues can only be received as "a cross for human ways of thought."[21]

Already we have been forced to try to articulate the specific nature of the trinitarian context of Orthodox theology so that we may delineate the basis for Lossky's criticism of the West's excessive Christocentrism. If the economy of the Holy Spirit is the missing factor in the Western paradigm, then this is due in Lossky's judgment to the Holy Spirit's subordination in the trinity, which is the product of its filioquist construction. How can the Holy Spirit be fully recognized in the economy of God if within the trinity its relationship of origination from the Father is also made dependent on the Son? What is the relationship between the Holy Spirit in God and the Holy Spirit in the work of God? In order to answer these questions we must say something about the distinction the Greek Fathers (and Lossky following them) make between "theology" and "economy."

The distinction is simple and one not completely unknown in the West. Theology proper concerns the divine being itself, God as the holy trinity. Economy refers to the exterior manifestations of God in the world in relationship to created being.[22] Its closest analogue in Western theology is the distinction made respectively between the immanent and the economic trinities. However, the similarity cannot be overdrawn. Here, a brief excursus is helpful.

Excursus on Karl Rahner's Doctrine of the Trinity

Ever since the publication of the Catholic theologian Karl Rahner's short book, *The Trinity*, much has been made of his fundamental axiom: "*The 'economic' Trinity is the 'immanent' Trinity and the 'immanent' Trinity is the 'economic' Trinity.*"[23] While the axiom itself would seem to contradict the absoluteness of the distinction made between the two sets of trinitarian realites—immanent and economic in the West, theology and economy in the East—the intent behind Rahner's axiom coincides with an aspect of the Orthodox construction that is not included in its Western counterpart. It serves to highlight the difference between the two traditions and will help us to elaborate the crucial disparity in their pneumatologies as well.

The Western distinction presupposes that in the difference between the immanent and economic trinity the relationship between the *ad intra* eternal processions and the *ad extra* temporal missions is not governed by necessity. In other words, even though Thomas Aquinas understood a trinitarian mission as an "eternal procession, with the addition of a temporal effect,"[24] the relationship between the person sent and the person sending in the trinity is not absolutely determined by the *ad intra* relations. St. Thomas makes the point in another article of the same *quaestio* of the *Summa Theologiae* that a person may be missioned by another person within the trinity who is not the intra-trinitarian principle of the person sent. In this case the basis of the sending is understood not in the relationship between the persons by way of the origin of the processions but in terms of the principle of the effects of the mission relative to created reality. The example he uses is that of the Son's mission in the incarnation, which is predicated on a sending not only by the Father but also by himself and the Holy Spirit.[25] This rules out any absolute correlation between *ad intra* processions and *ad extra* missions, since while it is true that the Son proceeds from the Father by way of generation there is certainly no procession of the Son from himself or the Holy Spirit (in fact, quite the opposite in light of the *filioque*). However, when the effects of the mission are considered—in this case, the assumption of human nature in the incarnation—then the eternal Son and the Holy Spirit can be considered as "senders," the former as one who from eternity chose to come forth from the Father[26] and the latter as the one through whom the Son became incarnate—i.e., *conceptus de Spiritu Sancto*.

It is against this background that the innovation represented by Rahner's axiom becomes clear. He, in fact, is suggesting that there is a necessary continuity between an *ad intra* procession and an *ad extra* mission. This in no way compromises in his view the freedom of God in creating and redeeming the world, a charge often made against his proposal.[27] Rahner is not disputing the utterly free act of God in sending the Son and the Spirit into the world. It is not as if the generation of the Son and the spiration of the Spirit are constituted by the economic relationship of God to the non-divine. Rather, he is arguing that the revelation of the Son and the Spirit in the divine economy reveal that God is indeed triune in the divine being itself, and this in such manner that is conceptually consistent. This would rule out the hypothetical possibility that a mission could entail a person being sent without any correlation with an intra-trinitarian procession. Such a possibility (affirmed by Aquinas in another *quaestio* when he allows the possibility for any of the three persons to have become incarnate—*ST* IIIa, 3, 5) in Rahner's view would introduce a conceptual break between God revealed and God in the divine being. It is safer and more cogent dogmatically to proceed on the principle of what actually is revealed rather than on the basis of hypotheticals that make the doctrine of the trinity only a matter of words ("a merely verbal revelation").[28] This latter option would be in contrast to his own thesis, which builds on the real relationship between the threefold differentiation in the divine economy and in the divine immanency.

The above summary also relates to another point concerning Rahner's proposal that is important to note before we return to the Orthodox distinction between theology and economy. Rahner's understanding of revelation is represented by the notion of the divine self-communication. In other words, revelation is not simply

words about God, and grace is not only the supernatural elevation of human nature
by created sanctifying grace, as in traditional scholasticism. Rather, in the event of
revelation and grace, God communicates the divine being to the creature as its own
fulfillment and is present to the creature in a manner that is intrinsic and constitutive
so that the creature may personally and immediately know and love God. In traditional Thomistic theology created grace as a supernatural created entity is prior to
uncreated grace, which is the presence of the divine persons.[29] Therefore, knowledge
of the divine persons is the consequence of the elevation of the human faculties in
knowledge and love. Rahner, on the other hand, conceives the knowledge of God
as based upon the experience of grace on the order of an ontological self-communication of God's triune being. More explicitly trinitarian, Rahner's construct envisages the Father as communicating the divine being in the missions of the Son and
the Holy Spirit, so that the latter two persons are not self-communications of divinity
in addition to the Father, but the two modalities of the one divine self-communication
of the Father.[30] This substantial difference between the two positions also relies on
the explication of different types of causality in the theology of grace. We shall return
to this in a later chapter. For the moment, we conclude this excursus on the different
positions of traditional Thomism and Karl Rahner by quoting William Hill's accurate
summary of the variance between them:

> Once energized with a created participation in God's own nature, the soul [accord-
> ing to traditional Thomism] is then able to relate to the uncreated Persons precisely
> as distinct subject-terms of its own knowing and loving. This is in marked contrast
> with Rahner's explanation wherein distinct relations to the Three in God are
> achieved in the ontic order prior to all knowing and loving.[31]

What relevance has this account for the Orthodox distinction between theology
and economy? A number of issues surface in the Western debate that are not a
problem for the East. For the latter this implies a more direct relationship to the
divine persons without the mediation of a created (albeit supernatural) entity, such
as created sanctifying grace. When the Greek Fathers distinguished between theology
and economy it is true, as it is in the West, that the divine being is considered either
in itself or in its activity in the work of creation, providence, and the temporal
missions of the Son and the Holy Spirit in redemption. However, it is not the case
that to posit an ontological participation in the divine nature one needs to adopt the
axiom proposed by Karl Rahner. It is the peculiarity of the Orthodox doctrine of the
trinity that such participation is strongly affirmed while at the same time theology
and economy are radically distinguished. The basis for this resides in the distinction
the Orthodox draw between the essence and energies of God. For this Lossky and
most other Orthodox theologians have utilized and developed the theology of St.
Gregory Palamas (1296–1359), Archbishop of Thessalonica.

Palamite Distinctions

The doctrine of the uncreated energies of God is derived from the premise that in
God there is an ineffable distinction between what is communicable and what is
incommunicable, between the divine essence or nature properly so-called, and the

"energies of divine operation," which, going forth from God, manifest, communicate, and impart the divine being to created reality.[32] The distinction preserves the apophatic structure of the Orthodox doctrine of God, ensuring that the divine essence is not only incommunicable but unknowable as well. This would meet the concerns of traditional Thomists who oppose Rahner's axiom on the basis that an identity between the economic and immanent trinities limits the freedom of God and therefore compromises the divine transcendence (although the knowability of the divine essence is still a serious point of disagreement between Thomists and Palamites). On the other hand, the Orthodox doctrine also identifies with the Rahnerian assertion that in the divine economy God communicates the uncreated divine being to humanity. According to Palamas, the communication of deifying grace is not the communication of a "created" supernatural entity but the communication of divinity itself. Specifically, it is the "uncreated" energy of God's own being proceeding from the divine essence (thus preserving the notion of divine simplicity even in the paradox of the ineffable distinction between the two) and in which God is wholly present as Father, Son, and Holy Spirit (what Palamas characterizes as "hypostatic energies"). Eventually this lays the groundwork for the strong pneumatological character of Orthodox soteriology and christology. But a few more important distinctions are in order.

First, one notes that what splits the Thomistic and Rahnerian interpretations is here held together. Both the transcendence and freedom of God are maintained in the inaccessibility and unknowability of the divine essence. So too, the priority of "uncreated grace" (scholastic terminology) and the "divine self-communication" (Rahnerian terminology) is upheld. One participates in the divine nature so that one is deified (the characteristic model for the Orthodox doctrine of sanctification) by being united to God through the uncreated divine energies. This is not a union with the divine essence (which is inaccessible), nor is it a union with the divine persons. Rather, it is a union with God in the divine energies that distinguishes this type of union from those appropriate to the union between a divine person and a created nature—e.g., the hypostatic union, or the substantial union of the three persons in the one divine nature. The union with God in the divine energies therefore is a deification of the creature by grace, in all respects a "becoming God" except for the identity of nature.[33]

Second, having preserved the distinction between God and the creature in the type of union effected by deifying grace, the doctrine of the uncreated energies also provides an important link between what the West describes as the economic and immanent trinities; here we return to the non-equivalence of this terminology with the Eastern "theology and economy." The energies are not simply the relation of God to the world. They are "natural" processions of divine forces flowing from the essence of God and that are inseparable from it.[34] This distinguishes them from the three hypostases, which are "personal" processions. The energies in particular manifest the glory of the divine being both *ad intra* and *ad extra*. The energies, therefore, occupy a middle ground between theology and economy. They exist independently of the creative act by which the non-divine is brought into existence; yet they are also the means by which God is externally related to the world. The *ad extra* acts of creation and redemption, it should be noted, are predicated solely on the divine will; this rules out, therefore, any neo-platonist theory of emanation as the basis for the divine operations *ad extra*. In addition, since the energies eternally flow from the divine essence, they cannot be separated from the three hypostases in either theology or the economy, although they are not identical to them. The energies manifest that the triune God who exists in the divine essence also exists outside of it. In a profound sense, with a view toward the divine economy, God—Father, Son, and Holy Spirit—whose ecstatic being is manifested to itself by virtue of the uncreated energies in theology proper, is also communicated to the world by means of creation "by" these energies and redemption "in" the energies, the latter signifying human participation in the divine nature—i.e., its deification through grace.[35]

When we turn to pneumatology proper, another very important distinction must be noted in the Orthodox doctrine that also sets the parameters for its version of pneumatic christology. The difference that exists between the divine essence and the divine energies also exists between the energies and the hypostases. As already stated, they are not identical. However, it is through the energies that the three hypostases are active in the divine economy, although not as three separate agents but as the one operation of God, possessing one common will. In one sense, the energies as the exterior manifestation of God (now extended to the divine economy) reveal the pluriform attributes of God—e.g., wisdom, power, justice, life, love, etc. These, however, are not identical with the hypostases. Therefore, this excludes the characterization of the Son and the Spirit as the divine hypostases who know and love, an attribution common to the psychological model of the trinity suggested by Augustine and refined by Aquinas; Lossky disparages this as "trinitarian psychologism".[36] The triune God is, it should be emphasized, wholly present within the energies and in a manner in which the distinction of persons is evident. The three persons as "hypostatic energies," posterior to the divine essence but communicating the very being of God, manifest in common the various divine attributes according to this patristic formula: from the Father through the Son in the Holy Spirit. Each person possesses the attribute in a distinct manner according to its own hypostasis. Thus, Lossky can summarize the working of the divine economy with respect to the revelation of the hypostases in the energies:

> In this dispensation, in which the Godhead is manifested in the energies, the Father appears as the possessor of the attribute which is manifested, the Son as the manifestation of the Father, the Holy Spirit as He who manifests.[37]

Lossky's interpretation of the formula is an intriguing one for it demonstrates the strong pneumatological emphasis within Orthodoxy—"the Holy Spirit . . . manifests"—and presupposes the basis in the Eastern doctrine for the intra-trinitarian distinction of the persons. To that we now turn. We will begin by way of contrast with the West.

Excursus on Latin Scholastic Trinitarian Categories

The Latin construction for the doctrine of the trinity distinguishes the persons on the basis of this formula: *In Deo omnia sunt unum, ubi non obviat relationis oppositio*— In God all is one except wherever the opposition of relation does not stand in the way. It posits that relative to the divine essence the only thing distinguishing the coequal persons of the trinity is their opposition of relation. At this point it is worth our while to explicate the logic of this formula. This demands another excursus with some attention to definitions and distinctions. However, it will serve in our attempt to understand the basis of Lossky's criticism of the West and will help clarify the dogmatic ground for the differing pneumatologies in the two traditions. We will then be able to return to our exposition of the relationship between pneumatology and christology in the East and examine why the West in its recovery of Spirit-christology is forced down another path.

The scholastic and especially Thomistic doctrine of the trinity rests upon the precision of a number of important distinctions. Before defining them, it is necessary to stress that the formalities proposed by the scholastics articulate the Thomistic insight that the trinitarian persons exist as "subsistent relations" within the one divine nature. This is meant to express the basic truth of the dogma of the trinity which is common to both East and West—namely, that of identity and non-identity in the triadic confession. Specifically, the three persons or hypostases are one (hence identity) and yet three (hence non-identity)—e.g., the Father is God and the Son is God but the Father is not the Son, and so, too, for all the other relations between the persons. The difference resides in the interpretation of how these relations are determined. The East prefers "relations of origin" or "relations of diversity" as the defining mode of differentiation among the divine persons, while the West chooses "opposition of relations." We turn first to the Western explication of the issues.

The doctrine of the trinity in Latin scholasticism owes more to the *De Trinitate* of St. Augustine than to any other Church Father. His psychological analogy of trinitarian relations has been one of the most influential proposals in the history of Western theology. It also underscores the entirely different approach adopted by the East. Augustine pursues primarily two lines of thought in his effort to distinguish the persons of the trinity. In addition to the psychological model just mentioned, he also proposed what may be termed a personalist model. This latter model, to which we shall return when we examine how a contemporary theologian attempts to recapitulate Augustine's effort in the light of a pneumatologically oriented christology, has its own trajectory in Western theology as well. Following the work of Betrand de Margerie, we may identify these two models as presenting two streams within the history of scholastic trinitarian speculative theology that were eventually synthesized by Thomas Aquinas. The psychological or essentialist model of personal intra-subjectivity utilizes the self-presence of the human spirit in knowledge and love as the analogy for the intra-trinitarian relations. Its path to Aquinas can be traced through Anselm, whereas the personalist model, which portrays the Holy Spirit as the mutual love of the Father and the Son, reached the Angelic Doctor through Richard of St. Victor.[38] Both models and the tension that arises in the effort to reconcile them are dependent on another term that we have hitherto used but not defined—namely, the concept of relation. Since the crux of the difference in trinitarian theology between East and West concerns the nature of relations, we shall reserve for a later chapter a discussion of the different Augustinian models of intra-trinitarian relations and their importance for Spirit-christology within the Catholic tradition. Here we shall concentrate on the difference between the more or less established Latin scholastic paradigm of these relations and that of Orthodox theology and their consequences for the relationship between christology and pneumatology.

It is only recently in the history of philosophy that the concept of relation has acquired some degree of metaphysical density—e.g., especially in process thought. In classical metaphysics, dominated by an ontology of substance, relation simply indicates the reference of a subject to another term (*respectus ad alterum*). It evokes no positive reality in and of itself.[39] Therefore, when it was utilized by the Cappadocians in the context of trinitarian theology, not only would the meaning of the term change but it would foreshadow a new advance in the understanding of the identity and distinction of the divine persons. The ground for this had already been prepared by the hard won efforts of Basil of Caesarea to distinguish hypostasis from ousia in the formula *treis hypostaseis en mia ousia*. Gregory of Nazianzus replied to the Arian criticism that if the Father signified either the essence or action of God, the Son could not be his equal in deity, with the following:

> O men so subtle! The name of the Father signifies neither essence nor action but it indicates a relation, that which the Father has towards his Son or the Son towards his Father.[40]

Gregory introduced a mediating concept between essence (or ousia) and person (or hypostasis).

In the West, beginning with Augustine (we shall return to the East shortly), relation functioned as an ideal middle term between the Aristotelian categories of substance and accident. Since nothing in God can be an accident and since to identify the persons as substance would be to negate their difference—except in the case of Arianism and Semi-Arianism where respectively the Son and the Spirit cease to be God—then relation designates that aspect of the divine being that is neither substance nor accident. The persons are not distinguished by their substance, for that exists *ad se* and is identical. They are differentiated by their relationships which exist *ad alterum* and are therefore not identical. The meaning of the terms "Father" and "Son" can be understood only in relation to one another—i.e., the Father is such because he has a Son and the Son is such because he has a Father. They are essentially relational terms of paternity and filiation; without each other they have no meaning. The category of relation, then, in the words of de Margerie "allows us to safeguard the plurality of hypostases in God without in any way denying the perfect unity of essence."[41]

There is another aspect of relation which is likewise significant for the further development of trinitarian doctrine. I stated previously that in classical philosophy the concept of relation does not bear any metaphysical or ontological density. A substance may exist in relation to another substance, but its being is not constituted by the relation. A human being, for example (in Aristotelian-Thomistic terms a composite substance having both a soul and body), exists in relation to other human beings, but its own act of being derives from the Creator, not from those relations. Therefore, in their primary substance human beings are unique and different by virtue of their independent acts of existence, while in their secondary substance—i.e., their quiddity or essence—they share the same human nature. In the case of the divine persons or hypostases the situation is quite different. Since their differentiation is not predicated on their substance (otherwise, we would end up in tritheism), we have said that it is determined by relation. Here is where the category of relation (taken from the realm of creaturely existence, as all philosophical and theological concepts are) truly functions as a theological analogy.

The General Council of Lateran IV (1215) stated: *inter creatorem et creaturam non potest similitudo notari quin inter eos maior sit dissimilitudo notanda*—one cannot note a likeness between creature and Creator without having to note a still-greater unlikeness. In God the divine persons not only exist in relation (as do human persons) but are constituted by relation (unlike human persons). Relation is the reality of the distinction of persons in the unity of the divine essence. Dissimilar to created reality, the non-identity predicated on relation in the divine being—e.g., the Father is not the Son and the Son is not the Father—does not entail non-identity in the absolute term of the divine essence; so therefore the Father is God, the Son is God, and the Holy Spirit is God. Finally, the relative terms in God—the Father, Son, and Holy Spirit—since they are identical with the divine nature or essence are bearers of the one divine being in the distinctiveness of their hypostatic persons, what Aquinas identifies as subsistent relations. In other words, relations in God do not lack metaphysical density. Their being subsists in the divine nature by virtue of their hypostatic identity, differentiating them from one another.

The utilization of the category of relation is shared by both Latin and Greek theology, although it occupies a more dominant place in the former than in the latter. What is peculiar to the Latin tradition is the prominence of relation as the determinative principle for distinguishing the trinitarian persons relative to the divine essence. This requires a fuller exposition of the various scholastic categories by which this is accomplished. Here we shall be brief and simply summarize what a typical neo-scholastic manual proposes in this area, based as most of them were on the work of Thomas Aquinas.[42] We shall then return to the Orthodox exposition of the issues and conclude with some theses on the challenge presented to the traditional Latin paradigm by the Eastern tradition and their implications for the development of Spirit-christology.

A series of terms require definition. The explication of these will clarify the basic structure of the traditional Latin scholastic paradigm of the doctrine of the trinity. We shall simply list the various terms and then define them: processions, relations, persons, properties, notions, appropriations, and missions.

Procession refers to the generic origin of one person from another through the communication of the numerically one divine essence.[43] I say generic because it covers the two internal divine processions (*processio ad intra* and *per immanans*) that in the language of the Nicene-Constantinopolitan Creed are respectively the begetting of the Son and the procession of the Holy Spirit. This already makes for some conflict with the Greek tendency to strictly limit the use of the word "procession" (*ekporeuesthai*) to the latter. The issue is clear. For the Latins *processio* does not in and of itself distinguish between the two, whereas for the Greeks begottenness (or generation) and procession are two different relations of origin from the Father. As will become clear later the Orthodox have never considered it particularly necessary to inquire beyond this biblical distinction (Jn 1:14; 15:26) or to explore the inner depths of God in order to define the difference between the two.

Relation, which I have already discussed to some extent, is understood as "the ordination of one thing to another (*respectus unius ad alterum*)" and is the basis for the distinction of persons in the Godhead.[44] They are consequent upon the processions and number as four "real" relations in God (as distinct from purely mental or logical relations, true in human conceptuality but not really distinct in the divine being). The relations and their reference to the specific divine persons are the following:

> a) the relationship of the Father to the Son: the active generation or paternity (*generare*); b) the relationship of the Son to the Father: the passive generation or filiation (*generari*); c) the relation of the Father and of the Son to the Holy Ghost: the active spiration (*spirare*); d) the relation of the Holy Ghost to the Father and to the Son; the passive spiration (*spirari*).[45]

Of these four, three (paternity, filiation, and active spiration) are really distinct relations in God, meaning that they stand in opposition to one another. Active spiration entails no opposition beyond that of passive spiration. It does not distinguish paternity from filiation. Therefore, it is only a virtual distinction in God, i.e., it is equivalent to a real distinction but only by effect, not in fact. Needless to say, this is due to the reception of the *filioque* in the Western version of the common symbol of Nicaea-Constantinople. This observation alerts us to the decisive role of pneumatology in these trinitarian constructions with which any version of Spirit-christology must contend.

The three mutually opposite relations constitute the *three persons* (or *hypostases*) of the Godhead. In addition to what was stated above concerning the three persons as subsistent relations, we reiterate that the persons are identical with the divine essence and non-identical with each other. The former rules out any quaternity in God (as if the essence is a fourth in God absolutely distinct from the three hypostases) and the latter underscores the incommunicability of each hypostasis. The relationship between the essence and persons may be described as follows. As subsistent relations the divine persons are the subject of being in God (*principium quod*—the basis which), while the divine essence or nature is that through which they act (*principium quo*—the basis by which).[46]

A *property* is exclusively attributed to a divine person and distinguishes it from the other two persons in the Godhead. There are four such properties, three of which are personal or person-forming properties: paternity, filiation, and passive spiration. These three are respectively predicated of the Father, the Son, and the Holy Spirit. The fourth, innascibility, is a distinguishing property (not personal or person-forming because it does not entail any relation) which in negative terms expresses the originlessness of the Father and is exclusive to the first person—the Son being in a relation of origin to the Father through passive generation and the Spirit to the Father and the Son through passive spiration.[47] This formality will be especially important in later chapters where it will be extended to the concept of mission defined below.

Notions are the distinctive characteristics by which the persons are known. These factually coincide with the properties and are sometimes identified as notional properties. Along with the previous category it will be noted that active spiration is not included because it is a relation shared by both the Father and the Son (according to the *filioque*) and therefore does not distinguish them as persons. This category will also figure significantly later, since one can distingush between notional acts in God and essential acts. The former are those acts that are predicated only of the persons, while the latter are those predicated of God in the divine nature without any distinction of persons. Although notional and essential acts are factually identical, they are virtually distinct in God.[48] When we return to the psychological analogy of intra-trinitarian distinctions we will have to ask whether the divine knowing and loving (correlated respectively with the processions of the Son and the Spirit) are essential or notional acts. This will help determine whether an orthodox Spirit-christology—i.e., one in which the Son and Spirit are still distinguished as persons—can be cogently associated with this model of intra-trinitarian relations.

Appropriation is a mode of predication in which the activity of God *ad extra* that is common to all three persons can on the basis of a similiarity between the activity and the property of a person be non-exclusively attributed to one of the persons.[49] It presupposes the scholastic formula *omnia opera Trinitatis sunt indivisa*—all the works of the trinity are undivided. Again, this category is important for our further inquiry. The question will arise in coordination with our next category as to whether appropriation theory is sufficient to distinguish the trinitarian persons in the divine economy.

Finally, many of the concerns expressed will converge on our understanding of *mission*. The divine missions are specifically missions *ad extra* and are two in number. They refer to the mission of the Son and the mission of the Holy Spirit in the economy of divine redemption. They are "temporal" missions in that they take place in time and are distinguished from the "eternal" processions described above in the definition and in our discussion of Karl Rahner's trinitarian axiom. The question in the latter discussion concerned the relationship between the two. We will return to that question in light of the Thomistic affirmation that a mission comprises the following two elements:

> a) a relation between the one sent and the sender as (*terminus a quo*) . . . b) a relation between the one sent and the object of the mission (*terminus ad quem*).[50]

At which of these points do the temporal missions reflect the notions of the divine persons, especially if we abide by this additional Thomistic affirmation?

> The Father sends only, but is not sent; the Son is sent and sends. The Holy Ghost is sent only, but does not send.[51]

In addition, we will also have to discuss the difference between visible and invisible missions. In usual scholastic nomenclature a visible mission includes the sensible perception of the person sent, either that of the Word in the incarnation (*missio substantialis*) or the Holy Spirit at Pentecost under the symbols of the dove and tongues of fire (*missio repraesentativa*). An invisible mission refers to the bestowal of sanctifying grace (sanctification) and the indwelling of God in the souls of the just (the divine inhabitation).[52] Whether or not this latter is ascribed to the Holy Spirit (or to the Son as well) and that by either appropriation or propriety, is one of our major questions. This will also include reference to the trinitarian perichoresis, or the reciprocal indwelling of the divine persons in one another. Latin scholasticism has translated this Greek patrological term by either *circumincessio* (emphasizing the Greek understanding of active penetration of the persons in one another) or *circuminsessio* (emphasizing the Latin idea of passive coinherence of the persons in one another).[53]

As it appears in this all too schematic summary, the Latin scholastic approach to trinitarian theology focuses on the logical explication of the basic principle that the divine persons are distinguished by their opposition in relation. It is a coherent paradigm, and on its own terms it maintains the integrity of trinitarian dogma, which must account for the identity of the persons with the divine nature and their non-identity with each other. I have noted in the summary the points at which controversy will arise when the elements of Spirit-christology are addressed within the context of this paradigm. To repeat, they will include the application of "property" and "notions" to the revelation of the divine persons in the temporal "missions." This will call into question the adequacy of "appropriation" theory in this regard. The broader question will investigate the relationship of intra-trinitarian "relations" and "processions" to the divine work *ad extra*.

The Basis of Orthodox Trinitarian Distinctions

When we turn to the Orthodox theology of intra-trinitarian distinctions, it is clear that the Latin model is quite foreign to its own trinitarian logic. In fact, this often leads to a misreading of the Latin position. For example, Lossky consistently and inaccurately renders the classic *relationis oppositio* as a "relation of opposition" rather than an "opposition of relation."[54] As Yves Congar has noted, this accentuates for Lossky an interpretation of the Latin position that seems to give priority to the divine essence before the distinction of persons,[55] a charge frequently made by Lossky and other Orthodox critics. Beside this accusation that Latin triadology posits "a pre-eminence of natural unity over personal trinity, as an ontological primacy of the essence over the hypostases," it also lays down the more serious indictment that "the origin of the persons of the Trinity therefore is impersonal."[56] Here we are at the heart of the matter. We may state it in the form of two questions that indicate the major problem for an orthodox Spirit-christology in the Western tradition: (1) How are the Son and the Holy Spirit adequately distinguished in the trinity so that the proper hypostatic character of the latter is fully revealed in the divine economy? (2) Where does the Holy Spirit figure in a christological construction that is thoroughly pneumatological without confusing the third person with the Son/Word? As we shall now see such problems do not arise for Orthodox pneumatology which because of its own unique character—based on its quite different paradigm of intra-trinitarian distinctions—lends a distinctly pneumatological cast to christology as well.

As Lossky points out, the concept of relation is important but not decisive for intra-trinitarian distinctions. Relations are not the cause of the distinctions but only their manifestation. They "serve to *express* the hypostatic diversity of the Three; they are not the basis of it."[57] This change of perspective, relative to that of the Latin position, cannot be overestimated. It entirely transforms how one proceeds theologically to articulate the ordering of the persons to one another. I have already noted the rubric for the Orthodox variation on the distinctions in the immanent trinity, "relations of origin" or "diversity" as contrasted to the Latin preference for the "opposition of relations." The Byzantine position can be narrowed down to two major differences with the Latin one: the monarchy of the Father and the greater emphasis given to what the Latin church considers as personal properties.

For the Orthodox, the Father alone (monopatrism) is the source of the eternal generation of the Son and the eternal procession of the Holy Spirit.[58] Therefore, the relations of origin between the two processions (using the term generically in Latin fashion) and the Father are absolutely differentiated and ineffable. There is no opposition of relations between the persons as is the case, for example, between the Spirit and the Son in the Latin filioquist construction. There the Spirit is distinct from the Son because it proceeds from the Son, an opposition of relation, not because the nature of their processions from the Father can distinguish them from each other. The Orthodox argue that the generation of the Son and the procession of the Spirit (both from the Father alone) are ineffably distinct because the persons are absolutely differentiated by their personal properties. One begins with this diversity—namely, the Father is without beginning, the Son is begotten, and the Spirit proceeds. It is this personal diversity that is the "primordial fact" of God's triune being, which because of the monarchy of the Father is also the basis for its unity in the divine essence. The latter is affirmed by the consubstantiality (homoousios) of the Son and the Spirit with the Father, from whom they derive the divine essence. He is the principle of their common possession of the essence, and it is to be noted that this origin is personal, not an impersonal one differentiated only by relation.[59] It is difficult in many passages of Lossky's work to distill his constructive exposition of the Greek Fathers from his implicit and explicit polemic against Latin theology. From Augustine onward, even in the filioquist doctrine of the Spirit's procession from the Father and the Son, the word *principaliter* has always been attributed to the Father to emphasize that the Son derives the property of active spiration from the first person. Also, whether the property of innascibility, which is exclusive to the Father, is conceived in strictly negative ("having his being from no one else"—Aquinas) or also in positive ("having the ability to give being to another"—Bonaventure) terms, the West has always affirmed that the Father is the absolute source of divinity (*fontana deitas* or *fons et origo divinitatis*), as Congar is patient to point out.[60] While agreeing with Congar that a careful and irenic reading of both Greek and Latin traditions not only does not prevent but indeed enhances the mutual recognition of the same trinitarian faith in the two traditions,[61] our concern in accentuating the difference is to point out that the task of establishing a pneumatological christology in the West takes on a different complexion and difficulty than what the East proffers rather easily. This is clearly evident when, after elucidating these important differences in trinitarian theology, we turn directly to the relationship between pneumatology and christology.

Orthodox Pneumatological Christology

A pneumatological christology in the Eastern tradition respects all the contours of its trinitarian theology. These include the distinction between theology and economy and the independent origin of the Holy Spirit from the Father. The former distinction ensures the cogency of the latter without reservation. It is common for the Greek Fathers when discussing the divine economy to speak quite strongly of the relationship between the Son and the Holy Spirit. Reference to the procession of the Holy Spirit "through the Son" (*dia Hiou; per filium*) must not be taken, however, for a moderated version of the *filioque*. The procession of the Holy Spirit from the Father alone (monopatrism) and from the Father through the Son (*per filium*) bespeaks respectively the hypostatic origin of the third person and the manifestation of the Spirit, "after the Word . . . [which] reveals to us the common glory of the Three, the eternal splendor of the divine nature."[62] The two should not be confused as neither should the essence and the energies of God nor theology proper and economy. Recalling that the divine energies are the means by which divinity is manifested, including the revelation of God in the divine economy, the Orthodox (and especially Lossky) simultaneously maintain a hierarchical relationship (not one, however, that implies subordination) between the Son and the Spirit in creation and redemption— i.e., "after the Word"—and the monopatristic structure of hypostatic origination. This has two beneficial results for pneumatological christology. First, it orders the work of the Holy Spirit to that of the Son. Second, it strongly affirms an independent proper mission of the Holy Spirit in the divine economy. We shall explore each in turn, but already it is evident that an Orthodox pneumatological christology will derive its strength from a viable and robust pneumatology.

The manifestation of the Holy Spirit "after the Word" points to a common problem that afflicts all pneumatology, both East and West. In comparison to the revelation of the Son the revelation of the Holy Spirit is always more obscure. It is not insignificant that St. Gregory of Nazianzus argued that recognition of the divinity of the Holy Spirit had to await clarification of the consubstantiality of the first two persons of the trinity:

> The Old Testament announces the Father clearly and the Son obscurely. The New Testament has manifested the Son but it has only indicated the divinity of the Holy Spirit. At present, the Spirit is among us and shows himself in all his splendor. It would not have been prudent, before one recognized the divinity of the Father, to preach openly the divinity of the Son, and as long as that of the Son was not accepted, to impose the Holy Spirit, if I may dare to express myself thus.[63]

Pavel Florensky, in a variation on this Cappadocian theme, ascribed such difficulty to the particular work of the Holy Spirit. After acknowledging that most Christians hardly know "the Holy Spirit as a Person, and then only dimly and in a confused way," he goes on to say that a vision of the Holy Spirit to created being would communicate "the full property of spirit-bearing, a full deification, a full enlightenment."[64] He draws on the work of another Cappadocian, Gregory of Nyssa, to underscore that the full manifestation of the Spirit awaits eschatological glory for the Holy Spirit is the "Kingdom of the Father and the Unction of the Son."[65] The same theme is pursued in a non-Orthodox context by Jürgen Moltmann.[66] Lossky, for his part, focuses on how in the divine economy the person of the Holy Spirit remains unmanifested or, due to the nature of the procession, confronts us with a certain anonymity.[67] If with respect to the latter we are confronted with the indefiniteness of what "procession" means—by way of contrast, generation (relative to the second person) implies a definite relationship of paternity and filiation between two persons—in regard to the divine economy, however, the Spirit does bear a definite relationship to the Son.

The economy of the Holy Spirit follows that of the Son because the Spirit is the image of the Son even as the Son is the image of the Father.[68] The Holy Spirit is the only divine person who does not have an image in another person of the trinity. This is why the Holy Spirit remains hidden even in the work of redemption. While the Spirit is the source of uncreated grace, the manifestation of God that radiates from the presence of the Spirit is that of the Son whose divinity the Holy Spirit displays. The perichoretic unity of the three persons is at the core of this understanding. The three persons share one will, nature, and substance; so what is manifested in the temporal missions by the Son (as image of the Father) and the Spirit (as image of the Son) is the divine nature "from the Father, through the Son, in the Holy Spirit." The Holy Spirit performs this will and imparts this divinity (through the divine energies) by indwelling believers whom he makes "the throne of the Holy Trinity," the Father and Son being present in the Holy Spirit. The image of the Holy Spirit, not borne by another divine person, becomes actual in created persons only through his deifying work.[69] In this sense the ministry of the Holy Spirit is associated with ecclesiology; some even make the argument that ecclesiology is best understood when it is a branch of pneumatology.

Although we have described the difficulty attending pneumatology by underscoring the hidden manifestation of the hypostatic identity of the Holy Spirit within the divine economy, this should not obscure the distinct mission of the Holy Spirit relative to that of the Son. In fact, the diversity of missions can be ascribed to their distinct hypostatic identities as just articulated by the trinitarian theology of images. Lossky, especially, is insistent that within the one divine economy the missions (or economies) of the Son and the Holy Spirit must be distinguished. The distinction may be noted on several levels. The Son's mission begins with the incarnation, the Spirit's at Pentecost. The latter is not a continuation of the incarnation. Precisely because the Holy Spirit derives its hypostatic existence independently from that of the Son, so, too, its pentecostal mission is likewise independent. This is not to deny the perichoretic unity discussed above; it is merely to assert that Pentecost is not a function of the incarnation but its sequel. Because of this, the Orthodox easily avoid any instrumental reading of the pneumatological mission that is so common in the West. The triune economy reaches its goal in the economy of the Holy Spirit, who like the Son undergoes his own kenosis in a temporal mission. Just as the Son emptied himself by becoming flesh through the union of his hypostasis to a human nature, so, too, the Holy Spirit empties himself by indwelling human hypostases through the impartation of uncreated grace. The former unifies common human nature in the one hypostasis of the Son; the latter diversifies God's gifts among many human persons or hypostases. Finally, it should be noted that the Holy Spirit is not identified with the uncreated gifts (or energies) he imparts. This again points to the perichoretic presence of all three persons in the divine work and underscores that human participation in God respects the distinction between the divine essence and energies.[70]

Having distinguished clearly between the christological and pneumatological missions, what remains of a pneumatological christology that I have already frequently alluded to? It may appear with the distinction just noted, especially the sequential pattern of incarnation and Pentecost, that the role of the Holy Spirit in christology proper is quite limited. Lossky does sharply distinguish between two communications of the Holy Spirit: one on Easter evening (Jn. 20:19-23) and the other on the day of Pentecost (Acts 2:1-5). These Johannine and Lukan "comings" of the Holy Spirit respectively indicate an instrumental and personal presence of the Spirit. Only the latter formally constitutes the Spirit's proper mission. The former is a part of the christological mission in founding the church by the communication of the priestly power ("binding and loosing") of the risen Christ to the college of apostles.[71] It is here, again founded on the basis of the trinitarian perichoresis, that one can speak of a pneumatological christology. It applies to each of the temporal missions. Thus, Christ becomes incarnate and fulfills his work by the Holy Spirit, and the Holy Spirit works through Christ having been sent by the Father and imparted by the Son.[72]

Other Orthodox theologians do not quite agree with the particular nuances of Lossky's distinctions between the missions. This raises the important issue of whether the missions are sequential or simultaneous. I shall return to this concern as a systematic question shortly. For the moment we just note that two other Orthodox theologians, John Zizioulas and Nikos Nissiotis, prefer not so much to distinguish the economies of the Son and the Spirit as to emphasize the christological and pneumatological dimensions of the one divine economy.[73] This position, in fact, lends itself more strongly to a more explicit pneumatological christology. In both cases, however, pneumatology serves to enrich our understanding of God's redemptive work in its full trinitarian context.

It now remains to examine summarily the model of pneumatological christology that emerges in the Orthodox tradition. We shall then take up specific systematic questions on the relationship between the christological and pneumatological missions. Finally, we will conclude this chapter with a précis of the direction of our study when we turn our attention to the Roman Catholic tradition.

Critical Dogmatic Issues for Spirit-christology

A pneumatological christology is integral to the tradition of Orthodox soteriology and ecclesiology. Under the rubrics of deification and communion, the communication of divine life in the Christ-event and in the ongoing work of salvation are present through the ministry of the church. The Holy Spirit is the giver of life and his personal presence from Pentecost onward is the eschatological completion (still outstanding) of the work of Christ. The Spirit's presence in the pentecostal mission cannot be understood, however, apart from the pneumatological aspect of Christ's own mission. Sacramental chrismation is an extension of the unction of the Holy Spirit upon Christ. As Nissiotis has commented: "Christ can never be separated from the Spirit of God. His Incarnation and Resurrection are the work of the Giver of Life, the Paraclete."[74] In another vein, this time in correlation with the understanding of salvation as deification, L. Gillet can refer to the Christian life as not only christocentric (by, with, and in Christ) but also as an act of Christification, an indication of the pneumatic dimension of Christology that may be summarized by identifying Christ as "of the Spirit," as well as its "bearer" and "sender" in the work of redemption.[75] In this respect, our original Irenaean theme ("the two hands of God") is thoroughly played out in Orthodox christology and pneumatology. Neither hand is subordinate to the other and neither replaces the other. The Spirit was present in the Son's incarnation, baptism, ministry, death, and resurrection and because of this is now sent by the risen and exalted Christ. The pentecostal Spirit, however, is neither a substitute for Christ (an extreme pneumatocentrism) nor merely the instrument of his presence (an extreme christocentrism). Rather, the Holy Spirit is the person of the trinity who "forms Christ within us and renders Him present to us," and by preparing us for Christ "achieves in us the Parousia, the eternal coming and Presence of Jesus the Lord."[76] Without the *Spiritus praesens* the reality of the *Christus praesens* would be an exercise in pious imagination instead of the communication of the divine being.

What systematic questions from an Orthodox perspective confront a Catholic version of pneumatological christology? As mentioned earlier, I have relied primarily on the work of Vladimir Lossky because he was one of the most trenchant of Orthodox critics. This has served to focus the areas of doctrinal construction that require our attention. We may now list them serially as follows:

1. How do we characterize the respective missions of the Son and the Holy Spirit? Whether we interpret them as distinct economies (Lossky) or as the christological and pneumatological dimensions of the one divine economy (Zizioulas and Nissiotis), it is imperative that their differentiation be dogmatically underscored. While it is true that the intra-trinitarian distinction of persons cannot be maintained on the basis of the divine economy alone, it is also true that such differentiation loses its cogency if theology cannot account for the contribution of each hypostasis in the work of the divine economy. More here has been introduced than has been directly addressed in the previous pages. A brief statement of the issues is in order.

We are here again distinguishing between theological reflection upon theology proper and economy, between God in the triune being and God as trinity in the work of redemption and deification. I have noted how Lossky sought to keep the two separate especially in regard to the Spirit's hypostatic identity in relationship to the Son—monopatristic in theology and "after the Word" in the economy. Despite the clear marking off from each other of these two loci, one need not adopt a filioquist trinitarian construction to recognize the relationship between the two realms, even in Lossky. It is precisely because the Holy Spirit proceeds monopatristically and not *ab utroque* that Lossky can so strongly posit a pneumatologically distinct economy and independent mission. As will be argued in subsequent chapters, the connection between the two realms must to some extent be upheld, especially in a Catholic context where we will need to contend with the implications of the *filioque*. At this point I will make the following three observations: First, the distinction in trinitarian missions in the divine economy is one gleaned from the New Testament. By this I do not mean that scripture provides us with a mature trinitarian theology. In fact, by most accounts the New Testament is rather limited in this regard. I do mean that the biblical revelation of a dual sending of Christ and the Spirit by the God of the covenant provides sufficient warrant to legitimately push theological reflection into the realm of the intra-trinitarian relations. Second, the purpose of this move is to develop the "theology" of the God of biblical revelation and the divine economy. It is an exercise in constructive speculation to give coherence to the biblical doctrine of God. Third, with the insights gained from this exercise, theology returns to the "economy" to further clarify the nature of the temporal missions. Here theology seeks a more specific delineation of the hypostatic character of the presence of the divine persons in the work of redemption and deification.[77] As is perhaps already clear, these three steps cannot simply be divided into hard-and-fast separate compartments. It is more a task of how the steps, which are theologically distinct, mutually influence and even correct one another.

2. Are the two temporal missions simultaneous or sequential? To answer "both" to this question is not necessarily to court contradiction. On the one hand, it is clear that the Holy Spirit is active in every aspect of the christological mission. At the same time it, is also clear that at Pentecost a new dimension of the Holy Spirit's mission begins. We will have to determine how the two are related as well as discuss the relationship to christology of the pentecostal mission, especially the relationship between the *Christus praesens* and the *Spiritus praesens*.

3. This next set of issues deals directly with Spirit-christology. We may pose it as the following question: How is Christ "of the Spirit"? Here we will have to discuss the relationship between the Word and the Spirit in the properly christological mission of the incarnation. This dovetails into the role of Christ in relationship to the properly pneumatological mission of Pentecost. Both will need to be correlated with a model of intra-trinitarian relations that preserves the identity and distinction among the divine persons.

Having listed the most important systematic questions that will guide our inquiry, we now turn to the contributions of Orthodox theology to Catholic reflection on these matters. Although I have previously used the method of comparison and contrast, giving full weight to Orthodox criticisms of the Latin trinitarian model, here I will simply list the contributions of the Orthodox tradition to the theology of the trinity and to pneumatological christology as they would appear in the light of Latin theological concerns. Then during the course of this study we shall note how the introduction of these elements into the Latin paradigm appears in slightly different guises but nevertheless are essential to the development of an orthodox Spirit-christology. We list these serially as well, with brief commentary:

1. The basis for pneumatological christology begins in the human reception of grace in which the communication of divine life is predicated on the temporal missions of both the Son and the Spirit. This means quite logically that the mission of Christ in the incarnation—the most obvious example of a proper mission of a divine person—is necessarily complemented by a proper mission of the Holy Spirit. While it is true that the Holy Spirit is sent "after the Word" and in the language of the Fourth Gospel the Holy Spirit "will not speak on his own, but will speak only what he hears" (Jn. 16:13), it is equally true that faith's reception of the christological

mission is only in the Holy Spirit (1 Cor. 12:3). In other words, the hypostatic presence of the Holy Spirit at Pentecost is as important as the hypostatic presence of the Son in the incarnation. Both "presences," so to speak, are proper to the respective person. Much will depend on what we mean by "proper."

2. The complementary missions of the Son and the Spirit—the "two hands of God"—also imply an integral relationship between the Son and the Spirit in all aspects of the divine economy in redemption and deification. Spirit-christology is after all a model that exegetes the divine economy. The risen Christ cannot be understood to be the "sender" of the Spirit if the incarnate Christ is not already the "bearer" of the Spirit. The dominical foundation for chrismation precedes the sending of the Spirit on Pentecost. In Latin terms this means an investigation into the pneumatological dimension of grace that is proper to the person of Christ.

3. The propriety of the Spirit's presence—meaning what is uniquely character-istic of the Spirit's ministry and person—in the divine economy is due in the Orthodox paradigm to the independent procession of the Holy Spirit from the Father alone. A recognition of this same pneumatological propriety in the Latin tradition would have to negotiate this affirmation within the context of the *filioque.*

4. Finally, as we direct our efforts to theology proper from the perspective of the divine economy, it is necessary—even despite the absolute Orthodox distinction between the two—that there be a correlation between the differentiation in missions and the differentation in processions. In Greek theology this is provided by the ineffable difference between the Son's generation and the Spirit's procession, both from the Father alone. We will have to explore whether in the Latin model there is a similar type of differentiation, especially in a tradition that distinguishes the pro-cessions (now used generically in Latin fashion) mainly on the basis of relational opposition.

These four points along with the previous three must now guide our investigation in the following chapters.

Notes

1. Moltmann originally criticized this unhealthy dichotomy in the context of a theology of the cross. See his *The Crucified God: The Cross of Christ as the Foundation and Criticism of Christian Theology* (San Francisco: Harper & Row, 1974), pp. 7–28. Subsequent work gave due attention to pneumatology: *The Church in the Power of the Spirit: A Contribution to Messianic Ecclesiology* (San Francisco: Harper & Row, 1977); *The Trinity and the Kingdom: The Doctrine of God* (San Francisco: Harper & Row, 1981); *God in Creation: A New Theology of Creation and the Spirit of God* (San Francisco: Harper & Row, 1985), and most recently *The Way of Jesus Christ: Christology in Messianic Dimensions* (San Francisco: Harper, 1990).

2. Such are the charges of Methodios Foyas, *Orthodoxy, Roman Catholicism, and Angli-canism* (Brookline, MA: Holy Cross Orthodox Press, 1984), pp. 204–09. Vladimir Lossky is especially harsh in detailing the consequences of the *Filioque*. The summary provided by André de Halleux is worth quoting: "The Spirit is here reduced to the function of a link between the two other Persons and one-sidedly subordinated to the Son in his very existence in contempt of the genuine perichoresis. He thereby loses, together with his hypostatic inde-

pendence, the personal fullness of his economic activity. The latter is henceforth seen as a simple means of serving the economy of the Word, both at the level of the Church and at that of the person. The goal of the Christian way of life therefore becomes the *imitatio Christi*, no longer a deification by the Holy Spirit. The people of God are subjected to the body of Christ, the charism is made subordinate to the institution, inner freedom to imposed authority, prophetism to juridicism, mysticism to scholasticism, the laity to the clergy, the universal priesthood to the ministerial hierarchy, and finally the college of bishops to the primacy of the Pope. Creative and renewing source as he is, the Spirit was nevertheless expropriated by the Catholic Church, which made that Spirit the supreme guardian of the dispensation set up by Christ in favour of his Vicar. The Orthodox Church, on the other hand, has preserved the mutual subordination and the fertile tension between the economy of the incarnation and that of Pentecost" Quoted in Yves Congar, *The Word and the Spirit* (San Francisco: Harper & Row, 1986), p. 113. Nikos A. Nissiotis makes a similar criticism of Vatican II, which he describes as positing "an ecclesiology without pneumatology": "The Main Ecclesiological Problem of the Second Vatican Council: And the Position of the Non-Roman Churches Facing It," *Journal of Ecumenical Studies* 2 (1965), p. 48. A corrective to this harsh criticism from an Orthodox perspective is provided by John D. Zizioulas. *Being As Communion: Studies in Personhood and the Church* (Crestwood, NY: St. Vladimir's Seminary Press, 1985), p. 127.

3. I utilize Lossky because of the severity of his criticism and to facilitate the identification of the most important dogmatic issues involved. However, one should note that there are more irenical voices among the Orthodox and that Lossky represents a particular strain in Orthodox thought—namely, one especially influenced by Palamism. See comments in L. Gillet, "A Monk of the Eastern Church," *Orthodox Spirituality: An Outline of the Orthodox Ascetical and Mystical Tradition* (Crestwood, NY: St. Vladimir's Seminary Press, 1978), pp. 105–107, 110, n. 3.

4. Vladimir Lossky, *The Mystical Theology of the Eastern Church*. (Crestwood, NY: St. Vladimir's Seminary Press, 1976), pp. 169–170.

5. Ibid., p. 64.

6. Lossky, *In the Image and Likeness of God* (Crestwood, NY: St. Vladimir's Seminary Press, 1974), p. 65.

7. Lossky, *The Mystical Theology of the Eastern Church*, p. 87.

8. Ibid., p. 65. Lossky pursues this theme relentlessly in *The Vision of God* (Crestwood, NY: St. Vladimir's Seminary Press, 1973).

9. Lossky, *In the Image and Likeness of God*. p. 65.

10. *Orthodox Spirituality: An Outline of the Orthodox Ascetical and Mystical Tradition*, p. 87.

11. Lossky, *In the Image and Likeness of God*, p. 187.

12. Ibid., pp. 189–190.

13. Congar is commenting on Augustine's analogy: "What the soul is in our body, that is the Holy Ghost in Christ's Body, the Church" (St. Aug., *Serm.* 187, *de Temp*) and its use by Pope Leo XIII in his encyclical on the Holy Spirit: *Divinum Illum Munus*, par. 7—"Let it suffice it to state that, as Christ is the Head of the Church, so is the Holy Ghost her soul." Additionally, when Pius XII wrote on ecclesiology (*Mystici Corporis*, par. 57), he quoted Leo XIII. It was this later encyclical that had the greater influence in advancing this ecclesiological model. For Congar's commentary see his "The Church and Pentecost," *The Mystery of the Church* (Baltimore: Helicon, 1960), pp. 35–36; *I Believe in the Holy Spirit*, Volume I: *The Experience of the Spirit*. (New York: Seabury, 1983), p. 154; *I Believe in the Holy Spirit*, Volume II: *Lord and Giver of Life* (New York: Seabury, 1983), pp. 17–20. The accurate interpretation of Augustine's analogy, Congar argues, is to take it as a functional and not as an ontological statement.

14. Lossky, op. cit.

15. Ibid., pp. 187–188.

16. Ibid., p. 115.

17. *Capita theologica et oeconomica* 2, 13; *Patrologia Graeca [J. P. Migne, Paris 1859–90, col. 1125A; quoted in Lossky,. The Image and Likeness of God,* p. 84.

18. Ibid., p. 29.

19. Ibid., p. 113. Also, p. 84.

20. Ibid., p. 29.

21. Lossky, *The Mystical Theology of the Eastern Church,* p. 66.

22. Ibid., p. 71.

23. Karl Rahner, *The Trinity* (New York: Herder & Herder, 1970), p. 22.

24. *Summa Theologiae* (henceforth, ST) Ia, 43, 2.

25. ST Ia, 43, 8.

26. This fits the definition of a mission as understood by St. Augustine, upon whom St. Thomas builds—"Therefore, to be sent, is to come forth from the Father, and to come into the world" (*De Trinitate* II.5).

27. See the criticisms of William J. Hill, *The Three-Personed God: The Trinity as a Mystery of Salvation* (Washington D.C.: The Catholic University of America Press, 1982), pp. 140–142; and Yves Congar, *I Believe in the Holy Spirit,* Volume III: *The Rivers of Life Flows in the East and the West* (New York: Seabury, 1983), pp. 11–17.

28. Rahner, *The Trinity.* p. 28.

29. ST Ia, 43,3.

30. For Rahner's explication of the notion of revelation as the divine self-communication, see Chapter IV ("Man as the Event of God's Free and Forgiving Self-Communication") of his work *Foundations of Christian Faith: An Introduction to the Idea of Christianity* (New York: Seabury, 1978), pp. 116–137.

31. Hill, *The Three-Personed God,* p. 294.

32. Lossky, *The Mystical Theology of the Eastern Church,* p. 70.

33. Ibid., p. 87.

34. Ibid., p. 86.

35. Ibid., pp. 89–90.

36. Ibid., p. 81.

37. Ibid., pp. 82–83.

38. Betrand de Margerie, S.J., *The Christian Trinity in History* (Still River, MA: St. Bede's Publications, 1982), pp. 315–319.

39. Ibid., p. 133.

40. St. Gregory of Nazianzus, *Patrologia Graeca* [(J. P. Migne), Paris 1857–1866], 36,96; Rouet de Journel, M.J., S.J., *Enchiridion Padrisdicum,* Rome, 1966–, 990. Quoted in de Margerie, *The Christian Trinity in History,* p. 135.

41. Ibid., p. 137.

42. For this I refer to a typical neo-scholastic manual. The purpose is strictly summary. Certainly the thought of Thomas Aquinas or that of major neo-scholastics such as Matthias Scheeben, whose work I shall examine in the next chapter, is much more profound than the schemas provided by any manual. However, for the sake of comparison, the manual's brevity is especially useful. The manual utilized here is that by Dr. Ludwig Ott, *Fundamentals of Catholic Dogma* ed. James Canon Bastible, D.D. (St. Louis: B. Herder Book Company, 1958).

43. Ott, *Fundamentals of Catholic Dogma,* p. 61.

44. Ibid., p. 67.

45. Ibid., p. 68.

46. Ibid., p. 69.

47. Ibid., p. 70.

48. Ibid., pp. 70–71.

49. Ibid., p. 72.

50. Ibid., p. 73, with slight emendation.

51. Ibid.

52. Ibid., p. 74.

53. Ibid., p. 71.

54. Lossky, *In the Image and Likeness of God*, p. 76. It should be stated that Lossky is not mistranslating the Latin. He is aware of the more common expression. For him it is a matter of theological emphasis with regard to this key term in the Latin paradigm. In his own defense, his explanatory footnote justifies his choice: "Thomas uses the expressions *relativa oppositio, oppositio relationis* (this above all with reference to the essence), *relatio* (or *respectus*) as *suum oppositum*, and *relationes oppositae* to signify what we here have called 'relation of opposition.' In using this expression, we do not in any way misrepresent Thomas' thought, for the idea of opposition is implied in his very definition of relation: 'De ratione autem relationis est respectus unius ad alterum, secundem quem aliquid alteri opponitur relative' (I, qu. 28, a.3)." n. 7.

55. Congar, *I Believe in the Holy Spirit*, Vol. III. p. 78, n. 11. Congar's point is the following: "To speak of a 'relationship of opposition' (as in the case of Father-Son or Son-Father) could mean that, for the Latins, the persons are pure relations in essence, but this would point to a lack of understanding, both of the idea of subsistent relationships and of the way in which the Latins think of the diversity of the persons in the unity and simplicity of the divine Absolute."

56. Lossky. *In the Image and Likeness of God*. p. 77.

57. Ibid., p. 79.

58. While some Orthodox will concede a procession of the Holy Spirit from the Father through the Son (*per filium*), Lossky is insistent that this only characterizes the economy and must be absolutely distinguished from the intra-trinitarian relations in theology proper.

59. Ibid., pp. 80–81.

60. Congar. *I Believe in the Holy Spirit*, Vol. III, pp. 134–140.

61. Ibid. See especially pp. 199–203.

62. Lossky. *In the Image and Likeness of God*, p. 93.

63. *Orat.* 31, 26. Quoted by de Margerie, *The Christian Trinity in History*, pp. 104–05, n. 153.

64. Pavel Aleksandrovich Florensky, "On the Holy Spirit," *Ultimate Questions: An Anthology of Modern Russian Religious Thought*, ed. Alexander Schmemann, (New York: Holt, Rinehart and Winston, 1965), pp. 139–140.

65. Ibid., p. 167.

66. See especially Moltmann's *The Trinity and the Kingdom*, pp. 122–128.

67. Lossky, *In the Image and Likeness of God*, p. 75.

68. Idem, *The Mystical Theology of the Eastern Church*, pp. 84–85.

69. Ibid., pp. 171–173.

70. For the most succinct summary of these points, see ibid., pp. 156–173.

71. Ibid., p. 167.

72. Ibid., p. 158.

73. John D. Zizioulas, *Being as Communion: Studies in Personhood and the Church*, pp. 123–142. Nikos. A. Nissiotis, "Pneumatological Christology as a Presupposition of Ecclesiology," *Oecumenica 1967*, eds. Friedrich Wilhelm Kantzenbach and Vilmos Vajta (Minneapolis: Augsburg, 1967), pp. 235–252. Both authors, it should be noted, in their reflections on the relationship between christology and pneumatology focus their attention on the im-

plications for ecclesiology. A similar intention has directed the work of Catholic theologian Yves Congar as well.

74. Nissiotis, "Pneumatological Christology as a Presupposition of Ecclesiology," p. 236.

75. Gillet, *Orthodox Spirituality.* pp. 57, 80–81.

76. Ibid., p. 64.

77. These steps represent the understanding of doctrinal development within trinitarian theology suggested by the Australian Catholic theologian David Coffey. Since his work is so central to this study, I will devote the entirety of Chapter 5 to an investigation of it.

2

"Christ and the Spirit:" Spirit-christology in the Neo-scholastic Tradition

In the previous chapter we concluded by listing the most important dogmatic issues that attend a pneumatological christology in the Orthodox tradition. We also kept in view the Catholic theological tradition, which we subjected critically to the insights of the East; or, more accurately, we let the East speak its most salient criticisms of its Western relative's pneumatology and trinitarianism. In that process a number of issues arose in these loci (including also the theology of grace) that we must now address directly out of the context of the Latin trinitarian tradition. Of the different choices possible I have chosen to focus on a particular trajectory within modern neo-scholasticism, mainly because it raises the specific issues that are germane to this study. It also raises them in an atmosphere of controversy and contestation. This works to our advantage, since we will be able to test by comparison with more traditional neo-scholasticism the warrants for the dogmatic positions taken. Two further points must be made concerning our choice and intention.

First, the choice of this neo-scholastic trend is not meant to be an exercise in theological obscurantism. The debates reviewed have perhaps long been forgotten by many Catholic theologians, and neo-scholasticism itself is a theological style and genre that for the most part is no longer practiced in the mainstream of Roman Catholic theology. However, since we are seeking to define some precise and nuanced issues in the area of trinitarian theology, pneumatology, and christology, this particular theological idiom serves us well. All of this, it should be noted, is aside from the fact that the much longer tradition of Latin scholasticism, reaching back to the Baroque period and ultimately to the High Middle Ages, was transmitted in the modern period by this nearly century-old tradition of neo-scholasticism (roughly the period between the two Vatican Councils: 1870–1963). For better or for worse it embodied this tradition of the great scholastics—Thomas Aquinas being foremost— and therefore is an excellent candidate to test the criticism voiced by modern Orthodoxy as reviewed in the previous chapter.

Second, our intention is to track a development in theology that eventually leads to the goal of Spirit-christology. The steps reviewed in this chapter are, it will be argued, necessary building blocks for this particular christological model. The theology of grace, the question of trinitarian propriety, and the presence of the divine persons will help clarify the relationship between the Son and the Spirit that is at the heart of any Spirit-christology. This claim, of course, must be tested dogmatically, since in analyzing these various building blocks it is this assertion that must be argued and justified, especially before the evidence provided by those who did not specifically consider the option before us. This rather indirect path to Spirit-christology is required, as we shall see, by the nature of the Latin trinitarian paradigm.

Neo-scholastic Dogmatics: A General Methodological Overview

Neo-scholastic thought when compared to much contemporary theology does not proceed along the lines of historical interest in the positive data of revelation, either in terms of critical investigation into the New Testament with its correlative understanding of the development of doctrine, or in terms of a more theological notion of salvation history—e.g., a biblical schema of promise and fulfillment (which gained ascendancy in the documents of Vatican II). It is true that within neo-scholastic dogmatic theology one could distinguish between positive theology which demonstrates the truth of dogma from the sources of revelation in scripture and tradition, and speculative theology which seeks through rational inquiry to penetrate the nature and principles of the dogmas themselves.[1] But neither of these could justify a critical approach either to the sources of revelation or to the evolution of dogma. These were strictly modernist aberrations. What the method did accomplish was to bequeath a fairly formalized, abstract, and rigorous framework for the dogmatic consideration of the trinitarian and christological mysteries.

A typical neo-scholastic manual would be loosely patterned after the *Summa Theologiae* of St. Thomas Aquinas (sometimes very loosely).[2] The pattern is speculative and encompasses the truths of salvation within the overall doctrine of God, with theology or *sacra doctrina* understood as "the science of God and the blessed."[3] It represents the *exitus* and *reditus* of all things in relation to God. The "manual tradition" of neo-scholasticism beginning in the late nineteenth century commences with the doctrine of God, first the divine unity and then the divine trinity. Only after establishing the existence and nature of God from the perspective of both reason and faith, along with the divine attributes and qualities, does one proceed to the strictly revelational knowledge of the trinity. Positive theology would demonstrate the triunity of God from scripture and tradition, and speculative theology would explain the trinitarian distinctions by way of the abstract categories of relations, persons, properties, notions, appropriations and missions as reviewed in Chapter 1. I shall return shortly to the significance of this procedure for our topic. However, it is important to note that this pattern reflects the Western tendency to begin trinitarian theology not from the distinction of persons as in the tradition of Eastern Orthodoxy, but from the unity of God in the divine essence, the implications of which have often caused the East (Lossky being an excellent example) to reproach Catholic theology for its dogmatic rationalism and (not inconsistent with this) its neglect of pneumatology.[4]

The manuals then continue with the doctrine of creation—i.e., the *exitus* of the created order—under which are considered creation itself, preservation, providence, angels, anthropology, the fall, and the relation of the natural to the supernatural orders. The doctrine of redemption follows with the specific rubrics of christology and mariology, then with the doctrine of sanctification, including grace (actual and habitual), the church and the sacraments, and finally eschatology.[5] The *reditus* begins with christology and culminates in eschatology; in other words, it charts the path of the return of the creature to God through supernatural grace.

It is the locus of christology that interests us. Formally divided into the doctrines of the person and work of Christ (or, respectively, christology proper and soteriology) the former considers the origins of the doctrine in scripture and tradition (the task of positive theology) and then proceeds to the speculative examination of the hypostatic union, Christ's attributes, and the states and mysteries of his life—e.g., abasement, glorification, death, and resurrection. The christological treatise concludes with the work of the redeemer, usually discussing atonement under the threefold office of Christ as prophet, priest, and king.

This formal method, long practiced by scholastics, was indirectly reaffirmed in the modern period (especially regarding its epistemological concerns—specifically, the relationship between faith and reason) by Vatican I's *Dogmatic Constitution on the Catholic Faith (Dei Filius,* 1870). Vatican I also emphasized that the divine mysteries (understood as discrete mysteries, not in terms of the basic mystery of the divine being, as Karl Rahner and those following him have emphasized) should be approached in terms of the relations that they bear to one another[6]—an exhortation not unrelated to our subject. Eventually, though, neo-scholasticism in the form especially of Thomist philosophy and theology was juridically mandated to be taught in seminaries and Catholic faculties by Pope Leo XIII's Encyclical Letter *On The Restoration of Christian Philosophy (Aeterni Patris)* (1879). Under the impact of this renewed Thomism, the conciliar dogmas of the ancient church were explicated through the subtleties of scholastic philosophy. So, for example, under the locus of christology, attention was focused on the relationship between the two natures (human and divine) and the one person of Christ as the Logos incarnate. Little concern was given to the historical Jesus or the narrative of the Gospels and the New Testament kergymata. It was strictly a speculative inquiry into the coherence of Nicaea and Chalcedon engendered by the introduction of dialectics and metaphysics into the dogmatic task (again, it should be stressed, by no means a new approach in Catholic theology). I will trace the influence of such an approach for pneumatology by examining another Encyclical Letter of Leo XIII, *On the Holy Ghost (Divinum Illud Munus),* published on the feast of Pentecost, 1897.

Although not a scholastic treatise, the Pope's letter reflects the insights of the Schools' theology of the third person and also highlights its connection to christology. There are also two other areas of pneumatology underscored by the Pope: the Spirit's intra-trinitarian relationships and the pneumatic dimension of the church. In each there is an ordering of the person and work of the Holy Spirit such that the rational coherence of the doctrine is maintained within the parameters of Latin scholasticism, with Augustine and Aquinas as the two most prominent teachers. As already mentioned, the main feature of Latin trinitarianism is the emergence of the persons from their unity in (or as) the divine essence. Augustine's well-known psychological model of the trinity, in which Word and Spirit proceed from God's inner knowing and loving as a self-related substance, was refined by Aquinas, who expanded the concept of relation beyond the psychological construct to a properly metaphysical one in which the definition of person as "subsistent relation" posits a genuine plurality in God while not disrupting the unity of the divine essence.[7]

Leo XIII reflects this theological heritage when he warns: "lest from distinguishing the Persons men should be led to distinguish the Divine Essence."[8] Therefore, the intra-trinitarian relationship of the Holy Spirit to the Father and the Son is based on the internal procession of the Spirit from both (the Latin *filioque*—thus preserving a "distinguishing" based solely on relation) and it is this procession that is the basis for his external mission in the economy of salvation. The mission is directed to the world's redemption; he is sent by the Father and the Son to complete the work of Christ in manifold power through the efficacy of his action and his indwelling in the "whole body of the Church and in the individual souls of its members, through the glorious abundance of His Divine graces."[9] When refracted back into the intra-trinitarian relations, the mission is assigned to the Spirit by virtue of appropriation.

This neo-scholastic doctrine, which the Pope utilizes, intends to underscore the indivisibility of the divine operations *ad extra* as well as the *ad intra* processions of the persons within the one divine essence. Since each person of the trinity is identical with the divine essence any action or operation of the trinity *ad extra* would be common to all the persons who together act as one. Although not formally adopted by Vatican I, the schema for *The Dogmatic Constitution on the Principal Mysteries of the Faith (De fide catholica)* did summarize with respect to the divine operations *ad extra* the following two scholastic theological axioms: (1) *omnia opera Trinitatis sunt indivisa*—all the works of the trinity are undivided; (2) *In Deo omnia sunt unum ubi non obviat relationis oppositio*—In God all is one except wherever the opposition of relation does not stand in the way.

> As there is one deity, nature and substance in the three divine persons, so there is one indivisible operation by which the Most Holy Trinity establishes, disposes, and governs all things outside it. For the divine persons act *ad extra*, not individually, but so far as in their essence, will, and power they are one God, one source of all things.
>
> If anyone should maintain that creation or any other action of God that terminates in creatures, is proper to one divine person in such a way as not to be one, undivided, and common to all of them, let him be anathema.[10]

In lieu of attributing an *ad extra* operation to one of the trinitarian persons on the basis of propriety—i.e., a property exclusive to that person—this doctrine allows for an affinity between an operation and the properties of the particular person; therefore, an operation can be *appropriated* to one person more than another. This manifests the peculiar uniqueness of the person as is evident, for example, in the tripartite distinction of causality that Leo XIII suggests: the Father is the efficient cause of all things, the Son is the exemplary cause, and the Spirit is the ultimate cause.[11]

More to the point of our investigation are the appropriated operations of the Holy Spirit relative to the incarnation and the church. The pope suggests that the incarnation is specially appropriated to the Holy Spirit in the work of Christ's conception, the personal union of his human nature with the divine Word, the sanctification of his soul, the works of his ministry, and the efficacy of his sacrifice.[12] In scholastic terminology this complex of events was explicated through a christological theology of grace—specifically, the grace of union (*gratia unionis*) in reference to the hypostatic union and the habitual graces (*gratia habitualis*) that sanctified his human nature; both here are attributed "through the special gift of the Holy Ghost."[13] In a similar fashion, a pneumatic ecclesiology is suggested. The Spirit is present in the church in twofold mission: visibly and outwardly through the institution of the church's sacramental ministry mediated by the hierarchy, and invisibly and inwardly through "His secret indwelling in the souls of the just."[14] The analogy to christology is maintained. The operation of the Holy Spirit in the person of Christ—viz., his natural generation as the incarnate Son of God—is also efficacious for believers— viz., their spiritual regeneration through baptism,[15] this being equivalent to the scholastic designation of the christological grace of headship (*gratia capitis*).

The influence of Leo XIII's letter would also be evident later in the ecclesiological model of the church as the Mystical Body of Christ. Adopted by Pope Pius XII in his encyclical *The Mystical Body of Christ and our Union in it with Christ (Mystici Corporis)* (1943), he further developed this twofold operation of the Spirit although in more christological terms—e.g., Christ governs the faithful invisibly and extraordinarily through interior guidance and visibly and ordinarily through the Roman Pontiff and the hierarchy.[16] Nevertheless, while the latter pope's emphasis is more christological than pneumatological, they both adhere to and expand on the Augustinian analogy that Christ is head of the church and the Holy Spirit is its soul, thus maintaining these two dimensions of the church's mystery.[17] However, it should still be emphasized that they strictly follow neo-scholastic patterns and therefore envision the mission of the Holy Spirit through the dogmatic construct of appropriation. This is true for both the presence of the Spirit's distinct hypostatic identity in the souls of the just and the distribution of graces relative to the divine operation *ad extra*. In addition, the respective pneumatological and christological emphases of Leo XIII and Pius XII pose for the theologian the significance of these different trinitarian orientations. If, for example, pneumatological and christological language can both be utilized to describe the mystery of the divine presence and agency in the church and the souls of the just, what is the necessary distinction between the two? An answer to this question is germane to the integrity of the trinitarian dogma.

While this gives a flavor of how neo-scholastic thought influenced universal papal teaching, we must recognize that they are encyclicals and not theological treatises. Two theologians within the neo-scholastic tradition, one from the late nineteenth century and one from the early twentieth century (writing in part during the respective reigns of the pontiffs), pursued in a highly refined manner a similar utililization of pneumatology, although each proceeded beyond certain traditional neo-scholastic explications of the doctrine. Their respective systems are important because they reveal both the limits and the depths to which one can develop pneumatology in this context. In the next two sections, I will examine their speculative constructs for the relationship between pneumatology and christology. While neither proposes a formal Spirit-christology, they are both sensitive to the unique relationship between Christ and the Spirit, with consequences for both ecclesiology and the theology of grace.

The Pneumatology of Appropriation: The Spirit-christology of Matthias Scheeben

Matthias Joseph Scheeben (1835–1888) was a student of the great neo-Thomist Joseph Kleutgen, S.J., at the German College in Rome. Upon his return to his native country, he became a significant force for the restoration of Thomism among the Catholic theological faculties of Germany.[18] Among his major works the most important include *Natur und Gnade* (*Nature and Grace*), *Die Mysterien des Christentums* (*The Mysteries of Christianity*), and *Handbuch der Katholischen Dogmatik* (*A Manual of Catholic Theology*). It is the last two that figure prominently for our study; they represent his most comprehensive investigations into the relationship between christology and pneumatology. I shall focus on three aspects of this relationship. I will examine first the trinitarian context for the distinction between the second and third persons; second, how these distinctions thus construed influence his theology of trinitarian missions and the consequences for a theology of grace; and finally, the implications he draws for the pneumatological dimension of christology proper. This will afford us a model of a pneumatologically minded scholastic theology that takes up the issues suggested by Orthodox theology in the previous chapter.

Relational Distinctions in the Immanent Trinity

Scheeben's method is an exemplary exercise in neo-scholastic trinitarian speculation. With the data of revelation in hand—specifically, the revelation of the divine trinity—one proceeds from God to the world. The immanent trinity, not the economic trinity, is the first subject for theological inquiry. One begins with the relations of the divine persons *ad intra* before turning to their missions *ad extra*. This procedure ensures that the nature of the missions, directed as they are to redemption, are consistent with the integrity and cogency of the distinctions within the intra-divine trinity. In other words, the speculative grasp of the triune mystery of God in the divine being itself apart from the relationship of God to the world cannot be violated when inquiry is then directed to the working of the divine persons in the economy of redemption. This is an inevitable consequence of beginning with the unity of the divine essence before distinguishing the persons, that distinction (relative to the divine essence) then being the inviolable construct when it comes to speaking of the temporal divine missions in the world.

Ensconced in this pattern Scheeben is as precise as any neo-scholastic:

Thus there are in God:
1. One Nature;
2. Two Productions;
3. Three Persons;
4. Four Relations; and
5. Five Notions.[19]

This summary serves to uphold the integrity of the "threeness" in God without subverting the "oneness." It follows the basic definitions that we have already reviewed. We will briefly repeat its most salient features. For example, the unicity and unity of God is found in the first person, who produces the other two persons and who in that production also communicates to them the single divine essence. This actually entails a dual production (or two processions) from the first person, those of generation and spiration. Logically, this requires four relations or two mutual relations when correlated with each act of production—active generation (or paternity), passive generation (or filiation), and active spiration, passive spiration. Each person can be distinguished from another (in the single divine essence) only on the basis of these relations. Add to these four relations the ingenerateness or innascibility of the first person and there are then five notions that appertain to the distinct identity or property of each person. To conclude: ingenerateness, paternity, and active spiration appertain to the Father; filiation and active spiration to the Son; and passive spiration to the Holy Spirit.[20] The success of this model depends on the distinction of the original two productions or processions from each other. This distinction, originally conceived in relation to the cogency and integrity of the immanent trinity, is determinative, as we shall see, for his theology of the divine missions, the theology of grace, and even for christology.

The distinction between the productions of generation and spiration relate directly to Scheeben's conception of the fecundity of the divine life. More specifically, it is the fecundity of "absolute and substantial Wisdom," which unlike the fecundity of the non-divine, is infinitely productive and within the immanent life of God can only communicate itself as the production and the intercommunion of divine persons.[21] The three are described as both hypostatic and personal, with hypostasis understood as a concrete, individual bearer of a nature, and person as an hypostasis whose nature is spiritual. The difference between a divine person and a created person is that the bearing of a rational nature by the latter entails the multiplication of the object possessed while for the former the divine persons communicate the one single divine essence. This being the case, that the divine persons possess the one divine nature, it must also be true that they are identical to it in different manners if they are to remain distinct. Therefore, they stand out as persons only by virtue of their relationship with one another as "relative proprietors of the divine nature"—i.e., "they are proprietors of the nature in and through their relationship to other proprietors of the same nature."[22]

What distinguishes the production of the Son from the production of the Spirit in addition to the relational distinctions elucidated above is their translation into the Augustinian psychological model of trinitarian distinctions. Therefore, Scheeben posits the internal divine productions in the familiar categories of cognition and love. By an act of self-consciousness and self-knowledge, the first person produces the second person as personal Word and the mutual love between them is the production of the Holy Spirit. In both cases it is understood that the divine nature is not produced but communicated in the productions through the distinct hypostatic relations. It is these relations and their respective origins that mark the major difference between the second and third persons and that require an explicit affirmation of the *filioque*. In sum, the first person is unoriginate, the second person proceeds from one person, and the third person proceeds from two persons. Or, relative to the distinct types of productivity, one can conclude not only to the distinction of persons but to their individual identity as well:

> The First Person's productivity through His cognition, and in conjunction with the Second Person through His love, must be the ultimate reason not only for the distinction of the persons, but also for all the individual distinctions and further determinations of the persons as well as their origins.[23]

In summary, Scheeben marks well the distinction of persons within the immanent trinity. Having their source in the fecundity of the divine life, the persons remain distinct in their unity through the opposition of relations, the relations determined by the nature and manner of the two *ad intra* processions.

Trinitarian Missions and the Theology of Grace

It is logical that this structure of hypostatic relational distinction in the immanent trinity would be determinative for the trinitarian missions *ad extra*. In fact, this is the case, although it also fixes certain restraints in the envisagement of the missions. Scheeben discusses this under the neo-scholastic rubrics that distinguish between appropriation and property in the missions. Scheeben defines a temporal mission of a divine person as a procession *ad extra* that "can be brought about only by a new manifestation of the substantial presence of the Person sent, and consequently by a new operation taking place in the creature, whereby the Divine Person reveals Himself externally [a visible or external mission] or enters into union with the creature [an invisible or internal mission]."[24] In other words, the mission reveals the distinctiveness of the person so missioned. He also holds to the concept of appropriation that can apply either to a divine attribute or to the divine activity in the missions. In both these cases, the attribute or activity in question is not exclusively applied to the person as if they could never be predicated of the other two persons, for all attributes and activity are common to all three persons—a traditional scholastic position. However, they do bear "a special connection and relationship with the proper character of the individual persons, and accordingly find in them their personal expression, their special representatives."[25] Appropriations, therefore, are relative to the trinitarian persons and never absolute as are the properties.

The precision of these standard neo-scholastic concepts does not, however, completely clarify the theological understanding of these divine formalities. One must consider the limitation of theological definition since even revelation does not provides access to the divine persons in themselves but only reveals them within the context of the divine economy.[26] Thus, when Scheeben considers the unique Christian confession of the incarnation, in which it is exclusively the second person who became flesh—i.e., the christological mission—he is compelled to supply a more nuanced version of the relationship between appropriation and property. This will have significant consequences for the pneumatological mission as well. To clarify this we must first return to the relationship between the immanent processions and economic missions.

The most obvious relationship between the processions and missions is in the hypostatic relational distinctions. The missions, for example, follow the same pattern as do the processions. The Father, who himself is not sent, sends the Son and the Holy Spirit. The Son is both sent (by the Father) and sends—i.e., relative to the Holy Spirit. The Holy Spirit does not send but is only sent (by the Father and the Son). These correspond to the notional acts of generation and spiration. But the correspondence is not absolute to the extent that the missions result in properties exclusive to the persons. In other words, the temporal missions of Son and Spirit, while they follow the pattern of the processions vis-à-vis the relations of the persons to one another, do not in the divine operations *ad extra* imply an activity exclusive to either one of them. There is, then, no formal property for a person in the missions as there is in the processions.

The neo-scholastic alternative to the proper identification of a person in a temporal mission is to resort to a theology of appropriation as defined above and as utilized by Leo XIII and Pius XII. Since all operations or activities of the trinity *ad extra* are common to the three persons one cannot exclude any person in the divine agency. Again, it must be emphasized that the reason for this resides in the Latin construction of the triunity. Only the relations distinguish the hypostatic identities. Therefore, when a person acts *ad extra*, it is by virtue of the single operation of the divine essence, whether that activity be applicable to the natural or supernatural order.[27] Scheeben can then conclude that "the divine persons . . . do not manifest themselves to the outer world formally by their operations and activity."[28] However, the results of this speculative construction are not entirely satisfactory as evidenced by Scheeben's following cautious remarks concerning a correct perception of the trinitarian missions:

> It must not be thought that the whole mission consists in a Divine Person coming down to the creature merely as representative of an operation appropriated to Him but common to the Three Persons, thus infusing not Himself but merely His operation into the creature, and consequently not proceeding *ad extra* in the character of a Person distinct from His principle as well as from His operations. As a matter of fact, in many texts of Holy Scripture the mission of Divine Persons implies no more than that They reveal themselves in creatures as bearers of an activity appropriated to Them and as Principle of an operation in the creature. Such is the case, for instance, where, in the spiritual order, every supernatural influence of God on the soul is ascribed to a coming of the Son or the Holy Ghost. But the theologians of all times agree in considering this kind of mission as an improper one, and assert the existence of another, to which the name of mission properly belongs.[29]

Here we are presented with a distinction between a proper and improper mission. Does this contradict the prevailing neo-scholastic paradigm to which Scheeben adheres? Or is Scheeben introducing an important nuance that goes beyond the prevailing theology of appropriation relative to the missions? To answer this, we begin with the most obvious question.

First, what is the modality for a proper mission if the divine activity as such does not formally reveal the distinction between persons? Divine operations *ad extra*, such as that of creation, do in fact entail the appropriation of different types of causality among the persons—e.g., power as efficient cause to the Father, wisdom as exemplary cause to the Son, and goodness as final cause to the Spirit;[30] however, this would be an example in which the distinction of persons is not made explicit in the activity.[31] This is not the case when we consider the supernatural works of the incarnation and of grace, which are properly missions. The distinction is as follows. An operation is common to all the persons and a mission is proper to the individual person. In the latter, the proper hypostatic and personal characters of the persons— respectively, the Son and the Spirit—are revealed. It is not by operation that the persons are revealed, for in each of these external works all three persons are active—commonly understood in the traditional formula: "The Father acts through the Son in the Holy Spirit."[32] Rather, Scheeben resorts to the principle that the divine persons are hypostatically revealed either by 1) prolongation and continuance, or 2) imitation and reproduction.[33]

The first instance of these two possibilities is the most exemplary and applies to the incarnation. The Son goes forth from the Father, and while preserving his relationship to the other persons in the interior of the Godhead, hypostatically unites himself with a human nature and enters the created world by means of this union.[34] To that extent the hypostatic union reveals the proper identity of the second person, commonly with the other persons in the operation of the incarnation—e.g., the Father sends the Son who is conceived by the Holy Spirit, but exclusively vis-à-vis its term in the God-human, Jesus Christ. I shall return to the incarnation to examine in more detail the role of the Holy Spirit. For the moment we now turn to the invisible missions of grace relative to both the Son and the Holy Spirit. The christological and pneumatological dimensions of these missions underscore their properly personal element.

The invisible and internal missions as real missions and not just as outwardly symbolic missions—e.g., the dove as a symbol of the Holy Spirit, are rooted in the internal processions that refer to the first model of the objective revelation of the divine persons—i.e., prolongation and continuance. This is clearly evident in the doctrine of adoptive filiation. Here both processions are active and are a direct prolongation of the immanent processions. They are also more than simply the modality of the creative power of God that is appropriate to God's presence in the world by virtue of the divine omnipresence, infinity, and immensity. The first mission is in the modality of God's generative power and the second in God's spirative power. In correlation with the *filioque*, the second mission of the Spirit is dependent on the first one of the Son (even with regard to interior grace). However, because the believer's filiation is by adoption and not by nature (as for the Son), the generative mission terminates in and is conducted by the pneumatic mission. In other words, the Son of God whose personal presence to the believer results in regeneration, is communicated by the Holy Spirit according to the liberality of God's grace, gift, and love. This underscores the important distinction between the processions and missions—namely, the absence of necessity in the divine-human relation enacted by the temporal missions. The necessity is only within the divine being and constitutes the eternal processional relations of the immanent trinity.[35]

Thus far, utilizing the concept of missions as the prolongation or continuance of immanent processions, Scheeben is able to distinguish between each respective mission while also affirming their inseparability. Regarding the distinction between the *Christus praesens* and the *Spiritus praesens*, within the ambit of these neo-scholastic constructions there is a precise articulation of the hypostatic identity revealed in the divine presence. In fact, all three persons are present in the one divine operation, but each in its own proper mode. So, for example, in the conferring of supernatural light and grace, "the eternal splendor of the Father is irradiated over us, and His consubstantial image, the Son of God, is imprinted in our soul and is reborn in us," and the Holy Spirit as the *donum Dei*, the gift of God, is the full outpouring of this inner divine life and its communication or channel to us.[36] This union and distinction within the divine presence also holds true for the second construct of how the divine persons are hypostatically revealed—namely, the imitation and reproduction of the divine persons in the creature.

The second conception of the trinitarian missions presupposes the first and goes beyond it. It is closely connected with the neo-scholastic understanding of sanctifying grace as both *habitum* and *habens*—i.e., the habits and acts of the supernatural life. The advantage of this model, which complements and completes the previous one, is that in addition to the impression and expression of the persons sent, their indwelling and possession is proffered through the imitation and reproduction of their hypostatic characters in the creature. As already mentioned in reference to the Son, this would entail the enjoyment and possession of him as the image of the Father. With respect to the Holy Spirit, he is not only *donum Dei* but *donum hypostaticum* as well. By the latter is meant that the Holy Spirit is not just the channel of divine love or is present through gifts, but that the Spirit is present in the creature as a hypostatic identity. Scheeben therefore proposes that the Spirit is present not just as donation but as person. In neo-scholastic terminology the Spirit is not only the efficient and exemplary cause of our sanctification through the mediation of sanctifying or created grace, but also the formal cause in terms of the divine giftedness (pledge of the divine love between Father and Son) and indwelling—i.e., uncreated grace. This proper or formal indwelling is not separable from union with Christ, for it makes us sons and daughters in the Son (*filii in Filio*).[37]

In conclusion, we note that Scheeben was able to hold to the strictures of the neo-scholastic model by not exceeding the doctrine of appropriation. The Latin *Inseparabilia sunt opera Trinitatis* was maintained by his distinction between activity or operation of the trinity and the revelation of the temporal missions. However, he also did not simply interpret the missions solely in terms of the theory of appropriation. Rather, he distinguished between appropriations generally applied that do not reveal the particular identity of the persons and those that include their own "proper" reference to a single hypostasis. In the supernatural works of grace—namely, the incarnation and the invisible missions of Son and Spirit—there is properly revealed the hypostatic character of the second and third persons. The doctrine of appropriations is not discarded in this case, for the proper missions of the Son and Spirit are not exclusive of the other persons. The innovation of Scheeben's speculative work lies precisely here—namely, in this proposal for a non-exclusive *proprium* theory.[38] Continuity with previous appropriation theory is also not severed. Therefore, the singularity of the divine operation is affirmed, although the distinct manner in which the several persons inhabit the creature—e.g., pertaining to the mystery of grace—is also maintained.[39]

What is especially noteworthy is his emphasis on the personal indwelling of the Holy Spirit that is proper. Scholastic and neo-scholastic theologians disagreed over this matter, and his argument for a formal personal indwelling proper to the Holy Spirit represented at the very least a renewed pneumatology in Catholic dogmatics. The neo-scholastic debate over the nature and propriety of the Spirit's mission and indwelling would reemerge with great vitality in the mid-twentieth century. We shall turn to this debate in the next chapter. For the moment I simply underscore the united but distinct christological and pneumatological dimensions of the divine indwelling (or presence) within the horizon of a neo-scholastic construction of trinitarian dogma. The distinction between the two is not incidental. Within the wider horizon of neo-scholastic thought it contributes to a more accentuated pneumatology. In order to pursue this further, relative to our query into Spirit-christology, we must now turn to Scheeben's formal christology—namely, his theology of the incarnation and hypostatic union.

"Anointing" and the Hypostatic Union

After having elucidated the trinitarian and anthropological mysteries in his magnum opus, *The Mysteries of Christianity*, Scheeben turned to christology. Situated between the mystery of God as a trinity of divine persons and the mystery of humanity originally called (in Adam) to supernatural union with God and sanctification by God but now separated through sin, is the mystery of the "God-man [who] stands in closest and most sublime relationship with all three." Scheeben goes on to further describe the centrality of the christological locus:

> In Him we find the most perfect prolongation and revelation of the interior productions of the Godhead, the restoration and the reestablishment of man's supernatural union with God, and finally full compensation for the extirpation and obliteration of sin.[40]

It is in Christ that the relationship of the triune God to the world and humanity is solidified including the communication of divine life through the Holy Spirit. In other words, the pneumatological dimension of the life of grace reviewed above is possible only as a result of the intrinsic pneumatic dimension of the incarnation itself.

As already mentioned, Scheeben distinguishes between the common role of all three persons in the incarnation and the exclusive role of the Son. The former share in the activity of God by which the Word becomes flesh, while with a view to the termination of the incarnation in the human being Jesus Christ it is exclusively the work of the Son, indeed a proper mission of the Son alone. This differs markedly from the temporal mission of the Holy Spirit, which is only appropriated, although Scheeben does posit a non-exclusive proper mission of the third person with respect to the divine indwelling through grace. The question now arises as to how the constitution of the person of Christ and the soteriological function of Christ as the source of grace is explicitly pneumatological.

Scheeben's christology is in the traditional sense a Logos-christology. A human nature is assumed and united with the divine person of the Word. Hence the Logos incarnate is not the union of human and divine natures to form a new or composite nature. The distinction in the Godhead between person and nature must be preserved. All three persons share the one divine nature or essence and are distinguished strictly by their persons (viz., the opposition of relations). Divine nature is united with human nature in the incarnation only in the sense that the hypostasis of the Word assumes a human nature.[41] This preserves the fourfold negation of Chalcedon—without confusion or change, without separation or division—as well as the anhypostasis of the human nature in the single person of the Logos incarnate—i.e., that the human nature of Christ is without its own hypostasis or person and exists as person only through the divine Son. But how is the human nature of Jesus united with the divine person of the Logos/Son? To answer this we must turn to the roles of the other two persons of the Godhead in the temporal mission of the Son's incarnation.

The Father, who is the origin of both processions in the trinity, is likewise the source of both temporal missions. The Father sends the Son and the Spirit into the world, and in each of these sendings he is present although not sent himself. In revealing himself the Father reveals the Son and Spirit; or, to use the language of Karl Rahner, the Father communicates himself to the Son and Spirit, who are God's self-communication to the world. In this sense, as the one from whom the Son is begotten, Scheeben can say that the Father "descends into the humanity [of the incarnation] along with the Son."[42] This indwelling of the Father in the incarnate Son is formally defined as "presence by concomitancy," which also applies to the Holy Spirit although the manner of the indwelling is different.[43]

The Holy Spirit's concomitance with the incarnate Son is predicated on the relationship between the persons in the immanent processions implying as it does the procession of the Spirit as defined by the *filioque*. So the Spirit descends with the Son into the assumed humanity as the one who proceeds from the Son (analogous to the Father descending as the one who generates and sends). In this capacity the Holy Spirit is regarded as playing a substantial role in the incarnation—one, however, that is only appropriated and not proper. Nevertheless, it is a role with direct connection to the actualization of the incarnation and the inner life and ministry of the incarnate Lord.

The former role is obvious from the creedal *qui conceptus est de Spiritu Sancto*. In this sense the Holy Spirit can be considered the cause of the incarnation with the appropriation understood as the breath of love communicated in any activity of the Word.[44] Therefore, the Holy Spirit performs a coordinate role with the Logos in the act of the incarnation, a role that continues in this same relation in the earthly and risen life of the incarnate Christ. The most common biblical image utilized by Scheeben to explicate this pneumatic dimension is that of "anointing." Two aspects of anointing are of moment: first, the agent who anoints, and then the scope of the anointing.

The agent of anointing is the Holy Spirit, an interpretation of this pneumatic dimension that was to be challenged later by those who revised Scheeben's work. In the present case the identity of the agent is determined by the immanent processional context of the *filioque* already mentioned. By proceeding from the Logos into the humanity of Christ, the Spirit anoints the humanity with the ointment of the

Logos' own fullness of divinity. Although the ultimate source of the anointing is the Father, the Spirit is active as the one who facilitates the full union of the divine Logos with an assumed human nature, the result of which is not a deified human but a true God-human. This distinction is important, for it both differentiates and connects pneumatic agency in the constitution of the person of Christ and that in the graced sanctification of human beings—i.e., the neo-scholastic distinction between *gratia unionis* and *gratia sanctificans*. In the latter case it is simply "the outpouring of the Holy Spirit in his deifying grace," while the former entails "personal union with the principle of the Holy Spirit." Or, as Scheeben states it: "the divine ointment is contained in the very make-up of Christ's being, and constitutes Him a divine-human being."[45]

The scope of the anointing encompasses, in addition to the mystery of the incarnation whereby Jesus' human nature is assumed into union with the Logos, "the transfiguration of the humanity and its assimilation to God by grace and glory" and the instrumentality of the humanity in the Logos' transmission of grace to others.[46] Thus, Jesus ministered in the power of the Spirit and eventually sacrificed himself to God "through the transforming fire of the Holy Spirit."[47] Precisely because of these first two pneumatic dimensions does the Spirit occupy such an important role in the life of grace. Only because of Christ's unique union with the Holy Spirit does the graced believer properly possess the Spirit in a manner qualitatively different from before the incarnation—e.g., Old Testament manifestations of the Spirit.[48] It is Christ who sends the Spirit at Pentecost, the Spirit who proceeds from his own divine heart[49] and whose divinity in humanity as the Risen One accords him the Pauline expression *Spiritus vivificans* (1 Cor. 15:45).[50] The latter also reveals Scheeben's deep affinity for the patristic understanding of Christ's activity as theandric—evidence of his profound reading of the Fathers with the beneficial result of an enriched scholasticism.[51] Through this explication of a pneumatic theology of anointing Scheeben has for all intents and purposes arrived at a Spirit-christology, one in which the Holy Spirit is central as a constitutive agent in the intrinsic relationship between christology and soteriology.

Conclusion

Matthias Scheeben's work in many ways represents a major innovation in neo-scholastic thought. Variously called the greatest dogmatic theologian of the nineteenth century and a theologian "*chez qui la science du dogma parle allemand et parle catholique*," nevertheless his opinions on pneumatology were considered by his critics to be hazardous and venturesome—specifically, the inhabitation of the soul by the Holy Spirit.[52] His suggestion of a non-exclusionary proper indwelling of the Holy Spirit and the formal causality of uncreated grace ran against the prevailing extrinsicism of neo-scholasticism's theology of grace and trinitarian appropriations.

Scheeben pushed at the edges of the neo-scholastic paradigm. Ever since Thomas Aquinas's commentary on Peter Lombard's *Sentences*, it was accepted that the latter's opinion was thoroughly negated. Lombard's preference in the theology of grace for the Holy Spirit's direct indwelling as love over love considered as an infused virtue in the just person was corrected by Aquinas with his insistence that grace must be created in order for the human person to be sanctified in his or her own nature (*per quemdam modum passionis*—through whatever manner of being acted upon).[53] Therefore, Scheeben's innovation involves new notions of causality concerning the workings of God *ad extra* and it emphasizes even more strongly the importance of uncreated grace, both of which result in the reconsideration of the structure of the hypostatic union and the proper mission of the Holy Spirit.

We may note that the theological terrain negotiated by Scheeben is considerably different from that familiar to Lossky and other Orthodox theologians. Although Lossky considers both "theology" and "economy" as subjects for theological investigation, one cannot help but highlight the difference in the two traditions represented by the speculative ethos of neo-scholastic dialectic. As one of the theologians we will examine later will affirm, one benefit of this approach is its precision. Neo-scholasticism is quite willing to distinguish and define where Orthodoxy may prefer to remain silent or simply allow biblical language to stand on its own—e.g., in not defining the meaning of generation and procession in relationship to each other.

Despite the difference between the two traditions, we can state that Scheeben's Spirit-christology and Orthodox pneumatological christology follow a similar pattern by accentuating the distinct hypostatic character of the Holy Spirit's mission, coordinating it with a trinitarian model that consistently distinguishes the persons, and by linking together the various decisive pneumatic moments in christology—i.e., where the Holy Spirit is a constituent agent in christology proper (the doctrine of the person of Christ in reference to the incarnation and the hypostatic union), soteriology (how Christ accomplishes and communicates salvation), and the theology of grace (as the basis for anthropology and the Christian life). This linkage neither confuses the persons nor obscures their presence. Both Christ and the Holy Spirit fully stand out as missions of divine revelation and salvation and are intrinsically related in the very event that marks out the particularity of the Christian gospel. If *Christus pro nobis* lies at the center of Christian creedal confession, then Christ is for us and our salvation only through the agency and power of the Holy Spirit. Such is the case because Christmas and Easter are as pneumatically informed saving mysteries as is Pentecost.

If Scheeben has succeeded in proferring a Spirit-christology within the context of neo-scholastic theology, one need also be mindful of that context. In the specifics of his proposal, Scheeben still operates within the prevailing paradigm even if he has explored some hitherto uncharted territory. Those specifics—i.e., a non-exclusionary proper mission of the Holy Spirit and pneumatic anointing—when taken together not only accentuate an underdeveloped pneumatology but contribute to a new christological construct. This construct, which I have labeled Spirit-christology, is more consciously trinitarian, dependent as it is on the inclusion of pneumatology in christological reflection. If for no other reason, Matthias Scheeben stands out as a pioneer in laying the foundation in Latin scholasticism for such an approach.

Eventually Scheeben's improvisation on the appropriated mission of the Holy Spirit to include a non-exclusionary proper mission of the Spirit's inhabitation of the just person would be revised by future pneumatologists. The direction taken by them includes the direct assertion of a proper mission and indwelling. This innovation, combined with the twentieth century debate over pneumatological and christological causality (efficient, formal, or quasi-formal), will be examined in the next chapter along with an investigation into the christological implications of this change. Finally, the combination of these three discrete but interrelated areas of dogmatic theology—the theology of grace, pneumatology and christology—resulted in new perspectives on ecclesiology. The Church as the Mystical Body of Christ is one outcome of this and it was soon reflected in papal teaching and in the work of many theologians. It is to this ecclesial model that we shall now turn by examining the proposal of a young twentieth century theologian who exploited it.

Pneumatology and the Mystical Body of Christ: The Spirit-christology of Emile Mersch, S.J.

The model of the church as the Mystical Body of Christ is not new to Roman Catholic ecclesiology. It was strongly suggested by Thomas Aquinas,[54] and by the time of Pius XII's famous encyclical *Mystici Corporis*, which formalized it in Catholic teaching, it had already passed through the hands of many theologians. Our interest is not the ecclesiology per se but the christological construct that informs it, especially in light of the harsh criticism directed against this model by Vladimir Lossky, as reviewed in the previous chapter. Specifically, we are interested in the development of the dogmatic construct that incorporates a pneumatic dimension in christology proper and by extension in ecclesiology. The pneumatic dimension offsets the dangers of ecclesiological monophysitism and the lack of "polyhypostasity" discussed by Congar and Lossky when only the second person is considered the basis for this model. This will also lead us to isolate the neo-scholastic conceptuality utilized to accomplish this. For this we turn to an early-twentieth-century Belgian Jesuit theologian who devoted his short career in theological scholarship to reviving this model.

   Emile Mersch published two complementary books covering the subject first from the perspective of historical theology—*The Whole Christ*[55]—and then as a formal dogmatics—*The Theology of the Mystical Body*. Mersch's ecclesiology bears a certain resemblance to Scheeben's, whose model for the church directs one to its "mystery."[56] They are even closer in emphasis through the analogy that they draw between Christ and the church. Both refer to the visible, empirical, and societal dimension of the church with its analogue in the incarnate and historical Christ and to the invisible, supernatural and divinized church corresponding to the divine and grace-filled Christ.[57] Although when the subject of ecclesiology is broached the accent is on pneumatology for Scheeben and christology for Mersch, the key for Mersch as it was for Scheeben is the mediatorial role of Christ proceeding from the very constitution of the hypostatic union, and one with a significant pneumatological dimension. However, let us begin by introducing a counterpoint—namely, that of Pope Pius XII.

   I have already alluded to *Mystici Corporis* and the position it takes on the governance of the church by Christ—i.e., invisible interior guidance and visible hierarchical guidance, and on the utilization of Augustine's analogy that the Holy

Spirit is the soul of the church as Christ is its head. These positions, along with similar ones on the nature of *ad extra* trinitarian operations, the theory of appropriation, and the theology of anointing in the hypostatic union, carved out authoritative papal opinions on disputed neo-scholastic debates on each of these issues. While it is not evident from the text of the encyclical, alternative positions had been proposed that differ from that of the pontiff's, not least of which are those of Emile Mersch.

There is a tragic and perhaps ironic element to this divergence of theological positions. Mersch was killed by a bomb on May 23, 1940, during the German invasion of France, which date that year also happened to be the feast of Corpus Christi. Having devoted his theological work to the revival of this ecclesiological model, he did not live to witness the publication only three years later of *Mystici Corporis* by Pius XII. The ironic element is that in the encyclical the positions taken by the Pope on the issues mentioned were not the ones suggested by Mersch in his book. His translator is at great pains to insist that Mersch, whose work was published posthumously from manuscripts, would have achieved greater precision in his theses if tragedy did not strike.[58] For our purposes this brief aside enriches this inquiry, since it highlights the diverse positions on pneumatological christology in the neo-scholastic tradition. That *Mystici Corporis* might be challenged should not be cause of great concern, since it is clear that Vatican II's *Lumen Gentium* (*Dogmatic Constitution on the Church*) likewise suggests alternative positions to the ones advocated by Pius XII.[59]

By beginning with Mersch's divergences from the encyclical we can dissect the various pneumatological elements in his own christology and their significance for our subject. We start with his position on the soul of the church. Although he makes certain allowances for the alternative stance eventually articulated by Pius XII, he prefers to identify the church's soul with sanctifying grace rather than with the Holy Spirit. He reasons on the basis of the neo-scholastic positions on causality, with each distinctive type portending a different mode of divine self-communication in the sanctification of the just person. Since neither Mersch nor the Pope advance beyond the theory of appropriation relative to the mission of the Holy Spirit and its correlative efficient causality, the difference between them resides in their conception of how the divine self-communication constitutes the church as the Mystical Body of Christ. In other words, the contrast in positions is not so much in regard to their pneumatology but to the application of pneumatology vis-à-vis their theology of grace and the notions of causality that inform it.

The distinctions regarding types of causality drawn by the scholastics, especially those in the Aristotelian-Thomistic tradition, are central to their theology of grace. They provide the basis for articulating a theological anthropology in which the human being receives (or is infused with) and increases in the grace of God. The major distinction that concerns us is between efficient and formal causality. In the case of efficient causality the agent acts but does not inform the term of its action with itself, whereas in formal causality the agent imparts itself to the recipient as a form. The danger perceived by the school theologians of attributing to God a formal causality in external operations is the reduction of the divine being (implying change) to the created term of its action. Therefore, to avoid in the Pope's words the elimination of "the immovable frontier that separates creatures from their Creator,"[60] only efficient causality can be the mode of divine operation in the world.

When Mersch considers Augustine's analogy—"What the soul is in our body, that is the Holy Ghost in Christ's Body, the Church"—(subsequently endorsed in more than analogical terms by both Leo XIII and Pius XII), he agrees that the Holy Spirit acts only by efficient causality in the divine operations *ad extra,* including the indwelling of the church and the believer. However, it is precisely for this reason that he prefers sanctifying grace rather than the Holy Spirit to be construed as the soul of the church, with the former conceived not in the modality of efficient causality but in terms of what he designates as "quasi-formal causality" or "causality of union," the same designated type of causality descriptive of the divine operation that actuates and constitutes the hypostatic union.[61] In other words, if for Mersch the church according to this metaphor is the "mystical continuation of Christ Himself,"[62] then the modality of divine agency must be the same in its causal relationship to Christ as is the case with the assumed humanity relative to the Divine Logos. Ecclesiology has direct implications for christology and vice versa. Interestingly enough, as we shall see, despite this difference with *Mystici Corporis,* Mersch suprisingly ends up in agreement on the formally pneumatological dimension of christology.

By quasi-formal causality Mersch means the actuation of being that does not communicate form (as in formal causality) but does impart subsistence. So, with respect to the hypostatic union, the Divine Word as the assuming agent formally actuates the subsistence of the human nature in the divine personality of the Word. As a quasi-formal cause the divine action does not constitute the human nature per se—this would be an exercise in efficient causality—but it does actuate and constitute the union so that the human nature is in fact the humanity of God vis-à-vis the person of the Son.[63] In the same manner Christ through sanctifying grace quasi-formally constitutes the church as his mystical body.[64] The church subsists in him so that one can say that Christ and his mystical body constitute the whole single Christ.[65] In a very real sense, the church as mystical body is a sort of prolongation of the incarnation.[66]

Nor does this exclude efficient causality either in the incarnation or in the constitution of the church. It is the Holy Spirit by appropriation who is the efficient cause of grace in Christ and the church.[67] In the former case, the *gratia unionis, gratia habitualis,* and *gratia capitis* (the three being the traditional neo-scholastic designations for grace in Christ) are the work of the Holy Spirit as the efficient cause (through appropriation) of the divine operations. Similarly, the God-human, Jesus Christ, through quasi-formal causality constitutes the church, while the Holy Spirit through efficient causality imparts created grace (both actual and habitual). According to the pneumatological aspect of this construction, Mersch does not deny the later position of Pius XII that the Holy Spirit is the soul of the church, but insists that the Spirit be conceived as the soul of the church only as the Spirit of the Son or, in the language of causality, as the quasi-efficient cause in correlation with the Son as the quasi-formal principle of the church's inner life.[68]

As with most neo-scholastic theologies (even if Mersch is not typical), analysis proceeds on a number of different levels. I have focused on the language of causality because of the innovation represented by the notion of quasi-formal causality, an innovation not recognized or acknowledged by *Mystici Corporis.* We now turn to a more explicit examination of his theology of grace and its relationship to pneumatology.

It was Karl Barth who criticized the Catholic theology of grace for its numerous distinctions:

> The heart and guiding principle of the Romanist doctrine of grace is the negation of the unity of grace as always God's grace to man, as His sovereign act which is everywhere new and strange and free. It is the negation of the unity of grace as His grace in Jesus Christ. It is the division of grace by which it is first of all His, but then—and this is where the emphasis falls—effected and empowered by His grace, it is also our grace. Against this we must at once and quite definitely set our face.[69]

Although he was somewhat more irenical in his concluding reflections,[70] such a strong confessional polemic gives serious pause to a theology of grace that seems to thrive on numerous distinctions, some of which we have already noted—e.g., uncreated grace, created grace, actual grace, habitual grace, etc. Since Mersch's theological project is determined by one overriding rubric—namely, the mystical Christ—his delineation of the theology of grace serves us well, in light of Barth's criticism, to evaluate such a theology in reference to the singularity of God's revelation in Jesus Christ.

Mersch's starting point is the consciousness of the believer considered not in the reception of many diverse graces but in the singular grace of filial adoption. By consciousness Mersch means the "possession of oneself in oneself, an immanence of all that a person is in all that he is, a perfect identity of being with himself . . . "[71] In other words, it is a notion of consciousness that has more in common with the reflexive self-knowledge of St. Thomas' agent intellect argued later by transcendental Thomists than with the immediate state of self-consciousness apprehended through "feeling" (*Gefühl*) as proposed, for example, by Friedrich Schleiermacher.[72] The distinction is important because Mersch implicates an ontology that directly suggests that Christian consciousness is formed not simply by the salvific experience of the believer within the context of a believing community, but by the hypostatic agents presupposed in a fully developed theology of the trinity. It is on this basis that the distinctions within the one grace of Christ are legitimate.

Christian consciousness is awareness of union with Christ, that through the communication and reception of grace from him one is a member of his body and is a child of God as he is. The inner witness that Christians possess in their consciousness is that of inner attachment to Christ and to God.[73] With Christian consciousness as a foundation, one may proceed through a series of reductions to the most basic intelligible of Christian theology—namely, the intelligible of Christ's own consciousness in which the formal object and *subjectum* of theology is God, but a God who for the Christian believer is "wholly in Christ."[74] Here resides the basis in Christian consciousness for the doctrines of the trinity and the hypostatic union. If one is aware of attachment to God through attachment to Christ, one can conclude to both dogmas.

Hence we must conclude that Christian teaching expresses the consciousness they have of themselves as Christians.

What is this consciousness? It is clearly something wholly unique, *sui generis*, and must possess the unique characteristics which theology recognizes in super-natural knowledge. What does this imply? The Christian, formally as a Christian, is a member of Christ, that is, of the Word, who is the Son of the Father and the co-principle of the Holy Spirit. The Christian lives as a member of that sacramental reality which is the Church. He lives in an immense redemption. He is made and animated by all that is expressed in the doctrine of Christianity. To express himself to himself, he must express this whole doctrine.[75]

It indeed may seem to be a rather large step from the consciousness of union with Christ to these formal and speculative doctrines. However, Mersch is concerned with a level of knowledge that entails a supernatural elevation of the person through the communication of supernatural life, or to use the language of the patristic church, the divinization of human being as one aspect of the incarnation—viz., the assumption of a human nature to be truly the humanity of the divine Word, and the communication of that divinized humanity to those joined to Christ in baptism. This returns us to the nature of grace and the distinctions within the one single grace of Christ.

Mersch in his use of school typology distinguished between sanctifying (or habitual) grace and actual grace. Both are subspecies of created grace, each of which is related to uncreated grace. Uncreated grace is best understood as the self-donation of God to humanity, whether it be that which enables the sacred humanity to be assumed in the hypostatic union or "what accounts for the presence of God which Christians enjoy, namely, the indwelling of the Spirit and the Trinity."[76] It is equivalent to the divine being itself; therefore, it is the basis of everything in the order of grace (as God is in the order of being) and consequently the foundation of all created grace, sanctifying and actual.[77] The latter are both species of created grace, and according to Mersch's soteriological schema can be defined as follows: actual grace is the power of divinization and sanctifying grace is divinization as present (albeit imperfectly) in believers.[78]

These different graces are really aspects of the divine operation, the origin of which resides in the trinitarian processions. If uncreated grace is the self-donation of God in the assuming Word and the indwelling Spirit (the latter only by appropriation), created grace is that effect within the human person that elevates and divinizes human acts and habits in the plenitude and perfection that is exemplified in Christ Jesus. Actual grace is a volitional enablement or other divine influence that is a product of uncreated grace and establishes an accidental entity that is a reinforcement of the union between Christ and the believer—an "accident" because it is truly instrinsic to human nature and exists in it as a subject of inherence.[79] This entitive union is sanctifying grace and is effected by the Holy Spirit, although the grace itself proceeds from Christ—i.e., his habitual grace communicated to the believer under the formality of Christ's grace of headship (*gratia capitis*). All grace, therefore, is a derivation from the threefold grace of Christ noted above.

The correlation between Christ and the Spirit at these levels of causality and grace can also be expressed in the explicitly hypostatic language of Son and Spirit.

The foundation for such is the *filioque*. While it is the Son alone who takes on flesh, the work of the incarnation is appropriated to the Holy Spirit; and while the mission of the Son is the basis for the adoptive filiation of believers (*filii in Filio*), it is a mission in the mission of the Spirit, who through grace effects the union between Christ and his body.[80] The Holy Spirit's work is always posterior to that of the Son, since he proceeds from the Son, who with and from the Father is the co-principle of the Spirit. If in the immanent trinity the procession by way of will and love follows the procession by way of knowledge and utterance, so, too, in the economic trinity, does the unity of divine love follow the fecundity of divine filiation.[81]

Even the assumed humanity shares in the spiration of the Spirit because of its union with the hypostatic principle of the Son. According to the logic of grace the assumed humanity of Christ possesses all the relations of the Word itself. This marks a unique innovation in Mersch, who draws to the forefront of the theology of grace the person of the Son. The grace of union bears a filial character, since the union between the divine nature and human nature in the person of the Son requires a genuine change (*mutatio,*) as do all relations that begin in time. The *mutatio* affects only the human nature (the divine nature being immutable) and is necessarily filial in character. If this was not the case, the real relation of the human nature to the divine Son in the hypostatic union would through the actualization of this *mutatio* bear no meaning.[82] The same thus follows for the grace communicated to believers. They are drawn into the filial relationship of Christ to the Father and are therefore sons and daughters in the Son (*filii in Filio*).

When refracted back into the trinity, a number of principles emerge that are important for Mersch's version of Spirit-christology. First, since the incarnation is the communication of the Godhead as trinity, the identity of Jesus Christ as "truly and exclusively the Son" must be fully appreciated.[83] With reference to the confession of his divinity, the "truth is that He is God because He is the Son, not that He is the Son because He is God."[84] So, too, regarding the other intra-trinitarian relations of the Son, by a purely rational priority one associates the man Jesus Christ with the personal and notional attributes of trinitarian identity before the essential ones. Therefore, in the order of identification Jesus Christ is first the Son (a personal identity), then the Spirator (a notional identity), and finally God (an essential identity). Following this, Mersch can then argue that believers who are united to the Son through grace in baptism likewise share through participation in Christ's filiation, spiration, and divinization. The second of these portends a strongly pneumatological dimension for the communion of Christians in the church, and one that is directly related to the intra-trinitarian relations, as we shall now see.

As with Scheeben, Mersch's pneumatic christology revolves around one key concept. Instead of the biblical and patristic image of anointing employed by the great nineteenth century theologian, Mersch has utilized the scholastic notional construct of spiration unique to the tradition of Latin trinitarianism. Dependent as this concept is on the *filioque*, it simply extends to believers the privilege enjoyed by the sacred humanity of Christ. Through that humanity's elevation in union with the person of the divine Word, it is able to share in the second person's co-spiration (with the Father) of the Holy Spirit; so, too, believers share in the co-spiration by virtue of their union with Christ—i.e., what Mersch labels a "a participated spiration that is communicated to them by Christ."[85] This presupposes that the sending of the Holy Spirit is a continuation in temporal mission of its eternal intra-trinitarian procession. It also points to the divine attribute traditionally appropriated to the Holy Spirit. As members of the co-principle of the Holy Spirit, Christians share in that theological charity, which is both Christ's charity and that spirating love in the Godhead that is the principle of the Holy Spirit. Through the incarnation "Christ's charity is the principle of our divine life because it is the human love of Him who is the principle of the Holy Spirit's divine life."[86] In other words, in the life of the church believers participate in the Son as spirator of the Spirit by their exercise of theological charity, thereby encapsulating within the mystical body the dual missions of Son and Spirit by virtue of the efficacy of "Christ and His love" and "the Holy Spirit and His sanctifying action."[87]

We can now return to the teaching of Pius XII. Even though the language of causality (in reference to the theology of grace) is different and there is no suggestion of quasi-formal causality in *Mystici Corporis*, the relationship articulated between Son and Spirit is nearly identical with that suggested by Mersch. The Son's activity as spirator of the Spirit does not exclude the hypostatic union. The Son spirates the Spirit as both the eternal Logos and in union with his assumed humanity, so that the Spirit's work can never be considered outside that of the Son.[88] In the language of the encyclical, the Son adorns or anoints his human nature with the Holy Spirit so that it might truly be an instrument of divine redemption;[89] or, in the language of the neo-scholastics and Mersch, the humanity of Christ is the instrumental cause of divinization through the efficacy of the Spirit.[90]

What emerges is a truly pneumatological christology even within the constraints of the Latin doctrine of the trinity that the neo-scholastics espoused. The limits of the theory of appropriation and of efficient causality for divine operations *ad extra* do not entirely inhibit the development of the pneumatolgical dimension. The introduction of quasi-formal causality on the christological side, similar to Scheeben's use of a pneumatological non-exclusive proper mission, certainly stretches the neo-scholastic paradigm. Pius XII, who does not endorse either of these innovations, nevertheless also develops the pneumatological side of christology in a manner similar to that of both Scheeben and Mersch. Whether his faithfulness to the paradigm is more theologically warranted relative to his intent remains to be examined. This we shall do in the following chapter by recounting the debate over causality in reference to the hypostatic union and the inhabitation of the Holy Spirit and then by querying a position that does in fact argue for the necessity of breaking open the paradigm on these issues, especially appropriation theory and efficient causality. In the meantime, one can make a preliminary judgment with respect to the rhetoric of the Pope's pneumatological christology. As the following excerpt from the encyclical illustrates, the pneumatological dimension of the pontiff's thought is certainly a strong factor in the salvific mystery that is Christ and the Church.

> If we examine closely this divine principle of life and power given by Christ, in so far as it constitutes the very source of every gift and created grace, we easily perceive that it is nothing else than the Holy Spirit, the Paraclete, who proceeds from the Father and the Son, and who is called in a special way the "Spirit of Christ" or the "Spirit of the Son." For it was by this Breath of grace and truth that

the Son of God anointed His soul in the immaculate womb of the Blessed Virgin; this Spirit delights to dwell in the beloved soul of our Redeemer as in His most cherished shrine; this Spirit Christ merited for us on the Cross by shedding His own blood; this Spirit He bestowed on the Church for the remission of sins, when He breathed on the Apostles; and while Christ alone received this Spirit without measure, to the members of the Mystical Body He is imparted only according to the measure of the giving of Christ from Christ's own fullness. But after Christ's glorification on the Cross, His Spirit is communicated to the Church in an abundant outpouring, so that she, and her individual members, may become daily more and more like to our Savior. It is the Spirit of Christ that has made us adopted sons of God in order that one day "we all beholding the glory of the Lord with open face may be transformed into the same image from glory to glory."[91]

In summary, we note the following points. Although Mersch concentrates on the christological locus for advancing his notion of the church as the Mystical Body of Christ, he has given considerable attention to pneumatology within the parameters of christology. As spirator of the Holy Spirit, Christ along with his body gives the central Christian confession as well as the life of the church a distinctive pneumatological flavor. Speculatively, the warrant for this pneumatically informed paradigm of christological ecclesiology is the filial character of grace. Both the sacred humanity of Jesus and the elevated humanity of baptized believers share in the singular relationship of the Word to the Father and the Spirit. This resolves the prevailing problem within scholastic theology—namely, "how to conceive the existence of a special and real relation of adoptive sons with the true Son and, through Him, with the Father and the Spirit, without disregarding the solidly established principle of theology that divine works *ad extra* are common to the three divine persons."[92] By emphasizing the filial character of the christological grace of union, Mersch is able to keep in perspective that the work common to the divine nature of the three persons *ad extra* in the incarnation of the Word does not prohibit but in fact lays the foundation for the subsistence of the assumed humanity of Christ (and by extension the participating humanity of believers) in the Word *ad intra*.[93] With this the grace of redemption does in fact reveal not just the work of the trinitarian persons in common but the real relation to the persons in particular—in this case, to the Son and vis-à-vis the intra-trinitarian relations of the Son to the Father and the Spirit.

Mersch, whose christological focus brings to the fore the possibility of a distinct and real relation of human nature to a divine person, nearly approaches Scheeben in the latter's pneumatic emphases. His Spirit-christology is as comprehensive as his predecessor's. It links together christology, soteriology, and anthropology. The Holy Spirit is an agent in the constitution of the God-human through the act of the incarnation and the sanctification of the assumed nature. Christ is the bearer and sender of the Spirit in the saving events signified from Christmas through Pentecost. Finally, Christians are joined to Christ and share in his saving work through the Spirit, who is spirated and sent. Mersch can therefore characterize his ecclesiological model in language that is both christological and pneumatological. On the one hand, the church is "Christ who forms himself in the mystical plenitude of his body,"[94] and on the other hand, "Everything begins in Christ through the work of the Holy Spirit who forms Christ and Christians: 'conceived of the Holy Ghost.'"[95]

Conclusion

In this chapter I have sought to explore patterns within neo-scholastic theology that lend themselves to the construction of Spirit-christology or what would approach Spirit-christology. Since this particular christological model was not explicitly advanced by any of the theologians examined, we have identified those suggestions within christology, pneumatology, and the theology of grace that could be used as building blocks for such a proposal. We may now summarize their content and identify the avenues down which our inquiry must proceed in order to arrive at a mature neo-scholastic Spirit-christology.

First, we introduced the neo-scholastic method in a framework wider than the definitions that were offered in Chapter 1. We also traced its influence through modern papal teaching on pneumatology and its relationship to christology. Although it was only a brief review of the issues, it does serve to highlight that at least by the late nineteenth century the theology of the Holy Spirit, especially in regard to ecclesiology, became a major concern in Catholic circles.

Second, we explored the work of Matthias Scheeben as exemplary for what this tradition might produce in the way of Spirit-christology. He presented us immediately with the most significant hindrance in neo-scholastic theology to the development of Spirit-christology—namely, how to distinguish the work of the individual persons of the trinity from that of the trinitarian persons in common. Appropriation theory was the traditional solution to this dilemma in neo-scholastic theology, although it was far from adequate. Does the identity of the person fully stand out if, in contrast to the hypostatic substance of the person, only the *operatum*—i.e., the effects of a divine person, still common to all three persons but simply appropriated to one—is infused through grace? Scheeben's solution was the suggestion of a non-exclusive *proprium* theory whereby the identity of the person is properly revealed and communicated. The importance of this issue cannot be overestimated irrespective of the ultimate cogency of Scheeben's proposal. A brief explanation is in order, since this debate will be our subject in the next chapter.

Latin scholasticism requires that the distinction of persons in the trinity be based on the opposition of relations (*relationis oppositio*). This has led to the dominance of appropriation theory relative to *ad extra* divine activity, wherein that opposition does not function since it is only applicable in reference to the intra-trinitarian processions. According to this paradigm, the distinct hypostatic identity of a divine person is not properly revealed *ad extra*—i.e., in reference to that person alone—except in the term of the incarnation, the man Jesus Christ. The inevitable consequence of this logic has been the subordination of pneumatology to christology, or in trinitarian language, the subordination of the mission of the Spirit to that of the Son.

Consider the revelation of the trinity through its works *ad extra*. Only the Son is properly revealed and communicated. The revelation of the Holy Spirit is limited to appropriation. An orthodox Spirit-christology—i.e., one that maintains the distinct hypostatic identities of each of the trinitarian persons and does not sink into modalism or theistic monopersonalism—must allow for a robust pneumatology to characterize its role in christology. Scheeben's non-exclusive *proprium* theory at least attempts that by arguing that some form of trinitarian *proprium* theory must undergird the theology of the temporal mission of the Holy Spirit to overcome the neglect of the third person in traditional Western theology.

More important, Scheeben maps the terrain for a Roman Catholic Spirit-christology. At least three dimensions of christology must be addressed for it to be thoroughly pneumatological as well. These include, first, the constitution of the God-human through the role of the Holy Spirit in the incarnation and the hypostatic union. Second, the soteriological implications of christology must be fully drawn out, with attention to how Christ effects salvation as the bearer and sender of the Spirit. Finally, the area traditionally appropriated to the Spirit—e.g., sanctification, the divine indwelling and the Christian life, must be linked integrally with the pneumatic christology emerging from the previous two dimensions.

Third, we investigated the work of Emile Mersch in exploring both an alternative neo-scholastic construct for Spirit-christology and, more importantly, in identifying the decisive role that the theology of grace plays within the overall neo-scholastic paradigm. Regarding the former goal, the key was to highlight the placement of the linking construct in the relation between the Son and the Spirit that allows for the articulation of a Spirit-christology. It clearly is located in the act of the incarnation, where, consistent with the descending model of christology—i.e., the Son becoming flesh—and the overall method of neo-scholastic theology—i.e., thinking from God to the world—pneumatic agency is determined in light of the intra-trinitarian relations, especially the *filioque*. Both suggested pneumatological models, anointing (Scheeben) and spiration (Mersch), attempt to offer cogent explanations of the Spirit's inclusion in the christological mission. Both proposals have been subject to criticism, and whether they can survive in the same form following such criticism will be discussed in Chapter 4.

Directly relevant for the next chapter is Mersch's innovation in the theology of grace. His insight that the event, act, or state of grace must be "filial" in character implies that the Christian experience of God is itself trinitarian. Without denying or in his mind contradicting the common *ad extra* working of the divine operation, Mersch has suggested that believers are really related to the divine persons because through the grace received in baptism they are sons and daughters in the Son (*filii in Filio*). Grace, which regenerates, adopts, and divinizes believers, unites them with Christ both in his filial relation to the Father and his spirational relation to the Holy Spirit. In effect, the *relationis oppositio* has become externalized through the ontological reality of grace. He seems to have thoroughly surmounted the neo-scholastic problematic that we briefly described in the preceding paragraphs. Is his solution cogent? To answer that we proceed to the next chapter.

Notes

1. This is the standard distinction from the "Manual tradition" in neo-scholasticism. For example: "When Theology expounds and coordinates the dogmas themselves, and demonstrates them from Scripture and Tradition, it takes the name of Positive Theology. When it takes the dogmas for granted, and penetrates into their nature and discovers their principles

and consequences, it is designated Speculative Theology, and sometimes Scholastic Theology
... " Joseph Wilhelm and Thomas B. Scannell, *A Manual of Catholic Theology: Based on
Scheeben's "Dogmatik"* (New York: Benzinger, 1899), p. xviii, from here on referred to as
MCT. For the same distinction in one of the last such manuals, see: Ludwig Ott, *Fundamentals
of Catholic Dogma*, Ed. James Canon Bastible, (St. Louis: B. Herder Book Company, 1958)
pp. 3–4, from here on referred to as *FCD.*

    2. I say loosely because both the methodological structure and the content differ in slight
but important ways. Whereas Thomas posed his inquiry in the form of *questiones,* the neo-
scholastics presented the dogmatic loci in thesis form. The emphasis on propositionalism is
certainly greater in the latter than in the former. In addition, the christological mystery is
handled by the Angelic Doctor under the "consideration of the Savior of all, and of the benefits
bestowed by Him on the human race," with attention not only to the mystery of the incarnation
in terms of the structure of the hypostatic union but also to "such things as were done and
suffered by our Savior"(ST IIIa, Pars.), a perspective that directs him to investigate the salvific
efficacy of the events of Christ's life as recorded in the Gospels. Therefore, attention to
scripture (in medieval perspective, of course) is greater in Thomas and other medieval scholastics than in the later neo-scholastics.

    3. Thomas Aquinas, *Summa Theologiae*, Ia Q. 1,2.

    4. This charge especially informs their consideration of ecumenism. See Methodios
Foyas, *Orthodoxy, Roman Catholicism, and Anglicanism*, pp. 204–205, 222. Vladimir Lossky
is particularly harsh in accusing Catholic trinitarian theology of descending to the realm of
religious philosophy—all of which is due to "Filioquism." See his "The Procession of the
Holy Spirit in Orthodox Trinitarian Doctrine," *In the Image and Likeness of God.* pp. 71–96.

    5. This order is basically followed by both *MCT* and *FCD* with only slight variations.

    6. *Dei Filius*, Chap. 4.

    7. I am following William J. Hill's argument in his *The Three-Personed God: The Trinity
as a Mystery of Salvation* (Washington, D.C.: Catholic University Press of America, 1982),
pp. 53–78. I shall return to Hill later in this work.

    8. *Divinum Illus Munus.* par. 3. English translation in *Official Catholic Teachings: Christ
Our Lord*, ed. Amanda G. Wallington. (Wilmington: McGrath Publishing Co., 1978).

    9. Ibid., par. 2.

    10. Chapter 1 and Canon 1,4. Present translation from quote in Emile Mersch, *The
Theology of the Mystical Body*, tr. Cyril Vollert, S.J. (St. Louis: Herder, 1951), p. 358.

    11. *Divinum Illus Munus.*, par. 4.

    12. Ibid.

    13. Ibid.

    14. Ibid.

    15. Ibid., pars. 9–10.

    16. Pius XII, *Mystici Corporis*, par's. 39–40. Also, in Wallington.

    17. *Divinum Illum Munus*, par. 7; *Mystici Corporis*, par. 57. Leo XIII quotes Augustine's
original analogy: "What the soul is in our body, that is the Holy Ghost in Christ's Body, the
Church" (St. Aug., *Serm.* 187, *de Temp*).

    18. Gerald McCool, *Catholic Theology in the Nineteenth Century: The Quest for a
Unitary Method* (New York: Seabury, 1977), pp. 168, 240.

    19. Scheeben. *A Manual of Catholic Theology*, Vol. I (henceforth, *Manual.* I), p. 315.

    20. Ibid., pp. 312–315.

    21. Ibid., p. 317.

    22. Matthias Scheeben, *The Mysteries of Christianity* (henceforth, *Mysteries*), tr. Cyril
Vollert, S.J. (New York: Herder, 1947), p. 81.

    23. Ibid., p. 88.

24. Scheeben, *Manual* I, p. 344.

25. Scheeben, *Mysteries*, p. 134.

26. "For us, who do not behold the persons in themselves, who for that matter are accustomed to judge all things in terms of their activities, this distinction and apportionment of activities is almost a necessity, if we are to distinguish the persons from one another and are to awaken in ourselves a living interest in each of them." Ibid.

27. Ibid., pp. 132–133. "The divine persons are distinct only in their mutual relationships, and these relationships, so far as an activity is connected with them, are actuated only among themselves. God the Father can operate with an action that is exclusively proper to Himself as Father, only in generating the Son; and Father and Son can operate with an action that is exclusively their own, only in spirating the Holy Spirit. As the spirating activity must be ascribed to the Son not in distinction to the Father, but in union with Him, so a fortiori every other activity must be ascribed to all three persons not according to their distinction, but according to their unity. As, therefore, according to the teaching of the Church, the Father and the Son are one principle of the Holy Spirit, so all three persons are one principle of all external works. On account of this unity in operation, which is based on unity of nature, one person does not have a greater function in any of the works than the other persons; they all act equally through one wisdom, one will, one power."

28. Ibid., p. 132.

29. Scheeben. *Manual* I, p. 344.

30. Ibid., p. 342.

31. The modality of this type of appropriation is explained as follows: " . . . all three persons have the same activity and the same mode of acting externally, but that they come into possession of it in different ways." Scheeben, *Mysteries*, p. 136.

32. Ibid., p. 135.

33. Ibid., p. 137.

34. Ibid.

35. Ibid., pp. 141–146.

36. Ibid., pp. 156–157, 161–162.

37. Ibid., pp. 163–168.

38. The term "non-exclusive *proprium* theory," which is a middle position between a strict *appropriatum* and a strict *proprium,* is taken from the work of Malachi Donnelly, S.J., who will be reviewed in the next chapter. See his "The Inhabitation of the Holy Spirit: A Solution According to de la Taille," *Theological Studies* 8 (1947), pp. 445–447. Scheeben expresses this middle position as follows: ". . . the end of the true mission of a divine person to the creature is not, strictly speaking, the activity which that person is to exercise there, because the activity is only an *appropriatum*, not a *proprium*; nevertheless this activity can be brought into harmony with the end of the mission. In carrying out His mission, the person who is sent is thought of as exclusively active in a twofold sense: first, so far as He Himself effects His union with the creature; and secondly, so far as, while sojourning in the creature, He puts forth an activity that corresponds to His union. But the appropriation of the activity does not negate the personal character of the mission, if we actually make the proper presence of the person who is sent the basis of this appropriation, and regard it as the center of the sending process." *Mysteries*, pp. 177–178.

39. Scheeben. *Mysteries*, pp. 173–180.

40. Ibid., p. 313.

41. Ibid., pp. 313–322. Scheeben. *Manual* I, pp. 90–95.

42. Ibid., p. 360.

43. Scheeben, *Manual* I, "Likewise the humanity of Christ is in the bosom of the Father, and the Father in Him as in His image, in a manner infinitely superior to what grace effects

in the sanctified. The special indwelling of the Father and the Holy Ghost in Christ is technically called 'presence by concomitancy.'" (p. 96.)

44. "The Holy Spirit is regarded, but only by appropriation, as the cause of the hypostatic union, which is a work of love. The substantial Word of God makes His appearance in a way that recalls the outward expression of our intelligible word. Our external word is formed through the agency of the breath streaming from the heart, and is propelled by love, which induces us to communicate our thoughts outwardly. But when our inner word, our thought, begets true and living love in us, our external word, too, bears this love within it, and breathes forth love. The pulsating of the Holy Spirit, by which the incarnation of the Logos is effected, and His pulsating within the incarnate Logos, are interconnected in a similar manner." Scheeben, *Mysteries*, pp. 360–361, n. 1.

45. Ibid., pp. 332–333. For the subtle distinction between the Spirit as agent of the anointing and his relationship to the Logos, Scheeben explains: "Not so much the Holy Spirit in Himself, as rather the source from which He issues, but including, besides this source, all its wealth and its overflow, is the unguent with which Christ is anointed. In other words, the ointment is not the *Spiritus Sanctus spiratus*, but the *Spiritus Sanctus spirans* together with His *spiramen*; it is not the latter's operation through the former, as with the saints, but the former's operation through the latter, that produces the Saint of saints. Moreover, the execution of the hypostatic union, which is the reason why the dignity of the Son of God pertains also to the Son of man, is ascribed to the Third Person, the representative of the divine love, only by appropriation." (p. 332, n. 7).

46. Ibid., p. 331.

47. Ibid., p. 439.

48. Ibid., p. 393.

49. Ibid., p. 395.

50. Ibid., p. 459.

51. Ibid., pp. 582, 585; *Manual* II, pp. 86–87.

52. See Malachi Donnelly, S.J., "The Indwelling of the Holy Spirit According to M. J. Scheeben," *Theological Studies* 7 (1946), p. 248, for reaction by his contemporaries.

53. David Coffey discusses this at great length in *Grace: The Gift of the Holy Spirit* (Manly, N.S.W., Australia: Catholic Institute of Sydney, 1979), pp. 55, 236.

54. *Summa Theologiae*, IIIa, q. 8.

55. Emile Mersch, *The Whole Christ*. tr. John R. Kelly, S.J. (Milwaukee: Bruce, 1938).

56. Scheeben, *Mysteries*, pp. 539–542.

57. "The Church is visible in the very way that its historical founder and head, the God-man Himself, was visible . . . The inner nature of the Church is absolutely supernatural, as is that of the God-man." Scheeben, ibid., p. 340. "As these two aspects [empirical reality and divinization] are found in Christ's humanity, they will also be found in the mystic perpetuation of that humanity which is the Church. The Church will likewise be an empirical thing and a mysterious reality." Mersch, *The Theology of the Mystical Body*, p. 482.

58. For his translator's (Fr. Cyril Vollert, S.J.) introduction on these matters, including the biographical information, see ibid. pp. ix–xv.

59. Specifically, on the position that the Holy Spirit is the soul of the church, *Lumen Gentium* reinforces the original analogical emphasis of St. Augustine, which both Leo XIII and Pius XII had transformed into a more literal assertion. *Lumen Gentium* on this matter reads as follows: "For this reason the Church is compared, not without significance, to the mystery of the incarnate Word. As the assumed nature, inseparably united to him, serves the divine Word as a living organ of salvation, so, in a somewhat similar way, does the social structure of the Church serve the Spirit of Christ who vivifies it, in the building up of the body (cf. Eph. 4:15)" (Art. 9). Cf. above, n. 32.

The second major issue of widely observed divergence between *Mystici Corporis* and *Lumen Gentium* concerns the relationship of the Roman Catholic Church with the true Church as the Body of Christ. As the following two quotes illustrate, Vatican II steps back from the virtual identity pronounced by Pius XII: 1) "If we would define and describe this true Church of Jesus Christ—which is the One, Holy, Catholic, Apostolic Roman Church . . . " (No. 13, *Mystici Corporis*)." 2) "This is the sole Church of Christ which in the Creed we profess to be one, holy, catholic and apostolic . . . This Church, constituted and organized as a society in the present world, subsists in the Catholic Church, which is governed by the successor of Peter and by the bishops in communion with him. (Art. 9, *Lumen Gentium*). For commentary on this divergence, due to Vatican II's introduction of the ecclesiological model of the Church as "the People of God," see especially Avery Dulles, S.J. *Models of the Church* (Garden City: Doubleday, 1978), pp. 56–57, 145–166.

Also, as will be evident in the next chapter, the debate over what exactly Pius XII resolved in the area of causality, the theology of grace and trinitarian appropriation was an open one.

60. *Mystici Corporis*, No. 9.

61. Mersch *Theology of the Mystical Body*, pp. 447–450, 484, 495–496.

62. Ibid., p. 486.

63. Ibid., pp. 208–209.

64. Mersch leaves open the conceptualization of this grace. "Whether we regard grace as an influx emanating from Christ or as Christ who infuses grace, it is present in all parts of the body and communicates to each part its own share and degree of life." Ibid., p. 448.

65. Ibid., pp. 484–485. "In any case we should note well that the soul of the Church, together with the body, forms a total entity, a single Church of Christ, just as soul and body constitute a single man or as the empirical aspect and the fullness of divinization make up a single Christ."

66. "The life of God Himself in Christ, or the Incarnation, and the life of Christ communicated to souls, or the mystical body, the totality of Christ: these two things seem to be but one, the second being no more than the fulfillment of the first." Ibid. p. 198, cf. p. 197.

67. Ibid., p. 448.

68. "Besides, our way of representing the doctrine does not imply a denial that the Holy Spirit is the soul of the Church. Since the Spirit is in the Son, He is an interior power incessantly infusing a life that has not yet reached its full perfection and forming an organism that is not yet completely constructed." Ibid.

69. Karl Barth. *Church Dogmatics 4/1* (Edinburgh: T & T Clark, 1956), p. 84.

70. "But we trust in that *communio in sacris* which—not made with hands—has already been achieved by the sovereign act of the God who reconciles us men with Himself and therefore with one another: on the far side of the Church's doctrine and practice, which even at its best (whether Evangelical or Catholic) can only be a witness made with the best of human understanding and conscience to the God who is greater than us all." Ibid., p. 88.

71. Mersch, *Theology of the Mystical Body*, p. 76.

72. Freidrich Schleiermacher, *The Christian Faith* (Philadelphia: Fortress, 1928), p. 6.

73. Mersch, *Theology of the Mystical Body*, p. 87.

74. Ibid., p. 89. In the language of Dorothee Sölle, Mersch's method can be labeled a "christological reduction." See Sölle's *Christ the Representative* (Philadelphia: Fortress, 1967). However, it is one contextualized by a fully developed doctrine of the trinity, whereas Sölle's theological contextualization is post-theist. Nevertheless, the reduction should not be minimized, as, for example, the following illustrates: "The task of theology is to reduce everything to the first intelligible, which is Christ and His consciousness." Mersch, *Theology of the Mystical Body*, p. 85.

75. Ibid., pp. 80–81.

76. Ibid., p. 607.
77. Ibid., pp. 599, 624.
78. Ibid., p. 595.
79. Ibid., pp. 608-609, 628-632.
80. Ibid., p. 363.
81. Ibid., pp. 421-422.
82. Ibid., pp. 362-362.
83. Ibid., p. 359.
84. Ibid.
85. Ibid., p. 437.
86. Ibid., p. 432.
87. Ibid.
88. Ibid., p. 428.
89. *Mystici Corporis*, No. 31—"Just as at the first moment of the Incarnation the Son of the Eternal Father adorned with the fullness of the Holy Spirit the human nature which was substantially united to Him, that it might be a fitting instrument of the Divinity in the sanguinary work of the Redemption, so at the hour of His precious death He willed that His Church should be enriched with the abundant gifts of the Paraclete in order that in dispensing the divine fruits of the Redemption she might be, for the Incarnate Word, a powerful instrument that would never fail."
90. Mersch. *Theology of the Mystical Body*, p. 229.
91. *Mystici Corporis*, No. 56.
92. Mersch. *The Theology of the Mystical Body*, p. 357.
93. Ibid., p. 372.
94. Ibid., p. 447.
95. Ibid., p. 446.

3

"Grace and Presence:"
Issues for a Catholic
Spirit-christology

In the previous chapter we introduced the neo-scholastic paradigm and explored its productivity for Spirit-christology. Popes Leo XIII and Pius XII strongly suggest the pneumatological dimension of ecclesial existence and hint at its formative influence in christology as well. Matthias Scheeben and Emile Mersch articulate the basics of Spirit-christology when they affirm and explicate the Spirit's role in the incarnation, the paschal mystery, the communication of grace, and the life of the church. The paradigm, while productive in this area, also sets the parameters for the focus of theological investigation into the further exploitation of a more fully developed Spirit-christology. Proceeding on the principle that the distinction of persons within the trinity is predicated on the *relationis oppositio* and that this holds for the *ad extra* operation of the trinity in the work of salvation vis-à-vis the temporal missions of the Son and the Spirit, we must now query the paradigm regarding the possibility for properly distinguishing the persons in those missions.

The logic of our inquiry directs that we proceed along a path that respects the developments within the paradigm. Spirit-christology as a viable construct within neo-scholasticism would have to maintain the orthodox distinction of the persons while not compromising either the transcendence of God or the essential unity of the divine operation *ad extra*—"from the Father through the Son in the Holy Spirit." At the same time, the integrity of the pneumatological dimension of the model can be maintained only if the Holy Spirit retains its own *proprium*. Otherwise, the role of the Holy Spirit would collapse into its traditionally instrumentalist position relative to the second person. Within a christological model especially, this would be self-defeating; the intent to integrate pneumatology into our understanding of Jesus Christ would fail. Unless the model upholds the full hypostatic integrity of the third person, Spirit-christology would lose its cogency within this tradition, except that an entirely revisionist option be taken where hypostatic distinctions in God cease to be meaningful. Such options must await the last two chapters of this book for evaluation.

In broader scholastic perspective we return to where Mersch proffered his most suggestive innovation—namely, that real relations to the divine persons are viable within a scholastic theology of grace. If this position is warranted and then explicated for both the christological and pneumatological missions, it will enable our model to uphold the integrity of the two missions without slipping into modalism. Therefore, our investigation will now focus on the cogency of this proposal, that real relations exist between the believer and the persons of the trinity, to the extent of understanding this relation within the perspective of a proper temporal mission that is applicable to the third person as well as to the second. As we shall see, the route toward such an affirmation was a rather slow one in neo-scholastic circles.

We will begin by reviewing a debate sparked by the innovative christological work of Maurice de la Taille, S.J. His theory of the hypostatic union as "created actuation by uncreated act" led a number of fellow Jesuits to apply the same metaphysical construct to the inhabitation of the Holy Spirit in terms very similar to those of Scheeben and Mersch. The subsequent controversy indicates two alternative paths for resolving the nature of trinitarian self-communication, one of which preserves an essentially Thomistic model and the other of which effectively goes beyond it. The first alternative is the subject of the remainder of this section; the second will be addressed as our only subject in Chapter 4. For the former we shall examine the trinitarian work of the Dominican theologian William J. Hill, and for the latter the recent work of Australian theologian David Coffey will be considered. With Coffey we shall have arrived at the transcending of the scholastic paradigm and, for all intents and purposes, at a maturely constructed Roman Catholic Spirit-christology. Following this, the construction of Spirit-christology will be studied and evaluated from outside the parameters of the scholastic method.

Debate and Controversy: The Metaphysics of Trinitarian Self-communication

Father de la Taille, already known for his theological work on the Mass, published a series of articles that were translated in one volume under the title *The Hypostatic Union and Created Actuation By Uncreated Act*.[1] The debate that ensued as a result of the book was motivated by the theory itself but also by the application of the theory to pneumatology. De la Taille had restricted his work primarily to christology, although it was argued (and indeed controverted) that the extension of it to pneumatology was theologically warranted. This is not difficult to comprehend after inquiring into his proposal, for de la Taille contends that his theological metaphysics is based on a similarity in the divine operation among the following three loci of supernatural agency: the light of glory, sanctifying grace, and the hypostatic union. The resemblance to similar linkages in Scheeben and Mersch, while not accounted for by de la Taille, betrays a basic like-mindedness among the three for an understanding of the theology of grace.

De la Taille's Theory of the Hypostatic Union

De la Taille was a speculative theologian with deep roots in Thomism. Much of the controversy was in fact an "in house" debate on the more accurate representation of

the Angelic Doctor's teaching. Amid the disputed territory of contemporary interpretations and traditional commentaries on St. Thomas, de la Taille laid out the
following problem for scholastic metaphysics when applied to the hypostatic union.
Assuming that the hypostatic union is a union of substances—e.g., body, soul, and
divine Word (the first two being incomplete substances)—one cannot presume that
the union results in some new substance or nature—e.g., a *tertium quid* between God
and humanity. Cognizant of this, de la Taille warns against the typical errors of
monophysitism and nestorianism. For the former, the human nature is absorbed by
the divine, and in the latter case the "man" (or person) born of Mary is strictly
coincidental with his human nature and therefore must be united to the divine Word
in a composite union. In both cases the confusion resides in the identification of the
person of Jesus Christ with his human nature. The correction mandated by orthodoxy
posits that the identity of the "person" of Christ is with his Godhead as contrasted
with his human nature. Christ is the divine Word who possesses a human nature and
alone subsists as person in a human nature.[2] In other words, going back to the
neo-Chalcedonic doctrine of the anhypostasis of Christ's human nature, the only
person present in the hypostatic union is that of the divine Word who became flesh.
A human nature, not a human person, was assumed by the Word in the incarnation.

This reaffirmation of patristic concerns in scholastic christology does not, however, resolve all the issues surrounding the question of how the human nature is
assumed. De la Taille posed a series of questions:

> The problem then is the following: how can a human nature be united to a
> pre-existent person? . . . how can a compound of body and soul, of a human body
> and a human soul, fail to be a Man, and therefore a subsisting individual, such as
> we call a person? And secondly, supposing even the possibility of such an anomaly,
> how can a pre-existing person become substantially one with an additional nature?[3]

To provide adequate answers, attention must be given to both the condition of the
nature that is assumed in the hypostatic union and the condition of the union itself.
With respect to the former, one is faced with a paradox—namely, how to posit a
change that is substantial but that does not also produce a change in substance; or,
in other words, how to maintain the integrity of the human nature that is at the same
time the human nature of the Son of God, already a divine person.

Being a Thomist, de la Taille searched for a positive accounting of the assumption
of the human nature relative to the issue of human personality. This is contrasted
with the traditional Scotistic resolution of this problem, a solution that is cast in
entirely negative terms. Duns Scotus had argued that the presence of personality in
human nature is simply the negation of ownership by another subject. So, in the case
of the hypostatic union, the presence of divine ownership of the human nature
through the Word's assumption of it means that there is no personality intrinsic to
it. The Thomistic solution has generally acknowledged that the negation of human
personality in the assumed humanity rests not simply on the negation vis-à-vis the
presence of divine ownership, but on something positive in the assumption itself.
An investigation of St. Thomas's commentators (Suarez, Cajetan, Capreolus) yields
at least three solutions when the positive side of the human nature's assumption is
considered.

The commentators' proposals require that the positive addition of personality to the human nature—proceeding only from the divine Word and not identical to the human nature—"is located either after, or before, or within the nature's *existence*."[4] The first solution, proposed by Suarez, argues that "personality follows upon the other substantial elements, whether existence or nature."[5] Basing his case on the impossibility of separating existence from nature, Suarez insisted that personality can only be an addition to the formal principle of the existence of the human nature. However, de la Taille questions whether such an addition can be substantial and not just accidental, as is the case with sanctifying grace.

Cajetan's solution is to argue that the personal modality of the God-human is a "prerequisite to substantial existence."[6] This anteriority of personhood to the substantial existence of Jesus Christ is based on the analogy of the correspondence of existence to nature on the one hand and of the actualizing principle to the potential element on the other. To be an existing substance is to actualize a potency in accordance with its nature. The modality of personality would then be on the side of potency, not identical with it as nature or substance but modifying it so that the substantial existence of a person would truly be its own. The positive addition of personality then would be found between nature as potential substance and existence as actualized substance, now with a personal dimension. De la Taille's problem with this construct is that it undervalues the completeness of nature. If nature needs to be modified in the transition to existence, that would mean that the nature itself would change. In the case of Jesus Christ, this stands against the positive data of the problem—namely, the assumption by the Word of a human nature that is consubstantial with all of humanity but is also contrasted to other humans' personal modality, since the sacred humanity is not connatural with creaturely human existence per se but is created supernaturally by the Word in the incarnation.[7]

Capreolus's proposal is the one that is most convincing to de la Taille and that therefore sets the agenda for his own constructive work. Here the personal factor is neither antecedent nor consequent to the substantial existence of Jesus Christ, but is found within it. More so than Cajetan's proposal, it presupposes the distinction between nature and person, and in the contrast between Jesus Christ and other persons this is especially pronounced. For Peter, Paul, or any other human person, the potency of human nature (a complex of body and soul) is endowed with existence by a formal principle of being that is commensurate and connatural. This is not true for Jesus Christ. His formal principle of existence is divine; it is supernatural, not connatural. Therefore, his principle of existence far surpasses the potency of his assumed human nature and is not ordered to it in absolute proportion, as is the case for other human beings.[8] Capreolus's solution, according to de la Taille, suggests a metaphysics of human personhood that can meet this challenge of difference between Christ and the humanity with which he is consubstantial. Its basic principle is clear: "the equation between *created personality* and *ownership of created being*."[9] A consistent and satisfactory explication of the issues is rendered by de la Taille as follows:

> Thus, if we compare the human nature and its manner of being, two cases are possible: either the human nature is the possessor, and existence is the possession;

or the human nature is held by the personal existence of one of the Trinity. Of the two terms, humanity and existence, the one that holds the other is the person. And, therefore, human nature is a person in our case; and, therefore, human nature is not a person in the case of Christ.[10]

When we pass on to the conditions of the hypostatic union, de la Taille builds on the foundation of Capreolus's theory with his own original insights. First, although the humanity of Jesus owes its existence to uncreated being, it must be stressed that it is not a divine existence common to all three persons of the trinity but one that is specific to the hypostatic and personal identity of the second person—this as distinct from the undifferentiated efficient causality of all three persons *ad extra*. Second, while the communication or actualizing principle of the union is uncreated and eternal and therefore absolutely supernatural, it did begin in time, and in its reception by the human nature it must be a created gift. In other words, the thing communicated is uncreated and the communication in its receptive power is created.[11] This is the principle behind his theory of the hypostatic union as "created actuation by uncreated act."

In order to further define what de la Taille means by this construct, it is necessary to understand the essentially metaphysical character of his proposal. His immediate concerns are not the psychology of Jesus or the theologal focus of his ministry, mission, and proclamation.[12] Rather, de la Taille works within the framework of Thomistic metaphysics to provide a satisfactory understanding of the structure of the hypostatic union. The theological consequences follow, as he is quick to note and as the debate over the reception of his work surely displayed. In any event, the issue is how an uncreated act communicates to a potency (by definition a created entity) so that the latter is truly possessed by the former. In the case of Jesus Christ this is realized when the subjective potency of the human nature is actuated or brought into substantial existence by the uncreated act of the divine Logos.

The major issue that de la Taille must clarify is whether the uncreated act informs the subjective potency of Christ's human nature. An act can be either a subsistent act or an act directed toward a subjective potency. In the former case, the perfection of the act is identical with the subject's essential being. In the latter case, a perfection is superadded to the essence of the potency of a being distinct from that of the subject. The communication of this type of act must be in a mode that the potency is capable of receiving. When there is a conjunction between an act and a potency, the latter is said to be actuated by the act—not, however, in the order of efficiency, generation or production, but as a union or self-donation of the act to the potency.[13] In the natural order this would entail formal and material causality—that is, information in the relationship between form (act) and matter (potency). In the hypostatic union, however, in which the act is uncreated being and the created potency is a human nature, this order does not obtain. While it possesses a higher degree of causality than efficiency, as is the case even on the natural level, it is not an operation of formal causality or information (on the side of the act) and material causality (on the side of the potency). Uncreated being cannot be made dependent on created being. However, there is a genuine change wrought in the created potency by the uncreated act—specifically, in the actuation as a created term that in the modality of a passive union undergoes an amelioration or traction in relationship to the uncreated Word.[14] Expressed in the terms of the hypostatic union, the Word is the act of the assumed human nature in the incarnation, adapting that nature through a created actuation to be receptive to the union and therefore to truly be the humanity of the Son of God.

To substantiate his claim, de la Taille turns to other activities of God in which a similar ontological structure is operative. For both the beatific vision attained through the light of glory and sanctifying grace already present in the life of believers, there is a disposition of the human soul to God that effects a union that can also be described as a created actuation by uncreated act. In these cases an "Act of divine life itself must come to actuate the receptive capacity of the soul, in order that the corresponding actuation may arise in the soul."[15] They involve an uncreated act and a created communication, resulting in a disposition that inheres in the soul, informing it to the point of union with its term either in uncreated grace (relative to sanctifying grace) or uncreated truth (relative to the light of glory). And, although the created actuations are accidental to human nature, they are nevertheless habitual (or dispositional in the beatific vision, that being within the order of intelligiblity) and permanent and portend nothing less than the indwelling of God.[16]

The major distinction of these graces from that of the hypostatic union is that the latter occurs in the substantial and not just the accidental order. The human nature is not anterior to the union and then actuated with the personhood of the Word. The substantial actuation, or grace of union, brings the nature into existence and conforms it as a perfective act (as distinguished from an informing act) into the now one theandric person of the Word become flesh.[17] Nor should this confuse the sense of how many existences there are in Christ, one or two. If considered in terms of the act by which the natures exist, there is one, but when analyzed with respect to the actuations, there are two, created and uncreated, temporal and eternal.[18]

Finally, two points especially must be stressed in de la Taille's accounting of this theory of the hypostatic union that also introduce its controversy. Both de la Taille and his opponents agree that the grace of union is supernatural in character (as is all grace). The potency to union in the human nature, therefore, is not natural but obediential. However, there is disagreement over whether the grace is created or uncreated. De la Taille insists on the former, which to others gives the appearance of compromising the integral humanity of Christ (which can only be created). They resolve the matter of union by assigning it to the efficient causality of the divine operation, which is totally uncreated in its agency and does not inhibit its immediate and substantial union with the created nature by the intermediary of another created entity. De la Taille replies by insisting that the relationship between the Word and the human nature is not one of causality but of act and potency. That relationship is not one of operation but of communication or self-donation by which the Word actuates the potency of the assumed nature. That actuation must be created (even as the act is uncreated) for there to be a substantial union (with respect to the human nature's reception of the communication). This leads to the second point, similar to that proposed by Mersch—namely, that efficient causality by operation common to all persons of the trinity is not excluded in de la Taille's theory but is "essentially presupposed to the presence of God by communication"; it is the anointing to the ointment of the uncreated act.[19]

Reception and Application of de la Taille's Theory

De la Taille's theory of the metaphysics of grace, "created actuation by uncreated act," provoked both agreement and opposition. His third article on the subject was a dialogue written specifically to take up the issues posed by his critics.[20] It was irenic in tone and served to clarify the key issues: that the grace of union is created; that it is the foundation of the relation between the uncreated person and the created nature; that the created actuation is not some third entity intervening between the two because it is an *ens quo* (being which), not an *ens quod* (being by which); and that it does not interfere with the necessity of habitual grace in the person of Christ. On this last point, the grace of union causes the passive potency of the soul to be actuated with respect to its substantial existence as the humanity of the Word, and habitual grace is that radical active potency enabling the operations of the human soul of Christ.[21] All in all, de la Taille's theory laid the groundwork for a renovation (not uncontested) in the scholastic concept of grace. Before reviewing the significant aspects of the debate, a few landmarks need to be noted so as to guide our inquiry in the direction of the relationship between christology and pneumatology.

In Chapter 2, I stated that both Scheeben and Mersch stretched the boundaries of the neo-scholastic paradigm. Specifically, Scheeben's theory of a non-exclusive proper mission of the Holy Spirit went beyond the appropriation theory of neo-scholasticism, and Mersch's introduction of quasi-formal causality for both the hypostatic union and the indwelling of the Holy Spirit challenged the strictures imposed by neo-scholasticism on these divine missions, which relegated them to the realm of efficient causality. In each of these cases, the way was opened to perceive more clearly the hypostatic identities of the second and third persons in the *ad extra* missions and even more decisively in the link between the two. In other words, the pneumatological dimension of christology proper became more explicit—e.g., in the theology of anointing (Scheeben)—as did the christological dimension of the divine inhabitation—e.g., the mission of the Holy Spirit, who is the Spirit of the Son (Mersch). The central fulcrum in each of these theories is the unity of God's grace in Jesus Christ, constituting his person, and communicated through the Holy Spirit in the inhabitation of the just.

The contestation over de la Taille's theory involved more than simply a dispute over the more accurate representation of St. Thomas's thought. De la Taille's contribution was original, and while he interpreted Aquinas and debated his commentators, the real issue was the adequacy of his proposal.[22] In addition to the criticisms that he himself took up, the other major charges included the following: ambiguity over whether the uncreated act is actually received by the created potency,[23] an implicit denial of the distinction between the natural and supernatural orders, and confusion between being and becoming and formal and efficient causality.[24] These were refuted by supporters,[25] and while it is not necessary to review the intricacies of the debate, it *is* necessary to underscore the importance of the issues directly applicable to the relationship between christology and pneumatology.

As already mentioned, one of the major thrusts of de la Taille's argument was the threefold link in the application of his metaphysics of grace to the hypostatic union and to sanctifying grace and the light of glory. In the first case, no one doubted the proper mission of the Son in the hypostatic union or the role of all three persons in the mission. The usual distinction was that the three persons shared in the divine work *ad extra* vis-à-vis efficient causality, while the term of that work in the assumed human nature properly belonged only to the Son. What marked out de la Taille's theory was the nature of the propriety of the second person in the hypostatic union and then the application of the same principle (by his followers) to a proper (although non-exclusive) mission of the Holy Spirit under the rubric of the divine inhabitation. To the extent that both efforts underscore the distinctly christological and pneumatological dimensions of the divine self-communication there is laid out for us a foundation for the construction of a Spirit-christology.

In addition to the objection that de la Taille interposed a fourth element in the complexus of the hypostatic union—a created actuation in addition to the uncreated person, the created nature, and the relation between the two—he was also charged with confusing the uncreated person with the divine nature. De la Taille countered by arguing that while it was true that the divine person became incarnate and not the divine nature, nevertheless the subject of the incarnation was the Son possessing this nature. In response to the further criticism that this would mean the divine nature, shared as it is by all three persons, would obscure the identity of the Son as the term of the incarnation, de la Taille argued that while the divine nature is common to all three persons, one cannot deny that the nature is possessed by each person individually and therefore cannot be separated from the terminal activity of the persons. For this he garners evidence from the Council of Rheims (1148): "*Credimus et confitemur ipsam divinitatem, sive substantiam divinam sive naturam dicas, incarnatam esse, sed in Filio*:" "we believe and confess that the Godhead itself, whether you call it divine substance or nature, is incarnate, but in the Son."[26] But the implications needed to be exploited.

In christology this meant that the hypostatic union was not simply the revelation of the second person (in terms of the knowledge of an object) but the communication of divine life that was proper to the union between divine and human natures in the one person of the Word become flesh. The mediation of divine life and grace through Jesus Christ approaches the theandrism of the Greek Fathers. When this metaphysics of grace is applied to the work of the third person, it likewise is clearer that there is a distinct and proper mission of the Holy Spirit in the doctrine of the inhabitation of the just person. Not exclusive of the other two persons, this more pronounced pneumatology (like that of Scheeben and Mersch) requires further clarification of the relationship between Christ and the Spirit. In other words, while it brings to the fore the distinctive missions of the second and third persons—for it is the Son and the Spirit who constitute the self-communication of the Father (who sends but is not sent)—the nature of that relationship in the unity of the divine grace and operation needs explicit dogmatic elaboration. That this would result in a Spirit-christology will become evident later; for the moment, we must now turn to the pneumatological development of de la Taille's theory.

It was fellow Jesuit theologians Malachi Donnelly, P. de Letter, and Francois

Bourassa who controverted this issue.[27] Donnelly was the first to suggest that de la Taille's theory of "created actuation by uncreated act" could be extended to the doctrine of the trinitarian indwelling. Already de la Taille had linked the self-communication of God in the hypostatic union with the light of glory (*lumen gloriae*) and sanctifying grace—the difference among them being that the former is of the substantial order and the latter two of the accidental. De la Taille did not, however, refer any of his examples to a proper mission of the Holy Spirit.[28] This particular task was taken up by Donnelly, who in a series of articles both proposed and debated the issue.[29]

In Donnelly's judgment two errors remained in Matthias Scheeben's otherwise innovative pneumatology: "The possibility of created grace without the accompanying inhabitation of the Blessed Trinity . . . [and the claim] . . . that the union [with the Holy Spirit (and with Son and Father) as a distinct Person] is a moral union and, consequently, that the sanctity resulting from uncreated grace is merely moral, i.e., external sanctity."[30] In other words, Scheeben had not gone far enough.[31] De la Taille offered the necessary remedy by intrinsically linking together the uncreated and created dimensions of the divine self-communication. By transcending the language of efficient causality, de la Taille (and Donnelly following him) was able to demonstrate the necessity for both the elevation of human nature to the transformative work of supernatural grace as a prerequisite for the divine indwelling (the work of efficient causality) and the uncreated and hypostatic act of God as the basis for all grace-filled transformations in the created order (created actuation by uncreated act). The implications of this transcend the limited options that are possible in strict neo-scholasticism.

It has already been remarked that much of Scheeben's theology was owed in no small part to his profound reading of the Greek Fathers and to his incorporation of those insights into a scholastic idiom. In the early part of the twentieth century, with its renewal of studies in the area of patristics and liturgy, many Catholic theologians sought to enrich their work with the results of such investigation. For our subject, both Donnelly and de Letter recognized that de la Taille's new scholastic theory opened up conceptual space for the introduction of the pneumatological emphasis of the Greek Fathers into Latin scholastic theology.[32] Karl Rahner, S.J., whose efforts in this area began a decade later than de la Taille's, summed up the two perspectives and the consequent theological task, which also could be descriptive of those who applied de la Taille's theory to pneumatology, as follows:

> Hence the question arises how the two ways of looking at things, that of Scripture and the Fathers on the one hand, and that of scholastic theology on the other, may be brought into harmony: there created grace as a *consequence* of God's communication of himself to the man whose sins have been forgiven, here created grace as the *basis* of this communication. There is not the slightest question of contesting the soundness of the positive aspect of the scholastic theory. Our only intention is to complete it by elaborating in more explicit terms a pattern of thought (already in principle to be found in scholastic theology) and applying it to our problem in such a way that the admissibility of the patristic formula should become clear too, and hence make available a more adequate appreciation of the nature of uncreated grace.[33]

Donnelly's appropriation of de la Taille's construct was an attempt to carry this out. His project could be described as a "suggest[ion toward] a tentative metaphysical solution for the non-exclusively *proprium* theory of the inhabitation of the Blessed Trinity in the just soul."[34] His definition of the theory, while revealing the influence of Scheeben, also displays the specificity of his own concerns: it "demands that each of the divine Persons be present to, and united with, the soul by a manner of presence and union that will in some way be different from the proper manner and presence of the other two divine persons."[35] He begins with the logical assumption that appropriation theory and its corollary mode of efficient causality is unable to distinguish between God's general work in creation and God's redemptive work through the missions of the Son and the Spirit. God is omnipresent in the natural order of creation through efficient causality, which is common to all three persons; therefore, the persons cannot be distinguished from one another. If efficient causality is the limit of God's supernatural work, then the distinctive identity of the trinitarian persons vis-à-vis the *ad extra* missions is obscured. If reason can demonstrate that the creature is related to *Deus unus*, the God of creation and conservation, surely in faith the grace-filled soul in the supernatural order is related to *Deus trinus* in a manner that is not simply nominal but genuinely hypostatic in modality.[36]

Donnelly does not deny that created grace is a product of efficient causality, but here the intra-trinitarian relations do not enter. They do enter by the reception of divine grace into humanity according to the Thomistic principle *per quemdam modum passionis*—through whatever manner of being acted upon. This was true, as de la Taille demonstrated, for the hypostatic union. The reception of divine being required a created actuation intrinsic to the human nature and predicated on the uncreated act of the Son. Donnelly makes the same argument for the inhabitation of the Holy Spirit. Created or sanctifying grace proceeds from the inhabitation of the Holy Spirit, not vice versa.

> . . . the conferring of created grace takes place by the impression on the soul of the divine seal of the Persons of the Blessed Trinity. Thus created grace becomes, so to speak, the concave impression of the convex divine seal.[37]

The impression referred to is of the same modality as the hypostatic union, except that it is an accidental rather than a substantial communication of the divine trinitarian life. Nevertheless, it is a communication according to "created actuation by uncreated act" (or quasi-formal causality in its Rahnerian adaptation). On the side of the divine, the *actio* is one and undivided but differs relatively and yet properly according to the hypostatic distinctions of the trinitarian persons. Conversely, on the human side, the reception or *passio* corresponds to the "active communication of the particular divine person."[38] So, too, the uncreated act that actuates does not inform the creature (due to the imperfection of act-dependence and act-limitation accruing to the uncreated being who informs), but the reception by the creature is a *passio* by way of information through the created actuation—the human person is made intrinsically just through sanctifying grace, as Trent declared.[39]

Donnelly's theology of the trinitarian indwelling is similar to Mersch's in the manner in which the persons are distinguished. The *ad extra* missions are consistent with the intra-trinitarian processions. Broadly speaking, the effects of quasi-formal causality (which includes an element of efficient causality) differ from the effects of efficient causality alone. The latter delimits the relationship between God and creatures to "the ordinary, natural substantial presence of God in creatures."[40] However, with quasi-formal causality, the effects in the creature entail a *passio, mutatio,* and *tractio.* Especially through the communication of a *tractio,* the creature is drawn "into the inner circuit of proper divine trinitarian life."[41] The union between God and creature is one determined by the hypostatic relations such that, in agreement with Mersch, Donnelly states that it "is not strictly an *opus ad extra,* but rather *ad intra.*"[42] In other words, the just person participates in the life of the trinity because the *ad extra* missions are consistent with and proceed from the *ad intra* relations and draw the creature into those relations that are immanent in the divine life.

Finally, along with Scheeben, Donnelly maintains that the propriety of the Holy Spirit's mission is non-exclusionary. All three divine persons are present in the inhabitation of the just person. Since the creature's relationship to the trinity is hypostatically determined, there is a distinct union with each of the persons. In this respect, there is an order of the persons in the divine indwelling. The Holy Spirit as breathed forth by the Father and the Son is in a sense the first to enter into union with the creature. Through him the other two persons enter into the union. Union with the divine persons is not a union in the unity of the divine essence, where the distinction of persons disappears, but a union in the "the love and harmony of the Holy Spirit."[43] Again, this is consistent with the intra-trinitarian divine processions and the identification of the Holy Spirit as the union of love between the Father and the Son. Thus, he can conclude that the appropriation of inhabitation to the Holy Spirit involves a true *proprium* distinctive to the person of the Spirit.[44]

Disagreement with Donnelly's application of de la Taille's theory came from various quarters. William R. O'Connor criticized him for substituting a notional act proper to a particular person in an effort to explicate the indwelling in place of an essential act of divinity common to all three persons.[45] This more traditional Thomistic position would be further elaborated by Bourassa. Among those who agreed with de la Taille and sought the application of his theory in the area of pneumatology was fellow Jesuit P. de Letter, who like Donnelly shared a basic dissatisfaction with traditional scholastic understandings of God's special presence through grace.[46] In fact, his agreement with Donnelly is nearly total on the most significant issues: the application to pneumatology of created actuation by uncreated act (use of de la Taille), the non-exclusive *proprium* of the Holy Spirit (Scheeben's basic thesis), and distinct relations possessed by the just soul to each of the divine persons (agreement with Mersch).[47] The dispute centers on the manner in which the soul is related to the persons.

De Letter took exception to Donnelly's description of this relationship when the latter referred to created grace as a kind of miniature trinity in us.[48] For de Letter the threefoldness of relation to the trinitarian persons is strictly an *esse ad,* not an *esse in.* In other words, the threefoldness is not in the foundation of the union, i.e.—the created actuation—but in the relationship produced by grace that is directed to the three divine persons as the "Uncreated Terminators" of the union.[49] Although our union with the persons is real, in God these relations of the trinitarian persons to the just soul are only relations of mere reason (*relatio merae rationis*); therefore, the threefoldness cannot extend to the constitution of the created actuation.[50] Donnelly's reply to de Letter was to correct the latter's understanding of relation by positing that God can exist in the soul only as he exists in himself, which is as a trinity of persons. Otherwise, if the union does not allow for "the *ind*welling of the Trinity as *distinct* Persons," then the threefoldness is extrinsic to the grace communicated.[51] It is not simply the termini of the union that are threefold; the *passio* itself must be threefold.[52] In a later article de Letter acknowledged Donnelly's clarification of the issues,[53] which was just as well, for the real criticism came from a more strict Thomist.

What Francois Bourassa and Malachi Donnelly shared in common was a recognition of the fundamental norms restated by Pius XII in *Mystici Corporis*: "First, this union of grace never destroys the radical distinction between Creator and creature; second, and by consequence, every exercise of divine efficient causality is common to the three persons."[54] Where they differed was on the scope of restriction implied by the norms. Donnelly believed that his adoption of the non-exclusive *proprium* theory of the inhabitation of the Holy Spirit and de la Taille's metaphysics of grace did not violate those norms. For that matter, neither did Karl Rahner, who stated with respect to the encyclical:

> As is well known, Pius XII in the encyclical "Mystici Corporis" has once more referred to this text as a starting-point for a consideration according to the *analogia fidei* so as to achieve a deeper understanding of the indwelling of the Spirit in the grace of justification. The Pope points out more clearly than before that the divine activity *ad extra* is common to the three Persons in the sense that this is to be understood of efficient causality; and at the same time draws attention to the *visio beatifica* as the starting-point for a more profound theology of grace. In this way he clearly points to a theology of grace which seeks to make full use of that notion of God's formal causality with respect to the creature which is a traditional possession of the schools in the theology of the *visio beatifica* and is quite inescapable in the doctrine of the hypostatic union. The circumstance that Pius XII clearly seems to wish to leave open the question whether the relations to the three divine Persons of the man to whom grace has been shown are really only appropriated cannot be discussed here. There is hardly any need to establish the fact that the solution here proposed respects the Pope's warning against every kind of pantheism.[55]

This passage serves to demonstrate how perspective informs such judgments. Whereas some understood the norms to have left open further exploration into the theology of grace by its hints and silences (suggested by the analogy with *visio beatifica*—also the tack taken by de la Taille before the encyclical was published), others clearly envision the restatement of the neo-scholastic position as definitive (recall the caution of Mersch's translator, Vollert).[56] Among the latter was Francois Bourassa.

Bourassa is quick to recognize the thesis of de la Taille's followers regarding the divine inhabitation. He agreed with Donnelly and de Letter that there is a formal causality that is distinct and proper in the incarnation. The disagreement concerns its extension to the Christian's union with the divine persons.[57] His line of criticism focuses on the mediation of such union through adoptive sonship, a principle that informs all the proposals for some sort of a *proprium* in regard to the Holy Spirit. As de Letter stated it, sanctifying grace is a sharing in Christ's *"gratia capitis*, the overflow into our souls of His own habitual grace." In this respect, "grace incorporates us in Christ, the Son of God incarnate"; we are therefore sons and daughters in the Son, *filii in Filio* (identical to Mersch's position as well).[58] The distinct relationship to each of the divine persons is evident in the effect of justifying grace—namely, adoptive sonship in Jesus Christ. The grace of adoption relates the soul differently to each divine person—e.g., to Christ as brother, to the Father in sonship, and to the Holy Spirit as indwelling guide.[59]

Bourassa's critique questions this model of adoption and the correlative doctrine that favors proper rather than appropriated trinitarian missions. Because of the difference between the natural sonship of Christ (through generation implicating the notional attributes of paternity and filiation) and the adoptive sonship of believers (through grace implicating the contingency of the divine freedom in love) Bourassa contends that it is more proper to designate believers as sons and daughters of the trinity rather than of the Father. The predicate for sonship (and daughterhood) is strictly efficient causality in which the divine persons are not distinguished by their properties. Even though we share in the habitual grace of Christ (*gratia capitis* in relation to us), this does not confer a title of sonship.[60] It is grace peculiar to Christ through the instrumentality of his humanity but communicated by all three persons in the unicity of divine efficiency.

Finally, Bourassa argues that this delimits our relationship to the divine persons to appropriation, and therefore does not include any propriety. Appropriation is a creaturely designation for the divine operations that are assigned to a particular person on the basis of characteristics proper to the hypostatic identity of the persons; therefore, appropriations are not arbitrary. However, since we are related to God (and to the trinitarian persons) *ab alio* (not *a se*)—i.e., always from another and not immanent in ourselves—our union with the persons is strictly on the basis of the operations of the intrinsic acts of a spiritual being in thought and love, not a proper indwelling of any of the persons. This preserves the distance between Creator and creature that Pius XII mandated, and it also finds refuge in the pontiff's reaffirmation of the Thomistic principle (*sicut cognitum in cognoscente et amatum in amante*) for our knowledge of the divine indwelling[61]: *"The Divine Persons are said to be indwelling* inasmuch as They are present to intellectual creatures in a way that lies beyond human comprehension, and *are known and loved by them* in a purely supernatural manner alone within the deepest sanctuary of the soul" (emphases are Bourassa's).[62]

Concluding Reflections

The debate rehearsed above represents two major options within a modern neo-scholastic framework for conceptualizing the incarnation and the indwelling of the Holy Spirit in reference to the *ad extra* divine missions. Both sides of the dispute over appropriation and propriety tried to respect the norms eventually taught by *Mystici Corporis*. Whether or not one abides by the limits of efficient causality has direct bearing on the nature of the missions relative to the hypostatic identities of the persons, at least with regard to human knowledge of those distinctions and their place in the believer's union with God. More to the point of this study, it also defines the parameters for the possibility of anything approaching Spirit-christology. Although this particular christological model is absent among these theologians, the relationship between Christ and the Spirit has informed much of their reflection.

In addition, the debate over an appropriated or proper mission of the Holy Spirit serves to highlight a distinctly Catholic approach to establishing a foundation for Spirit-christology. In contrast to the proposal by Geoffrey Lampe, who dispenses with hypostatic distinctions (his work will be reviewed in Chapter 5), the identity of the Holy Spirit as a distinct hypostasis is more decisive for a Catholic pneumatology than a generalized ascription of Spirit signifying the divinity of Christ. Lampe delimits Spirit to the relational and immanent activity of God. This designation of the divinity of Christ in terms of Spirit is a substitute for an existent hypostatic identity of Spirit in God as well as for the traditional identity of Christ as the Logos incarnate. Spirit functions as the medium by which Jesus is divine because he acts divinely. In the scholastic model, this type of Spirit ascription would be equivalent to the common efficiency caused by all three persons (thus maintaining the distinct hypostatic identities) and appropriated to the Holy Spirit. So, for example, the incarnation can be appropriated to the Holy Spirit—*incarnatus est de Spiritu Sancto*—but remain properly the terminal mission of the divine Word. However, most of our theologians went beyond this restriction or at least exploited it so as to emphasize in a more pronounced manner the pneumatic dimension.

Both Scheeben and Mersch suggested that the unity of God's grace in Jesus Christ can be ascribed to the efficacy of the divine operation appropriated to the Holy Spirit and present in the incarnation and redemptive work of the Son of God. Mersch and de la Taille contended that there is a genuine communication of supernatural life to humanity in the great events of grace—e.g., to the sacred humanity in the hypostatic union and to the just soul in sanctifying grace. Donnelly and de Letter argued that the latter is appropriated to the Holy Spirit and that without exclusion the divine inhabitation that effects our union with God is a pneumatic *proprium*. Those who abided by the more traditional scholastic positions—i.e., Leo XIII, Pius XII, O'Connor, and Bourassa—nevertheless affirmed our relationship to the trinitarian persons through an appropriation predicated on distinct hypostatic properties[63] and our union with them through the divine operation, reproducing in us the likeness of the trinitarian processions in intellect and love.[64]

The two models of proper or appropriated missions, the former more than the latter, do in fact link the indwelling of the Holy Spirit in the soul of the just person with his presence and efficacy in the hypostatic union. In the language of Scheeben and Pius XII, the Holy Spirit proceeding from the Father and the Son anoints the human soul of Christ with the ointment of divinity (actually the divinity of the Logos through the *spiramen* of the *Spiritus Sanctus spirans*—especially with reference to Scheeben). In other words, it is the overflow of the Spirit in Christ (John 3:34-"the Spirit without measure") that is the predicate for the gift of the Spirit to believers (John 7:39). Or, in the language of grace, Christ's habitual grace (*gratia habitualis*) becomes the grace of headship (*gratia capitis*) for the members of his mystical body (their own sanctifying grace). But this is only a general agreement among them, for differences on the nature of grace and the role of the Spirit with respect to appropriated or proper inhabitation result in different pneumatologies based on divergent analyses of creaturely relations to the persons of the trinity.

It is therefore clear that a Roman Catholic Spirit-christology would need to negotiate the more general framework of trinitarian theology. By this I mean that the relation of the graced soul to the individual persons of the trinity and the relation of the trinitarian persons to one another cannot be separated. Spirit-christology offers a dogmatic construct in which these two sets of relations are joined. In other words, if the pneumatological dimension of Christian salvation is to be fully articulated— e.g., that the Christian life is life in the Spirit—then it is necessary to explicate how the being and event of incarnation/redemption is pneumatological. Spirit-christology affirms the constitutive agency of the Holy Spirit in the confession of Jesus Christ and in those homologies and eventual doctrinal constructions that express the meaning of his person and deed.

A necessary stage in this process is the recognition that the Holy Spirit is conjoined with and yet distinct from the Son or Word: conjoined because of the intrinsic pneumatic dimension of revelation and redemption; distinct in opposition to any subordinationist or docetic tendencies. The former concern is at the heart of any Spirit-christology. Jesus Christ is the redeeming Word of God because in and by the Spirit he is the efficacious and reconciling presence of God in the world. The latter concern studiously avoids modalist options in this christological construction. These can conflate the person of the Spirit into that of the Son in a subordinationist direction that too quickly reduces the *Spiritus praesens* to the *Christus praesens* and thus renders the pneumatological mission meaningless. It becomes simply an extension of the christological mission and effectively transforms the trinity into a binity. Or it may conflate the person of the Son into that of the Spirit, where the *Christus praesens* is reduced to the *Spiritus praesens*. Here the corporeal reality of the *Christus praesens* disappears (with grave consequences for sacramental theology) and the role of christological anamnesis can easily be neglected (itself an important factor in the origins of New Testament christologies[65]).

In the neo-scholastic tradition the temptation to modalism is quite limited, considering its solid commitment to Catholic orthodoxy. However, its tendency to implicitly subordinate the role of the Spirit in comparison to that of the Son is great. Certainly the debate over an *appropriatum* or *proprium* regarding the pneumatological mission can be read in this light. No matter the oftentimes cogent reasons advanced for the former more traditional construct—e.g., the unicity of the divine operation *ad extra*—it nevertheless deemphasizes the revelation of the person of the Holy Spirit in comparison to that of the Son, the latter unquestionably revealed in a proper mission. To that extent, the model that builds on de la Taille's metaphysics of grace (in the area of pneumatology) and proceeds to a proper mission of the Holy Spirit is more amenable to the task of Spirit-christology, which is founded upon the more pronounced role of the Spirit than that suggested by a more traditional Thomist pneumatology. The reason is as follows: Unless the Holy Spirit is given a proper mission (even if non-exclusive) relative to the divine inhabitation and sanctification, as is the case with Scheeben and Mersch, then the grounds for the inclusion of the Spirit in the christological locus are limited. For Scheeben, Mersch, Donnelly, and others, the propriety of the Holy Spirit's indwelling establishes a fundamental link with Christ's own person. In other words, the manifestation of hypostatic identity in the Spirit's temporal mission in the indwelling relates directly to the pneumatic dimension of Christ's person, and this would be the decisive link to any Spirit-christology.

In light of the above logic, it is no suprise that traditional Thomists have taken to affirming a *proprium* for the Holy Spirit while maintaining their still-strict accounting of the nature of the union between believers and the trinitarian persons. It remains, then, to compare this option with the one suggested by the innovators reviewed above. By examining two proposals that both affirm a *proprium* for the Holy Spirit but differ in regard to the manner of union between the Christian and the Holy Spirit, we hope more accurately to depict the options for a pneumatic christology. As we shall see, the option for the Spirit as self-communication is more conducive to the particular christological model we have in mind.

The *Proprium* of the Holy Spirit in Thomism: The Pneumatology of William J. Hill, O.P.

William Hill entered the debate under discussion with the publication of his dissertation, *Proper Relations to the Indwelling Divine Persons*. Working within the framework of St. Thomas's thought, Hill vigorously defended the traditional relationship to the divine indwelling as the Angelic Doctor originally suggested—*sicut cognitum in cognoscente et amatum in amante* (a position similar to those of O'Connor and Bourassa). However, he also proposed a proper relation to the divine persons that does not detract from the doctrine of appropriation (a position departing from them). As he sums up his project he intentionally extracts the propriety of relationship to the trinitarian persons on the basis of a prior appropriation.

> . . . the justified soul is related to the Trinity as object and end, and here it is conformed and joined to each of the distinct Persons. The foundations for these relations are the gifts of grace appropriated to one or another of the Persons. But through the appropriated gift there is effected a proper relationship in knowledge and love terminating at the particular Person in His proper hypostatic character.[66]

The question then arises concerning the distinct *proprium* of the Holy Spirit and how this informs christology. To answer this we turn to Hill's more recent work, *The Three-Personed God: The Trinity as a Mystery of Salvation*.

The fact that much of the discussion thus far has focused on the nature and means of the divine indwelling should not appear strange except apart from the context of scholastic thought. Inevitably our topic, which explores the relationship between Christ and the Spirit under the model of Spirit-christology, requires both a foundation in positive theology and a significant degree of speculative theological inquiry. For most neo-scholastics the tendency is toward speculation, and Hill is no exception. But before proceeding, it is necessary to state what is perhaps already obvious. Access to a new dogmatic model (in this case Spirit-christology) entails for the researcher a prospect of inquiry into the sources (in our case modern and contemporary Roman

Catholic theology) for the building blocks for such a model. In the speculative world of neo-scholastic and neo-Thomist theology, where the model is not presented, one analyzes the subtle shifts in the dominant paradigm toward a more pronounced pneumatology and then gleans from the material and reconstructs its import for christology. In the case of William Hill the shift is toward a proper relationship to the Holy Spirit without, however, the more significant shift toward a new metaphysics of grace that informs the work of Rahner, de la Taille, and their followers. For that shift, we will examine the work of David Coffey in the next chapter.

Hill's later work preserves the basic argument of the earlier one, although he is more open to some of the insights of Rahner and de la Taille. However, he still seeks to correct their notion of a formal (even if quasi-formal) relationship between the divine persons and the believer. The relationship of union between the two is of the order of intention, not that of being—viz., a quasi-formal cause or created actuation by uncreated act. It is a union of intention regarding the term of the relation—in the case of St. Thomas, through knowing and loving the divine persons. But despite this disagreement, Hill along with Donnelly and Rahner are agreed that this "proper" relationship to the divine persons exceeds their common and undifferentiated efficient causality in the unity of the divine operation.[67]

The Thomistic proposal of Hill does seek to articulate the distinctive and proper mission of the Holy Spirit. His procedure is grounded in the classic Latin paradigm beginning with the divine unity and then through the negotiation of trinitarian metaphysics marking out the distinction of persons. This needs to be emphasized, for in contrast to other methods we will examine, this is the most traditional. In effect, this means Hill still preserves the dogmatic tract *De Deo Uno* prior to *De Deo Trino*, a method abandoned by many theologians who are critical of the gap between these tracts and who are persuaded that trinitarian theology should be ensconced more within the framework of salvation history.[68] Nevertheless, Hill is firm in this regard for the weighty reason that theologians who fail to broach metaphysics—i.e., the metaphysics of trinitarian unity and triunity—yield to a failure of nerve with the end result of superficiality in their projects.[69] Whether this entails following his traditional method merits further investigation. Now we must examine his reasons and its implications for pneumatology. They are noteworthy.

Hill argues his case on the basis of two methodological triplets concerning the *ordo* pertaining to the dogma of the trinity. First, since theology does proceed from the situation of faith seeking rational understanding, the theologian must be cognizant of both the origin of encounter with God in Christian experience and the decisive role that the church's hermeneutics of transmitted texts and symbols plays in such faith experience. It is the latter—i.e., the sources testifying to divine revelation—that prevent theological analysis of Christian experience from being reduced to religious anthropology. These two steps, however, are incomplete and lead to theological atrophy if the final step requiring the constructive use of speculative reason is neglected. It is this step in the service of faith—i.e., guarding against pure logicism and other forms of rational reduction—that enables theology to probe the inner intelligibility of its subject matter.[70]

When this method is applied to the doctrine of the trinity we are confronted with a second triplet of issues in need of resolution. These are various "moves" that constitute a speculative theology of the trinity. They are as follows: 1) to move from the divine unity to triunity; 2) to move from trinity in God to trinity in the world; and 3) to move toward the integration of trinitarian theology's appropriation of metaphysics and psychology.[71] It is the third move that solidifies the first step and that provides grounds for the affirmation that the recognition of God's plurality in the temporal missions of Son and Spirit warrant the identity between the economic and immanent trinities. It must be emphasized that these metaphysical and psychological appropriations provide the speculative foundation for true trinitarian distinctions—that is, that God is both one in essence and plural in hypostatic and personal identity. The explication is likewise threefold.

First, Hill argues that St. Thomas's identification of divinity as *Ipsum Esse* and *Actus Purus* means that God is neither a self-enclosed absolute nor part of the worldly process. In other words, God is neither Being as a substantive nor Becoming as creative process. Between the Aristotelian construct of the former and Whitehead's latter revision of it, Hill's exposition of Aquinas's position conceives "deity as the Pure Act of Be-ing, unreceived by any constricting essence . . . [which] locates God noetically beyond all concepts."[72] This participial construction suggests God as dynamic actuality, not static divinity, and intentionally self-related, not relatively dependent on another. It is this dynamism of the fullness of be-ing that is the ground for the divine self-relationship in the intentionality of knowledge and love.

Second, the overflow or abundance of be-ing into knowing and loving produces an immanent term relative to each of these activities that is distinct from the knower and lover. Neither can be reduced to the other or to their origin. Nor are they simply the result of an operation (*per modum operationis*) by the subject. Rather, they are the terms that emanate from the activity of the subject (*per modum operati*), which qualifies its be-ing in the richness of dynamic self-diffusion. The term of knowing displays the indigenous self-expression of be-ing as "the *conceptus* of the known in the 'womb' of the knower," and that of loving as a "conative *élan* that orients the lover" in a procession that is self-unitive.[73] Both of these "intelligible emanations" are intrinsic to the interiority of dynamic be-ing and bespeak metaphysical relationality and opposition at the core of divine existence, one that does not deny the unity and simplicity of the divine essence but does reveal a relative distinction between the origin of such activity and its term. These terms are subsistent and not transient or accidental, for they are not a qualification of divine essence but are identical with it. Therefore, in addition to the activity of relation (an *esse ad* suggesting plurality in God) and its being the actuality of the divine essence (an *esse in* suggesting unity in God), there are hypostatic distinctions in God as the proper terms of such activity and actuality (hypostastis understood in the original patristic sense as "a concrete [objective] presentation of an essence, with connotations of existence and actuality as opposed to form or idea"). Hill sums up this sequence as follows:

> from (i) Be-ing, to (ii) Knowing-Loving, to (iii) immanent processions, to (iv) really distinct terms, identified as (v) Subsistent Relations, that answer to (vi) the concept of person in the metaphysical sense.[74]

Finally, it remains for Hill to establish the psychological dimension within the divine plurality. This distinguishes his theology of the trinity from those whom he claims tend toward neo-modalism—e.g., Barth and Rahner, with their preference for describing the trinitarian identities respectively as "modes of being" and "ways of existing," and not as persons.[75] To fully justify the plurality of persons in God, Hill broaches the issue of divine consciousness. Rather than beginning with the dynamic diffusion of be-ing in knowing and loving, Hill turns to the subjects exercising the acts of "to be," "to know," "to love." His concern is to prevent any return to a-personalism or uni-personalism in God that does not give due attention to the plurality of persons. To resolve the issue without falling into tritheism, Hill argues that the three persons constitute a divine intersubjectivity in which there is a mutual communication among three centers of consciousness. This avowal of psychological plurality guards against the error mentioned due to the distinction between essential and notional acts of consciousness. All three persons know and love the divine truth and goodness in the one selfsame divine nature, except where such knowing and loving can be distinguished by the notional acts that constitute the persons—e.g., paternity, filiation, active and passive spiration. The latter classifications simply direct the appropriation of the psychological dimension to each proper divine person.[76]

Having established a thorough metaphysics of trinitarian relations and personhood—one which for all its speculative density is constructed a posteriori relative to the unique Christian revelation of the trinity—Hill is then able to acknowledge as he did in his earlier work, the presence of the trinity in the proper missions of Son and Spirit, based as they are on an *appropriatum*. More pertinent to this more recent work (and to our subject matter) is his emphasis that as the trinity is revealed in the mystery of salvation enacted by the Christ-event, so, too, an "integral trinitarianism is, of course, not only christological but pneumatological."[77] Consistent with his exposition of intra-trinitarian relations, Hill correlates the *ad extra* gift of the Spirit with the *ad intra* procession of the Spirit as the mutual love in the communication between the Father and the Son. Since the personal identity of the Spirit in God proceeds from that dynamism of the divine be-ing to consummate itself in love, then in the temporal mission of the Spirit this unitive activity manifests itself in God's love for his adopted children in grace. As the Father sends the Spirit through the Son, so, too, the Son returns the Spirit to the Father bearing with him all those who have received grace.

In relation to believers Hill's logic leads to a certain priority of the Spirit in the missions *ad extra*. It is in the Spirit that believers participate in the uncreated mode of God's being through grace, especially with respect to the divine indwelling where in questions of God's presence the Spirit is preeminent.[78] Whereas in the trinity the Father communicates himself through the Son and in the Spirit, the believer enounters God in inverse order: "first to the Spirit, then to the Son, and lastly to the Father."[79] In addition, the two temporal missions connote different aspects of the divine activity. The Father works through the Son and Spirit in order to obtain the communion of adopted children: the former in the unique freedom and individual history of Jesus, and the latter transhistorically in the "communal freedom of all believers."[80] This ecclesial note constitutes a continuing history not yet finally thematized, which Hill underscores as being thoroughly pneumatological.

> God's active presence in history—a history whose horizon has been set by the
> Resurrection of Jesus, but which remains an open history and a human project—is
> not in the "person" of the Father but in the "person" of the Spirit.[81]

Hill is also able to confirm from the positive sources of revelation in the New Testament that in conjunction with his speculative efforts one can proceed from the concept of the Spirit as the divine immanence and the source of life to a distinct personal presence of the Spirit whose mission as divine agent (or source of that agency) bears the marks of "interiority, anonymity, and community formation." With these he thus emphasizes the effect on the deeply personal level of the following works of the Spirit: the Spirit's subjective work in believers, the enlisting in freedom of those joined to the Father through the Son in love and their commitment to be co-creators in the new creation, and the essential relationality of the Spirit's work embodied in the ecclesial community.[82] This final point demands full attention to the presence of the Spirit evident communally and existentially in the gifts of the Spirit.[83]

In summary, William Hill has constructed trinitarian theology with equally definitive christological and pneumatological dimensions. Recalling the image of Irenaeus, the Son and Spirit are the two hands of God in the mystery of salvation.[84] God communicates and redeems through the Son and in the Spirit, which according to Hill's model reveal respectively the manifestive and unitive aspects of the divine being.[85] This is certainly an accurate correlation of the two missions, especially as they relate to the *ad intra* processions that Hill has meticulously examined. However, the strength of his proposal is also its weakness. Hill restricts the role of the Holy Spirit to that which is proper vis-à-vis the schema of trinitarian relations that he has constructed. This is determined almost wholly by the divine self-diffusion in knowledge and love. To that extent, the relationship between Christ and the Spirit is formalized only in reference to these relations, even as that pertains to the work of salvation. He does begin to explore the latter's role in the adoptive sonship and daughterhood of believers, but with his criticism of this position in the earlier work ("The term of adoptive filiation is not the First Person, but the entire Godhead")[86] and the undeveloped suggestions made in the more recent one, it is difficult to conceive how he would exploit this in christology proper. However, one suspects from the close relationship between Christ and the Spirit in the New Testament (especially the Pauline and Johannine material) that if the fullness of pneumatology is to be emphasized there must be a more integral relationship between the second and third persons than the formalized one suggested by Hill. Perhaps these are the limits of this particular theological paradigm. If such is the case, it remains to be proved. A more explicit relation between the two is proposed by our next theologian, who will also challenge the received paradigm relative to some of the more innovative steps in pneumatology undertaken by Hill, and whom we will employ as an interlocutor with him.

Conclusion

In this chapter, I have examined the basis for the unqualified affirmation within neo-scholasticism of a proper temporal mission of the Holy Spirit, this being a prerequisite for an orthodox Spirit-christology. That basis was whether or not within the metaphysics of grace a real relation exists with the trinitarian persons. Against the background of neo-scholasticism's emphasis on appropriated missions and efficient causality for the divine operation (with its correlative created grace on the side of human reception), the work of de la Taille and his interpreters represents a turn to the alternative constructs of proper missions, formal causality, and uncreated grace to explicate the nature of the divine-human relation in the hypostatic union, sanctifying grace, and the beatific vision. The basic similarity of grace in each of these relations, that it involves a real relation to a divine person beyond that of efficient causality common to all three persons, links together the vitality of the two temporal missions, christological and pneumatological. Three summary observations can be made in this regard.

First, a proper temporal mission of the Holy Spirit is dependent on a real relation of the sacred humanity to the divine Son in the hypostatic union. The proposal in the area of pneumatology was never intended to supplant the centrality of christology for the mystery of salvation. Only by arguing for a "created actuation by uncreated act" or a "quasi-formal causality of grace" as the means by which a human nature is assumed by the divine Word in the incarnation is it possible to posit an analogous relationship between the believer and the Holy Spirit in the grace of sanctification effected by the divine indwelling. In both cases, a relation of self-donation by a divine person toward a created term is at the heart of the divine-human relation. Trinitarian self-communication becomes the basis for the theology of grace, and as this involves the dual missions of Son and Spirit the equality of the two as both properly related to the graced creature is underscored.

Second, the work by Donnelly to extend de la Taille's theology of grace to the third person was a conscious effort on his part to expand upon the pneumatology of Matthias Scheeben. The difficulty of the scholastic tradition with Scheeben's original proposal, it will be recalled, was his non-exclusive *proprium* theory applicable to the third person. The controversy surrounding Donnelly's proposal focused on his adaptation to the third person of de la Taille's revised metaphysics of grace. Combined, these two emphases depart significantly from standard neo-Thomist theology. In doing so, they offer the possibility of returning to the relationship between Christ and the Spirit in christology proper. If the Spirit is properly revealed and related to believers through the instrumentality of the incarnate Word, it may then be appropriate to query the manner of relation between the assumed humanity and the Spirit. This is the question of Spirit-christology already broached by Scheeben and Mersch. The clarification afforded by de la Taille and Donnelly is that the very nature of grace necessitates the communication of divine life as a communication effected not only by an undifferentiated divine agency (the efficient causality common to all three persons) but by the "presencing" of the divine persons as well. If the incarnation and the divine inhabitation respectively and properly reveal the Son and the Spirit— having now attained a *proprium* for the third person—one might well ask the following two questions: (1) How is the Holy Spirit present to Christ constitutively in the incarnation, efficaciously in his ministry and paschal mystery, and redemptively in his exaltation? (2) If the Spirit is present to Christ, how is Christ present to or in the Spirit? In other words, is there any differentiation between the *Christus praesens* and the *Spiritus praesens*? The answers to these questions are germane to the cogency (question 1) and the implications (question 2) of Spirit-christology and will be pursued in later chapters.

Third, the chapter closed with the challenge by a traditional Thomist (Hill) that accepts a *proprium* for the third person but still differs on the nature of the union with the divine persons effected by grace. I was critical of this position and would argue that it stands as a major barrier to Spirit-christology, since the latter construction requires a relation between created reality and the divine persons that is not restricted to intentionality. In other words, the relation to, union with, or presence of the divine persons involves an *esse in* and not simply an *esse ad*. However, I do not underestimate the strength of Hill's position and argument. After all, the very distinction of the divine persons from one another within the Latin paradigm is a *relationis oppositio*—i.e, an intra-trinitarian *esse ad*.[87] Is this an insurmountable barrier to the construction of Spirit-christology, especially if modalism lurks as danger in any Spirit-christology that does not expressly affirm a proper presence of the "person" of the Holy Spirit? If at the end of the last chapter we were left with the question of the justification for the trinitarian nature of grace—i.e, Mersch's filial conception of grace—we are now confronted with the modality of the intra-trinitarian relations themselves. Although the various Jesuit neo-scholastics examined were able to develop their pneumatology, christology, and theology of grace within the overall theological method of the schools, we now turn to a theologian who questions the paradigm itself as to whether its foundations are secure enough for the innovations thus far suggested.

Notes

1. West Baden, 1952 (hereafter referred to as *The Hypostatic Union*). The three articles were previously published separately: 1) "The Schoolmen," first given as a paper at the Summer School of Catholic Studies held at the University of Cambridge, England (July 25–31, 1925) and published as a part of *The Incarnation*, ed. Rev. C. Lattey, S.J. (Cambridge: W. Heffer & Sons, 1925), 152–189; 2) "Created Actuation by Uncreated Act," tr. Cyril Vollert, S.J., originally published as "Actuation créée par acte incréé," *Recherches de Science Religieuse* 18 (1928), pp. 253–268; 3) "Dialogue in the Grace of Union," tr. Cyril Vollert, S.J., originally published as "Etretien amical d'Eudoxe et de Palaméde sur la grâce d'union," *Revue Apologétique* 48 (1929), pp. 5–26, 129–145.

2. Maurice de la Taille, *The Hypostatic Union*, pp. 7–9.

3. Ibid., p. 13.

4. Ibid., p. 16.

5. Ibid.

6. Ibid., p. 17.

7. Ibid., pp. 16–19.

8. Ibid., p. 19.

9. Ibid., p. 20.

10. Ibid., p. 19.

11. Ibid., p. 21.

12. In using the term "theologal" I am following Edward Schillebeeckx, who defines it as "a vital human activity of which God himself is the object and the motive, and in the perfecting of which God is coactive: namely, the life of grace in faith, hope and love, the only virtues which of their nature bring about a personal relationship with God." *Christ the Sacrament of the Encounter with God* (New York: Sheed & Ward, 1963), p. 16, n. 14. It

obviously differs from "theological," which implicates the more reflectively critical act of faith seeking understanding.

13. De la Taille, *The Hypostatic Union* p. 29.

14. Ibid., pp. 30, 59.

15. Ibid., p. 33.

16. Ibid., p. 34.

17. Ibid., p. 35.

18. Ibid., p. 40.

19. Ibid., p. 38.

20. "Dialogue in the Grace of Union," tr. Cyril Vollert, S.J., originally published as "Etretien amical d'Eudoxe et de Palaméde sur la grâce d'union," *Revue Apologétique* 48 (1929), pp. 5–26, 129–145.

21. De la Taille, *The Hypostatic Union and Created Actuation but Uncreated Act*, pp. 42, 47, 63, 76.

22. P. de Letter, S.J., perhaps sums up the attitude of his supporters when he states that de la Taille's fidelity to Aquinas was more formal than literally material and that neither St. Thomas nor his commentators "were fully aware of the basic intuition that inspires de la Taille's theory." "Created Actuation by the Uncreated Act: Difficulties And Answers," *Theological Studies* 18 (1957), p. 74.

23. William R. O'Connor, "The Theory of the Supernatural: A Critique of P. de la Taille," *Theological Studies* 3 (1943), pp. 410–413.

24. Thomas U. Mullaney, "The Incarnation: de la Taille vs. Thomist Tradition," *The Thomist* 17 (1954), pp. 1–42.

25. The first charge was already partially addressed by Malachi Donnelly, S.J.: "The Theory of R.P. Maurice de la Taille, S.J. on the Hypostatic Union," *Theological Studies* 2 (1941), 510–526. De Letter refuted Mullaney's criticisms: "Created Actuation by the Uncreated Act: Difficulties And Answers," pp. 75–92.

26. De la Taille, *The Hypostatic Union and Created Actuation by Uncreated Act.* p. 12.

27. This has been noted by Robert L. Faricy, S.J.: "The Trinitarian Indwelling," *The Thomist* 35 (1971), p. 370; Karl Rahner, "Some Implications of the Scholastic Concept of Uncreated Grace," *Theological Investigations I* (New York: Crossroad, 1982), p. 319, n. 1; Petro F. Chirico, S.S., *The Divine Indwelling and Distinct Relations to the Indwelling Persons in Modern Theological Discussion* (Rome: Pontificia Universitas Gregoriana, 1960); and William J. Hill, O.P., *Proper Relations to the Indwelling Divine Persons* (Washington, D.C.: Thomist Press, 1955). Chirico's work, as the title suggests, is the most comprehensive, including both a précis of each position (including many others—e.g., Mersch and Rahner, to name just two), critique, and his own proposal. Since my interest is to glean from this debate the pattern for possible building blocks toward a constructive Spirit-christology within the larger paradigm of neo-scholasticism, I will not examine his analysis. However, it should be noted that it stands on its own and provides an excellent summary of the issues and possible solutions to the question of the divine inhabitation.

28. William R. O'Connor is quick to point this out in his response to Donnelly's proposal. O'Connor, a traditional Thomist, maintains exclusively the appropriation theory of the Holy Spirit's indwelling. "Discussion of *The Inhabitation of the Holy Spirit*," *Proceedings of the Catholic Theological Society of America* 3 (1949), pp. 85–86.

29. After preparatory work in his articles, "The Theory of R.P. Maurice de la Taille, S.J. on the Hypostatic Union," *Theological Studies* 2 (1941), pp. 510–526; "The Indwelling of the Holy Spirit according to M. J. Scheeben," *Theological Studies* 7 (1946), pp. 244–280, he directly dealt with the issue at hand: "The Inhabitation of the Holy Spirit: A Solution according to de la Taille," *Theological Studies* 8 (1949), pp. 445–470; "The Inhabitation of the Holy

Spirit," *Proceedings of the Catholic Theological Society of America* 3 (1949), pp. 39–77; "Sanctifying Grace and our Union With the Holy Trinity: A Reply," *Theological Studies* 13 (1952), pp. 190–204 (this last article was a reply to de Letter).

30. Donnelly, "The Indwelling of the Holy Spirit according to M.J. Scheeben," pp. 279–280.

31. It is interesting that Donnelly on the one hand seeks to guard Scheeben from charges of association with Petavius's theory and on the other desires to push him in the direction of a more substantial union between the just person and the Holy Spirit. Petavius (or Petau), a seventeenth-century Jesuit theologian who pioneered the development of positive theology, argued that the Holy Spirit possessed an exclusively proper mission such that the Father and Son are present in the soul only through the Holy Spirit. This along with Peter Lombard's theology of grace, which asserted an identity between infused charity and the Holy Spirit, was rejected by the majority of scholastic theologians. Scheeben had to negotiate this territory, which he did with his non-exclusive theory of the proper mission of the Holy Spirit. Donnelly, whose criticism of Scheeben is more in the line of shoring up his insights, accomplishes that with the help of de la Taille in the very language and conceptuality of scholasticism.

32. Donnelly, "The Inhabitation of the Holy Spirit: A Solution According to de la Taille," p. 450; P. de Letter, "Sanctifying Grace and the Divine Indwelling," *Theological Studies* 14 (1953), pp. 247–249, 251, 257–258. Karl Rahner did the same with a theory more similar to that of Emile Mersch. In his essay "Some Implications of the Scholastic Concept of Uncreated Grace," *Theological Investigations* I, pp. 319–346, Rahner argued that through the application of a "quasi-formal causality" both the traditional Greek and Latin views could be upheld.

33. Rahner, ibid., p. 325.

34. Donnelly, "The Inhabitation of the Holy Spirit: A Solution According to de la Taille," p. 445.

35. Ibid.

36. Ibid., p. 450.

37. Ibid., p. 463.

38. Ibid., p. 465. Note Donnelly's summary of each side of the communication: "The reality communicated by each Person is, absolutely speaking, the same: the one, indivisible, finite, accidental, created communication of their common trinitarian life. Nevertheless, each Person communicates this one reality wholly and entirely, and that as a Person distinct from the other two divine Persons.

"Created grace, therefore, may be considered as the passive reception, in an accidental, finite, and created manner, of proper trinitarian life."

39. Ibid., p. 456.

40. Donnelly, "The Inhabitation of the Holy Spirit," p. 43.

41. Idem, "The Inhabitation of the Holy Spirit: A Solution According to de la Taille," p. 458.

42. Ibid., p. 459.

43. Ibid., p. 69.

44. Ibid., p. 470.

45. O'Connor, "Discussion of *The Inhabitation of the Holy Spirit*," p. 86.

46. De Letter sums up these approaches: 1) St. Thomas's explanation that God is present in the just soul through grace: *"sicut cognitum in cognoscente et amatum in amante"*; 2) the "friendship theory" of Suarez in which God and the soul are united through the virtue of love; 3) Lessius's theory that grace is the bond that unites with the Holy Spirit; 4) Vasquez's dynamic theory of God's presence through the effects of created grace; and other more modern variations on these. "Sanctifying Grace and our Union with the Holy Trinity," *Theological Studies* 13 (1952), pp. 38–41. Other articles on this subject by de Letter include: "Sanctifying Grace

and the Divine Indwelling," *Theological Studies* 14 (1953), pp. 242-272; "Grace, Incorpora-
tion, Inhabitation," *Theological Studies* 19 (1958), pp. 1-31; "Sanctifying Grace and Divine
Indwelling: Fr. de la Taille and St. Thomas," *Gregorianum* 41 (1960), pp. 63-69; " The
Theology of God's Self-Gift," *Theological Studies* 24 (1963), pp. 402-422.

47. Ibid., pp. 46-50, 56-58.

48. Donnelly "The Inhabitation of the Holy Spirit," p. 466.

49. De Letter, "Sanctifying Grace and our Union with the Holy Trinity," p. 46.

50. Ibid., pp. 49-51.

51. Donnelly, "The Inhabitation of the Holy Spirit," pp. 195-197.

52. Ibid., p. 200. "From its threefold (not absolute, but relative [a point of agreement with
de Letter]) character, created grace gives rise to three distinct relations, one to each divine
Person, who *ad modum passionis* communicates trinitarian life to, and impresses His own
likeness upon, the soul."

53. De Letter, "Grace, Incorporation, Inhabitation," p. 13, n. 49: "Fr. Donnelly's critical
remarks have been helpful in reenvisaging our relationship to the Blessed Trinity as triune
(rather than as threefold or as three distinct relations)."

54. François Bourassa, "Adoptive Sonship: Our Union with the Divine Persons," *Theological Studies* 13 (1952), p. 309. Also Donnelly, "The Inhabitation of the Holy Spirit: A
Solution According to de la Taille," p. 445.

55. Rahner, "Some Implications of the Scholastic Concept of Uncreated Grace," *Theological Investigations* I, p. 335, n. 1. This apology is relevant not only for himself but for de
la Taille and his followers. Interestingly, Rahner claims that his conclusions on quasi-formal
causality, so similar to those of de la Taille, were arrived at independently; he being unaware
of the latter's important essay. Apart from that, it does assure that Rahner's comments on
Mystici Corporis hold for those who advocate the theory of "created actuation by uncreated
act." Ibid., p. 340, n. 2.

56. Pius XII does seem to leave open such investigation and certainly rules out any
censure of theological opinion not directly indicted by his two norms. Chirico in his accounting
of this debate favors this interpretation along with the majority consensus of theologians (*The
Divine Indwelling and Distinct Relations to the Indwelling Persons in Modern Theological
Discussion*, p. 7). The full paragraph from the encyclical is worth quoting: "For indeed We
are not ignorant of the fact that this profound truth—of our union with the Divine Redeemer
and in particular of the indwelling of the Holy Spirit in our souls—is shrouded in darkness
by many a veil that impedes our power to understand and explain it, both because of the
hidden nature of the doctrine itself, and of the limitations of our human intellect. But We
know, too, that from well-directed and earnest study of this doctrine, and from the clash of
diverse opinions and the discussion thereof, provided that these are regulated by the love of
truth and by due submission to the Church, much light will be gained, which, in its turn will
help to progress in kindred sacred sciences. Hence We do not censure those who in various
ways, and with diverse reasonings make every effort to understand and to clarify the mystery
of this our wonderful union with Christ. But let all agree uncompromisingly on this, if they
would not err from the truth and from the orthodox teaching of the Church; to reject every
kind of mystic union by which the faithful of Christ should in any way pass beyond the sphere
of creatures and wrongly enter the divine, were it only to the extent of appropriating to
themselves as their own but one single attribute of the eternal Godhead. And, moreover, let
all hold this as certain truth, that all these activities are common to the most Blessed Trinity,
insofar as they have God as supreme efficient cause." No. 78 (Boston: St. Paul Editions).

57. Bourassa also mentions Scheeben and Mersch in this regard. "Adoptive Sonship: Our
Union with the Divine Persons," pp. 309-310.

58. De Letter, "Grace, Incorporation, Inhabitation," p. 1.

59. Ibid., pp. 30. It must be understood that for de Letter this distinct relationship to the persons is through quasi-formal causality as that terminates in the persons, while for Donnelly it resides in the actuation itself.

60. Bourassa, "Adoptive Sonship: Our Union with the Divine Persons," pp. 312-313.

61. Ibid., pp. 318-322, 328-335.

62. Pius XII, *Mystici Corporis*, No. 79. Quoted by Bourassa, "Adoptive Sonship: Our Union with the Divine Persons," pp. 333-334.

63. See especially Bourassa: ". . . even in appropriation the Person who is the subject of the appropriation is considered in His hypostatic property, for the perfection predicated of Him is appropriated precisely because of its similitude to that property." Ibid., p. 323.

64. Again, Bourassa: "Habitual grace, or assimilation to God, explains one aspect of the mystery of our deification; but the full meaning of the latter is not grasped until one realizes how habitual grace results in communion with the divine essence through operation, thus developing in us the divine trinitarian life of thought and love." Ibid., p. 331.

65. See especially Petr Pokorny, *The Genesis of Christology: Foundations for a Theology of the New Testament* (Edinburg: T & T Clark, 1987), pp. 179-184: "Christian theology arises out the tension between the present experience of the faith and the above-mentioned tendencies that lead to the remembrance (ANAMNESIS) of the earthly Jesus" p. 181).

66. Hill, *Proper Relations to the Indwelling Divine Persons*, p. 116.

67. Hill, *The Three-Personed God: The Trinity as a Mystery of Salvation*, pp. 287-296.

68. Again, Karl Rahner is most influential in this regard. See his *The Trinity*, pp. 15-21.

69. Hill, *The Three-Personed God: The Trinity as a Mystery of Salvation*, p. 247.

70. Ibid., pp. 241-251. Hill summarizes his project as follows: "A systematic theology of the Trinity, then, cannot be only hermeneutics in the sense of mere reflection on the corpus of sacred Scripture; nor simply dogmatics, in starting with the orthodox formula of the Church whose meaning it then seeks to explain. It will rather be a rational exploration, at once critical and constructive, but working within the intentionality of faith. Its immediate focus will be the experience of contemporary faith as this gains expression in the symbols of the Christian community." Ibid., pp. 250-251.

71. Ibid., pp. 255-259.

72. Ibid., p. 260.

73. Ibid., pp. 262-263.

74. Ibid., p. 267.

75. For his critique, see ibid., pp. 111-124, 130-145.

76. Ibid., pp. 268-272.

77. Ibid., p. 286.

78. Ibid., p. 296.

79. Ibid.

80. Ibid., p. 290.

81. Ibid., p. 301.

82. Ibid., pp. 297-303. The following is even more emphatic: "The Holy Spirit is active within believers, then, as they constitute the community of believers which is the New Creation, the *ekklesia*. In uniting men to God, the Spirit unites them to one another. In this way, the outpouring of the Spirit appears as the very constitution of the people of God as a community of trinitarian love. That outpouring is at once the sending of the Spirit by the Father and Son and the Spirit's forming of the assembly of saved mankind. The New Creation is thus the immanence of God to humanity; that immanence, however, is the special prerogative of the Holy Spirit." (p. 307).

83. Ibid., pp. 303-307.

84. Irenaeus, *Against Heresies* bk. 5, chap. vi, par. 1.

85. Hill, *The Three-Personed God: The Trinity as a Mystery of Salvation*, p. 287.

86. Hill, *Proper Relations to the Divine Indwelling Persons*, p. 72.

87. It should be recalled that the doctrine of trinitarian circumincession, where the divine persons coinhere in the divine essence and in one another, presupposes in its Latin version the prior differentiation of persons through the opposition of relations. Logically, the divine persons are related by an *esse ad* before they coinhere as an *esse in*. Therefore, the concept of *relationis oppositio* must be addressed before the benefits of circumincession can be fruitfully applied in Spirit-christology.

4

"Beyond Neo-scholasticism:"
The Spirit-christology of David Coffey

By examining the work of David Coffey, a secular priest of the Archdiocese of Sydney (Australia), we continue to follow the development of the same themes within the particular trajectory of neo-scholasticism that was reviewed in the previous two chapters. We have attempted to discern a pattern in the work of Scheeben, Mersch, de la Taille, Donnelly, and Rahner, which when taken collectively provide the necessary building blocks for the construction of Spirit-christology within the broad scholastic tradition of Roman Catholic theology and one that is compatible with the pneumatological christology of the Orthodox tradition. Coffey, for his part, accepts the basic correctness of these theologians' innovations in the theology of grace and pneumatology, especially as these point to the priority of the Holy Spirit in the divine inhabitation. These two foci, the theology of grace and those dogmatic constructions that interpret the trinitarian missions with an emphasis on pneumatology, serve to anchor the new model of Spirit-christology around which our inquiry has been focused. A brief review of their relevance for the required doctrinal construction is helpful.

By suggesting that the relation between the divine persons and the creature can be articulated as a "created actuation by an uncreated act" or as "quasi-formal causality," these theologians strove intentionally to overcome the tendency in neo-scholasticism to limit that relation to efficient causality and created grace. The more traditional neo-scholastic position states that the creature knows God primarily through the created effects of the divine working that is common to the entire Godhead and in which the individuality of the divine persons is not discernible. Knowledge of the divine persons is attained through the elevation of the human faculties by created grace as they are directed to the term of its created effects, that term being the Son and the Spirit in their respective missions. On the other side, it should be noted, however, that the theologians who opt for a more intrinsic notion of the presence of the trinitarian persons in the communication of grace do not deny or undervalue the role of created grace in the divine-human relation. For them it is simply the consequence of a prior uncreated grace through which, they argued, the knowledge of the trinitarian persons is more directly apprehensible.

Created grace occupies a venerable place in the history of Catholic doctrine. It emphasizes that the divine self-communication must be received by the creature under the conditions of the creature's own metaphysical structure of being. This is why the Catholic doctrine of justification (as Trent formalized it) has always insisted that the divine righteousness is an infused grace resulting in an actual ontological change in the sinner's condition. This transformation can take place only within the contingent realities of the human condition; hence, created grace. The innovations in the theology of grace proposed by the theologians whom we have examined has to do with (as Rahner put it) whether created grace is the consequence or basis of uncreated grace, the latter more broadly understood as simply the presence of the divine persons. According to the revised model, created grace is the consequence of the presence of the divine persons, based as it is on the metaphysical reconstruction of the divine-human relation exemplified by "created actuation by uncreated act" and "quasi-formal causality." This is contrasted to the more traditional scholasticism, where created grace (mediated by common efficient causality) is the basis for knowledge of the divine persons that is communicated not within the metaphysical structure of grace itself (Mersch and Donnelly) but by virtue of the elevation that grace enables in the intentionality of knowledge and love (Bourassa and Hill).

The second innovation concerned the nature of the temporal divine missions. According to the traditional model, the theory of appropriation was sufficient to highlight the prominence of any one of the trinitarian persons in the divine operation *ad extra*. This simply meant that all three persons are involved in the divine operation through common efficient causality. Because there was a similarity between the particular operation and a property of one of the persons, it could be appropriated to that person without excluding the other persons. However, starting with Scheeben the question was raised if appropriation theory alone was sufficient to characterize the christological and pneumatological missions. In the case of the former, it is universally agreed that the term of that mission properly belongs to the Son exclusively, since he alone assumes a human nature in the incarnation. The debate therefore centered on the pneumatological mission that hitherto was conceptualized as an *appropriatum*. By suggesting a non-exclusive *proprium* for this mission, Scheeben and those following him argued that the hypostatic identity of the Holy Spirit comes to the fore in the divine inhabitation of the just person; otherwise, there is no real basis for the differentiation of the third person in the pneumatological mission.

These two dogmatic innovations, I have argued, are necessary for the construction of Spirit-christology within the scholastic tradition. Such a statement makes sense only within the purview of an orthodox construction of Spirit-christology. By that I mean one that preserves the integrity of hypostatic differentiation within the trinity. Other, more revisionist models, wherein such differentiation is no longer a concern, are possible—e.g., the works of Geoffrey Lampe and James Mackey (mentioned in the next chapter)—but scholasticism within the Roman Catholic tradition thrives on its preservation of orthodoxy. This, however, presents its own problems, some doctrinal and others conceptual. On the doctrinal side, orthodox trinitarianism is in part the result of the gradual displacement of Spirit-christology by Logoschristology in the ancient church. Since some pre-conciliar (before Nicaea and Chalcedon) Spirit-christologies tended toward heterodoxy and Spirit movements likewise had similar proclivities—e.g., Montanism, Joachimism, the Spiritual Franciscans, the Beguines—Catholic dogmatics has been hesitant to reconsider the merits of this christological model. The conceptual hindrance revolves around the Latin model of intra-trinitarian relations, which presupposes that hypostatic differentiation is only predicated on the opposition of relation. This has made the task of differentiation difficult when it comes to the *ad extra* missions, especially since any christology begins there rather than in the *ad intra* relations. For example, if we take the Gospel narratives, a primitive triadology is evident when Jesus prays to the Father and is anointed with the Spirit. Without these basic "evangelical data" no trinitarian theology would have ever emerged. Here the heuristic device of the "opposition of relation" is not even necessary. If that is true for kerygmatic anamnesis, how does one then apply the *relationis oppositio* to the differentiation in the communication of grace between the missions of the risen Christ and the Holy Spirit—i.e., the *Christus praesens* and the *Spiritus praesens*?

The combination of these two hindrances delimits the possibilities for Spirit-christology in this tradition. While maintaining the integrity of hypostatic differentiation the new model must also bring to the fore the identity and function of the Holy Spirit within christology proper. In this manner, therefore, the two points with which I concluded the previous chapter can be affirmed—namely, that a real relation exists between created humanity (in both the hypostatic union and the sanctification of the just person) and the trinitarian persons, and that the Holy Spirit can be the bearer of this relation in a proper mission. As stated before, however, these are only building blocks for Spirit-christology. The success of the model is dependent not only on a fully developed pneumatology (hence the need for a pneumatological *proprium*), but also on the application to the humanity of Jesus of this pneumatological mission (a specific but different application of the revised theology of grace). It is also necessary that this application of the pneumatological mission—i.e., the relation of the Holy Spirit to the sacred humanity—be differentiated from the properly christological one—i.e., the relation of the Son to the sacred humanity. In this way the proposal remains within the scope of Catholic orthodoxy and on the speculative level requires that the construct be related explicitly to the theology of the intra-trinitarian relations.

In light of the above issues, David Coffey's work is especially well suited to be the subject of our inquiry. One can trace the development of his thought through a series of publications that outline not only a distinct pneumatology but also its relation to christology, the theology of grace, and trinitarian theology, including the question of trinitarian propriety relative to the pneumatological mission. As already stated, his work can be placed within the particular scholastic trajectory thus far reviewed. However, it is a trajectory that upon the successful development of Spirit-christology demonstrates the limitation of the scholastic method and the necessary transcendence of it. Therefore, I will begin thematically, attempting to explicate his new trinitarian and christological constructions while also noting along the way important shifts away from the scholastic tradition, which, as I shall argue, eventually push Coffey beyond the received paradigm. I will also note the shifts in his own work (in earlier and later publications) where, in his efforts to advance his proposals, he wrestles with different ways of offering constructive alternatives to the traditional trinitarian paradigms common to Latin scholasticism.

Background Issues: Grace, the Eastern Fathers
and Trinitarian Models

Coffey began work in an article, "The Gift of the Holy Spirit," that argued for the distinctly pneumatological dimension of the doctrine of grace.[1] Although written well after the original proposals of de la Taille and Rahner, Coffey concurs with the judgment of Flemish Jesuit Piet Fransen who wrote in 1969 that the theories of de la Taille and Rahner had made their mark and that, while many (especially in Europe) sought to improve on their intuition, they had substantially contributed to rescuing the treatise on grace from its decline in the manual scholastic tradition.[2] This unfortunate situation was the result of two main scholastic constructs relative to the theology of grace, both of which Coffey addresses in his various studies on pneumatology. First, Coffey and those in the tradition that he develops do not conceive of grace as primarily "created." Although the scholastic tradition acknowledged the role of uncreated grace, primary attention was given to created grace. For Coffey, as with the others reviewed, there must be a direct explication of the relationship between uncreated and created grace. Second, the indwelling of the Holy Spirit is not restricted to a trinitarian appropriation (as in neo-scholasticism), but is identified as a pneumatic *proprium*.

As an aside it should also be noted that, as Fransen comments, the initial success of de la Taille and Rahner was due to their utilization of the scholastic idiom, methodology, and philosophical presuppositions (usually of the Thomistic variety).[3] They worked from within that tradition even if at points they revised it. Such was not the case for others who either worked outside of it or attempted to expand it from within. As Coffey notes with regard to the works of Petavius (the early-seventeenth-century Jesuit theologian who argued for the primacy and exclusivity of the Holy Spirit in sanctification and the divine inhabitation) and Scheeben, they were largely rejected when they attempted from within scholastiscism "to ingraft the theology of the East into the Western *corpus theologicum*," especially in the area of pneumatology.[4] Coffey's position, which is loyal (not uncritically so, as we shall see) to Scheeben and the others, places him within the framework of the general scholastic paradigm, but like Scheeben he pursues a line of inquiry that is compatible with the pneumatological emphases in Eastern Orthodoxy. It is this trajectory within neo-scholasticism that we have traced in the previous two chapters. Because of this, Coffey is at some distance from those, like Hill, who advocate only a strictly Thomistic model of relationship to the divine persons—*sicut cognitum in cognoscente et amatum in amante* (just as the object known is in the knower and the beloved in the lover).[5]

The obstacle to the above-mentioned reception of the pneumatological insights of the Eastern Fathers was the neglect of the relationship between created and uncreated grace and the exclusivity of efficient causality in the divine operations *ad extra*. This provides the warrant for Coffey's turn to de la Taille and Rahner in an effort to utilize the notion of formal (or quasi-formal) causality and resolve the difficulties cited. At this point, however, he goes beyond the two Jesuits to apply the theory not to all three persons in their relationship to the just soul (as in Rahner and

Donnelly), but strictly to the Holy Spirit as the one person who is the author of sanctifying grace (a position closer to that of Scheeben). As he explains in his own words, the reason for this dogmatic shift is related directly to the integrity of trinitarian theology.

> It is the contention of this essay that the concept of divine formal causality in the context of the Blessed Trinity is patient of still further development, in which it can be shown that the works of this causality (of which there are, and can be, only two) must in each instance be attributed to *one divine person alone*, so that sanctifying grace not only is, but must be, the Gift precisely of the Holy Spirit. It is further contended that this task must be undertaken if we are both to avoid a unitarian or only nominally trinitarian conception of grace and to attain a genuinely trinitarian conception of it.[6]

Underlying his proposal are a series of basic points that betray his debt to Scheeben and Rahner. The first is the appeal to Scripture and the Eastern Fathers to substantiate that there is warrant in the primitive and patristic Christian traditions for his claim that what Catholic theology has labeled "sanctifying grace" is "at the same time the Gift of the Holy Spirit and the indwelling of the Blessed Trinity."[7] This strategy, attributable to Scheeben, is then complemented by two Rahnerian insights: the identification of the economic and immanent trinities, and the theory of quasi-formal casuality. On these points (especially the latter two) the contrasts with Hill's positions are quite strong, each of which needs to be identified and evaluated as we proceed.

The return to the Eastern Fathers is a common theme for many Catholic theologians for obvious reasons—the profundity of reflection on the Holy Spirit by Athanasius and the Cappadocians. The appropriation of their insight into the dominant Latin paradigm, however, raises serious questions. A hint of this is surely seen in the critiques of the Latin position often made by Orthodox theologians—for example, as we reviewed in Chapter 1, Vladimir Lossky's charge that "Filioquist" considerations bespeak not just a divergency of starting points in a theology of the trinity—e.g., the divine unity for the West and the divine triad for the East—but also betrays an unnecessary rationalization of the doctrine of the trinity. By a preference for the ontological primacy of the divine essence over the divine hypostases, one inevitably introduces a positive rationalist qualification into the mystery of the divine being—an intrusion of the God of the philosophers into the Christian mystery of the divine triunity.[8] The issue for Catholic theologians, even if they may not fully accept Lossky's critical deductions from the *filioque* (or, for that matter, his interpretation of the Latin position), is to what extent the Latin paradigm requires revision or simply needs to be complemented by the insights of the Greek Fathers.

Coffey is among those Catholic theologians who attempt sympathetically to listen to the Orthodox East. In fact, when it comes to Palamism, Coffey, unlike Yves Congar, who otherwise is one of the strongest proponents of dialogue with the East, reaps a more fruitful harvest.[9] He argues for a parallel development between the insights of the specifically Palamite doctrines and the trajectory in neo-scholastic thought that we have reviewed in Chapters 2 and 3. The main difference between the two theologians is that in regard to the theology of grace Congar remains a much more traditional Thomist. Coffey, on the other hand, exploits the Palamite insight on the distinction between the divine essence and energies in the direction of de la Taille's "created actuation by uncreated act" and Rahner's quasi-formal causality. Both the Orthodox doctrine of the divine energies and the innovations of de la Taille and Rahner intend to highlight the presence of the divine persons in the work of grace—i.e., the priority of uncreated over created grace.[10] Coffey also goes beyond Palamas, as he does with Rahner, but more of that later.

In the broader context, Coffey asserts that both Greek and Latin theologies of the trinity shared an original undifferentiated consciousness in the apostolic and post-apostolic church that God was both one and three, as evidenced in various baptismal and creedal formulas. Later, a tripartite symbol emerged which did not further specify the nature of the unity and the triad beyond the identity in substance implied by the *homoousion*. While heretical alternatives grew out of Greek subordinationism on the one hand and Latin modalism on the other, the beginnings of theological dialectic could be seen in each side's utilization of terminology that only gradually acquired theological exactitude—e.g., *prosopon, hypostasis, ousia, substantia, persona,* etc. In the West it was Augustine who began the next stage of the dialectic, to be completed by Aquinas, who, as his heir, thoroughly complemented the insights of the Fathers with the rigor of the schools. This "scholastic" approach was able to surmount the tension created by the existence of two trinitarian formulas (East and West) through the density of its metaphysical innovations, which in their Thomistic explication were reviewed above.[11]

Like Hill, Coffey remarks that the danger attending Greek trinitarian theology is subordinationism and that Augustine's starting point in the unity of the divine essence sufficiently counters this.[12] To this extent Coffey is indebted to the Latin tradition and operates within the perspective framed by the scholastic development of patristic theology. These can be reduced to the two theological axioms already mentioned, known also to the East but not affirmed with the same degree of magisterial authority as in the West. First is the principle that because of "the unity of the divine operation the triune God acts as 'one principle' in relation to the world" (*omnia opera Trinitatis sunt indivisa*); and second, "that distinction in the Godhead is explained by the opposition of relationships" (*In Deo omnia sunt unum, ubi non obviat relationis oppositio*—expressed by the Council of Florence, 1438–1445).[13]

Even though Coffey does acknowledge these Latin developments, he envisages his own project as an attempt to construct a theology of grace rooted in the Eastern tradition and, as he eventually delineates it, one that is able to negotiate the lacuna of pneumatological neglect characteristic of Western trinitarian theology. Here he differs substantially from William Hill. In his assessment of the need to incorporate the insights of the Eastern Fathers he argues for the introduction of another model of trinitarian relations to balance the one dominant in the Latin West. Descriptively, he labels this as the "bestowal model" of trinitarian relations that complements the scholastic "procession model" (the Latin *filioque*). More responsive to the framework of biblical salvation history and its corresponding "ascending christology," the bestowal model is also conducive to the viability of a more explicitly pneumatic christological construction. We shall examine each of these claims. We shall also need to define these terms and note that in his later work Coffey prefers to rename the new model as the "mutual love" or "return" model in place of his original "bestowal" designation. The reason for this is directly relevant to the observation that Coffey inevitably must step beyond the neo-scholastic paradigm in order to exploit his insights into pneumatology and trinitarian theology.

In his original efforts, however, Coffey examined the steps within the ambit of scholastic trinitarian theology that had to be undertaken to provide a base for expansion beyond it. Therefore, although his inspiration stems from the Eastern tradition, his conceptual framework at this early stage was that of Catholic scholasticism. His interlocutors are both classical and modern, with the result that he assesses the former in preparation for the critical innovations of the latter, eventually leading to his own proposal. Thomas Aquinas is the subject of his investigation into the classical paradigm, read critically in the light of Augustinian, Anselmian, and Victorine strains in his thought. The modern teachers, especially Matthias Scheeben, Heribert Mühlen, and Karl Rahner, are those who from within or on the edges of scholastic thought suggest the dogmatic innovations that Coffey considers necessary for a fully developed trinitarian theology, one that accentuates the pneumatological dimension of christology and is most compatible with the insights of the Eastern Christian tradition. We begin with his speculative reworking of the intra-trinitarian relations, including the introduction of alternative models and later refinements. As we have argued in previous chapters, Spirit-christology is linked dogmatically in two directions: to the communication of redemption in the divine economy and to the relations of the divine persons in the immanent trinity. Since Coffey's original contributions span both these areas, we begin in good scholastic fashion (as he does) with the more speculative locus—namely, intra-trinitarian relations.

The Speculative Reworking of Intra-trinitarian Relations

Coffey's speculative work in trinitarian theology leads him to examine the basis for the traditional Latin filioquist understanding of intra-trinitarian relations (procession model in his usage) and, even more important, to propose an additional model for conceiving the relationship of the divine persons to one another. Coffey does not intend this additional model—which he variously labels as the bestowal, mutual-love or return model—to be a replacement for the traditional one. Rather, it is meant to account for aspects of the divine economy that are not sufficiently explained by the inherited paradigm. The new model complements the older one, and for our purposes it leads to the development of Spirit-christology. It also serves to clarify the distinct mission of the Holy Spirit, and this paired with his reception of Rahnerian insights into the theology of grace enables Coffey to offer an original contribution in pneumatology proper—i.e., a theology of the Holy Spirit. We now turn first to the reasons why Coffey pursues a new model for understanding the intra-trinitarian relations, and then examine the relationship between the two models.

Like many Catholic theologians following the Second Vatican Council, David Coffey is an advocate of methodological pluralism in theology. His own work operates on an intellectual terrain that includes Thomism, neo-scholasticism, transcendental theology, personalism and the fruit of New Testament and patristic scholarship. In fact, we may characterize the intellectual genesis of his own thought as proceeding along the path of the neo-scholasticism that we have thus far traced (he makes mention of Scheeben and de la Taille); and then, with the help of Rahner's transcendental theology and in conversation with personalism he forges his own original proposals, which will also account for the insights of Orthodox trinitarian theology with which he is in conversation as well. Although he does not use the term "Spirit-christology," it is clear that his attention to christology, pneumatology, trinitarian theology, and the theology of grace can converge under this rubric.

The real basis for his innovations in constructive doctrinal work is not, however, simply the articulation of traditional theological loci in a new intellectual idiom. By stating this we do not underestimate the hermeneutical dimension of shifting from one idiom to another. Coffey is aware of this and it serves as a major focal point for his understanding of the development of doctrine, to which we shall return. Nevertheless, despite some problems this causes within his own constructive work, Coffey is definitely motivated by genuine doctrinal concerns. In the light of both recent scholarship (especially biblical) and the Gospel itself, he believes there is a need to explore new speculative models to do full justice to the mysteries of the faith, especially the trinitarian loci and christology. With this in mind, we turn now to a brief schematization of the progress of his thought with an eye toward the relationship between methodology and doctrine.

Coffey confronts us with a series of methodological couplets. He advocates two models for understanding the trinity, correlated with two types of christologies (determined by contrasting methodological approaches), both of which are based on the speculative work that is the fruit of the interaction between the biblical proclamation and the need for doctrinal definition. We will start with Coffey's characterization of the latter. We will then proceed to the first of the trinitarian models—i.e., the traditional Latin filioquist one—and following that to the new model he proposes.

It would be an understatement to suggest that the relationship between biblical scholarship and systematic theology in the modern era has not been an entirely comfortable one. Although Protestant theology has attempted to assimilate the results of New Testament investigation since the last century, Roman Catholic theology has been similarly engaged on a wide scale only since Vatican II—excepting the efforts of such modernists at the turn of the century as Alfred Loisy, whose work was condemned by the church's Holy Office. The tensions in this relationship have not been more pronounced than in field of christology. Only beginning in the 1960s and 1970s did Catholics begin to sort through the issues raised by the classical christological debate concerning the relationship between the Jesus of history and the Christ of faith that emerged among New Testament exegetes and theologians and their counterparts in the field of dogmatic theology, represented especially by the "old" and "new" quests for the historical Jesus. As a systematic theologian emerging out of the speculative ethos of neo-scholasticism, David Coffey addresses the major issue that the diversity of New Testament christologies now raises for dogmatics—namely, how to conceptualize the divinity of Christ. Our examination will focus on the systematic construct that Coffey employs to fruitfully link the later church doctrine with the biblical testimony.

Amid the various New Testament christologies Coffey is quite willing to acknowledge that the only one that lends itself to a traditional "descending christology" from which the dogma of the incarnation is derived is that of the Johannine corpus. The Fourth Gospel's prologue (Jn. 1:14) contains the most direct New Testament proclamation of the descent of the divine Logos into flesh, interpreted almost universally by the patristic church as a metaphysical becoming-human of the pre-existent Son of God.[14] But is this later church teaching the correct exegesis of the passage? Coffey's answer is negative; yet despite his alternative exegetical conclusion, he does not discount the later teachings of either Nicaea or Chalcedon. How he constructively links the two provides us with a key insight into his systematic work.

The immediate question regarding the Johannine prologue concerns the identity of the Logos. Coffey argues that the reference is actually to the man Jesus who pre-existed with God from eternity, not to a pre-existent divine person who assumes human flesh. What was originally a hymn to the Logos as the pre-existent divine Wisdom—most likely originating out of the Hellenistic Jewish tradition of Alexandria—was taken over by the Johannine community and Christianized. Jesus was identified with the Logos by that community to express its christological faith.[15] While biblical scholars may debate the accuracy of this exegesis, what is interesting from a systematic point of view (to be distinguished from the perspectives of either biblical theology or historical theology) are the steps taken by Coffey to demonstrate how in the development of doctrine this christology led to the later conciliar definitions. To do so he distinguishes between functional and ontological predications of divinity and between ascending and descending christologies. Each requires explanation and will figure importantly in its relationship to the pneumatology that he proposes.

The first distinction is between "functional divinity" and "ontological divinity." Both are used christologically and basically distinguish between the biblical and patristic understandings of the person of Christ. Coffey follows Oscar Cullman when he describes the functional divinity of Christ as rooted in salvation-history with a focus on the words and deeds of Jesus (including death and resurrection).[16] There is no reference at this stage to the being or nature of Christ—that is, to a properly ontological christology, which would so occupy the church after it had passed thoroughly into the Greco-Roman world. In the New Testament, where christological language is limited to a functional notion of divinity, one may also distinguish between its use by means of either an ascending or descending christology. Each of these types is descriptive of the direction taken by christology, either from God to humanity (descending) or from humanity to God (ascending). It is similar to the terms used originally by Wolfhart Pannenberg when he distinguished between christologies "from below" and "from above,"[17] except that Coffey is not so much concerned with advancing reasons for "the confession of Jesus' divinity"[18] as he is in elucidating the manner in which divinity is acknowledged and conceptualized. Here, as in most of his work, his debt to Rahner is much greater. As posed by the latter, the main distinction between the two types of christology (descending and ascending) aside from direction (from above or below) is whether or not Jesus' divinity is conceived in terms of saving history (functional divinity) or metaphysics (ontological divinity).[19] Coffey is interested in recovering the former for christology and eventually even for trinitarian theology.

In the combination of the two ascriptions of divinity and the two types of christology, Coffey suggests four distinct stages in the development of dogmatic christology. First, scripture presents us with a functional christology in the ascending mode—namely, that Jesus is one with God by virtue of his saving activity, a christology that is common, for example, to the synoptic Gospels. This is followed by a functional christology in the descending mode characteristic of the highest christology in the New Testament—i.e., Jn 1:14—where the man Jesus is identified with the divine Logos who becomes flesh within the perspective of saving history. Coffey contends that in this passage there is only a functional identification between the man Jesus and the pre-existent Logos or Wisdom. The introduction of ontological christology, where the focus switches to the being of Christ, begins in the post-apostolic era and culminates in the homoousion of Nicaea (third stage). The full recognition of the assumption of a human nature by the Logos in a metaphysical incarnation (fourth stage) would await the developments following Chalcedon, especially the enhypostatic christology of Leontius of Byzantium in the sixth century, where the only hypostasis in the person of Christ is that of the assuming Logos, not the assumed humanity. This resolves the metaphysical relationship between the man Jesus and the divine Logos. Coffey summarizes these four stages as follows:

> We move step by step from functional divinity via functional incarnation and ontological divinity to ontological incarnation.[20]

How do these christological distinctions bear on pneumatology? Here we return to the wider trinitarian context. In our study thus far, while we have distinguished between the immanent and economic trinities (and the similar but not equivalent "theology" and "economy" in the East), we have not brought these into relationship with the biblical material. This is precisely what Coffey argues is necessary to mediate between these two perspectives on the trinity. In fact, what emerges is a methodological principle that guides the speculative thrust of trinitarian theology and that highlights pneumatology as the key factor in a fully mature theology of the trinity. The principle harks back to his affirmation of the Latin theological axioms that the works of the trinity are one and that only the opposition of relation distinguishes the persons. From these Coffey concludes that "the only ground for distinguishing the divine persons is strictly *innertrinitarian.* "[21] How does this reflect on the relationship between the biblical material and the later perspectives on the trinity?

Coffey contends that the order of doctrinal development begins with the biblical understanding of the trinity, proceeds to the immanent trinity, and ends with the economic trinity. Therefore, without diminishing the role of speculative and constructive theology—in fact, that is where Coffey makes his contribution—the import of biblical theology for trinitarian reflection is much greater than in the traditional approach, where the two axioms mentioned are the sole guides. As just reviewed, the biblical perspective on christology is expressed in functional terms. The same is true for the trinity:

> ... the "biblical" doctrine of the Trinity. This is a doctrine in which the Father is called Yahweh, called Father by Jesus because of the unique nature of his relationship to Him, a relationship which combines authority with intimacy; a doctrine in

which the Son is Jesus, though his Sonship is not yet understood as an ontological reality requiring an incarnation in the metaphysical sense; and a doctrine in which the Holy Spirit appears now impersonally as the spirit, or power, of God, and now as this same power impregnated with the human personality of Jesus, though not yet grasped as a person in his own right.[22]

From this biblical account, which is by no means uniform, considering that both ascending and descending christologies are included in Luke and John, respectively, the doctrine of the immanent trinity is inferred. Consistent with his appreciation of doctrinal development, Coffey denies that the immanent trinity is directly revealed in the New Testament.[23] The manner of this doctrinal inference is therefore important. Again, Coffey approaches this as a systematic theologian, not as a historical theologian. The steps taken in theological reflection from the biblical doctrine to the immanent trinity sets up the doctrinal parameters for further development. Important to Coffey are the limits of this process according to the model utilized. This is impetus enough, in his view, for further theological exploration into trinitarian theology.

The initial step from the biblical doctrine to the more speculative one is the inference drawn from what later theology would call the missions of the Son and Spirit. Because Christians are united to the Son through the Holy Spirit, it is concluded that the incarnation of the Son and the gift of the Holy Spirit are prolongations into the world of their own processional relationships within the trinity. This speculative step entails "reversing the epistemological order (i.e., the order of discovery) to acquire the ontological order (i.e., the order of givenness)."[24] The Christian experience in the Spirit of Christ as the saving revelation of God—Spirit, Son, Father—is inverted in an effort to understand the nature and being of the triadic identity in God—Father, Son, Spirit. This leads to the traditional filioquist model of intra-trinitarian relations. To summarize, the givenness of the missions of the Son and the Spirit lead one to infer that the Son proceeds from the Father and the Holy Spirit from both the Father and the Son.

Although many are content with the theological inference implied in this inversion, Coffey is not. The reasons are several. In view of the axiom that the work of God *ad extra* is indivisible, it would seem impossible that the persons of the trinity could be distinguished in their missions. However, if this is the case, then the problem is with the speculative axiom, or at least its application, since the givenness of the incarnation of the Son and the gift of the Holy Spirit cannot be denied in their specificity without diminishing the deposit of the faith. Therefore, to assume that the immanent relations of the divine persons to one another according to the filioquist pattern of the procession model can be inferred from a simple inversion of the experience of grace is to misapply this particular model of intra-trinitarian relations. To clarify this, we turn to the correlation between the procession model and descending christology.

The descending christology of Jn. 1:14 became the paradigmatic christological model for the church of the Fathers. The descent of the Logos into human flesh in the incarnation also clearly indicates that the Son or Word of God proceeds from the Father, or more accurately is generated by him as the only begotten one. The Holy Spirit is also presented in the same modality of descent. Whether or not the *filioque* is accepted, it is also clear that the Paraclete proceeds from the Father and (at the least) is sent by the Son. Even as the breathing-forth of the Holy Spirit follows the generation of the Son, so, too, the mission of the Son in the incarnation leads to the mission of the Holy Spirit at Pentecost (whether that be the Lukan or Johannine versions). This portrayal of the missions of the Son and the Spirit in the economic trinity indicate their processional relations in the immanent trinity. However, this procession model of relations in the immanent trinity and of missions in the economic trinity is not simply the inversion of the order of the believer's relation to the divine persons in the experience of grace—i.e., in the Spirit through the Son to the Father. The problem with the inversion of these terms is not that the two orders—i.e., the order of intra-trinitarian relations and the order of relation to the trinitarian persons through the grace of salvation, are not connected but rather that the conceptualization of this particular model of relations does not provide for such an inversion. As Coffey notes, it is methodologically incorrect; a "wrong reason is provided for the right answer."[25]

Coffey's critique of the utilization of the procession model and descending christology reverts back to the restrictions implied by the two Latin trinitarian axioms quoted above. If the persons of the trinity cannot be distinguished on the basis of the divine operation *ad extra*, where the *relationis oppositio* does not function since the work of God is common to all three persons, then how are the persons distinct in their respective missions, since they are an *ad extra* manifestation of the divine working? Thomas Aquinas states that a mission of a divine person "includes the eternal procession, with the addition of a temporal effect;"[26] hence the relationship between the procession model of intra-trinitarian relations and the external divine missions. Coupled with the descending christology of Jn. 1:14 and the sending of the Paraclete in the same Gospel by both the Father (14:26) and the Son (16:7) and by the Son in dependence on the Father (15:26), there is warrant in the biblical texts for concluding that the Son and the Spirit are sent from the Father into the world because there is already a relationship between each of them and the Father, a relationship that can be described broadly in terms of "proceeding from." Coffey contends that it is this notion of "proceeding from" implying also the modality of a descending christology, that does not offer a convincing construct to imagine the relationship of the creature to the divine persons in their distinctiveness.

The distinct relationship to a divine person can be predicated only on the basis of "the *assimilation* of the creature into the Trinity."[27] In other words, the offer of grace in the incarnate mission of the Son and the Pentecostal mission of the Holy Spirit does not in the offer alone constitute that assimilation. Both of these missions conceived along the lines of the procession model are "outward-moving" or centrifugal sendings of the Son and the Spirit. As the communication of divine life they are the basis for the reception of that life by the creature, but they are not identical to that reception. Only in the reception is the creature united to a divine person in a manner that assimilates it to that person and then by the extension of the intra-trinitarian relations to the other persons of the trinity as well. In the case of the incarnation the creaturely element is the human nature assumed by the divine Word, and in the pneumatological mission it is the gift of the Holy Spirit that unites many human persons to his own person and thus to the risen and glorified Christ. From this perspective the temporal missions are interpreted in the modality of return—that is, as an "inward-moving" or centripetal operation of the divine presence.[28]

Christologically, the modality required for union in the divine-human relation is one of "ascent." Pneumatologically, the Holy Spirit is not understood as proceeding from the Father (and the Son), but as bestowed by the Father on the Son and by the Son on the Father. Therefore, the inversion of the order of the divine persons is not dependent on a "sending forth" as the economic correlation to the immanent "proceeding from." Strictly regarding the modality of direction—i.e., from God to humanity and from humanity to God—the procession model cannot account for the ascension of the creature to God. The Father who sends the Son who in turn sends the Spirit does not invert to the Spirit returning the creature to the Son and then to the Father. The Holy Spirit, it will be recalled, is only sent and does not send; therefore, by "proceeding from" it does not return to the Son and the Father. Only if the Father and Son mutually bestow the Spirit on one another is there a basis in the immanent trinity for this economic manifestation of the divine persons, wherein pneumatology is the key for the return of all things to God. As we shall now see, the working out of this theory requires considerable effort on Coffey's part; the fruit of it, however, is a mature Spirit-christology. We turn now to his early efforts in the realm of scholastic theology. He will later abandon this perspective, since with many others he recognizes that "the day of scholastic theology is over."[29] For the moment, his efforts serve to highlight the limitations of the scholastic approach.

Coffey's initial inquiry into the cogency of the traditional model—i.e., the procession model—and the possibilities for a complementary one focuses on a study of Thomas Aquinas, especially the earlier and later reflections of the Angelic Doctor on the nature of the Holy Spirit's procession. When Thomas adopted Augustine's psychological analogy of the trinity, he also affirmed his more interpersonal model of trinitarian relations. Logically, the two models do not necessarily coincide. For example, according to the former the Son and the Spirit are identified with the essential operation of the divine knowing and loving. In the latter model the Holy Spirit is identified by Augustine as the mutual love of the Father and the Son, a relational description that exceeds the unitary subject of the psychological analogy. As adopted by Aquinas, the situation is further complicated by the Anselmian and Victorine influences that develop each of these emphases respectively.

Anselm extended the psychological analogy into a properly metaphysical construct. The knowing and loving of the divine subject are defined as essential acts that become the basis for the formal reasons of the divine processions—the first procession of the Son as the divine knowing and the second procession of the Holy Spirit as the divine loving. But as Coffey points out, to maintain the differentiation of the persons the analogy shifts from the psychological operations of the divine subject—i.e., knowing and loving—to the biblical metaphors of generating and breathing-forth.[30] This is evident in the *Monologium* where Anselm, after having identified the two processions with the divine knowledge and love (and the first person with memory—he extends the psychological analogy to include all three of the faculties), must then further delineate the personal distinctions on the basis of the one who begets, the one begotten and the one who is breathed forth—this so that he does not deny that each person possesses memory, intelligence, and love.[19] In other words, the necessary co-equality of the persons forces Anselm to buttress the psychological analogy with the biblical metaphors—i.e., generation and breathing-forth (John 1:14; 15:26)—which are also the traditionally Eastern reasons for the trinitarian distinctions beyond which they have not normally ventured.[32] When we return to Aquinas, however, and examine the traces of Anselmian trinitarianism in his *corpus* we are presented with a number of problems that in particular motivate Coffey to introduce his new model from within the parameters of the old one.

As explicated in his book *Grace: The Gift of the Holy Spirit*, Coffey argues that in Thomas there is both a complementarity and a tension between these two strains in his trinitarian thought. The shift in his understanding of the procession of the Holy Spirit (in analogy with the procession of the Son) is evident in the comparison of the early works (the *De Veritate* and *In I Sententiarum*) with the *Summa Theologiae*. The issue is whether or not the second procession—i.e., the Holy Spirit, can be conceived in the same manner as the first—i.e., the Son—specifically as a *processio operati* (procession of the thing operated). In the early work this ascription was assigned only to the procession that constitutes the Son. Correlating the procession of the Son with the divine knowledge (Augustine's psychological analogy), Thomas posits it as a *processio operati* because it requires an immanent term. It is a centripetal operation of the knower—i.e., one that returns to the subject—because it culminates in the thing known. In other words, in knowing the knower objectifies within the intellect the thing known through the necessary abstraction of the object of knowledge; this process constitutes the act of knowledge itself. The abstraction produced as an immanent term within the intellect remains distinct from the knowing subject. The correlation with the subsisting relations of Father and Son is clear and already traditional in the Latin West—namely, that God's self-knowledge, in which the knower and the known can be distinguished, is analogous to the Father's begetting of the Son, in which the begetter and the begotten are also distinguished, with the recognition that by the terms of the analogy the *Verbum* in God is never simply an abstraction. The same does not hold for the second procession of divine love correlated with the subsisting relation of the Holy Spirit. This volitional operation (as distinguished from the intellective nature of the first procession) bears no immanent term. It is a centrifugal operation—i.e., strictly outgoing—and therefore must be described as a *processio operationis* (procession of the operation). The act of loving, while it may come to rest on another—e.g., the Father loving the Son—does not in the process of loving produce something in the loving distinct from the act itself. With these distinctions Coffey is in agreement.[33] The problem arises with the change in Aquinas' understanding of the comparison between the two processions, a change followed by Hill as reviewed in the previous chapter, but now severely disputed by Coffey.

In the *Summa Theologiae* St. Thomas identifies the second procession as a *processio operati*. Instead of being contrasted, the two processions are now parallel, each with an immanent term and both centripetal in operation.[34] The act of loving does produce an immanent term, and the only thing that distinguishes the divine loving from the divine knowing is the faculty exercised, not the manner of its exercise. Within the horizon of the psychological model of the trinity, this confines the distinction between the two processions to a difference in the subjective operations of the divine essence; that is, Son and Spirit are not identical because the divine knowing and loving are not identical. However, if, as the later Aquinas argues, both processions are parallel in operation except for the faculty expressed (intellective or volitional), the warrant for the distinction between the two processions is considerably lessened in view of the fact that the attribute of divine simplicity prohibits an undue separation of faculties. In other words, given that the primary analogue of the psychological model is the human spirit and secondarily God as infinite spirit, one cannot argue without mediation from one to the other. The Thomistic principle for the distinction and relatedness of the faculties—"nothing can be loved by the will unless it is conceived in the intellect"—can be applied to both analogues only with the provision that the operations of the human spirit are not simply identical to the notional distinctions of the trinitarian persons. In fact, the analogy sought is between the operations of the human spirit and the divine processions that explain the manner of origination for the second and third persons. Here again, the divine simplicity requires that this not entail real distinctions in God, for the only distinctions warranted by revelation are the persons themselves. What is at issue is the theo-logic in human thought that best renders these revealed distinctions. It is at this point that Coffey attempts a breakthough in the prevailing neo-scholastic and Thomistic paradigm.

According to the psychological model, it was generally argued that the divine knowing and loving are predicates of the divine essence and are the formal reasons for the production of the second and third persons. If the interpersonal model was introduced, as it was by Augustine and Aquinas in order to posit the Holy Spirit as the mutual love of the Father and the Son, this was usually subordinated to the psychological model's emphasis that it was the self-love of the divine essence that originated the procession. The distinction between essential and notional acts must, however, be emphasized. Essential divine acts are those common to the Godhead; notional acts are those not common to all three persons and are therefore constitutive of any one divine person as distinct from the others.[35] It is at this point that the strictly essential procession of divine love implied by the psychological model breaks down if that love is intended as the basis for the procession of the Holy Spirit. It could never be a purely essential act of divine self-love, because the Holy Spirit as a product of this love is not included within its agency. According to the theological fund of the Latin tradition, with its inclusion of the *filioque,* the second procession does require the agency of the Father and the Son. These are notional acts, for they correspond to the notion of active spiration peculiar to both the Father and the Son. Can they be translated into a notional (as contrasted to an essential) act of divine self-love? If so, then we have reason to differentiate the trinitarian persons not only by their opposition of relation (the Latin model) but by their manner of origin (the Greek model). This will figure importantly in Spirit-christology, where the differentiation of processions must be maintained relative to the one person of Jesus Christ and where likewise the context of a theology of grace wherein there is a real relation between human reality and the divine persons of the trinity is presupposed.

The positive answer to this question represents the innovation in Coffey's work, especially with regard to that of Aquinas.

The difference between the position of Aquinas and that which we are taking here
. . . is that he judged the essential plane to be primary and the notional plane to be
secondary, whereas in the argument that we present the notional plane is primary
and the essential plane secondary.[36]

Specifically, the argument is that notional statements are particularly appropriate in
speaking of the trinitarian processions and their formal reasons.[37] This does not
necessarily invalidate or contradict essentialist statements "but rather makes an
advance on them," for they stand as "the determination or specification" of essentialist language about God.[38] Without neglecting the basic orientation of the Latin
model, Coffey is able to bring to the fore the distinct identity of each of the persons.
By giving priority to notional differentiation within the trinity, the context for christological reflection is more immediately trinitarian than is the case with an essentialist emphasis. For example, to speak of the *verbum Dei* when put in the language
of notional predication is to confess that it is the Word of the Father who becomes
flesh and not simply the divine Word, or, better yet, that the divine Word (essentialist
language) is the Father's Word (notional language). This manner of conceptualizing
the intra-trinitarian relations is more accessible to a salvation-history approach
whereby one begins with the economy of redemption revealed in Jesus Christ and
proceeds to his relationship to the God he addressed as Abba and the Spirit with
whom he was anointed. Needless to say, the possibilities for the exploitation of this
emphatic shift to notional predication in the direction of Spirit-christology, where
the inter-relation of the trinitarian persons is primary, is much greater than is the
case with the essentialist model.

   In terms of the argument, this innovation accomplishes three things for Coffey
immediately. First, it establishes the distinction between the two processions as clear
notional acts of the divine persons. Second, it upholds a solid connection between
the psychological analogy and the interpersonal one, thereby paving the way for the
introduction of his new model of trinitarian relations. This model, to which we shall
shortly come, is both the end result of his reconsideration of the intra-trinitarian
relations and the necessary basis for Spirit-christology. Finally, it provides the proper
foundation for a theology of grace that is predicated on the proper indwelling of the
Holy Spirit as the grace of God. I shall return to this latter point, with its important
consequences for pneumatic christology. For the moment we need underscore the
significance of the first two points.

   In his initial critique of the later Aquinas's understanding of the nature of the
two processions, Coffey had taken issue with the presentation of the second procession as a *processio operati*. This basically negated the distinction between the manner
of the processions (not their origin where one person begets and two persons spirate)
except for the difference in faculties, which while real cannot be overemphasized—
"knowledge and love are not simply distinct in God."[39] In addition, if we reason
from operation to being (the converse—from being to operation—is not a legitimate
form of inductive reasoning) it is clear from ordinary language use that knowledge
does bear an immanent term—i.e., the thing known as a concept or word—but not
so clear that the same follows for love—e.g., the one loved as what? The beloved
is the object of love, but love is simply the operation of the lover with no immanent

term present to the lover as the concept is to the knower. In view of this, the warrant for a notional origination for the processions is more cogent than a strictly essentialist one.

If the two processions are distinguished respectively as a *processio operati* and a *processio operationis,* then not only are the processions themselves distinct but the origin of the processions cannot simply be the unitary divine subject (qua the divine essence). Rather, the distinction in processions (between the thing operated—i.e., the Word—and merely an operation—i.e., the Spirit) requires a multiplicity in the divine subject, both because accidents are excluded from the divine being and real distinction in God among the persons is based on the opposition of relations. The former translates into the subsistent relation of the Son produced by the notional act of the Father's self-knowledge—the concept in the Father's act of knowledge cannot be accidental but substantial. The latter means that the divine self-love as proceeding is likewise a subsistent relation distinct from both the immanent intellective term and its origin. As an operation, it presupposes the procession of knowing ("nothing can be loved by the will unless it is conceived in the intellect") and yet is distinguished from it by the manner of its own procession (one without an immanent term). In addition, while the act of love is to be distinguished from the act of knowing, this love nevertheless proceeds from its notional origin in the knower and its immanent term. This is the basis for the *filioque* (and the Eastern *per filium*) and the correlation between the biblical metaphors of generation (begetting) and spiration (breathing-forth) and the psychological model's utilization of knowledge and love. The only true notional acts are the former, since each person of the trinity knows and loves; but as has been illustrated, one can and indeed must also speak of the divine knowing and loving in notional and not merely in essential terms.[40] To do so is to recognize the necessary distinction between the two processions that are constitutive of the second and third persons—or, more exactly, the first procession as constitutive and productive of the Son and the second procession as constitutive (but not productive) of the Holy Spirit, this due directly to the contrast between a *processio operati* and a *processio operationis*.[41]

Having demonstrated the difference between the two processions based on notional acts in God, Coffey, quoting the early Aquinas, further distinguishes between the "procession" and the "manner of the procession" of the Holy Spirit.[42] The Holy Spirit subsists as a divine person on the basis of the "procession" itself, with the Father and the Son constituting the single principle of the procession whether it be envisaged on the basis of the *filioque* or the *per filium*. Coffey designates this as the procession model of the trinity. But this does not address the question of the third person relative to the relationship between the Father and the Son. Here the "manner of the procession" is significant. If the Holy Spirit is the notional love of Father and Son, then the mutuality of that love is underscored. The Holy Spirit as the mutual love of Father and Son is bestowed first from the Father upon the Son and then from the Son back to the Father. Coffey identifies the resulting analogy as the bestowal model of the trinity—i.e., the Father bestowing love on the Son and the Son then bestowing it on the Father, this mutual love being the Holy Spirit. He has thus arrived at the new model by examining the nature of the processions within the old model in order to give a more adequate accounting of the mutuality of the inter-personal relations within the trinity. As he will later argue, this model is also more conducive to an Orthodox understanding of the intra-trinitarian distinctions—i.e., starting with the divine persons, while at the same time keeping within a Latin perspective—i.e., Augustine's mutual-love model.

In comparing the two models we note that they differ in that the procession model is based on the productive and constitutive origin of the persons. The bestowal model, on the other hand, emphasizes the inter-personal relationship of the persons rather than their constitutive relationship. The relationship of the persons is based not on principiality—i.e., that the Father by generation is the principle of the Son and that by spiration the Father and the Son are the principle of the Holy Spirit, as in the procession model. Rather, mutuality is at the basis of these relations. The Father loves and bestows that love on the Son, with the Son answering in love to the Father. The Spirit as the mutual love between Father and Son exists differently as person than either the Father or the Son, the Spirit not being an active agent of love but love itself. This corresponds to the notional attribute of the Spirit in the procession model that is strictly passive in nature—i.e., passive spiration. The two models complement one another, and in regard to a comprehensive doctrine of the trinity the bestowal model completes the procession model by emphasizing the self-enclosure and self-sufficiency of the trinity vis-à-vis the mutuality of its relations, mediated by the person of the Holy Spirit, by which the Father loves the Son and the Son loves the Father.[43] In other words, as Coffey claims, it gives meaning and purpose to the procession of the Holy Spirit, who is breathed forth not into a void but in the mutuality of love terminating "at the Father (in receiving the bestowal of the Son's love), from whom it began (in generating the Son)."[44]

One might be well satisfied to ponder this new trinitarian model, and especially the turn in emphasis from essential to notional predication for the two intra-trinitarian processions. As has been stated, this shift is conducive to the nature of personal distinctions emphasized by the Eastern church (although notional and personal predication are still differentiated on the basis of the *filioque*—e.g., the Father and Son are distinguished from the Holy Spirit but not from each other by the notional distinctions of active and passive spiration). However, Coffey seems to reconsider aspects of this proposal in a later article without explanation.[45] There he restricts the correlation of the psychological analogy to the procession model and does not extend it to his new bestowal model, as he did in the earlier work.[46] He even suggests that the procession model serves to clarify the *essential* unity of the Godhead, while the bestowal model's emphasis is on the *personal* unity.[47] Does this mean that Coffey in his later work has abandoned his proposal concerning notional predication for the two intra-trinitarian processions? And what significance does this hold for his overall pneumatology? The answer to these questions, at least to the first one, can only be speculative, and without further word from Coffey need not concern this study. The second question, however, is more serious and will be examined in the next section, where we will investigate how this new model of intra-trinitarian relations constructively informs Coffey's christology and theology of grace.

Incarnation and Grace: A Pneumatic Interpretation

Method

David Coffey understands himself as standing within the recent tradition of a new theological methodology articulated by a number of Catholic theologians. Enunciated by Piet Schoonenberg and repeated by Walter Kasper it can be stated as follows:

> Our whole thinking moves from the world to God, and can never move in the opposite direction . . . We never conclude from the Trinity to Christ and his Spirit given to us, but always the other way round.[48]

However, his work reviewed thus far implicates the more traditional method in scholastic speculative theology—i.e., to move from God to the world, the *exitus* and *reditus* of all things in relation to God. This is true only in a provisional sense; it enables Coffey to advance to his more constructive dogmatic work. He remarks in a later article that there are at least three ways of conceptualizing the trinity: the biblical, procession, and bestowal models. New Testament triadic formulas, christological titles, and references to the Spirit focus on the redemptive activity of God rather than on the nature of the ontological relationship that obtains between the one and the three. An ontologically developed conceptualization of the trinity was attained only through the procession model constructed by the great scholastics, with their reception of patristic insights and an emphasis on the immanent trinity. Coffey's own bestowal model, although it pertains to the immanent trinity (relative to the intra-trinitarian relations), is really the product of going back to the biblical understanding with the insights of the procession model and then, from the perspective of the economic trinity (the product of this going back), reconceiving a new understanding of the relations. By introducing the bestowal model of trinitarian relations from within the parameters of the basic scholastic paradigm and its interaction with biblical categories, Coffey has accomplished a necessary foundational step for a Spirit-christology that is consistent with the Catholic tradition for at least two reasons. First, the integrity of the trinitarian dogma is maintained only with the distinction of persons. Second, the specific presence and work of the third person can be accentuated only if the distinctiveness of his procession is cogently upheld. Having accomplished that, Coffey is then able to proffer his proposal for a pneumatic christology. To that we now turn.

We proceed by examining what Edward Kilmartin, in following Coffey, has described as the "yield" of each trinitarian model—i.e., procession and bestowal— for the theologies of incarnation and grace.[49] Each model is correlated with a mode of christological method, and each must account for the scholastic distinction between formal and efficient causality. Descending christology, the traditional creative pattern of God's salvific action in the world since the patristic era, is the expected corollary for the procession model. As the Son proceeds from the Father, he assumes a human nature in his *ad exra* mission directed to human redemption. Ascending christology, by which the incarnate Jesus is related to and returns to the Father, follows the unitive pattern of the bestowal model. In each model, the incarnation is the revelation of the trinity and grace its operation, with both models including the exercise of efficient and formal causality. This engages the trinity respectively in centrifugal (outward-moving) and centripetal (inward-moving) activity relative to created reality. In other words, both models, to the extent that causality is predicated of the divine persons, points to the economic trinity whose efficacious and formal agency results in the foundational Christian witness to the incarnation and the grace of God. The models also establish the correlation between the *ad extra* missions and the *ad intra* relations, although in the immanent trinity causality is excluded, motion being foreign to pure immanence. The intra-trinitarian relations are predicated not on causality but on the principiality—i.e., the productive origin, of the divine self-communication as Word and Spirit.[50] In the case of the bestowal model, a similar distinction between the immanent and economic trinities is maintained by reference to different types of "bestowal" by the Father and the Son of the Holy Spirit. While in the immanent trinity the Holy Spirit is simply bestowed as the mutual love of the first and second persons, in the economic trinity the Spirit is "given" gratuitously in the context of redemption wherein the humanity of Christ is both recipient and giver of the third person.[51] As will be discussed below, this means that the Holy Spirit when conceived in reference to Christ as recipient is understood as the Spirit of Sonship and in relation to Christ as giver the Spirit becomes incarnate in the human love of Jesus for both God and neighbor.

Coffey owes his utilization of formal causality to the work of M. de la Taille and Karl Rahner as explicated in the previous chapter. Combined with the latter's notion of the divine self-communication as the self-communication of the Father in the Word and in the Spirit (the latter two persons then not being self-communications of divinity in addition to the Father but the two modalities of the one divine self-communication of the Father), Coffey is able to establish proper and exclusive missions for the second and third persons in the incarnation and grace, respectively. Neither excludes the complementarity of efficient and formal causality. Efficient causality is the creative work of all three persons undifferentiated as the single divine operation that creates the sacred humanity (relative to the incarnation) and infuses created grace (relative to sanctification). "Efficient causality [therefore] provides the basis and condition of possibility of formal causality."[52] This centrifugal operation lends itself to the centripetal operation of formal causality by which God as communicator assimilates to the divine being the sacred humanity and graced believers. By formal causality the Son and the Spirit are received as proper and personal communications of the trinity in the modalities respectively of the hypostatic union and the divine indwelling.

Application or "Yields" of the Models

RECONSTRUCTION OF THE SCHOLASTIC PARADIGM

As we turn now to the specific contributions, or "yields," of each model for the doctrines of the incarnation and grace, it is important to note the major shift that Coffey's work advances within the overall framework of Catholic trinitarian theology. Still working with the scholastic idiom, Coffey is quick to acknowledge the deficiency of its adaptation of Aristotelian infra-personal categories—specifically, the rendering of religious event and experience in the language of substance, motion, and causality rather than in that of the human subject or interpersonal relations. So, for example, when the divine agency is limited to efficient causality and grace is described as an entitive habit, both the biblical testimony to the "favour and merciful love of God" and the personal integrity of the recipient of grace recede into the background. To that extent his dialogue with modern Catholic theologians Heribert Mühlen and Karl Rahner is decisive for the end result of his work, a product that attempts to combine the precision of scholasticism with the biblical emphasis on a more personalistic mode of divine agency.

From Mühlen, whose now classic works have led to a renewed pneumatological emphasis in ecclesiology,[53] Coffey accepts the insights of an interpersonal model of trinitarian relations, although not without severe criticism. Suffice it to say that Mühlen's well-known pronominalization of the trinitarian relations (i.e., the Father as the I-relation, the Son as the Thou-relation, and the Holy Spirit as the We-relation) is rejected by Coffey, but the personalistic suggestions for the intra-trinitarian relations implicated by it is accepted. Thus, Coffey's reworking of the psychological model vis-à-vis notional predication of the divine knowing and loving—i.e., the two constitutive acts of the processions—can be expressed in terms similar to Mühlen's pronominalization:

1. I (the Father) know myself in Thee (the Son);
2. We (the Father and the Son) love each other (this love being the Holy Spirit).[54]

This ensures that the trinitarian distinctions are able to assimilate the modern concept of person as "a spirit rooted in relationship." However, it must be recognized that such an assimilation is possible only on the "level of secondary Trinitarian data" i.e, how the persons occupy the trinitarian self-consciousness that belongs not to the persons as such but to the divine essence.[55] On the level of primary trinitarian data, the ancient notion of person as a "spiritual subsistent being" still prevails since the processions implicate only subsistence and not consciousness.

Having extracted this personalist emphasis from Mühlen, Coffey is even more indebted to Karl Rahner. Neo-scholasticism not only was ensconced within the infra-personal categories of Aristotelian-Thomistic philosophy, but likewise was concerned to maintain the transcendence of the Creator relative to the creature. As we have seen, this restricted the divine agency to the realm of efficient causality. Coffey's appropriation of the Rahnerian concepts of (quasi-)formal causality and revelation as the divine self-communication in the two modalities of Word and Spirit enables him to demonstrate that the events of revelation—i.e., the incarnation and grace—are respectively the communications of the proper missions of the Son and Spirit and likewise respectively entail unity and union between each and their created terms. The pneumatological mission does not reproduce the christological mission. The sacred humanity is united with the Son so that Jesus Christ *is* the Son of God, whereas the just person is only brought into union with the Holy Spirit, without constituting an incarnation of the third person. Regarding the divine missions, the "self" that is communicated must not be reduced to its explication on the human level, where only a "part of the self" is communicated—e.g., a word or thought. The nature of divinity allows for the totality of divinity to be communicated in the modalities mentioned—namely, as the persons of the Son and the Spirit.[56] As with all analogies of the divine the dissimilarites as well as the similarities make for the nature of the analogy—in this case, the scope of communication of the self.[57]

By the time Coffey articulates the fruit of the trinitarian missions in incarnation and grace, the scholastic idiom has already been transformed by Mühlen's personalism and Rahner's transcendental theology. The originality of his project lies in the extent to which scholasticism can go before it must be transcended, even if from within. In fact, Coffey by no means abandons the insights of scholastic speculative theology. He argues for the complementarity of the different theological traditions rather than the displacement of one by the other. Even in his later work where he admits that the day of scholasticism is over, he is also concerned that one fully understand the implications of positions that scholasticism was defending and not simply dismiss them out of hand. Concretely, it would be inadvisable in his view, for example, to rely only on personalist categories to provide a foundation for the reception of the proper missions of the Son and Spirit. The precision and clarity of scholastic distinctions are still important, and one ought not simply to set in opposition the infra-personal and the personal, as has been done by personalism. The need for dialogical models in epistemology does not negate the necessity for the categorization of the content of knowledge claims. Transcendental method, with its emphasis on the priority of the human subject as knower, is able to incorporate both of these concerns. In this regard, it is transcendental theology that guides the dialectic between these two traditions.[58]

This is clearly evident in his utilization of the procession model to explicate the self-communication of God in the incarnation and the doctrine of grace. Two dimensions of the issue are addressed: first, the active communication of the modalities from the side of God, and second, the reception of these modalities in the created order. The former leads Coffey into a profound revision of neo-scholastic and Thomistic doctrine. In the *Summa Theologiae* St. Thomas asks whether each person of the trinity can assume a created nature. His positive answer excludes any necessity in attributing the incarnation to the procession of the Son.[59] Coffey, on the other hand, argues precisely for such a necessity, and this with respect to both processions in the trinity. Here again his debt to Rahner is evident, but he differs from him on the exclusivity of the divine self-communication mediated by the processions. We shall examine the significance of each of these points in detail.

In his short work, *The Trinity*,[60] Rahner essayed his position on the necessity of the second person's assuming a created nature. It was implicated by a more general trinitarian axiom, which we mentioned in the first chapter: *"The 'economic' Trinity is the 'immanent' Trinity and the 'immanent' Trinity is the 'economic' Trinity."*[61] The axiom begins with the conviction that the salvific work of the trinity is revelatory of the trinity's nature, therefore assuring the dogmatic certainty that only the Logos could become incarnate in Jesus. The question as to whether any divine person might have assumed a human nature (hypothetically affirmed by Aquinas) is negated by Rahner, because a positive answer would render the trinitarian mystery speculatively irrelevant to the history of salvation. This position of St. Thomas is heavily criticized by Rahner, and when taken logically to its conclusion it asserts that what is predicated of one divine person in the hypostatic union bespeaks nothing of the intra-divine relations that constitute the triune God. Such a consequence, while notionally still preserving the hypostatic distinctions within the trinity, does not account for those distinctions within the missions. However, this is a contested judgment and raises the question concerning the justification for Rahner's position, and by implication Coffey's innovation of it.

Rahner's argument depends on the establishment of three crucial points implied by the axiom. The first concerns the "Special Nature of the 'Hypostatic' Union."[62] It is acknowledged in scholastic theology that the incarnation is exclusively the mission of the second person when understood in reference to its term in Jesus Christ. However, utilizing the principle (also affirmed by Coffey) that one can reason from operation to being but not from being to operation, it is objected that the specific instance of the incarnation of the Son cannot be the ground for speculation concerning intra-trinitarian relations. In other words, the dogmatic certainty of the incarnation of the Son does not necessarily lead to any general speculative principle relative to the two trinitarian processions. If this be the case, the assertion of a necessarily exclusive mission of the Son vis-à-vis the incarnation is no longer justified. According to this rule, one would argue in the opposite direction—namely, that other persons in the trinity are capable of hypostatic union with created reality, this based on the axiom that all things in God are one except where there exists an opposition of relation. Therefore, all the persons by virtue of their unity in the divine essence and their equality in divine power could assume a human nature. The most that can be ventured in order to specify the relationship between processions and missions is the standard position of Thomas Aquinas, which on the one hand assumes an appropriate relation between the processions and the actual missions, and on the other hand maintains the freedom of all the persons in assuming any one of the missions.[63]

Rahner, however, in a dialectical reversal of this rule, utilizes it to define what speculative judgments are prohibited from the certain instance of the incarnation. The incarnation of the Logos does not imply the incarnation of another divine person, because one cannot assume that the descriptive terms are identical. For example, can it be presumed that "hypostasis" possesses an identical meaning for its trinitarian and christological ascriptions? If not, and the rule cannot deliver an answer one way or another, we encounter an instance of distinction between a hypostatically special relation, as any divine person may have with created reality, and a hypostatically unitive relation—i.e., the uniqueness of the hypostatic union. The latter is an instance of the former, but the former does not always translate into the latter.[64] This being the case, one must seek a wider horizon of issues to define the relationship between processions and missions.

Second, Rahner alerts us to the difficulty implied in assuming an undifferentiated relationship (even if only hypothetically) of the divine persons to created reality. If the distinction of divine persons does not translate into distinct relations or missions to the creation, this would mean that in the history of salvation nothing in reality is revealed about the Logos. The trinity is revealed only nominally, not substantially. If another divine person could constitute the subsistence of the human reality of the incarnation, then the incarnation does not reveal an extension into created reality of an intra-trinitarian relation but only a mere verbal revelation of what is true about God in general. The notion of hypostasis would be univocal and nothing could be said of the Son's unique property as the Word who reveals the Father—and this without adequate demonstration to suggest that another divine person bears the same capacity. Or, with reference to the event of grace, the believer's sonship and daughterhood in grace is not at all related to the Son's sonship by generation.[65] It is more convincing, Rahner argues, to propose "that the Logos is really as he appears in revelation, that he is *the one* who reveals to us (not merely *one* of those who might have revealed to us) the triune God, on account of the personal being which belongs exclusively to him, the Father's Logos."[66]

The third point implied by Rahner's trinitarian axiom concerns the relationship between the humanity of Christ and the subjectivity of the Logos. If for the previous point Rahner argued that it is the distinctiveness of the Logos relative to the other divine persons that is the basis for the subjectivity of the incarnation, here the issue is the manner in which the human nature is assumed. For the Logos truly to reveal himself in Jesus Christ, a relationship limited to an abstract formal subjectivity on the part of the Logos is not sufficient. By this is meant that the human nature that is assumed is understood only in the universal or general sense of its essence and not as particular to the Logos in the union. By way of contrast, since the Logos is the utterance of God, the human nature is not added to the Logos but is posited and constituted by the Logos as the means of its expression in the world. Because the Logos can exteriorize itself and even empty itself into the non-divine, the human nature of Christ is the concrete real symbol of the Logos.[67] From this dogmatic certainty—"what Jesus is and does as man reveals the Logos himself"—one can conclude to the christological version of his original trinitarian axiom—namely, "the immanent Logos and the economic Logos are strictly the same."[68]

All of these points are accepted by Coffey, who extends the propriety of the first procession (relative to the mission of the Son) to the second procession (relative to the mission of the Spirit). The basis for each is Rahner's notion of the divine self-communication, which he also applies to both processions. However, Coffey goes beyond Rahner by stipulating the difference in processions in reference to their mode of operation (as discussed above) and in the nature of their relationship to created reality. Finally, he also specifies the exclusive propriety of each mission in the exercise of formal causality. Despite these differences the agreement is substantial, especially on the most basic level of positing a necessary connection between processions and missions. Here the breakthrough of transcendental theology is accepted by Coffey as a step beyond the limitations of scholastic trinitarian theology. Coffey's argument for this necessity, while not identical to Rahner's, bears certain similarities that are worth noting.

First, Coffey employs the notion of self-communication to articulate the meaning of divine revelation and formal causality to explain its event from the side of the divine. As already stated, the divine self-communication is from the Father in the two modalities of Son and Spirit, each consistent with the nature of the intra-trinitarian processions. Even though this would still be the case with "appropriation" theory (regarding the appropriateness of a mission as the temporal manifestation of an eternal procession), Coffey, like Rahner, argues that the propriety of these two missions relative to the processions cannot be otherwise without reducing the trinitarian distinctions to a nominal theological predication of divine reality. To substantiate his argument, Coffey must first explicate the nature of the missions and then correlate "by necessity" their link with the two trinitarian processions.

The missions are the self-communication of the Father to created reality, or, considered from the perspective of the persons sent, they are the communication of Son and Spirit, each bearing a proper and unique relationship to the non-divine. In contrast to Thomas Aquinas, Coffey questions the consistency between the proposition that the temporal missions include the eternal procession (mission defined as an "eternal procession, with the addition of a temporal effect"—*ST* Ia, 43, 2) and one that asserts that any divine person may have assumed a human nature in the hypostatic union ("Therefore the Divine power could have united human nature to the Person of the Father or of the Holy Ghost, as It united it to the Person of the Son. And hence we must say that the Father or the Holy Ghost could have assumed flesh even as the Son"—*ST* IIIa, 3, 5). The hypothetical possibility of the latter seems to deny the distinction of persons presupposed by the former, especially with regard to the Father, who is innascible and cannot be sent. In effect, the only possibility available that Aquinas affirms would be the incarnation of the Father without a mission—i.e., without being sent, since a mission is predicated on the manner of the procession. Such a possibility seems absurd.

The critique thus far exercised by Coffey is pertinent only on the speculative level. A more severe critique pertains to the noticeable lack of reference to salvation history in Aquinas. Although theoretically one might argue that the divine freedom is preserved through the hypothetical possibility of a person other than the Son becoming incarnate, one can equally argue that such freedom resides not in the indifference of the relational distinctions in the trinity to specific temporal missions but in the divine decision to create and redeem non-divine reality. This indifference would have to be the case if the manner of being person in the trinity that is distinctive by virtue of the notions is not distinctive in the concrete temporal missions. The speculative distinction implied by the negation of this indifference would also be reinforced by initiating trinitarian theology on the basis of the external missions known from salvation-history. This is more explicit in Coffey's later work where he justifies the use of the bestowal model without reference to the traditional psychological model, preferring instead conclusions drawn from an ascending christology "from below."[69] The shift is important, although as noted above it is defended only in brief. The most significant point is that Coffey now distinguishes the two models more clearly according to methodology. The processions model (in its psychological specification) begins with the essential unity of God and posits the distinctions on the basis of the nature of the processions. The bestowal model begins with the distinction of persons and moves toward the personal unity of the trinity based on the mutuality of love (between Father and Son), that being the Holy Spirit. In both cases, the distinction of persons is affirmed and directly related to the *proprium* of the two temporal missions, which can be sketched as follows according to each of the models.

The procession model (in its psychological specification) emphasizes the distinct processions according to knowledge and love. The Son and the Spirit are, respectively, the Word/Image and Love/Gift of God. As such, the temporal missions of incarnation and sanctification correlate by necessity with these processions. Relative to the Father who, is innascible and incapable of being sent, the Son and the Spirit are receptive as communications of the Father's self-communication. Relative to created reality they are actuating, each through formal causality and each in the specific manner of their procession. Therefore, the Son as the self-knowing of God actuates in a hypostatic union with a single human nature the irrevocable and unsurpassable revelation of God. The Holy Spirit, as the mutual bond between Father and Son and as the Gift of God, actuates in a graced union with many human persons (who through the union are sons and daughters in the Son—*filii in Filio*) the indwelling and sanctification of God.[70] In the former case, formal causality operates as a substantial form in the sacred humanity of Christ, whereas in the graced union predicated on the formal causality of the Holy Spirit the form is merely accidental vis-à-vis already existing human persons.[71] Each mission is distinct, proper to the divine person implicated, and regarding its term directed to a different ontological entity—i.e., to a human nature or to a human person.[72]

Even though Coffey is clear that the two missions are in fact two modalities of God's self-communication, one must understand these modalities as really two moments of the one operation of God's revealing and saving action in the world. In the language of the missions one can say that the incarnation by its very nature drives beyond itself to the mission of the Spirit. Its inner dynamism as the revelation of God enfleshed is directed to the communication of God as grace. Or, in the language of Aquinas's appropriation of the psychological model, "nothing can be loved by the will unless it is conceived in the intellect." But here Coffey is more concerned with the concrete temporal missions. Therefore, God's self-communication in the Son's incarnation is "the highest possible actuation of human nature" and leads beyond that single assumed human nature to lesser actuations of human persons in union with God actuated by the Holy Spirit.

Thus far, much of what Coffey has articulated follows the basic thrust of Rahner's trinitarian theology. However, there are also two significant divergences from Rahner. First, Coffey takes exception to Rahner's position that each of the divine persons communicates itself by formal causality to the believer. In contrast, Coffey contends that only the Holy Spirit enters into such a union. Therefore, the Holy Spirit properly indwells the just person, while the Father and the Son indwell the believer not by formal causality but only by perichoresis with the Holy Spirit.[73] Second, if the temporal mission properly identified with the Holy Spirit is prior in the divine inhabitation, then the uncreated grace of God can likewise be identified with the third person. Coffey, without denying the necessity for created grace, does consider the communication of the Holy Spirit to be the grace (uncreated) of God. This brings us back to the yields of each of the trinitarian models.[74]

By "yields" we mean the advantages that each trinitarian model provides in furthering our understanding of the central mysteries of the Christian faith. In addition to the criticism of the Catholic doctrine of grace by Karl Barth rehearsed above, another major criticism of Roman Catholic dogmatic theology was the unrelatedness of the various dogmatic loci. To what extent, especially in the neo-scholastic manual tradition, did the dogma of the trinity essentially and not just incidentally undergird the loci concerning grace and the sacraments or even christology? Coffey in contrast to the deficiencies of this tradition, attempts to demonstrate the direct linkage among such loci, beginning with the trinity, then christology, the theology of grace, and the sacraments. Each trinitarian model contributes to the explication of these doctrines in a necessary and complementary manner. Our focus will be limited to his account of how a new pneumatic christology is the fulcrum that integrates the dogma of the trinity with the theology of grace and the Christian life.

"YIELD" OF THE PROCESSION MODEL

The procession model is predicated on a descending christology as the mode of revelation and divine self-communication for the temporal missions of Son and Spirit. Understood from the perspective of the human reception of these missions, they effect (or yield) the realities of sonship and grace, specifically the sonship of Jesus and the Holy Spirit given as the Spirit of Sonship (Gal. 4:6). Jesus' own sonship is the basis for believers' sonship and daughterhood in him (*filii in Filio*). Here Coffey distinguishes between the sonship of Jesus and that of believers. Included in this comparison is a delineation of the ontological and psychological levels of divine interaction with the human. In each case, the divine self-communication is objectified ontologically as sonship and correlated with its human psychological reception as faith. If, as the tradition has usually stated it, the sonship of Jesus is by nature and that of believers by adoption, the question arises as to whether faith is proper to the natural and immediate sonship of the former. In other words, is it proper to speak of the faith of Jesus if that is the psychological human response to the agency of God objectified in sonship? The question concerns the uniqueness of Jesus' sonship relative to that of believers in general, of whom it is confessed they receive their adoption through the mediation of the exalted and glorified Christ.

Coffey answers this query by qualifying the traditional theologumenon that asserted the absence of faith in Jesus, to whom it was also attributed (in another theologumenon) that he possessed the beatific vision during his earthly life (the latter logically excluding the need for faith). Here again his debt to Rahner is evident. By accepting Rahner's conclusion on the latter issue—namely, that the earthly Jesus possessed only the beatific vision in an unobjective manner that is therefore perfectly reconcilable with the historical development of all human experience—Coffey is able to articulate a concept of faith consistent with the exceptionality of the hypostatic union.[75] Defining faith as the "steadfast adherence to God and his will in the face of opposing difficulties and temptations," it is clear, Coffey argues, that Jesus is not only the object of faith but the supreme model of faith as well.[76] However, the difference between the faith of Jesus and that of believers is also asserted. In the case of Jesus, faith proceeds from the grace of union, itself the basis of sonship. For Jesus faith is not a predicate of the hypostatic union, as it is of the union that obtains between believers and the Holy Spirit. Therefore, for persons in general sonship begins with the formation of faith, whereas in the case of Jesus, divine sonship entails the creative assumption of a human nature from the first moment of its existence. Faith can be said to proceed from this union in the existential and historical working out of this sonship over the entire course of Jesus' life and death.[77]

When we turn to believers' sonship and daughterhood, there is a different accounting of the psychological reception of faith and its formative role in the ontological action of grace. Although Coffey's discussion of the issue revolves around the integrity of free will and the avoidance of Pelagianism, suffice it to say that the offer of grace culminating in adoptive sonship and daughterhood requires regeneration as a work proper to the procession of the Holy Spirit.[78] When expressed in the language of scholasticism, the difference between the two types of sonship is explicated in regard to being and operation or in the distinction between substance and accident. It is the former that most appreciably implicates the distinction in processions according to that model. Without being redundant, it is enough to state that by Coffey's explication the two processions would by their difference in operation—i.e., respectively a *processio operati* and a *processio operationis*—result in quite different relationships to its term in the created order. The first leads to a unity in being—i.e., the hypostatic union—and the second to a union of operation—i.e., the operation of grace constituting the believer's sonship or daughterhood. The term of the first procession is intrinsic to that procession and therefore subsists as person in the assumption of human nature that constitutes the incarnation. The second procession does not end in a term, but rather inititiates an operation in the subject that corresponds to the operation that the Holy Spirit is as a unique and distinct procession in God.

If we follow the trinitarian reasoning as just elucidated, it is also clear that divine sonship is sacramental for believers but non-sacramental for Jesus. In the former case it is the Spirit of sonship that initiates believers into the saving mystery as that is sacramentally enfleshed in the crucified and glorified Christ. The Holy Spirit is the necessary medium and bond between believers and the Father. As the Spirit of sonship, the third person is sent by the Father through the Son (*per filium*) and with the Son (*filioque*) in the indissoluble union of the Son with his sacred humanity—in other words, through the very sacramentality of the Son. But this sacramentality of the Son signifies the revelation of the Son as the self-communication of the Father, not his own divine sonship in the constitution of the hypostatic union, which is not sacramental nor dependent on the medium of the Holy Spirit, since Jesus as the divine Son is already *homoousios* with the Father.[79]

This concludes the yield gleaned from the procession model of trinitarian relations. It links together the mysteries of the trinity, the person of Christ, and the life of grace. The offer of God's self-communication as grace to humanity is identical to the offer of divine sonship, itself predicated on the Spirit of sonship sacramentally mediated to believers through the incarnation of the Son. The processions, while distinct both in themselves and in their temporal missions, are also united as two modalities of the one divine operation that effects salvation and redemption. It now remains to complete this picture by an examination of the even more fruitful yield that the bestowal model of trinitarian relations offers.

"YIELD" OF THE BESTOWAL MODEL

It is clear that David Coffey considers the pneumatological emphasis to be much greater in the bestowal model of trinitarian relations. Without the focus on the person of the Holy Spirit as the love bestowed by the Father on the Son and vice versa, the model would not be viable. It is in effect a pneumatologically determined model of trinitarian relations that utilizes an ascending christology and the theology of anointing to explicate this pneumatic dimension in the doctrines of the incarnation and grace. This more explicit pneumatology provides a christo-logical construction that for all intents and purposes can be described as Spirit-christology while at the same time preserving the distinctions between the proper missions of Son and Spirit. With this last point Coffey avoids a modalism of the second and third persons, always a danger when considering the "invisible" tem-poral missions—i.e., the mission of the glorified and exalted Christ and that of the indwelling of the Holy Spirit.

In the previous model the problem of modalism was countered because the distinction of processions each properly led to a distinction of missions: the Son in the incarnation and the Holy Spirit in grace. These were constituting missions whereby either the incarnation or the union of the believer with the Holy Spirit was actualized. The *proprium* of each mission is exclusive to the trinitarian person so missioned—i.e., sent by the Father. This is not the case for the bestowal model. This model does not consider the "constitution in being" of the mission but rather its "formation in becoming." It is the contrast in scholastic terminology between the *in facto esse* of a mission and its *in fieri*, with the latter especially being the province of the Holy Spirit.[80]

Beginning with an ascending christology, the bestowal model does not differen-tiate between the proper missions of the Son and the Holy Spirit to distinguish between their respective roles in the incarnation and grace, as does the procession model. Since the concern in this model is not the constitution of the object of the temporal missions—i.e., the hypostatic union of the Son with a human nature and the graced union of the Holy Spirit with believers—but with the historical outwork-ing of these respective unions in the salvation history of Christ and the church (the formation, or *in fieri*, of these divine operations), the major locus of reflection is upon the Holy Spirit as the formative agent for both the incarnation and grace.[81] The pneumatic basis for both missions underscores the unity of God's redemptive work in the world as well as the unique and necessary mediating role of Christ. In other words, the bestowal of the Spirit in its christological referent is similar to but different from its bestowal in its ecclesial referent. Here we can simply note Coffey's account of the matter in an important, although lengthy, quote:

> . . . the Holy Spirit is the Spirit precisely of Sonship (cf. Rm 8.15). As such, he constitutes both Jesus and other men sons of God, even if divine sonship changes greatly (though not totally) in meaning and content from the former instance to the latter. The Father makes the man Jesus his Son, one in person with his eternal Son, by bestowing the Holy Spirit on him in a uniquely radical way. This makes Jesus the very paradigm of divine sonship. The Father makes other men his sons also, but in a much humbler sense, viz. sons in the Son, by bestowing on them the same Spirit, who is offered to them in the sacrament of Christ. The difference between the two instances may be stated succinctly as follows. The Father bestowed the Holy Spirit on the humanity of Jesus in an act by which at the same time that humanity was created, sanctified and united in person to the divine Son. He bestows the Holy Spirit on other men in an act which finds them already constituted as human persons (sinners however), but with their co-operation sanctifies them and

unites them to Christ the divine Son as sons in the Son, in the sense that they now possess the same Spirit who made him unique Son of God in humanity.[82]

It is important to note that despite the similarity of sanctification in both communications of the Holy Spirit the ontological order relative to the union is quite different. The sanctification of the man Jesus is prior to union with the divine Son, while the sanctification of believers proceeds from union with the risen and glorified Christ. Here Coffey remains thoroughly orthodox in the innovations introduced by his pneumatological theology of anointing.

The theology of anointing that is the ground for the strong pneumatological emphasis of the bestowal model was already introduced into modern Catholic theology by Matthias Scheeben, as reviewed in Chapter 2. Coffey's critical reading of Scheeben along with that of Heribert Mühlen prepares the way for his own constructive proposal. He reviews their use of various patristic references, compares their results, and evaluates them in light of the biblical material. This overview of his methodology only highlights the dialectical nature of his constructive dogmatic work. Coffey's originality lies in his ability to synthesize the insights of the two most significant Catholic pneumatologies of the nineteenth and twentieth centuries and integrally link the resulting product to christology and the theology of grace within the horizon of a new model of trinitarian relations.

By critically utilizing the work of Matthias Scheeben, Coffey again negotiates the familiar territory of the scholastic idiom. As we have seen, Scheeben quite profoundly resurrected a theology of the Holy Spirit within the speculative project of neo-scholastic theology. Its formative influence on christology was mediated by a theology of anointing, which is the point where Coffey exercises his critical reception of Scheeben's pneumatology. Scheeben is especially appealing to Coffey because he more than others in the neo-scholastic tradition was able to unify the doctrine of grace by proffering to some degree a pneumatologically informed christology. His shortcoming in Coffey's estimation was that he confused the filiological and pneumatological predicates in the theologies of anointing and incarnation. The specific factors informing Scheeben's dogmatic construction and Coffey's criticism may be summarized by the following three observations.

First, there is an integral link between the incarnation and the anointing of Jesus in his humanity with the divine ointment. Second, the title of anointing—i.e., the Christ—signifies not just the ministry or function of Jesus but his inner being as the God-human. Third, the Logos is the agent of anointing, anointing the sacred humanity of Jesus with the divinity of his own person. It is this last point with which Coffey disagrees and, in his critical revision of Scheeben's proposal, he moves in a more pneumatological direction.

Scheeben, as we have seen, does not exclude the work of the Spirit in the incarnation. On the contrary, it is emphasized but distinctly subordinated to the Son when the referent is the hypostatic union. For Scheeben, the Spirit mediates between the Logos and his humanity, proceeding from the Son by virtue of the *filioque*, and this only by appropriation. Scheeben's interpretation of the theology of anointing (gleaned from the Fathers) is to identify it with the act of the incarnation, and within this perspective secondarily to orient the work of the Father and the Holy Spirit to that of the Son in this his proper mission. Therefore, the Father is said to be an agent of the anointing only insofar as he eternally generates the Son, and the Holy Spirit's appropriation just described is only a corollary to or a symbol of the basic anointing which is that of the Son himself.[83]

Before returning to Coffey's evaluation of Scheeben, we turn first to Mühlen, who likewise figures critically in Coffey's constructive proposal. Mühlen differs from Scheeben on each of the three major points of the proposal, thereby offering a strong counterpoint that Coffey will dialectically sublate. First, the anointing is not identified with the incarnation but only refers to the endowment with power that accompanies Christ's mission and ministry inaugurated at his baptism (although in a hidden sense it is present at the first moment of the incarnation to the extent that the Son even as incarnate is together with the Father the origin of the Holy Spirit). In other words, in contrast to Scheeben, the anointing of Jesus is quite distinct from the incarnation. In this regard Mühlen borrows heavily from New Testament exegete Ignace de la Potterie, whose article on anointing strictly maintains this distinction.[84] The second counterpoint then follows. The title "Christ" is precisely that, a title connoting the office of Jesus and not descriptive of his inner being. Thirdly, Mühlen is clearer than Scheeben that the agent of the anointing is the Father who anoints the Son with the Holy Spirit. Because the anointing is not referred to the incarnation, Mühlen asserts the propriety of the Holy Spirit's mission in the anointing as well as affirming the role of the Father, whose presence to Jesus in the anointing through the Holy Spirit is distinguished from his presence in the incarnation through divine sonship. In scholastic language, the latter is the proper work of the Son in the grace of union at the basis of the incarnation, while the former in the person of the Holy Spirit is associated only with the created grace of Jesus' humanity, giving a strong pneumatological cast to the consequent grace of headship mediated by Christ to all humanity.[85]

Coffey's critical dialogue with these theologians on the theology of anointing results in the combination of Scheeben's emphasis on the incarnation as the locus for the anointing with Mühlen's clear assertion of the propriety of the Holy Spirit's mission. Faced with these variant theologies of anointing along with the somewhat unsystematic statements of the Fathers, Coffey attempts to clarify its ambiguity by setting it strictly within the limits and options of an ascending christology. This will make for clear references to the agent, the occasion, the content, and the object of the anointing.[86] One further note distinguishes Coffey's proposal. Although the final product is a thoroughly pneumatological christology, as I will argue, he nevertheless does not envisage his project as a restoration of early pre-conciliar Spirit-christologies. He presumes the Athanasian *homoousion* as a prerequisite for both the christological and pneumatological predicates.[87]

Coffey, who otherwise disagrees with the dogmatic implications of Mühlen's use of de la Pottiere's biblical exegesis, does agree with the following key aspects of a theology of anointing.

We have established that when the New Testament, specifically Luke, speaks of the anointing of the man Jesus, the occasion of the anointing is the baptism in the Jordan, the agent is the Father, the ointment is the Holy Spirit, and the objective achieved is the constitution of Jesus as the Prophet.[88]

However, while this undermines the basis of Scheeben's theology of anointing—
e.g., the Son is excluded as agent and the ointment is not the divinity of the Logos
but the Holy Spirit—it is meant as more of a corrective to an otherwise sound
approach. Coffey's more profound difficulties are with Mühlen, and have already
exercised him with regard to the latter's pronomialization of intra-trinitarian relations. Therefore, it is quite right to suspect that Coffey is simply revising the great
Catholic neo-scholastic pneumatologian of the nineteenth century by critically un-
seating one of the more prominent Catholic pneumatologians of the twentieth century.

Take, for example, the meaning of the title "Christ." Although Coffey acknowledges that Mühlen is clearly more correct, the instincts of Scheeben are more in
keeping with an integral relationship between christology and pneumatology. The
revelation of the office of "Christ" to which the anointing at Jordan attests does
bespeak the inner constitution of the hypostatic union. Even though Mühlen acknowledges that the anointing at baptism is the revelation of a prior though distinct
anointing in the act of the incarnation, the latter effects only the created grace or
sanctification of the already assumed human nature of Jesus. Coffey does distinguish
between the incarnation and anointing; the pre-existent Son becomes incarnate, and
it is with the Holy Spirit that the sacred humanity is anointed. However, the distinction between incarnational anointing (effecting created grace or the sanctification of
Jesus' humanity) and baptismal anointing (effecting prophethood), along with the
exclusive use of descending christology that excludes the Holy Spirit from the grace
of union (that being effected by the divine Son), does not do justice in Coffey's
estimation to the pneumatological dimension of the incarnation and its relationship
to the gift of the Holy Spirit for believers.[89] I shall take up each of these points with
a focus on Coffey's constructive proposal.

The relationship between incarnation and anointing or between ontology and
function cannot be sidestepped. What is at stake is the "full sacramentality of God's
economic action."[90] Rather than separating person and office in christology, Coffey
argues that the person of Christ is revealed in his office or in the language of salvation
history, "in the baptismal anointing the incarnation stands revealed."[91] In order to
ensure this, Coffey revises and pneumatologizes the traditional Thomistic paradigm
for the christological locus of the theology of grace that is employed by both
Scheeben and Mühlen. We are speaking of the threefold christological grace already
elaborated in previous chapters: *gratia unionis, habitus gratiae, gratia capitis.* The
distinction of these graces entails both an order of precedence—"in the order not of
time but of nature and understanding"[92]—and an order of relationship—e.g., that the
habitual grace of Jesus is the basis for his grace of headship to believers. The
argument made by St. Thomas for the precedence of the grace of union over habitual
grace is a cogent one within the framework of a descending christology and the
procession model of the trinity. Three reasons are advanced by the Angelic Doctor,
each of which illustrates the mode of operation of the traditional trinitarian paradigm.
First, since the Son is the principle of the grace of union and the Holy Spirit that of
habitual grace, the relationship between these two persons determined by the *filioque*
requires the precedence of the Son.[93] Second, in terms of causality grace follows the
presence of the divine person; in this case, habit would follow the union of a human

nature with the divine Son. Third, the teleology of grace dictates that grace is ordered to the operation of a suppositum and the individual, thereby requiring the union of a divine person with a human nature before the operation of a supernatural habit in the human faculties.

Coffey's revision of the Thomistic order of christological grace, which reverses the order of precedence between the grace of union and habitual grace in the person of Christ, clearly intimates the priority he affords to the new trinitarian model. As a yield from the bestowal model of trinitarian relations, Coffey is not simply complementing the procession model but transferring and then substantially revising the traditional construct for understanding the act of the incarnation. The reversal of precedence in christological grace excludes the traditional rendering, even if the more classical procession model is still maintained. Therefore, in response to the Thomistic argument Coffey explicates the inclusion of the third person as agent in the incarnation by stating that the Holy Spirit first creates, then sanctifies (habitual grace), and then unites (grace of union) the human nature of Jesus in person to the pre-existent divine Son.[94] This means that the habitual grace of Jesus and his grace of headship are not directly related as in descending christology (a product of the procession model), which according to that paradigm ensured unity between the mysteries of the incarnation and the more general theology of grace. Coffey prefers that unity to reside in the gift of the Holy Spirit, whom Jesus possessed in fullness through its bestowal on him by the Father.[95] The question still remains, however, concerning the viability of this model when compared to the more traditional one, especially regarding the order of precedence and the propriety of the trinitarian missions.

The order of precedence in christological grace results from a critique at two levels of the Thomistic doctrine. First, Coffey argues for the necessity of habitual grace as arising from the hypostatic union itself—this in contrast to some Thomistic renderings whereby it is possible for Jesus to have possessed the grace of union without habitual grace. This hypothetical possibility stems from the recognition that nothing greater can be attained through grace than personal union with a divine person.[96] If this is already accomplished through the grace of union which precedes habitual grace, it can in an alteration of the paradigm make the habitual grace of Christ superfluous. St. Thomas defends the necessity of habitual grace not on the basis of the constituting act of the hypostatic union but on the necessary perfection of the human operation (as distinct from the already perfect divine operation) in the God-human.[97] When de la Taille and others, as reviewed in Chapter 3, interpret the hypostatic union as a union predicated on an uncreated act of the divine Son, they also posit the grace of union as a created grace to ensure the full humanity of Jesus Christ. Habitual grace follows from the hypostatic union but is not a constituent part of it. The grace of union actuates a passive potency for existence, while habitual grace actuates an active potency directed toward the active operations of the now existing subject.[98] It is Coffey's argument that the disjuncture between the constituting act of the hypostatic union and habitual grace devalues the role of habitual grace in the person of Christ because priority must always be given to the preceding grace of union.

To more firmly establish habitual grace as a necessary dimension of the hypostatic union, Coffey posits "the sanctification of Jesus' humanity (the resultant sanctity being identical with his habitual grace) . . . [as] a necessary stage towards his unity in person with the Son, which is the grace of union."[99] This functions as one of three stages, each of which can be identified with the agency of the Holy Spirit. The Holy Spirit creates, sanctifies, and then unites the humanity of Jesus to the divine Son. When viewed "from below," from the perspective of an ascending christology, the hypostatic union is an anointing or bestowal by the Father of the Holy Spirit on the humanity of Jesus. As such, Coffey is not compelled to link the personal sanctity of Jesus—i.e., his habitual grace—with the grace of headship to demonstrate that the grace experienced by believers is rooted instrinsically in the person of Christ as its source. In his own right, Christ is personally holy because he fully possessed the Holy Spirit, and it is this same Spirit sent by him that is the grace of Christians.[100]

This pneumatization of the theology of grace is at the center of Coffey's proposal, and it can only be justified on the basis of the bestowal model of the trinity. Scheeben and Mühlen both emphasize that the believer's relationship to God proceeds in inverse manner to the trinitarian processions. The Christian encounters first the Holy Spirit, then the Son, and finally the Father. However, as reviewed above, the procession model is speculatively unable to sustain this order. True, the Father sends the Son and they send the Holy Spirit; but the reversal of this order demands another construct than that of "proceeding from." The "bestowing of" the Holy Spirit provides this construct while at the same time possessing the virtue of perspective from the side of created reality—i.e., from below. In the case of the unity between the reality of the incarnation and the grace of believers, this is provided by the model of divine operation understood as divine sonship predicated on the Holy Spirit as the Spirit of sonship. The Spirit unites the humanity of Jesus to the divine Son in a union of person (a profound reception by the sacred humanity of the Son), and likewise in a simple manner (entailing a difference in kind and not just degree) unites believers as sons and daughters in the Son through their reception of the same Holy Spirit.

This returns us to the language of anointing, which also serves to distinguish the explanatory regimes of each of the models. Incarnation and anointing are the appropriate terms for the procession and bestowal models, respectively. In the traditional procession model the Holy Spirit is offered (only to believers, this being exclusive of Jesus, on whom it is simply bestowed); in the bestowal model the Spirit is in reality "bestowed." In the procession model no significant role is assigned to the Holy Spirit in the incarnation. In the bestowal model Jesus is anointed to divine sonship with the Holy Spirit. In the procession model the Son is co-principle of the Holy Spirit, while in the bestowal model the bestowing of the Holy Spirit is alternatively carried out by the Father upon the Son and then by the Son upon the Father. In neither model does the Son communicate the Holy Spirit to his own humanity; this would entail an undue separation between divinity and humanity in the hypostatic union.[101] In sum, in the anointing theology of Coffey, the Father anoints Jesus with the Holy Spirit to divine sonship, this being identical with the incarnation.[102] Therefore, the Spirit-christology that this model of trinitarian relations motivates identifies the agent of anointing as the Father, its occasion in the incarnation, its content as the Holy Spirit, and its object as the humanity of Jesus.

The bestowal model also affords Coffey a paradigm that affirms the proper mission of the Holy Spirit while at the same time preserving the freedom of God relative to the world. Coffey has already argued for the necessity of the *ad extra* missions' being linked to the *ad intra* processions. Against the prevailing position in neo-scholasticism that the divine freedom required a non-necessary appropriation of the temporal missions to the divine persons, Coffey contends that such freedom figures only in the divine decision to communicate in and to the created order. In the same manner, Coffey demonstrates that the procession model alone would compromise the freedom of the Father in sending the Holy Spirit if its only purpose was the gracing of humanity, since the model does not provide a construct for conceiving the Holy Spirit as the mutual love of Father and Son (the only other purpose of the Spirit's procession according to the traditional model would be a procession into the void!). The bestowal model, on the other hand, allows for the mutual bestowal of the Spirit by the Father and the Son upon each other, thereby demonstrating the trinity's self-sufficiency. The extension of this bestowal to include the sending of the Holy Spirit upon humanity—i.e., the temporal and proper mission of the Holy Spirit in the freedom of God—is an expression of the Son's love for the Father now recapitulating all creation into the communion of the trinity.[103]

The extension of the mutual love of the Father and the Son, who is the Holy Spirit, into the economy of the trinitarian missions incorporates a distinction between the Father's sending of the Spirit and that of the Son. Already Coffey distinguished between the bestowal of the Spirit on Jesus and the bestowal upon human beings. In the latter case, the bestowal is sacramental—i.e., mediated by a categorical historical agent—while in the former case it is strictly a transcendental action of God without any mediation. When he further examines the sending of the Holy Spirit by Christ and the Spirit's bestowal by the Father—the terms respectively preferred by Coffey for each person's role—he distinguishes the transcendental and categorial aspects of the outpouring of the Holy Spirit upon believers. The Father is the agent of the transcendental anointing and the Son of the categorial anointing. Whereas the exalted Christ is a "co-sender" of the Holy Spirit, this is predicated through the agency of his glorified humanity and may be described as a theandric operation of the one who is historical and visible (through the sacramentality of the church). This is united to but differs from the sending of the Holy Spirit by the Father who remains transcendent and invisible. In the latter case, the Father not only sends but actually bestows the Spirit through the sacrament of Christ's sending. Herein lies the unity but not identity of these two dimensions of the divine operation. This unity and distinction is best expressed in Coffey's own words:

> Thus we may say simply that the offer of grace by Christ is the sacrament of its bestowal by the Father, or, more comprehensively, that the offer of grace by Christ, when accepted, is the sending of the Holy Spirit by him, and this in turn is the sacrament of the bestowal of the Holy Spirit by the Father.[104]

Also regarding the relationship between the two:

> The anointing of men by the Father is a purely divine or transcendental act, since it is the communication by the Father of his Spirit to the spirit of man. Since no creature could be the medium of this act without reducing it and hence destroying

it, this communication must be direct. This, however, is no obstacle to its sacramentality. The role of Christ in this act is theandric—i.e., human-divine, which requires it to be human at base, and therefore categorial. When man accepts the offer of Christ, it becomes for him a sending of the Holy Spirit by Christ. This, however, is the limit of Christ's function. We can say that in all confidence, for we know that the Holy Spirit as sent by him makes men not his sons, but sons of the Father. This shows that the sending by Christ is no substitute for the sending, or bestowal, by the Father; nor is it a medium through which the Father's act is filtered. Sacrament of the Father's act, it draws this act into history, without destroying its transcendentality.[105]

Summary and Addendum

In summary, Coffey's new trinitarian model, along with his revision of the classical model, unites through an accentuated pneumatology what we may identify as the deep structure of the Christian doctrines of God, Christ, and grace. Incarnation and grace actualize the proper missions of the Son and the Spirit according to the procession model and its corresponding descending christology. Likewise, they actualize the anointing with the Holy Spirit in two different ways (non-sacramentally and sacramentally) according to the bestowal model and its corresponding ascending christology.[106] What believers receive as the grace of God through the presence and power of the Holy Spirit is constitutive of the person of Christ and consistent with the self-communication of God, itself an expression of the intra-trinitarian relations.

In later articles Coffey further refines his thesis. Only three points need be mentioned. First, in an article titled "The 'Incarnation' of the Holy Spirit in Christ,"[107] Coffey expands on his notion that the Holy Spirit is the Spirit of sonship. Using the model of Rahner's transcendental christology, which argues that the divinity of Christ is a determination of his humanity and is therefore not ontologically different from it, Coffey goes on to make the case that the divine sonship that constitutes the hypostatic union is progressively actualized in Jesus during the course of his life and ministry and is fully realized through his death and resurrection. This same notion of "progressive actualization" can also be applied to the Holy Spirit who is Jesus' transcendental love of the Father. Since the bestowal model envisages the Holy Spirit as the mutual love of the Father and Son, in the historical reality of Jesus' life and death the Holy Spirit becomes progressively actualized or incarnated in the categorial acts of his human love. Analogous with the incarnation of the Son, so, too, the Holy Spirit becomes fully incarnated and singly concentrated in that act of Jesus' love for the Father which is the paschal mystery.[108] Consequent upon this is the sending of the Holy Spirit by Christ in which his love of the Father now includes his love for humanity, which Christ unites with the Father.[109]

Second, in his later article, "A Proper Mission of the Holy Spirit,"[110] Coffey argues for a more precise rendering of the fundamental basis for the bestowal model. As noted above, in contrast to his earlier work Coffey disassociates the bestowal model from the psychological model altogether. Although the procession model bears affinity to the latter, the basis of the bestowal model is now considered by Coffey to be entirely different. The former derives from "the two great ordered events of salvation history: the mission of Christ by the Father, and the mission of the Holy Spirit by Christ from the Father."[111] Ontologically, its basis would be Jesus' experience of being sent by the Father. The bestowal model, on the other hand, is more directly related to his experience of being united to the Father, which Coffey then argues is the more basic "phenomenon from which the Christian religion itself takes its origin [that being through grace the Christian experiences a union with the saving God], and not, as with the procession model, from something consequent upon this."[112] This change in perspective provides Coffey with a more solid basis for his utilization of distinct trinitarian models.

Finally, in his most recent article to date, "The Holy Spirit as the Mutual Love of the Father and the Son," Coffey attempts to fully recover the "mutual love" theory of Augustine, but now corrected by the biblical perspective. Consistent with his sensitivity to the development of doctrine, Coffey acknowledges that this theory "cannot simply be demonstrated from Scripture."[113] However, the foundations for it are contained in the New Testament, especially when interpreted in terms of the structure of gift and response wherein the Holy Spirit can be proposed as the Father's love for Jesus and the same Spirit as his answering love for the Father. Much of this is already contained in his earlier work, except that here Coffey is more emphatic in attending to the ascending christologies of the synoptic Gospels as an alternative to the descending Johannine christology. This New Testament foundation provides the warrant for the mutual-love theory as a new model for the economic trinity, for it can be correlated with its formulation at the level of the immanent trinity. The major innovation represented here is that with the biblical data in hand the theory begins with the distinction of persons, in contrast with its original Augustinian formulation where the starting point is the divine essence. Two important benefits can be derived from this approach, one ecumenical and one doctrinal.

The mutual-love theory of intra-trinitarian relations cannot be subordinated either to the filioquist or monopatristic models of the Holy Spirit's relation to the other persons of the trinity. Since the theory does begin with the distinction of persons and then proceeds to their unity, it opens a door of conversation with the East. However, it should also be noted that the theory calls both the Latin filioquist and the Greek monopatristic models beyond the limits of their own capacity to fully absorb the implications of New Testament ascending christology and theology. Therefore, the two traditions can meet on doctrinal ground that is complementary to both their traditions of trinitarian theology, the source of which—i.e., the scripture—is the common foundation for them.[114] This ecumenical path also highlights the particular doctrinal innovation suggested by Coffey.

The doctrinal benefit can be viewed both christologically and pneumatologically. On the christological side, the theory emphasizes that Christ is both the recipient and mediator of divine blessing.[115] On the economic side of trinitarian understanding, this points to the subsistence of the divine person of the Son in his humanity, not strictly in the trinity alone. Likewise, the Holy Spirit is considered not only in the intra-trinitarian relationship but as the Spirit of sonship who unites a human nature to the divine Son (and believers to Christ) and as the Spirit of Christ who fully manifests the love of the incarnate Son for the Father in the union of all believers with God. In this latter respect, the Holy Spirit in its christological role is "the sacrament of the action of the same Spirit as Spirit of God."[116] Therefore, both the mediate and immediate nature of the believer's relationship to God is brought out, which also demonstrates the continuity and distinction on the pneumatological plane between the immanent (Spirit of God) and economic (Spirit of Christ) trinities, each correlated with its appropriate christological truth—i.e., the love of the incarnate Son for the Father being a manifestation of the love of the eternal Son for the Father.

Conclusion

David Coffey's work in dogmatically establishing a pneumatological christology represents the culmination of a distinctive tendency in the pneumatology of traditional Roman Catholic neo-scholastic theology. Beginning with Matthias Scheeben and then proceeding through the work of the Jesuit neo-scholastics who followed M. de la Taille, the transcendental Thomism of Karl Rahner and the personalist pneumatology of Heribert Mühlen, Coffey has recapitulated many of their most important themes and offered a new and innovative theological construct. One could even suggest that Coffey's proposal is a latter-day representation of a Petavian pneumatology thoroughly refined by scholastic dialectic and then applied to a coherent rethinking of the basic mysteries of the Christian faith. The methodological horizon has been the scholastic idiom, although as we have seen he has gone well beyond the traditional scholastic presentation of the doctrines of the trinity, Christ, the Holy Spirit, and grace.[117]

   I have followed this tendency in scholastic thought in an effort to highlight the most pneumatologically focused route that can be taken in neo-scholasticism. As will be explored in the following chapter, this is considerably different from other possible approaches, especially as many more theological methodologies have flourished since Vatican II. Recently, Hans Küng's comment that Karl Rahner was "the last great (and stimulating) Neo-Scholastic" serves only to confirm that despite the innovations of his transcendental theology (considered nearly heretical by some stalwart traditionalists), the method is still familiar.[118] However, there is still a strong counterpoint within this common horizon. I have provided that in our examination of the work of the more traditional Thomist, William Hill, in Chapter 3. In the following concluding paragraphs I will attempt to summarize the major differences between Coffey and that position and then list the significant dogmatic warrants for a Spirit-christology provided by Coffey. These will serve to guide our investigation into non-scholastic proposals for Spirit-christologies in the following chapter.

   Before specifying the differences and their dogmatic consequences between Coffey and Hill, it is worth noting the commonality they share within the wider scholastic horizon. It concerns an aspect of methodology that when applied to the dogmatic locus under consideration is clearly the hallmark of scholastic method. On the precise issue of trinitarian distinctions, both Coffey and Hill consider this to be an exercise in speculative dogmatic theology, since in the words of Coffey "the only ground for distinguishing the divine persons is strictly *innertrinitarian.*"[119] Hill, likewise, affirms this logic, since the constructive use of speculative reason seeks a "transtemporal intelligible ground" in its attempt to follow "the path of truth in the thinking of Being."[120] This is the mark of theological consciousness when compared to religious consciousness—i.e., the immediate consciousness of faith in its origination. They result in two different epistemological orders in relationship to the doctrine of the trinity that Hill explicates as follows:

> *Religious consciousness*: . . . moves from the Trinity encountered in the events of saving history to the inner-divine Trinity and thence to an awareness of the Trinity operative in creation.

> *Theological consciousness*: . . in its reflective act seeks the order of things in themselves rather than involved in our discovery of them; it seeks to approximate (obviously in a highly limited way) something of the standpoint of God himself. This is dictated by its search for intelligibility; that God is a Trinity in himself "explains" the trinitarian characteristics first of creation and then of salvation— granted that the Trinity is manifest merely inchoatively in the former and fully so only in salvation history.[121]

However, it is also in this elucidation of method that a significant difference emerges between Hill and Coffey. Coffey has argued consistently that the bestowal model of trinitarian relations, while still adhering to the principle that the distinction of persons must be intra-trinitarian, nevertheless grounds the model in the perspective of an ascending christology—a direction of thinking from the world to God that is quite the opposite of Hill's proposal. The consequences for their respective trinitarian theologies are not incidental, placing Coffey slightly beyond the horizon of scholastic theology.

The implications of this shift in method between the two theologians is best illustrated where the shift is least operative. Coffey and Hill, as we have seen, disagree on the psychological variant of the procession model of trinitarian relations. The question of whether or not the second procession as the divine loving bears its own immanent term is strongly disputed. Hill opts for the later Aquinas in his affirmative answer to the question, and Coffey argues in favor of the early Aquinas in his denial of the same. Note, however, that both are on the same speculative ground of thinking from God to the world. In answer, then, to Coffey's objection that in ordinary language use there is no word to describe the immanent term of love, Hill can easily but profoundly reply:

> Since the term coming to origin within love comes forth as Spirit rather than as Word in understanding, the procession is called "spiration" rather than (intellectual) "generation." In a further linguistic nicety, just as *intelligere* (to understand) is distinguished from *dicere* (to bring to interior expression what is understood), so *amare* (to love) is distinguished from *spirare* (to breathe forth a perduring impulse towards the beloved). Ceslaus Velecky distinguished *amare* from *spirare* as "the act by which the lover fixes his attention upon the beloved [differs from] the act of conscious endorsement of the affective preference which leads to a permanent union between the lover and the beloved." . . . What is important is that there is a real term posited by the spirative act, one that remains immanent to the consciousnesses of the lovers—in spite of a poverty of language in the attempt to name this term.[122]

Although no reference is made by Coffey, this type of objection may be the reason for his abandonment of the attempt to distinguish the processions on the basis of the psychological model. Whether Hill or Coffey is correct on this point is not important. What is significant is that the processions must be distinguished if distinct proper missions for the Son and Spirit are to be maintained. Coffey's stronger reliance on the bestowal model in his later work to ground this claim is evidence of its dogmatic necessity within the perspective of his larger project. We may also conclude that it is the change of direction for dogmatic thinking—i.e., from world to God rather than vice versa—that best justifies Coffey's constructive proposals.

Regarding the specifics of their proposals that differ from each other, the most important concerns the nature of the union between the believer and the divine persons, and these likewise are dependent on their respective understanding of divine revelation. Hill contends that two models present themselves in contemporary Catholic theology and both interpret the role of creation relative to the incarnation. One, which is Rahnerian in perspective, "views creation as a mere condition for God's personal communication of himself as Word and Spirit."[123] The other, more traditionally Thomist perspective "gives logical priority to God's intention to communicate not himself but a created participation in his own being, which, through man, is personal in its own finite way."[124] In continuity with his "moderate realist" Thomism, Hill envisages the Rahnerian goal for creation as a theology of divine self-enactment, while the traditional position allows for the integrity of the non-divine world in and of itself, even if its goal and its glory is to commune with God. That each of these positions should result in differing theologies of the nature of union with the divine should be of no surprise. The critical question then ensues: Which of these options best exemplifies the integral relationship between Christ and the Spirit that we have described as Spirit-christology?

Again we begin with Hill, for he offers a critical perspective on the type of proposal advanced by Coffey with its Rahnerian roots. According to Hill's model of trinitarian relations, the union with the divine persons in their proper missions include both an essential and personal dimension. The former is the only realm entailing causality in the relationship between human and divine. It is a common and efficient causality elevating the soul to union with the divine persons. The latter cannot be described in causal terms, for this would reduce the divine persons to a form. Against this Hill argues that the transcendence of God must be preserved for two reasons. First, the intra-divine trinity must be self sufficient in itself and not dependent upon the creature for its self-enactment. His understanding of the Rahnerian notion of quasi-formal causality as the means by which the just soul is united to the trinitarian persons seems to imply the latter. Second, the creature must exist for its own right with its own integrity. An ontic union between the divine persons and the just soul would seem to deny this if uncreated grace (as the trinitarian persons in their hypostatic uniqueness) is logically prior to created grace. By arguing for this priority, Hill contends that Rahner (and others) makes God a structural element intrinsic to the constitution of finite reality, a violation of both of his enunciated principles.[125]

The alternative offered by Hill is dependent upon his definition of the trinitarian persons as subsisting relations whose actualization of the divine consciousness in the intentionality of knowledge and love is both essential and personal. There is no logical or ontological priority between the essential and notional. All three persons simultaneously know the divine truth and love the divine goodness essentially in the unity of the divine being and distinctly in the relations of the divine persons to one another. In the divine intersubjectivity they both constitute three centers of consciousness in perichoretic communion and are "the subjects and centers of one divine conscious life."[126] Their relationship to the creature is then one not of self-enactment but of altruistic self-communication, which is both essential and personal.[127] Since the non-divine already reflects the creativity of the divine nature, including the divine processions—this being the ground in human nature for the attributes of knowledge and love—once elevated by created grace (through efficient causality) "the soul is then able to relate to the uncreated Persons precisely as distinct subject-terms of its own knowing and loving" (and this inclusive of the Holy Spirit in its own proper mission as reviewed in chapter three).[128] Only in this way is the active dialogic character of person as spirit (as contrasted to the infra-personal nature of causality, including formal or quasi-formal causality) preserved in the human-divine relation, according to Hill.[129]

I have elaborated on Hill's critique and proposal to isolate what is unique in Coffey's project. This should not obscure what is common to the two of them. Each affirms a proper mission for the Son and the Holy Spirit. Both emphasize (in Hill's language) that the christological mission is directed toward the manifestation of God and the pneumatological mission actualizes union with God.[130] When the issue of divine presence is broached, the Holy Spirit is given preeminence in both proposals, although the manner of such preeminence is contested.[131] Finally, the divine self-communication mediated through the two temporal missions bears distinct manners of operation. The mission of the Son is accomplished historically and visibly, while that of the Spirit is transhistorical and invisible although engendering the communal freedom of believers in their "continuing history that cannot be finally thematized."[132]

Also, many of the objections of Hill are already met by Coffey. Specifically, the utilization of the procession and bestowal models attempts to clarify the difference between the essential and personal unity of the trinity. In addition, Coffey is concerned that the procession model in and of itself is unable to guard against the total gratuity of the divine missions if there is not an intra-trinitarian purpose to the divine processions. This, obviously, is a criticism that can be directed against Hill, including his lack of demonstration that the unitive aspect of the Spirit's mission can be cogently upheld by the procession model, especially since for all its metaphysical density Hill's use of the procession model is one largely dictated by its psychological variant. The most important issue, however, is one of disagreement, and it concerns the nature of the divine communication in grace. Hill's critique of Rahner touches Coffey as well, and a response was in fact forthcoming. By turning to it we will be in a better position to evaluate the merits of Coffey's project.

First, it must be said that both Coffey and Hill agree that the manners of union enacted by the two missions are ontologically distinct. The hypostatic union is a union between natures in the person of the divine Son. The union of the Holy Spirit with the just soul is a union between already existing persons, prompting Hill to describe it in the language of intentionality and Coffey (vis-à-vis formal causality) in the terminology of accident. The more serious issue is whether or not the divine self-communication mediated in the two missions (with a focus on the mission of the Holy Spirit) requires a reception of the divine person beyond that of the Thomistic *sicut cognitum in cognoscente et amatum in amante* utilized by Hill.

Interestingly enough, Coffey retreats from the language of causality in his latest article. Fortunately, he gives a slightly more expanded reason for the change than he offered in the case concerning his abandonment of the manners of procession in the psychological variant of the procession model as the basis to distinguish the processions. His concern is similar to that of William Hill. He wants to accentuate the personalism inherent in the divine self-communication of the, pneumatological mission. Briefly, Coffey acknowledges his debt to the development of the idea of divine formal causality for the theology of revelation as God's self-communication. However, this theology can now stand on its own without the help of this once seminal concept. More important, it marks for Coffey the abandonment of the scholastic idiom. What he once heralded as the necessary complementarity of personalism and scholasticism, combining the power of the former with the precision of the latter, is now recognized as an unnecessary task in a changed theological atmosphere. His concern now is to preserve the idea intended by this terminology. However, he still needs to respond to the criticism of Hill to accomplish this.[133]

Coffey's evaluation of Hill's criticism is brief but precise. Acknowledging that for Hill the actuation of grace involves an elevation of the soul to participate in the divine nature, nevertheless this elevation is disjoined from any reception on the part of the created intellect. The reader will recall that the debate (initiated by M. de la Taille) had originally begun with a focus on the beatific vision wherein the grace of the *lumen gloriae* elevating the intellect is decisive and then proceeded by deduction to analyze the grace of justification. Coffey, who now contends that this instance of the divine self-communication—i.e., the beatific vision—is the one "which we know least about and for which much of the 'knowledge' that we do have is highly speculative," argues that a surer path for dogmatic conclusions ought to begin with the missions of the Son and the Holy Spirit. In both cases, however, Hill should realize that regarding grace there should not be "a total disjunction of reception and elevation" and that "the fact of the matter must be that the elevation *includes* reception" (emphasis his).[134]

We thus arrive at the most significant departure of Coffey from the norms of the Thomistic theology of grace and trinitarian missions—namely, a starting point in the trinitarian missions and the pneumatic reception of those missions by created reality as the basis for the theology of grace.[135] When he states that the "ultimate innertrinitarian ground" for the proper mission of the Holy Spirit is "the love of the Father for the Son, which is the Holy Spirit,"[136] he has thoroughly recapitulated the speculative moment in theological inquiry on the foundation of the immanent trinity and with a view to the economic trinity. One should not underestimate this accomplishment, for like Hill he agrees that the distinction among divine persons ultimately must be intra-trinitarian. This is the speculative moment where the distinctions are intelligible in themselves. But by beginning with the temporal missions he has ensured that the distinctions proceed from the reality of the divine economy. More specifically, since the economy is communicated in the Spirit, he has constructed his proposal on the basis of a sound and thoroughly retrieved pneumatology. Such a pneumatology is inclusive of the proper mission of the Holy Spirit, one in which the full personhood of the Holy Spirit is manifested, the alternative of a strictly appropriated mission being for Coffey "a reduction of the content of the deposit of faith."[137]

We may thus summarize Coffey's project as the pneumatization of a Rahnerian theology of revelation and grace. In the reception of grace and in the revelation of God as the divine self-communication through the trinitarian missions, the Holy Spirit emerges as the agent of divine operation toward created reality. Its culmination is in the divine sonship of Jesus, who in his love for the Father is the sacramental mediator of our adoption as sons and daughters of God. Both the person and mission of Christ and that of believers' participation in the divine sending into the world are thoroughly pneumatological in nature. Therefore, by virtue of divine revelation and redemption both Son and Spirit are distinguished and yet united in what Coffey has proffered in the construction of what I have described as Spirit-christology. It now remains for us to examine this same paradigm of relationship between Christ and the Spirit among theologians in an entirely non-scholastic framework. In the concluding chapter, we will proceed to a critical assessment of Spirit-christology as a contemporary Roman Catholic dogmatic christology.

Notes

1. David Coffey, "The Gift of the Holy Spirit," *The Irish Theological Quarterly 38* (1971), pp. 202–223.

2. Peter (Piet) Fransen, *The New Life of Grace* (Tournai: Desclee, 1969), pp. 96–97. Fransen, in fact, was quite severe: "The doctrine of grace, as set forth in classrooms and textbooks, was reduced to an uninviting short chapter on what had come to be called 'sanctifying grace' and long chapters dealing with the endless disputes on the subject of 'actual grace.'" Also Coffey, "The Gift of the Holy Spirit," p. 204.

3. Conversely, this likewise informed the resistance to other theologians who attempted to utilize the language of the Fathers and the mystical tradition. Such include Leonard Lessius, Cornelius a Lapide, Ruysbroeck, Denys Petau, Christian Thomasius, and in the nineteenth century Scheeben and Théodore de Régnon. Ibid., p. 97. This is a typical list of those whom traditional Thomists name as having departed from the dominant tradition and who in one way or another repeat the error of Peter Lombard, who equated infused charity with the Holy Spirit.

4. Coffey, "The Gift of the Holy Spirit," p. 203

5. Hill's only comment on Coffey's work which predates his is relegated to an exemplary footnote. Coffey is one of those who "have emphasized the special role of the Spirit to the point of making the inhabitation exclusive to the Third Person—not denying thereby a presence of Father and Logos but reducing their presence to something derivative from that of the Spirit, and explained by the inseparability of the Three." Hill, *The Three-Personed God,* p. 292, n. 21.

6. Coffey, "The Gift of the Holy Spirit," p. 204.

7. Ibid., p. 205

8. Lossky, *In The Image and Likeness of God.* pp. 85–90. It is interesting that Lossky quotes approvingly of Fr. Th. de Régnon, who also sought a retrieval from the Greek Fathers: "Latin philosophy envisages first the nature in itself and then proceeds to the expression;

Greek philosophy envisages first the expression and then penetrates it to find the nature. The Latin considers personality as a mode of nature, the Greek considers nature as the content of the person." p. 78, n. 10 (from *Études de théologie positive sur la Sainte Trinité I* [Paris, 1892] p. 433). This issue will arise again in Coffey's discussion of the relationship in contemporary Roman Catholic theology between scholasticism and personalism.

9. Congar's qualifications concerning Palamism revolve around the distinction between the divine essence and energies. Actually, he does not quarrel with the intention of Palamas but does state his disagreement: "I do not dispute the underlying intention of Palamas' teaching, but find myself in disagreement with the concepts that he uses and his metaphysical mode of expression." *I Believe in the Holy Spirit, Vol. 3. p. 66.* Coffey's investigation of the matter is essayed in his article: "The Palamite Doctrine of God: A New Perspective," *St. Vladimir's Theological Quarterly 32* (1988), pp. 329-358.

10. Coffey, "The Palamite Doctrine of God: A New Perspective," pp. 334-42.

11. Hill, *The Three-Personed God,* pp. 252-253.

12. David Coffey, *Grace: The Gift of the Holy Spirit* (Sydney: Catholic Institute of Sydney, 1979), p. 6.

13. Ibid., pp. 8-9.

14. David Coffey, "The Pre-existent and Incarnate Word," *Faith and Culture: Contemporary Questions* (Sydney: Faith and Culture, 1983), pp. 62-76.

15. Ibid., pp. 68-69.

16. David Coffey, "The Incarnation: Fact Not Myth," *Faith and Culture,* vol. 1 (Sydney: The Catholic Institute of Sydney, 1978), p. 18.

17. "For Christology that begins 'from above,' from the divinity of Jesus, the concept of the incarnation stands at the center. A Christology 'from below,' rising from the historical man Jesus to the recognition of his divinity, is concerned first of all with Jesus' message and fate and arrives only at the end at the concept of the incarnation." Wolfhart Pannenberg, *Jesus— God and Man,* 2nd ed. (Philadelphia: Westminster, 1977), p. 33

18. Ibid., p. 34

19. Karl Rahner, "The Two Basic Types of Christology," *Theological Investigations,* vol. XIII. (New York: Crossroad, 1983), pp. 213-223.

20. Coffey. "The Incarnation: Fact Not Myth," p. 19.

21. David Coffey, "A Proper Mission of the Holy Spirit," *Theological Studies* 47 (1986), p. 229.

22. David Coffey, "The Holy Spirit as the Mutual Love of the Father and the Son," *Theological Studies* 51 (1990), p. 195.

23. Ibid.

24. Coffey, "A Proper Mission of the Holy Spirit," p. 231.

25. Ibid, p. 130.

26. *ST* Ia, 43, 2.

27. Coffey, "A Proper Mission of the Holy Spirit," p. 230.

28. Idem, "The Holy Spirit as the Mutual Love of the Father and the Son," p. 220.

29. Idem, "A Proper Mission of the Holy Spirit," p. 243.

30. Idem., The Gift of the Holy Spirit. p. 20. This shift will figure in Coffey's own change of mind, as we shall see.

31. *Monologium,* 47,51, in *St. Anselm: Basic Writings,* trans. S. N. Dean (La Salle, IL: Open Court, 1962).

32. As Vladimir Lossky states, we are only permitted to distinguish the persons on the basis of "relations of diversity," not as in Latin scholasticism on "relations of opposition." It is sufficient to follow Gregory of Nazianzus: "To be unbegotten, to be begotten, to proceed— these are the features which characterize the Father, the Son, and Him whom we call the Holy

Spirit, in such a way as to safeguard the distinction of the three hypostases in the one nature and majesty of the Divinity . . . Or. 30, 9: *Patrologia Graeca* [(J. P. Migne), Paris, 1857–1866], 36, col. 141D–44A." Lossky, *In the Image and Likeness of God,* p. 79 and n. 14.

33. Coffey, *The Gift of the Holy Spirit,*. pp. 12–13.

34. Coffey quotes from I,37,1: "As when someone knows something there proceeds in the knower a certain intellectual conception of the thing known, which is called the word, so when someone loves something there proceeds in the affection of the lover what might be called an impression of the thing loved, according to which the thing loved is said to be in the lover, just as the thing known is in the knower" (pp. 12–13). This as contrasted with the earlier *De Veritate* 4,2, and 7: "This is the difference between the intellect and the will, that the operation of the will terminates at things, in which are good and evil, whereas the operation of the intellect terminates in the mind, in which are truth and falsehood, as is said in the Metaphysics 6.8. Therefore, the will does not have proceeding from it anything which is in it after the manner of an operation, but the intellect does have in itself something proceeding from it, not only after the manner of an operation, but also after the manner of a thing operated. Therefore, the word is signified as a thing proceeding, but love is signified as an operation proceeding." p. 12.

35. Ibid., pp. 22–24.

36. Ibid., p. 25.

37. By "formal reasons" Coffey means the following: "The formal reason of a thing is its exact, precise and immediate explanation. Properly speaking, therefore, it indicates not the thing itself, but what is immediately prior to it, not in time but in logical sequence." Ibid., p. 19.

38. Ibid., p. 25.

39. Ibid., p. 15. Although analogously, there is a "fundamental contrast that exists between knowledge and love" (p. 20).

40. Ibid., p. 23.

41. Ibid., p. 29.

42. *In I Sententiarum* 10,1,2: "In the procession of the Holy Spirit there are two things to be considered, viz. the procession itself and the manner of the procession. And because the Holy Spirit proceeds as something distinct and self-existent, he does not have it from the procession as such that he is from the Father to the Son or *vice versa,* but he has it that he is subsistent in himself. But if the manner of the procession is considered—i.e. that he proceeds as love (as we said in the preceding article in reply to the second objection), since according to the nature of the intellectual process the loved one is that in which love is terminated, and the lover that from which love goes forth: since the Father loves the Son, the Holy Spirit can be said to be the love of the Father for the Son, and since the Son loves the Father, the Holy Spirit can be said to be the love of the Son for the Father." (Ibid., p. 29).

43. It should also be emphasized that there is a certain order to the models, as the following illustrates: "As the procession occurs only in its concrete mode, the order of encounter or what we might call the epistemological order, is first the bestowal, then the procession; the logical order, however, is the inverse, first the procession, then its mode, bestowal of love." Ibid., p. 30.

44. Ibid., p. 31.

45. "A Proper Mission of the Holy Spirit," *Theological Studies* 47 (1986), 227–250.

47. Ibid., 234, n. 12.

48. Ibid., p. 2. Quoted from Walter Kasper. *Jesus the Christ* (New York: Paulist, 1976), p. 180.

49. Edward J. Kilmartin, S.J. *Christian Liturgy: Theology and Practice, I. Systematic Theology of Liturgy* (Kansas City: Sheed & Ward, 1988), pp. 135–179.

50. Coffey, *Grace: The Gift of the Holy Spirit*, p. 40.

51. Idem, "The Holy Spirit as the Mutual Love of the Father and the Son," p. 221.

52. Coffey, *Grace: The Gift of the Holy Spirit*, p. 38.

53. Heribert Mühlen *Der Heilige Geist als Person* (Münster, 1966). Idem. *Una Mystica Persona* (Paderbo

n, 1968).

54. Coffey, *Grace: The Gift of the Holy Spirit*, p. 38.

55. Ibid.

56. Ibid. p. 39.

57. Offically defined by the Fourth Lateran Council (1215) as normative for any theological method: "For between Creator and creature no similarity can be uttered without this having to embrace a still greater dissimilarity between the two."

58. Coffey still admits the role of philosophical anthropology within dogmatic theology, as did scholasticism. Thus the following: "These brief remarks will, it is hoped, suffice to show that there is a great need for a theology of grace which is as systematic as the efforts of scholasticism but which surpasses them by presenting grace in genuinely personal terms. Scholarly works of biblical theology of grace, though indispensable, are no substitute for this. They constitute only the first and preparatory stage of a comprehensive theology of grace, which must interpret the biblical truth in the light of contemporary culture, particularly philosophical culture." Ibid., p. 47. Also: "Personalism . . . has not succeeded in comprehending the whole of reality, and has finished up by placing infra-personal and personal being in opposition. . . . likewise . . . personalism . . . can contribute to a more comprehensive future philosophy, but only if it resists the temptation to erect itself into an absolute, and makes a concerted effort with transcendental philosophy." Ibid., p. 49.

59. *Summa Theologiae*. IIIa q. 3,5.

60. Karl Rahner, S.J. *The Trinity* (New York: Herder & Herder, 1970).

61 Ibid., p. 22.

62. Ibid., p. 24f.

63. Compare *Summa Theologiae*, I, q. 43, 1 with III, q. 3, 5.

64. Rahner. *The Trinity*, pp. 26-27.

65. Ibid., pp. 28-30.

66. Ibid., p. 30.

67. Ibid., pp. 31-33.

68. Ibid., p. 33.

69. David Coffey, "A Proper Mission of the Holy Spirit," *Theological Studies* 47 (1986), pp. 234-235.

70. "As we have seen, within the Trinity the Son proceeds as self-knowledge of the Father, and the Holy Spirit as the bond of love between the Father and the Son. Because of the necessary consistency of God, when the Father communicates himself to the world by projections of the ways in which he communicates himself in the Trinity, the Son and the Holy Spirit as thus communicated to the world must retain their respective identities as given in the Trinity, the Son must be communicated as the revelation of the Father to men, and the Holy Spirit must be communicated as the bond of love between the Father and his sons, sons in the Son." Coffey, *Grace: The Gift of the Holy Spirit*, p. 67.

71. Ibid., pp. 63-64. It should also be understood that the distinction in form is metaphysical and not logical. In other words, accidental form here means the union of the Holy Spirit with human persons where divinity and humanity are distinguished, not that the gift of the Holy Spirit is extraneous to the essential being of the human person.

72. In this respect Coffey is traditional in that he understands that the term assumed in the incarnation is a human nature and not a human person. It is the singular person of the

divine Son who subsists in the human nature assumed in the hypostatic union. Coffey explicates the difference with reference to distinct types of union: "Thus we see that the two basic verbs 'to be' and 'to have' exhaust the possibilities of the ways in which men can be united (by divine formal causality) to divine persons, and that 'to be,' corresponding to substantial form, pertains of necessity to the incarnation of the Son, while 'to have,' corresponding to accidental form, pertains of necessity to the Gift of the Holy Spirit in grace." Ibid., p. 70.

73. Ibid., p. 62.

74. Ibid., p. 70. Also: "Grace is the Father's Gift of the Holy Spirit . . . ," (p. 80).

75. Rahner's thesis is summarized as follows: "Furthermore, it is a perfectly theologically correct interpretation of this direct vision of God to understand this vision, not as an extrinsic addition to the Hypostatic Union, since—after all—it is held to be necessary to understand the Hypostatic Union itself ontologically and not merely ontically. It is then legitimate to be of the positive opinion that such an interpretation can understand the vision of God as a basic condition of the created spiritual nature of Jesus, a basic condition which is so original and unobjective, unsystematic and fundamental, that it is perfectly reconcilable with a genuine, human experience; there is no reason why it should not be perfectly reconcilable with a historical development, understood as an objectifying systematization of this original, always given, direct presence of God, both in the encounter with the spiritual and religious enviroment and in the experience of one's own life." Rahner, "Dogmatic Reflections on the Knowledge and Self-Consciousness of Christ," *Theological Investigations*, Vol. V. (New York: Crossroad, 1983), p. 215.

76. Coffey, *Grace: The Gift of the Holy Spirit,* p. 73.

77. Ibid., p. 74. Coffey summarizes: "We summarize our treatment of the relation of divine sonship and faith in Jesus by saying that to him was given a unique grace, the incarnation, which established in him a unique divine Sonship, which both came to expression in and was realized through his faith, which was established in the common freedom and darkness experienced by men in this life, and also in the full mastering of concupiscence, so that in him the unique Son of God was expressed, revealed and realized as fully as possible in the limits of humanity." (p. 78).

78. The Catholic understanding of the postlapsarian integrity of the free will confessed by Trent *(The Decree on Justification,* Chapter I) is affirmed by Coffey: "Grace is the Father's Gift of the Holy Spirit, the Spirit of sonship, who forms willing men into sons of God." Also: "We repeat, human freedom, on which responsibility depends, is not annihilated by grace." Ibid., p. 80.

79. Ibid., pp. 83-84.

80. Ibid., pp. 91-92.

81. Coffey is unambiguous on this matter: ". . . it is clear that in formation the incarnation and grace can both be communications of the Holy Spirit while in constitution the former is the communication of the Son and the latter the communication of the Holy Spirit." Ibid., p. 92.

82. Ibid., pp. 91-92.

83. Ibid., pp. 94-95.

84. Ibid., p. 97. De la Pottierie's article makes four major points. First, no text in the New Testament "refers to an anointing of Christ at the moment of the incarnation." Second, there is no question of a sacerdotal anointing but only of a prophetic anointing. In other words, anointing is associated with the beginning of Jesus' ministry as prophet, not in relationship to his priesthood. Third, there is no connection in the New Testament between the title "Christ" and the theology of anointing. Anointing refers to the function of Christ, not his being or nature. Fourth, there is no doctrine of a "double anointing" of Jesus during his earthly life in the New Testament—e.g., at the incarnation and at his baptism—but only a baptismal anoint-

ing for ministry. Therefore, the association of anointing theology with the incarnation (as in the Fathers) or with the threefold office of Christ as prophet, priest, and king loses the specificity of this theology as portrayed in the scripture, especially the connection in the Lukan corpus between the prophetic anointing of Christ at his baptism with eschatological nuances that link it to the gift of the Holy Spirit poured out upon the whole church at Pentecost. See Ignace de la Potterie, S.J., "The Anointing of Christ," *Word and Mystery: Biblical Essays on the Person and Mission of Christ*, ed. Leo J. O'Donovan, S.J. (New York: Newman, 1968), pp. 155–184.

85. Coffey, *Grace: The Gift of the Holy Spirit*, pp. 96–100.

86. Coffey admits that in the Fathers there are many variant referents in anointing theology—e.g., the identification of both the Father and the Son as agents of anointing, anointing with, by or in the Holy Spirit. These can be interpreted in the context of both ascending and descending christologies leading to the conclusion that there is no homogenous theology of anointing in the Fathers. Ibid., p. 102.

87. Coffey states in reference to these christologies: "However, our Christology has little in common with it. The patristic Christology out of which our own grows is not this primitive one, but the one forged by Athanasius with his homoousion, and therefore distinct personhood, of the Holy Spirit." Ibid., p. 105

88. Ibid., p. 106.

89. Ibid., pp. 107–108.

90. Ibid., p. 108.

91. Ibid.

92. *Summa Theologiae*, III, q. 7, a. 13.

93. This is also true with regard to their appropriated faculties. The Holy Spirit proceeds from the Son even as love proceeds from wisdom.

94. Coffey, *Grace: The Gift of the Holy Spirit*, p. 109.

95. "The grace of union is therefore the Gift of the Holy Spirit bestowed by the Father in all fulness on Jesus, creating his humanity, sanctifying it and uniting it in person to the pre-existent divine Son; and the habitual grace of Jesus is the unsurpassable sanctity of his humanity brought about by the Gift of the Holy Spirit as uniquely bestowed on him." Ibid., p. 110.

96. *Summa Theologiae* III, q. 7, a. 12.

97. Ibid., III, q. 7, a. 1.

98. M. de la Taille, *The Hypostatic Union and Created Actuation by Uncreated Act*, p. 76.

99. Coffey, *Grace: The Gift of the Holy Spirit*, p. 109.

100. "The commonly advanced argument that Jesus must have possessed habitual grace, and indeed in its fulness, in order to be the source of grace for men begs the question, as it assumes that it is this grace that is the 'grace of head' (*gratia capitis*), which Christ communicates to the members of his mystical body; whereas the grace of head is better conceived as the Holy Spirit, possessed by Jesus in all fulness and sent by him upon the Church and therein offered to men through his continuing ministry, the more so as his habitual grace was proper to himself as a man and therefore incommunicable." Ibid., p. 109.

101. Ibid., pp. 114–118.

102. All hints of adoptionism are avoided because the anointing creates the humanity of Jesus as well as uniting him to the divine Son. It is therefore situated at the conception of Jesus. Ibid., pp. 120, 127, 130.

103. Ibid., p. 148.

104. Ibid., p. 160.

105. Ibid., p. 174.

106. Ibid., p. 175.

107. David Coffey, "The 'Incarnation' of the Holy Spirit in Christ," *Theological Studies* 45 (1984), pp. 466–480.

108. This is in a real sense the completion of Jesus' human love for the Father. Speaking of the death of Jesus, Coffey says: ". . . there is no further place for elicited acts of love of the Father on Jesus' part, since his whole being is now concentrated in a single act of love which would render such acts superfluous even if they were not ruled out already on anthropological grounds. Here, then, we have the perfect 'incarnation' of the Holy Spirit in Christ. It is the incarnation of divine love in human love." Ibid., p. 477. It should also be noted that Coffey is indebted to James Dunn, who will be mentioned in the next chapter. Specifically, he cites him for his insight into "the Christological character of the Holy Spirit." (p. 478).

109. One further insight of Coffey's concerns the possible compromise of the divine transcendence concerning the incarnation of the transcendental love of the Son in the human love of Christ. Coffey responds with an explanation approaching the *extra calvinisticum:* ". . . in the human love of Christ which is the Holy Spirit the divine love does not come to that absolutely perfect expression which it receives in the immanent Trinity in the love which the Son acting in the divine nature returns to the Father, but only to the perfection that is relative to the capacity of human nature under God's grace. Only thus is a true, if analogous, 'incarnation' of the Holy Spirit guaranteed." Ibid., p. 479. But this similarity does not extend to his theology of grace. There he thoroughly rejects the Calvinist *finitum non capax infiniti* in favor of the patristic understanding of divinization. See "The Proper Mission of the Holy Spirit," p. 245.

110. David Coffey, "A Proper Mission of the Holy Spirit," *Theological Studies.* 47 (1986), pp. 227–250.

111. Ibid., p. 232.

112. Ibid., p. 233.

113. Coffey, "The Holy Spirit as the Mutual Love of the Father and the Son," p. 201.

114. Ibid., pp. 227–228.

115. Ibid., p. 216.

116. Ibid., p. 224.

117. The same could be said for the sacraments. See Chapters 11 and 12 of *Grace: The Gift of the Holy Spirit.*

118. Hans Küng, *Theology for the Third Millenium* (New York: Doubleday, 1988), p. 188.

119. Coffey, "Proper Mission of the Holy Spirit," p. 229

120. Hill, *The Three-Personed God. pp. 274–275.*

121. Ibid., p. 274.

122. Ibid., p. 263, n. 24.

123. Ibid., p. 275.

124. Ibid.

125. Ibid., pp. 276–77, 288–295.

126. Ibid., p. 272.

127. Ibid., p. 276.

128. Ibid., p. 294. Hill follows this statement with the following critical comment: "This is in marked contrast with Rahner's explanation wherein distinct relations to the Three in God are achieved in the ontic order prior to all knowing and loving."

129. Ibid. One should also note that when the referent for divine-human union is the hypostatic union, Hill contends that this also is not an instance of formal causality, since "the Word of God communicates existence *simpliciter* to that humanity so that it exists as the humanity of God." (p. 293). It is a union of natures achieved ontically on the level of person,

while the union between the Holy Spirit and the believer is a union not of natures but of persons.

130. Ibid., p. 287.

131. Ibid., p. 296.

132. Ibid., p. 290. Also Coffey, "The Proper Mission of the Holy Spirit," p. 243.

133. Ibid., pp. 243–244. Hill, it should be noted, has been a long-standing critic of Rahner's innovations, going back to his article "Uncreated Grace—A Critique of Karl Rahner," *The Thomist* 26 (1963) pp. 333–56. That he continues to be so even in his own somewhat post-scholastic work, *The Three-Personed God* is a testimony to the enduring value of this intra-scholastic debate, which we examined in Chapters 2 and 3. I say "post-scholastic" book because, while he is still very much within the horizon of that theology, his interlocuters throughout are non-scholastic theologians. Hill is one of the few Thomists who have been able to maintain an informed and profound theological conversation in the present post-scho-lastic era of Catholic theology. His is no longer simply an "in-house" debate.

134. Coffey, "The Proper Mission of the Holy Spirit," pp. 245–246.

135. At one time such a departure was considered very seriously. In his original critique of Karl Rahner, Hill ended his article with the following sentence: "But the directions which Father Rahner here suggests do seem to break continuity with the rich traditions of the past, even to come close to overstepping the norms of orthodoxy." "Uncreated Grace: A Critique of Karl Rahner," p. 356. His later work, while still critical, does not suggest such danger in the Rahnerian theology of grace. There, his purpose is simply "to register a reservation on the category of 'quasi-formal causality.'" *The Three-Personed God*, p. 292. Despite such disagree-ments, Hill always gave credit to the profundity of Rahner's work. In the earlier article he recognized that his critique "contain[ed] an implicit acknowledgement that perhaps his [Rahner's] efforts have opened up a whole new direction to theological speculation on grace, justification, glory, the Incarnation, and the supernatural." "Uncreated Grace: A Critique of Karl Rahner," p. 333.

136. Coffey, "The Proper Mission of the Holy Spirit," p. 239.

137. Ibid., p. 228

5

Spirit-christology: Dogmatic Issues in Trinitarian Perspective

In this chapter we will attempt to provide a perspective on the model of Spirit-christology that is an alternative to what we have thus far examined. By stepping outside of the circle of Roman Catholic neo-scholastic thought, we hope to test the viability of Coffey's model against the concerns of other contemporary theologians and in light of biblical and patristic precedents for it. We shall then turn, in the final chapter, to a critical evaluation of the project in general.

Biblical Perspectives

The relationship between New Testament pneumatology and christology is best assessed in light of the debate, begun with D. F. Strauss, that ensued regarding the priority of the Jesus of history or the Christ of faith for Christian religious experience.[1] This debate, which became the object of the old and new quests for the historical Jesus, resurfaced with vigor after the advent of the kerygmatic and existential theology of Rudolph Bultmann and his students. At the turn of the century, dogmatic theologians Wilhelm Herrmann and Martin Kähler had debated the issue, and their concern, as is ours, can be framed accordingly as whether the object of Christian faith is the religious personality of Jesus or the proclamation of the risen Christ in the church's kerygma. We may translate this into the systematic terms used by Coffey. The distinction between Jesus as the recipient of divine blessing or as its mediator respectively represent the perspectives of ascending and descending christologies and their correlate procession and bestowal models of the trinity. To what extent can this debate in New Testament theology enhance our understanding of Spirit-christology as developed by David Coffey out of the context of the Catholic neo-scholastic tradition? To answer this question we turn to the contemporary British exegete James D. G. Dunn, who in particular has examined the relationship between the historical Jesus and the Christ of faith in light of New Testament testimony to the experience of the Holy Spirit.

Following Hermann Gunkel's classic work *The Influence of the Holy Spirit*, Dunn recognizes the development of pneumatology in the New Testament and would agree with Gunkel's own evaluation of biblical pneumatology. In his preface to the second and third German editions, Gunkel had remarked that "the real task of my little work was to ascertain the symptoms by which an 'effect' of the Spirit was recognized, and in face of the modernizing of exegetes who, without historical reflection and influenced by rationalism, know nothing of the 'effects' of the *pneuma* and render 'Spirit' a pure abstraction."[2] In the face of the idealistic overtones of "spirit" in the German philosophical tradition, this represented a recovery of the biblical notion of Spirit.[3] By reference to the activity of the Spirit in the biblical sources, Gunkel was able to contrast pneumatic effects in and through persons with spirit as a metaphysical or religio-ethical principle.

Subsequent work in New Testament theology and exegesis basically confirmed Gunkel's findings in marking out an authentically biblical pneumatology.[4] However, the relationship between the risen Christ and the Holy Spirit remained somewhat ambiguous. Most positions oscillate between what Gunkel labeled as either a complete or partial identification between the two. For example, he had argued that in Paul the identification between Christ and the Spirit is only partial. While the exalted Christ works through the Spirit, there is also an area of Christ's activity that is greater than that of the Spirit.[5] Also, in contrast to the later doctrinal tradition, he distinguished Christ from the Spirit as the difference between person and power.

> Accordingly, the teaching concerning the *pneuma* and the teaching concerning *Christos* are parallel. What each has to say differs from the other merely by the fact that in the one the supernatural is derived from a divine power; in the other, it is derived from a divine person who has this power in himself.[6]

Much early work in the "History of Religions School" (*Religionsgeschichtliche Schule*) is illustrative of this, especially their emphasis on the Christ-mysticism of Paul. Adolf Diessmann could speak of the "Christ-experience of the Apostle" as the experience of the "Spirit-Christ," thus identifying Christ as the Spirit.[7] Albert Schweitzer, after dismantling the "life of Jesus" theology, rescued his apocalyptic Jesus' "simple Gospel of the Kingdom of God" through the "authentic Primitive-Christian eschatological Paulinism" in which Christ-mysticism is mediated through possession of the Spirit.[8] For Wilhelm Boussett, in his classic *Kyrios Christos,* the major foundation for Paul's Christ-mysticism is the cult of Christ as *Kyrios,* which emerged out of Hellenistic Christianity and which established an "intimate connection between pneumatic experience and community cult" through a similar identification of Christ and the Spirit.[9] Although this notion of Christ-mysticism has been criticized by Bultmann and others, such identification between Christ and the Spirit merits further examination.[10] Dogmatically, and directly relevant to our inquiry, it raises the issue that if one unduly separates the Jesus of history from the Christ of faith, with the latter interpreted according to a pneumatic mystical construction, then the groundwork has certainly been laid for a modalistic identification of Christ and the Spirit. We shall come back to this issue in subsequent sections.

A much more detailed and in-depth examination of this relationship between New Testament pneumatology and christology is offered by Dunn.[11] Dunn recognizes the diversity in New Testament kerygmata and investigates the relationship of these kerygmata to the historical Jesus. It is a given that these kerygmata, representing "many kerygmatic Christs," entail not only diversity among kerygmata but contradiction as well.[12]

> In short, *"the kerygmatic Christ" is no single or simple formulation, but a fairly wide diversity of formulations which embrace quite a broad spectrum of different understandings of "the Christ event," which are not always wholly compatible with each other, and which change and develop as the first century progresses.*[13]

Although this indeed presents problems for the affirmation of continuity between the historical Jesus and the Christ of faith, Dunn argues for continuity amid the diversity on the basis of the following factors: Jesus' expectation of vindication, Jesus' sense of sonship, Jesus' experience of the kingdom and of the Spirit of God.[14] In each case, Dunn notes points of continuity between the self-understanding of Jesus and that of the first Christians. This does not mean that one can establish continuity on the basis of the utilization by early Christian kergymata of the kerygma, or teaching, of Jesus. Rather, there are elements of understanding in the various early Christian kergymata that help conceptualize the relation of the early Christians to God. These elements are then correlated with the self-understanding of Jesus in his relation to God. In addition, this correlation functions in such a manner that "the link between Jesus the proclaimer and Jesus the proclaimed, is *Jesus proclaimed as the proclaimer.*"[15]

The correlation between Jesus and the kerygma of the early Christians functions as follows. In the case of Jesus' expectation of vindication, an expectation envisaged vis-à-vis the imminent consummation of the kingdom, the early Christians recognized such vindication in his resurrection from the dead. Second, Jesus' sense of sonship was the theological basis for the sonship and daughterhood experienced by his disciples both before and after Easter. Finally, Jesus' experience of the kingdom in eschatological reserve (already—not yet) was mediated by the Spirit and manifest in his works of power, exorcisms, and healings. This experience of Jesus' anointing by the end-time Spirit (Luke 4:18) can be similarly correlated with the Spirit's reception by the early Christians, who understood their experience of the Spirit as a pledge of its fullness in eschatological consummation. In each case the correlation of the early Christians' experience with that of Jesus is necessarily mediated by the risen and exalted Christ. In other words, their experience is itself dependent on Jesus (now risen and exalted), a dependence and mediation that is implicit in the pre-Easter ministry of Jesus. Dunn concludes:

> In short, *there are sufficiently clear foreshadowings of the centrality of the kerygmatic Christ in the self-understanding of Jesus during his ministry for us to recognize the kerygmata of the early churches as a development from Jesus' own proclamation in the light of the resurrection.*[16]

Once having established this unity, Dunn is able to affirm that it is precisely this identity of the historical Jesus with the kerygmatic Christ that is "*the one basis and bond of unity which holds together the manifold diversity of first-century Christianity.*"[17] Even though "*this unifying core is an abstraction,*"[18] it nevertheless underscores the entirety of the New Testament and through his emphasis on pneumatology also contributes new insights not only to resolving the tension that has existed in the theological understanding of the relationship of the Jesus of history to the Christ of faith, but also to the problems surrounding the relationship of the Holy Spirit to the *Christus praesens*. It is to this issue that I will now turn.

Dunn's analysis of New Testament pneumatology in his study *Jesus and the Spirit* examines the broad range of religious experiences in the New Testament, especially as these focus on pneumatic and charismatic experiences. His query particularly seeks to answer the question whether early Christian experience merely repeats Jesus' experience or derives from Jesus as its source (Coffey's Christ as either recipient or mediator of divine blessing).[19] This approach is the pneumatological version of the christological question discussed above—namely, how does one conceive the relationship between the Jesus of history and the Christ of faith? As already noted, a pneumatic interpretation is included in the strictly christological discussion. The fuller pneumatological discussion sheds further light on this theological issue.

When Dunn examines the religious experience of Jesus he does not mean that one can trace "*development*" in the consciousness of Jesus. He intends only to "*see something of the experiential basis of Jesus' faith in God.*"[20] Specifically, this basis can be described as a "*consciousness of eschatological power, of God's Spirit upon him and working through him . . . [as] . . . a distinctive and even unique element in his own experience of God.*"[21] It is this awareness that enables us to speak of the "'divinity' of the *historical* Jesus"—i.e., *his relationship with the Father as son and the Spirit of God in him.*"[22]

Although Dunn does not expand on this, except to note that it grounds the christological claims of the early Christians in the historical Jesus, this pneumatic awareness on the part of the historical Jesus does portend the constructive possibilities of a pneumatic christology. More than this, it also establishes the framework for understanding early Christian kerygmata relative to the pneumatic experiences of the primitive church. Dunn, in fact, follows Gunkel by distinguishing between the understanding of pneumatic experiences in Luke—Acts and in Paul, noting that Paul curbs the narrowly enthusiast interpretation of Luke. For our purposes I will focus only on the christological dimensions of the respective pneumatologies.[23]

It is clear that in both cases the experience of the Spirit focuses on the risen and exalted Christ. For Luke—Acts this applies particularly to the issue of charismatic authority. Thus, while the eschatological Spirit was experienced by both Jesus and the early Christians, in the case of Jesus, authority is centered in himself; but for the early Christians authority is centered in Jesus in their dependency upon his exaltation.[24] Although for Paul the nature and import of pneumatic experiences are interpreted differently, this same structure holds. The Pauline communities, for example, experience charismata (as pneumatic events and energies) in dependence on "*Christ the Lord and his Spirit.*"[25] However, the association of Jesus and the Spirit in Paul goes a significant step further. Dunn characterizes the Pauline understanding of this relationship in terms of identity, as the following descriptive statements reveal:

Christ the life-giving Spirit.[26]

Paul equates the risen Jesus with the Spirit who makes alive.[27]

. . . the Spirit has himself taken on the character of Christ.[28]

If Christ is now experienced as Spirit, Spirit is now experienced as Christ.[29]

... the distinctive mark of the Christian is experience of the Spirit as the life of Christ.[30]

... experience of Spirit identified and distinguished as experience of Christ.[31]

... when Paul wants to find the distinctive mark of Spirit-given experience, he finds it not in the charismatic Spirit as such, nor in the eschatological Spirit as such, but in the Jesus Spirit, the Spirit whose characteristics are those of Christ.[32]

the distinctive mark of the Spirit becomes his Christness. The charismatic Spirit is brought to the test of the Christ event ... as the Spirit was the 'divinity' of Jesus, so Jesus became the personality of the Spirit.[33]

This last quote is the most important, for it establishes both continuity between the historical Jesus and the Christ of faith and identity between the Spirit and the *Christus praesens.* It is Dunn's contention that there is indeed a trinitarian pattern to the experience of the believer, but one that can only be acknowledged on the basis of the experience of the Spirit of sonship and daughterhood, something different from the ponderings of a speculative metaphysics.[34] Finally, while deutero-Paul and the Pastoral epistles lose something of Paul's pneumatic vitality, the Johannine writings present a comparable pneumatic vision. The Spirit is John's other Paraclete and is the same as Paul's Spirit of Jesus, affording "an immediate and direct continuity between believers and Jesus" and betraying the fact that "the personality of Jesus has become the personality of the Spirit."[35]

In conclusion, Dunn has utilized pneumatology to resolve the tension between the historical Jesus and the Christ of faith by examining New Testament religious experience in its self-testifying pneumatic dimension. This is the most creative aspect of his work. However, in the process he highlights another problem, the question of identity or distinction between the risen Christ and the Holy Spirit. Following Paul, he equates the Spirit with the risen Jesus, the only "personal" element of the Spirit being Jesus himself.[36] Although there is a trinitarian structure to Christian experience—Christians experience a dual relationship to God and the risen Jesus that is attributed to the Spirit—this is not the same as an experience of the trinity. The Spirit is the subject of one's experience, not of one's speculation. Interestingly enough, Dunn is willing on the basis of scriptural testimony to recognize that "there is more to the risen Jesus than life-giving Spirit (cf., e.g., Rom 1.3f; 8.34; I Cor. 15. 24–8)."[37] The same is not conceded to the Spirit; in fact, to return to his reading of Paul, pneumatology is "immanent christology."[38] Therefore, we simply note that the contribution of Dunn's pneumatological approach relative to the issue of the Straussian problematic solves the problem of continuity or discontinuity between the historical Jesus and the Christ of faith while leaving the dogmatic issue of trinitarian identification unresolved. Because the latter point is decisive for the issue posed in this chapter, I conclude by quoting fully his summary constructive proposals:

> Moreover, if christology is the key to Christianity, then the teeth of that key are not only the historical Jesus and the kerygmatic Christ but also the life-giving Spirit. The new "Quest" and interest in the "titles of majesty" must not detract attention from the further dimension of christology—'Christ in me, the hope of glory." In the debate between those who seek to ground an understanding of faith

in the historical Jesus and those who start from 'the kerygma', the *experiential* basis of early Christianity must not be ignored. Men believed in Jesus as Christ and Lord because they experienced a to them supernatural vitalizing power—power whose character, if Paul is to be our guide, directed them to the conclusion that Jesus was its living source. Paul's understanding of the exalted Christ emerged out of his experience of the Spirit, not *vice versa*.[39]

In terms of the modern debate and of our opening question the significant feature to emerge from our study is that although Paul thinks almost exclusively in terms of the present Jesus experienced now as Spirit, he does not thereby ignore or deny the relevance of the historical man Jesus. For it is precisely the Jesus-, that is, the historical Jesus-, content and Jesus-character of the present experience of the Spirit which is the distinctive and most important feature of the experience. Christ has become Spirit, *Christ is now experienced as Spirit*—that is true. But it is only because *the Spirit is now experienced as Christ* that the experience of the Spirit is valid and essential for Paul. The centrality given to the experience of the exalted Lord does not deny the relevance and importance of the historical Jesus for Paul; on the contrary it reinforces it, by binding the historical Jesus and the exalted Lord together in the single all-important experience of the life-giving Spirit.[40]

We may conclude that in the resolution of the relationship between the Jesus of history and the Christ of faith through pneumatology as proposed by Dunn, we also have the beginnings of Spirit-christology in the New Testament itself. Yet we are also confronted with a problem for dogmatic christology that we may identify as the danger of modalism regarding the relationship of the second and third persons of the trinity. As Dunn phrased it in one of his earlier articles, the New Testament perhaps provides warrant to speak only of a binity in God and not a trinity.

This naturally raises the question as to how appropriate it is to speak of a *Trinity* rather than a *Binity*. Before the incarnation Logos and Spirit were hardly to be distinguished. After incarnation the divinity of Jesus was a function of the Spirit. And after the resurrection the risen humanity of Jesus was a function of the Spirit.[41]

If dogmatic christology is to maintain the integrity of trinitarian distinctions, then it must be able to account for the difference between the Son and the Spirit in each of the categories mentioned by Dunn—i.e., between Logos and Spirit before the incarnation and between the Spirit and the predication of divinity and humanity in the incarnate and risen Christ, respectively. Does Coffey's construct answer to this query?

The first set of relations implicates the doctrine of the immanent trinity. Even though Coffey turns to the *ad extra* missions of the Son and the Spirit to explicate his new bestowal model, he agrees with the traditional Latin position that the distinction of persons can be maintained only on the basis of their "innertrinitarian" relations. How, then, are we to evaluate his claim that this distinction is necessary in light of Dunn's exegetical work? Since Coffey does not argue that the immanent doctrine of the trinity is found in the New Testament, it is only appropriate that we examine his argument in comparison with a dogmatic christological model that does not proceed to these intra-trinitarian distinctions. This we shall do in the next section by critically comparing his dogmatic proposal in Spirit-christology to one suggested by Piet Schoonenberg.

The second and third options, which express the relationship of predication between the Holy Spirit and the humanity and divinity of Christ, also can be examined and evaluated in comparison with other contemporary dogmatic proposals. Geoffrey Lampe's Spirit-christology can follow Dunn's statement that the divinity of the incarnate Christ is a function of the Holy Spirit, while proposals by Dietrich Ritschl and Peter Hodgson relative to a christology of presence are similar to the correlate statement that the risen humanity of Jesus is also a function of the Spirit, although they raise this more from the christological side than from the pneumatological one. Since each of Dunn's points can be associated with a dogmatic christological construction that differs significantly from that of Coffey's, we shall now utilize them to help evaluate his proposal from theological perspectives completely outside the tradition of Roman Catholic neo-scholasticism.

An Alternative Catholic Spirit-christology

Exposition

Other Roman Catholic variants of Spirit-christology have emerged in addition to that of Coffey's. Many of them offer a construction that may be summed up by the thesis of biblical theologian F. X. Durwell, C.S.S.R.:

> The Spirit is the agent of salvation in Jesus Christ in the same way as he is the intimate movement of God by which the Father begets *his Son* through the sanctity of the Spirit.
>
> *The salvific mystery is identical with the personal mystery of Jesus. It is the mystery of a man who, in his life and death, is begotten through the Holy Spirit and receives divine personality through this Spirit.*[42]

In other words, harking back to the indications of Spirit-christology in Matthias Scheeben and Leo XIII—e.g., the role of the Spirit in the incarnation and the paschal mystery—contemporary Catholic theologians are now developing those pointers in recognition that there is an integrated dogmatic relationship between christology and pneumatology. In recent years a number of articles by Roman Catholic systematicians have either directly or indirectly broached the subject of Spirit-christology.[43] Kilian McDonnell, O.S.B., John O'Donnell, S.J., and Philip Rosato, S.J., have especially raised the key dogmatic issue that has been our concern—namely, the identity of each of the trinitarian persons in this particular christological construction. McDonnell argues for pneumatology as an entrance point into christology to keep theology Christocentric but not pan-christological or Christo-monistic. If "the Spirit belongs to Jesus constitutively and not merely in a second moment," then there must be a particular type of precision to articulate the identity and non-identity between Christ and the Spirit.[44] O'Donnell suggests, with an emphasis similar to that of Coffey, that a descending christology of the incarnation must be complemented by an ascending christology of the Spirit to link together an ontological mode of thinking and that carried out in salvific-historical perspective.[45] Rosato directly addresses the issue concerning whether or not

Spirit-christologies can avoid the tendency evident in pre-Chalcedonian Spirit-christologies to blend a Father theology and a Spirit theology to the exclusion of a Son theology—specifically, to apotheosize humanity apart from the particularity of Jesus.[46] All in fact affirm a Spirit-christology that at the same time preserves Catholic orthodoxy.

This is not necessarily the case with James Mackey, who combines Spirit-christology with a revisionist proposal for a binitarian theology. By demythologizing both the New Testament kerygmata and the development of trinitarian and christological dogma, he identifies the Spirit as the presence of God in Jesus and in the church. Because he interprets the trinitarian distinctions—i.e., hypostases—in a purely economic modality, he rules out speculation concerning pre-incarnational intra-trinitarian differentiation or existent persons in God.[47] His reconstructed binitarian theology then proffers the Spirit as God transcendent and immanent, as Father and as the definitive presence of God in Jesus, now present through Jesus in the eucharistic community.[48]

Similar in its revisionary impulse are the suggestions of Roger Haight, S.J. Here we are confronted with an either-or position:

> By a Spirit Christology I mean one that "explains" how God is present and active in Jesus, and thus Jesus' divinity, by using the biblical symbol of God as Spirit, and not the symbol Logos. It is the contention of those who propose such a thoroughgoing Spirit Christology that it expresses in a more adequate way for our time what has been expressed through a Logos Christology.[49]

Haight is convinced that this model more adequately deals with the major cultural and religious issues that modernity poses. Historical consciousness, existential awareness, and religious pluralism all require a new approach to christology that Logos christology is unable to deliver on. At the same time, he argues that the doctrinal norms of Nicaea and Chalcedon are honored and that Spirit christology is able to enact a "strict coherence between Christology, the life of grace, ecclesiology, and Christian spirituality."[50] As Haight is quite dependent on Geoffrey Lampe, to whom we shall come, comment will be reserved except for the following question, which has been the framework for our inquiry: Can the benefits so ascribed to Spirit-christology be reaped without opting for the either-or approach?[51]

Another alternative, this time more orthodox but still revisionary, is provided by Piet Schoonenberg, S.J. By examining his proposal in contrast to that of Coffey's, it will help us to evaluate the necessary inclusion of theological speculation concerning the immanent trinity, so crucial to Coffey's project, as a part of an overall pneumatological christology and to test whether such a dogmatic development is legitimate in the light of the absence of this notion in New Testament christologies and pneumatologies.

Since his book on christology (see Appendix for exposition), a major work in the new Dutch christology,[52] Schoonenberg has written two significant articles specifically on Spirit-christology and the doctrine of the trinity.[53] There, Schoonenberg attempts to retrieve the early tradition of Spirit-christology and utilize it to complement the traditional Logos-christology.[54] With this in mind, he compares the two christologies in search of answers to the following four questions:

1) What is the proportion between Christ's divinity and humanity in both christologies?

2) Is this proportion different because of their different point of departure?

3) How to conceive of the divine person in both christologies?

4) How both christologies are related if we consider the relationship between the Logos and the Spirit themselves?[55]

The questions bespeak Schoonenberg's interest in dialoguing with and reinterpreting the conciliar tradition—a interest partly informed by the uniquely Roman Catholic situation of both intense collegial and magisterial response to new christologies.[56] If the advantage of Spirit-christology is its stress upon the "full humanity" or "human personhood" of Jesus, its danger is its neglect or limited assertion of Christ's divinity—e.g., in adoptionism. Schoonenberg's initial response (specifically, to question #1) is to recall a Thomistic principle that greatly informed his work in christology.

> The creature, says St. Thomas, is from God and of God in its totality: "*secundum omne quod est, Dei est.*" . . . God's work and that of his creatures are not in inverse, but in direct, proportion.[57]

That is to say, one cannot set up an opposition between divinity and humanity as if the assertion of one negates or diminishes the other, a principle that is applicable to both Logos- and Spirit-christologies. In fact, if one acknowledges that the positional difference between the two christologies is the "descending" direction of the former and the "ascending" direction of the latter, it is clear that even in the New Testament ascending Spirit-christologies assume the form of descending christologies—e.g., the infancy narratives (on this point Coffey would disagree).

The question of starting points (question #2) further illumines the issue of proportionality in the christological predicates. Whether one starts with the divine Word incarnating itself in Jesus (descending christology) as an "enfleshed God" (*theos sarkotheis*) or the human Jesus filled with the Holy Spirit (ascending christology) as a "God-bearing human" (*anthropos theophoros*) one is obliged to attend to the lesser-emphasized christological predicate to respect the double *homoousion* of Chalcedon. Since the burden of proof is greater for the newer Spirit-christology vis-à-vis the inherited tradition, Schoonenberg proposes two qualifications for the presence of God in Jesus enunciated by Spirit-christology.

First, this presence is supreme, final, and definitive—that is, messianic and eschatological. Second, it is also reciprocal. Reverting to the neo-Chalcedonic doctrine of the enhypostasis of Jesus's human nature in the divine Logos, Schoonenberg inverts it, accepting the traditional meaning in only a qualified sense. Jesus' human nature is present in and sustained by the Word (qualified acceptance), which itself is enhypostatic or "in-person-ed" in the human person Jesus (the inversion).[58] Although originally an issue in Logos-christology, Schoonenberg sustains its applicability to Spirit-christology to the extent that the Spirit not only is present in Jesus and is thus communicated to his followers through his glorification, but the human

Jesus is embraced by the Spirit. Because the Spirit pervades Jesus, Schoonenberg posits an ontological and not simply a functional relationship between the Spirit and Jesus. Schoonenberg's proposal for Spirit-christology maintains the *vere Deus* of Chalcedon, with the intended orthodoxy that Jesus is not simply divine adverbially (because Jesus acts divinely) but "*is*" divine.[59]

The issue of divine personhood (question #3) even more directly broaches the question of the dogmatic relationship between Spirit-christology and the doctrine of the trinity. Schoonenberg, even as he does not advocate displacing Logos-christology with Spirit-christology, also does not intend to discount the traditional trinitarian distinctions but rather reinterpret them. However, he does raise a theological problem that has informed our own query in this study. It concerns the application of "personhood" or "hypostatic identity" to the divine Logos and Spirit as they apply to christological formulation and interpretation. Schoonenberg states it thus:

> How can the divine person of the Spirit mediate between the other divine person of the Logos and his humanity without interrrupting their hypostatic union? Or, if we prefer to see the [Spirit] Logos (*sic*) at work alongside of the Logos, do we avoid making Jesus' human nature a sort of condominium of two persons?[60]

Schoonenberg's answer to this dilemma betrays a strong revisionary proposal—namely, "Both Logos and Spirit-christology invite us to rethink the personhood of Logos and Spirit."[61]

Schoonenberg's solution can be gleaned both from the present article under review and from his earlier article: "Trinity—The Consummated Covenant: Theses on the Doctrine of the Trinitarian God."[62] Following his rule that reflection on the trinity must proceed from God's self-communication in history, Schoonenberg eschews any point of departure that does not proceed from the economic revelation of Christ and the Spirit (theses 1–4 of the article). The question at this point is not how speculatively to resolve the numeration of divine persons with respect to the oneness of God, but how to relate such numeration to the oneness of the human person of Jesus. Two principles figure in the solution. First, theologically, one cannot reduce such numeration of the divine persons or that of God's relation to Christ and the world to a strict mathematical equivalence. In support of this, Schoonenberg cites Edward Schillebeeckx's restatement of the scholastic maxim "*plura entia sed non plus esse*, more beings but not more being."[63] One might just as appropriately quote Basil of Caesarea:

> When the Lord taught us the doctrine of Father, Son, and Holy Spirit, He did not make arithmetic a part of this gift! . . . He blessed us with the knowledge given us by faith, by means of Holy Names. We are saved through faith; numbers have been invented as symbols of quantity. . . . Numbers cannot change the nature of anything, . . . But the Unapproachable One is beyond numbers, wisest sirs; imitate the reverence shown by the Hebrews of old to the unutterable name of God.[64]

Second, the only dialogical relationship in scripture is between Jesus and the Father, not between Jesus and the Logos/Son or the Spirit. On this basis, the only legitimate inference to the existence of persons in God is an inter-personal relation. The conclusion from these points is that numerical and dialogical distinctions should not be assumed back into the trinity apart from the mediation of salvation-history—i.e., one should start exclusively from the economic trinity.

On a more constructive level, Schoonenberg posits that since one cannot assume a dialogical relationship of the Logos and the Spirit to Jesus, one must infer that they "meet him (since his very origin) certainly as divine but not as divine *persons*."[65] Prior to the incarnation, the Logos and Spirit are active not as persons but as extensions of the person of God.[66] In the incarnation and glorification of Jesus Christ, the Logos and the Spirit respectively "become" persons. Specifically, the Logos assumes a dialogical relation to the Father vis-à-vis its enhypostatization in the human person Jesus and thus becomes the divine Son,[67] and the Spirit through its communication as the "Pentecostal Gift" and "the Paraclete" in the glorification (resurrection/ascension) of Christ likewise becomes a person, although in a less determined way than the Logos—a reflection of the New Testament's utilization of both personal and impersonal representations of the Spirit. The Spirit is person in the mode of God's being as the personal presence and outpouring of the Father through Christ's person, which sustains and sanctifies the church (thesis 35). In this role as the church's Paraclete, it faces the Father and the Son (thesis 28); thus, in a qualified sense it assumes a dialogical posture. [68]

Schoonenberg is aware that his rather innovative theory that distinguishes between a pre-incarnational and post-incarnational economy of God could be subject to criticism. However, he claims he is neither compromising the divinity of the Logos or the Spirit, nor assuming a modalistic procedure (thus also excluding Patripassianism—thesis 27). He does admit a trinity of persons only "after" the Christ event and bases this upon co-existence of mutability and immutability in the divine being.

> God is immutable and mutable, and both at the same time. He is immutable in his divine being and mutable in his self-communication, which coincides with his being. These statements are not contradictory if we notice that "becoming" and "change" in God are quite different from becoming and change in creatures. Here they indicate a transition from potency to act, but God proceeds from act to act.[69]

Therefore, God can change interiorly to become a trinity of persons, i.e., "having been one person and becoming three persons," without in that process (mediated through the history of salvation in which God becomes the God of the covenant) becoming "more God." Rather, in freedom, God becomes more "*our* God."[70]

Finally, Schoonenberg elucidates the relationship between the Logos and the Spirit (question #4) by distinguishing between the protological and eschatological dimensions of God's presence. The Logos in connection with the Old Testament conception of Wisdom is associated with the former—i.e., God's creating, founding, and protological outpouring, and the Spirit with God's prophetic, messianic, and eschatological power. They coincide in Christ and penetrate his entire human reality. In the Old Testament the Spirit was contained in God's Word or Wisdom; in and through the incarnate and risen Christ both the Spirit and God's Wisdom/Word are personally realized and released. The Spirit was the overflowing of the Logos's self-communication *in* Jesus during his earthly life and then overflowed *from* Jesus since his glorification, the gift received by the church.[71] In a dynamic affirmation of the Greek Fathers' doctrine of perichoresis, Schoonenberg can conclude with the following:

Hence they [Father, Logos and Spirit] give up their enclosedness and go out of
each other. So the Logos goes out of the Father and becomes Son at the incarnation.
And the Spirit, filling the Son together with the Logos, goes out from the Son at
his glorification and becomes the Water flowing into eternal life and the Paraclete
guiding to the full truth.[72]

Critique and Evaluation

The preceding pages provide a detailed exposition of Schoonenberg's position so
that we may delineate the variations in dogmatic construction between his work and
the work of David Coffey. Two points of agreement should be noted first. One is
methodological and the other is doctrinal. Schoonenberg and Coffey both agree that
theological reflection on the trinity should proceed from the world to God—i.e., from
the revelation of God in salvation-history to God in the divine being, and not vice
versa. Second, although they differ on the interpretation of enhypostatic christology—Coffey's enthusiasm for it reflects his more positive assessment of patristic
and scholastic categories—they do agree that the doctrine of the incarnation should
not be explicated in dualistic categories. As Coffey is wont to say, the divinity of
Christ is realized in his humanity, not alongside it.[73] However, despite these agree-
ments, it is also in relation to these points that a different path of doctrinal construction is pursued by our authors. To this we now turn.

The methodological move from salvation-history to the divine being, while
affirmed by each, also presents two very distinct possibilities for trinitarian theology.
Schoonenberg takes the Rahnerian axiom—*"The 'economic' Trinity is the
'immanent' Trinity and the 'immanent' Trinity is the 'economic' Trinity"*—and con-
verts each of the terms into an absolute identity. In effect, speculation concerning
the immanent trinity is excluded on the basis that it is precisely that, mere speculation. Schoonenberg contends that whether or not God is triune apart from salvation-
history can neither be denied nor presupposed. To answer more definitively would
demand insight into the relationship between God's immutability and self-determination.[74] More to the point of our concern in trinitarian doctrine and its implications
for Spirit-christology is his revision of the basis for the distinction of persons. Here
he rejects the notion that the persons are distinguished by their relations to each other
in favor of a purely economic accounting of this issue. Only in their relation to the
world in salvation-history can we determine their relation to each other, and this
only insofar as we restrict ourselves to christology and pneumatology as the extension of God's self-communication and presence to the world.[75]

The difference in perspective from Coffey may be framed in the form of a
question: Is the *relationis oppositio* necessary to preserve the integrity of trinitarian
distinctions, and what are the consequences for Spirit-christology? Indeed it is
Schoonenberg's contention that one may proceed directly from the biblical testimony
to the economic doctrine of the trinity without the intermediary of an immanent
trinitarian construction. Directly at odds with this is Coffey's assertion that a doctrine
of the economic trinity is the product of a reconception of the immanent trinity on
the basis of the biblical testimony. While this eventually led to his new model of
intra-trinitarian relations, it also was consistent with the scholastic tradition's em-

phasis that only the opposition of relation can distinguish the persons. In fact, it has been the argument thus far that from within the perspective of the traditional Latin paradigm, it is necessary that a properly pneumatological mission be developed that is consistent with a coherent doctrine of intra-trinitarian distinctions in order for Spirit-christology to be a viable theological construct.

To evaluate the different options presented by Schoonenberg and Coffey, we can test the viability of the connection made between the pneumatological dimensions of each aspect of their proposals. By this we intend to underscore the hypostatic distinctiveness of the pneumatological mission in relation to the christological one in each of their theologies, even as we assume the common ground of beginning one's constructive efforts from the perspective of salvation-history. Thus, for example, Schoonenberg maintains that according to a strictly economic model of the trinity the Holy Spirit is no longer "portrayed as a 'middle-person' within the hypostatic union of Logos and Jesus" (which was the case in Scheeben's neo-scholastic model of Spirit-christology) but as an "emanation, sanctifying power, and gift of self in God" (which Scheeben and those following him also affirmed).[76] This is argued on the clear evidence of the biblical witness, but also without any reference to any intra-trinitarian relations.

For David Coffey, on the other hand, the Holy Spirit as the mutual love of the Father and the Son can also appeal to the biblical witness, but only indirectly. By means of inference from the ascending christologies of the New Testament he develops an immanent construct of the trinity and only then proceeds to a formal doctrine of the economic trinity. For example, the unity of Jesus with the Father in ascending christology is predicated on descent of the Spirit upon him whom he receives from the Father, as the Gospel narratives attest. From this Coffey infers that the Holy Spirit is the mutual love of the Father and the Son in the immanent trinity. The next step is to return again to the divine economy and posit the Holy Spirit as the incarnate love of Jesus for the Father, leading to the post-Easter economy wherein in response to the risen Jesus' sacramental sending of the Spirit to the church the Father bestows this same Spirit upon believers. Herein lies the mutuality of the Spirit between the Father and the Son, now with the provision that this mutual love includes many sons and daughters as the fruit of the trinitarian economy. As was explicated in Chapter 4, the cogency of this model depends on its grounding in the immanent life of the trinity. The gratuitous giving of the Spirit in the economy of salvation between the Father and the Son—which works itself out as both a Spirit-christology and a pneumatological theology of grace—is possible only because within the trinity the Spirit is mutually bestowed by the first and second persons on each other.[77] Finally, we may note that in a critical comparison of Coffey's and Schoonenberg's positions that the unitive dimension of the Spirit's work—i.e., how the Holy Spirit unites believers to the Father and the Son—is emphasized by both authors, although more strongly by the former than by the latter. Schoonenberg considers giftedness and sanctification the more appropriate marks of the Spirit.

The manifestation of the Spirit in the economy of salvation is consistent with the pneumatological dimension of trinitarian doctrine in both their positions. Since the Spirit becomes "person" in the divine economy for Schoonenberg, he need only affirm that before the incarnation the Spirit is simply a "mode" of the divine presence.

In correspondence with his Spirit-christology, he explicates its role as the eschato-logical overflowing of divine presence from the glorified Jesus into the world who becomes "person" because it now faces the Father and the Son through its indwelling in the church. One might here concede that Schoonenberg escapes Coffey's criticism directed against the procession model that in reasoning from the experience of salvation one cannot simply reverse the sequence of persons from the order of their sending—i.e., from the Father through the Son in the Holy Spirit—to the order of their reception in the life of grace—i.e., in the Spirit through the Son to the Father. After all, Schoonenberg argues that the "inner-divine 'proceedings' (*processiones*) are known to us only as missions. The missions are the processions, and vice versa."[78] Without the necessity of an immanent construction of the trinitarian processions, the justification for a theological inference from the missions to the processions is not required. However, we may also query the adequacy of a strictly economic model of the trinity.

We begin first by noting the pattern of theological judgment that informed the christological and trinitarian thinking of the Church Fathers. Soteriological im-plications were certainly the most important factor in the great christological and trinitarian controversies. If the rule of beginning theological reflection from the perspective of salvation-history is rigorously adhered to, one may still proceed to speculation concerning the immanent trinity on the basis of one of two reasons. Either one's economic trinitarian model logically requires it, as is the case with a filioquist conception of the relationship between the Spirit and the Son; the second and third persons can be distinguished only on the basis of an intra-trinitarian relation. Or, in the absence of such a logical necessity—which I admit is the case with Schoonenberg's proposal—an immanent construction deepens our understand-ing and perception of what takes place in salvation history. Admittedly, this is not an absolutely necessary reason, but it is a sufficient one for theology's task of reflection on the church's proclamation of the full counsels of God (Acts 20:27).

From consideration of Schoonenberg's position we may now turn to Coffey to test his inclusion of an immanent doctrine of the trinity in light of his acceptance of salvation-history as a starting point for theological reflection. As already stated, Coffey accepts the implications of the traditional Latin trinitarian axioms that the divine persons can be distinguished only on an intra-trinitarian basis. Therefore, we would have to invoke the first of the reasons just mentioned—i.e., logical neces-sity—for the inclusion of an immanent construct in his trinitarian thinking. By virtue of the inferences that Coffey makes from salvation-history, indeed it is required that an immanent contruction should be proffered. So, for example, when Coffey infers from the New Testament that the conferral of the Holy Spirit is the basis of Jesus' union with the Father, it is necessary to explicate that pneumatological relationship in reference to the mutuality of the Father and the Son in the immanent trinity. Otherwise, this unitive dimension of the divine economy effected by the trinitarian missions is not grounded in the nature (both essential and personal) of the divine being itself. When we turn to the comparison of models—i.e., Coffey's with Schoonenberg's—it is our contention that this logical requirement cannot be raised to an absolute principle. This, however, does not rule out an application of the second reason mentioned above.

If it is possible to assert that the inclusion of an immanent construction of the trinity is necessary in one model of trinitarian theology (Coffey's) but not in another (Schoonenberg's), it is not because this important issue can simply be consigned to the realm of either dogmatic relativism or speculative incoherence. We are in fact dealing with theological truth of the highest order, and some sort of position should be marked out in the process. Our justification for this assertion is the relative value of the various models utilized to explicate the truth of the trinitarian mystery. At its most basic level, and one that does indeed set parameters for Christian dogmatics, the doctrine of the trinity requires that the three hypostases are both one (in the divine essence) and non-identical (in their personal differentiation). This is a necessary inference drawn from the Christian experience of salvation in which both Christ and the Spirit are referents in testimony to the revelation and redemption of God (the question of binitarianism will be addressed in a subsequent section). If, as is the case with Schoonenberg, a model of trinitarian predication is advanced that is strictly economic in character, it is not inconsistent to accept the differentiation of persons on the basis of distinct divine missions alone (especially where the reality of divine "persons" is realized in the divine economy). To that extent, Schoonenberg does not intend an attentuation of the trinitarian mystery. In his speculative agnosticism concerning the immanent trinity, he desires to underscore the reality of the divine persons and missions within the context of salvation history. This defense of Schoonenberg is meant only to justify his exclusion of an immanent trinitarian construct as a matter of logical necessity. However, in reference to a more comprehensive explication of the mystery of God revealed in salvation history he is to be criticized.

Schoonenberg's exclusively economic model of the trinity is founded on the premise that the "relations between Father, Son, and Spirit are accessible to us only in their relation to us."[79] True enough. However, does their relation to us reveal anythng about their relation to each other? In other words, do the christological and pneumatological missions reveal a hypostatic distinctiveness relative to the persons of the Son and the Spirit? Do, for example, Christ and the Spirit inhabit their economic missions in the same manner, and if not, does this reveal something about the divine being vis-à-vis the relation of the persons to one another? These questions implicitly raise doubts about Schoonenberg's restrictive trinitarian principle. They also point to the possibility of being able to extract a principle of trinitarian theology beyond the comparison and critique of these two particular trinitarian models.

In the chapters devoted to the development of Spirit-christology in the neo-scholastic tradition, we argued that the new model was possible only on the basis of a proper pneumatological mission, its clear distinction from the christological mission, and a trinitarian model with which these were consistent. This preserves the integrity of the trinitarian distinctions and thus ensures that poles in Spirit-christology, the filiological and the pneumatological, are essential for an understanding of the person of Christ. Through the Spirit of sonship, the humanity of Christ is assumed by the divine Son. Through the power of the Spirit, Jesus ministered and entered into his passion. By the same Spirit he was raised up, and now as the risen one he communicates divine life by the Spirit. All of this follows because in its hypostatic being the Spirit is not only gift and sanctifying power (as Schoonenberg argues) but also the communion or love of the divine persons for one another (Coffey's point). In other words, the distinctiveness of the Spirit's economy is predicated on the distinctiveness of the Spirit's hypostatic relation to the other persons in the trinity.

If the above argument is correct—namely, that the role of the Spirit in christology is determined by the unique relation of the Spirit to the Father and the Son—then clearly the warrant for speculation on the intra-trinitarian relations is justified. To apply this principle in criticism of Schoonenberg and in support of Coffey, we are arguing the following points. First, while accepting that in Schoonenberg's strict economic trinitarianism it is not logically required that one proceed to an immanent construction of the trinity, it is theologically fruitful to consider such a move when it is merited by understanding gained at the level of the temporal missions in the work of the divine economy. So, for example, in Coffey's constructive work the logic of the scholastic construct with which he is working requires this step; nevertheless, it also raises a dimension of the strictly temporal missions alone, which provokes reconsideration of Schoonenberg's restriction. This concerns what I have described as the manner in which the Holy Spirit inhabits his mission in the work of salvation.

Second, the "properly" distinctive aspects of the *ad extra* missions do in fact distinguish the work of one person from another—specifically, the work of the Son from that of the Spirit. Since the work of God is one, this would also require that the relations of the persons in the divine economy are also significant. For example, the filiological relationship of Jesus to the Father in salvation-history is decisive for understanding the work of the Spirit, which then incorporates a filiological dimension—e.g., as the Spirit of sonship—and also for soteriology proper, in which those who receive grace are adopted as sons and daughters in Christ (*filii in Filio*). However, and this is the major point, these three subjects (the Son, the Spirit, and believers) each inhabit this filiological dimension differently—e.g., by nature (the Son), inspiration (the Spirit), or adoption (believers).

Third, the economic attributes assigned to the Holy Spirit by Schoonenberg—i.e., the Holy Spirit as gift and sanctifying power—may also yield to a greater attribute that is distinctive to the Holy Spirit—namely the Holy Spirit as the mutual love of the Father and the Son. For example, in the divine economy in which incarnate and adoptive filiation are descriptive of the christological and anthropological dimensions of redemption respectively, it seems appropriate to explicate the pneumatological dimension in terms of the divine love. The incarnation of the Son and the adoption of sons and daughters in the Son implicate the Holy Spirit as the agent of both events, and that not merely in terms of the Holy Spirit as a "middle-person" between the Logos and Jesus or between the risen Christ and believers (against which Schoonenberg argues), but as the hypostatic dynamic—i.e., literally the spiration, or breathing-forth, of the more comprehensive relationship between the Father and the Son that is the theological basis of the relationship between God and creation. In other words, the pneumatological dimension of the divine being revealed in creation and redemption is itself a relational distinction when considered in reference to the relationship that obtains between the Father and the Son in the immanent trinity and between God and creation when considered in the *ad extra* economic order. To restrict that dimension to the economic order is to reduce creaturely appreciation of the divine work even in that order (with all the attendent implications for worship) of the communion that obtains between the creature and God as a result of the reception of grace. The filiological relation of the believer (predicated on the grace of adoption) to God in Christ bespeaks a pneumatological agent in whom a further hypostatic relation is implicated. Furthermore, if this hypostatic relation is properly explicated as the mutual love between God and Christ, it also follows that this implicates the same relation between the Father and the Son in the divine being itself, considering the inclusion by redemption of the created order in that relation through adoptive grace, wherein that inclusion also effects a discrete relation to each of the persons.

Finally, we focus our conclusions on the issue of Spirit-christology. The discussion thus far has reflected both the economic and immanent orders of the trinitarian relations. In fact, it has been argued in previous chapters that Spirit-christology is a dogmatic construction that is descriptive of the convergence between christology and pneumatology in the divine economy. Schoonenberg's own proposal in this area restricts itself to this context, whereas Coffey's does not for the reasons elucidated above. It is our conclusion that once it is deemed appropriate to extend our reflection on the divine missions into the immanent trinity and its *ad intra* relations on the basis of the creature's insight into and appreciation of the divine being resulting from such a move, we also suggest that the only dogmatic christological construction that fully explicates this position is one that advances a Spirit-christology. Only when the filiological and pneumatological dimensions of christology are related to each other have we done justice to the doctrine of God that is substantially and not just nominally trinitarian, as well as to soteriology, wherein we understand that the divine self-communication effects the union of the creature with God in a reception of grace that bears witness to Christ in the Spirit and to the Spirit as resting upon and sent by the risen one. What this means in reference to the filiological and pneumatological dimensions of Spirit-christology is the subject of the next two sections.

Spirit-christologies: Pre- and Post-Chalcedonian

In this section I shall examine Spirit-christology as a dogmatic construct in antiquity and as a contemporary theological project with a view toward a non-Chalcedonian understanding of the predication of divinity in the person of Christ. As our study has demonstrated, it is in Spirit-christology that the most pressing problems concerning the relationship between Christ and the Spirit are concentrated. Focusing on models of Spirit-christology, ancient and modern, will help us note and evaluate the utilization of "Spirit" for christological formulation and interpretation, as well as address the issue raised by Dunn that the divinity of the incarnate Christ is a function of the Holy Spirit. According to the contemporary model developed dogmatically by Geoffrey Lampe, a non-hypostatic pneumatology displaces a filiological predication of divinity in Christ. Instead of the pre-existent divine Logos or Son becoming flesh in Jesus Christ and that being the foundation for the Christian confession of his divinity, the Spirit is understood as that which inspires Jesus to act divinely. By comparing this proposal with David Coffey's, we hope to evaluate more clearly the relationship between the filiological and pneumatological aspects of christology. The review of the pre-Chalcedonian patristic model will provide perspective for our examination of the innovation represented by the contemporary model and its comparison with the more traditional (relative to this revision) suggestions of Coffey.

Pre-Chalcedonian Spirit-christologies

Among the Spirit-christologies prevalent in antiquity before the dominance of Logos-christologies and the conciliar definition of Chalcedon (451), there were both heterodox and orthodox variations. Jean Daniélou has distinguished between these two characterizations among predominantly Jewish-Christian groups. He characterizes as heterodox the christology of the Ebionites, who although acknowledging Christ as prophet or Messiah did not confess him as Son of God, while the orthodox include the Jerusalem community—i.e., the Nazarenes, and other Jewish Christians and even Gentile Christians whose thought forms were borrowed from Judaism.[80] If we compare their respective uses of Spirit-christology, we begin to see the different forms that Spirit-christology has taken. This will also help us evaluate the import of the contemporary utilization of Spirit-christology. As an introduction to the issues that have surfaced in the modern debate, here I will limit myself to delineating the distinction in Spirit-christologies between the more orthodox variety and the heterodox Ebionites.

Ebionite christology characterized the person of Jesus by a number of titles similar to those used in other primitive christologies in the New Testament, such as Son of Man, the Righteous One, the True Prophet, but that were not developed by early Catholicism or the later Orthodoxy.[81] It was a clearly adoptionist christology, with Jesus' baptism as the beginning of his consecration to the messianic office. This elevation of Jesus is due to the agency of the Holy Spirit, who descended upon him and called him to divine sonship in a strictly human sense (psilanthropism). In contrast to the canonical tradition of the primitive church, there is no soteriological interpretation of Jesus' death. Rather, soteriology is focused on two other dimensions of their christological confession. First, their apocalyptic-eschatological expectation of Jesus as the coming Son of Man possessed a distinctly millenarian flavor. Here, adoptionist Spirit-christology merges with an Angel-christology in which Jesus is identified with a supernatural angelic being who fulfills the millenarian expectation.

Second, and even more soteriologically determinative, is the christology of Jesus as the prophetic Messiah after the pattern of Moses (Deut. 18: 15-22). It was the Ebionites' strong conviction that the "True Prophet" had arrived in the person of Jesus. In this office Jesus both purifies and fulfills the Mosaic covenant delivered at Sinai. Purification required the abolition of the sacrificial cult, the condemnation of the Israelite monarchy, and the depreciation of prophecy. Fulfillment entailed the intensification of food laws and purity regulations and the high valuation of baptismal practice and poverty.[82] In both cases, the prophetic office is a fruit of the divine Spirit (*theion pneuma*) of true prophecy who is active throughout Jewish salvation-history. Jesus figures as the last in a line of bearers of the Spirit or Shekinah (divine presence), following the biblical figures of Adam, Enoch, Noah, Abraham, Isaac, Jacob, and Moses. The teaching of this prophetic

Spirit culminates in Jesus, its final revelation, and can even be understood as incarnate to the extent that the teaching has been completely realized in the prophetic ministry of Jesus. Thus, Jesus is the last pillar of revelation; he is the Messiah and bearer of the divine will and is witness to the monarchy of God (*monarchia tou theou*). It is interesting to note that this Ebionite Spirit-christology is anti-Gnostic in that it does not supersede prior revelation, but confirms it while also delimiting any pneumatic movement in congregational life. Pneumatic activity was limited to the bearers of divine revelation; Ebionite Christian life consisted of halakhic observance, not pneumatic experience.[83]

The Ebionites were not the only Jewish-Christians to utilize Spirit-christology. Orthodox Jewish-Christians and even Gentile-Christians of the emerging Catholic Church employed spirit language to confess Jesus Christ. Orthodox Jewish-Christians, however, were similar to the Ebionites in their utilization of angelology for christological formulation. Both Ebionites and Orthodox Jewish-Christians identified angels—e.g., Michael or Gabriel—with the Word or the Spirit, where both express a divine status. This can be found in Old Testament Pseudepigraphia (*II Enoch, Ascension of Isaiah*), New Testament Apocrypha (*Gospel of Peter, Gospel of the Hebrews*), and the Apostolic Fathers (*The Didache, The Shepherd of Hermas*).[84]

A major difference, however, between the two groups of Jewish-Christians concerns their understanding of the present work of the Spirit. The Ebionite Spirit-christology of inspiration, in which the bearers of the Spirit are likewise the bearers of divine revelation in the exclusive sense—i.e., the activity of the prophetic spirit does not continue in the Christian community beyond Jesus—is contrasted with the present reality of the Spirit in the life of the church. Even in the *Didache* where itinerant charismatic apostles and prophets are subjected to at least partial control by local churches, the activity of the Spirit is still identified with the reality of Christ (11:7—12:5).[85] Also, in contrast to the Ebionites, most of the Apostolic fathers acknowledge Jesus' birth through Mary and the Holy Spirit (Ignatius—*Letter to the Ephesians* 18:2[86] and Justin Martyr—*First Apology*, ch. 33).[87] More important, spirit is identified as the mode of Christ's pre-existence (Clement—*Second Letter to the Corinthians* 9:5)[88] or as the divine element of Christ in the incarnation. The latter concept is explicit in the *Shepherd of Hermas*. In his Fifth Similitude (6:5–7) Hermas depicts the mode of incarnation as a union of flesh with the pre-existent Spirit.

> The holy, pre-existent Spirit, that created every creature, God made to dwell in flesh, which He chose (Similitude V: ch. 6).

However, the precise interpretation of this mode of confessing the divinity in Christ through the use of spirit language is sufficiently ambigous to merit further reflection.

J.N.D. Kelly interprets the passage as an instance of early "Spirit-christology," the definition of which he gives:

> By this is meant the view that in the historical Jesus Christ the pre-existent Son of God, Who is divine spirit, united Himself with human nature.[89]

Indeed, this definition may be described as an ontological utilization of Spirit in christology. The Spirit is the pre-existent Christ, which represents the divinity in the later christological equation *vere Deus, vere homo*. Another commentator on Hermas introduces an alternative interpretation of this Spirit-christology. Lage Pernveden, in disagreement with Kelly, contends that the relationship between Spirit and Son of God in Hermas is not ontological, but purely soteriological. It is not a question of the consubstantial nature of the Son of God, but of the activity of the Spirit vis-à-vis "the role of the Son of God in the economy of salvation."[90] In other words, the pneumatic dimension of christological language must be understood in reference to Christ's saving work rather than in terms of the person of Christ. In the older dogmatic categories, the work of Christ (soteriology) and not the person of Christ (christology) is the proper place for pneumatological attribution. It is also similar to the distinction suggested by Coffey when he differentiates between the ontological and functional predication of divinity in Christ in the context of his understanding of the development of doctrine.

Clearly, it is difficult to classify Hermas in any of these categories, or for that matter most pre-conciliar christologies—i.e., before Nicaea and Chalcedon. Much of the terminology utilized by the patristic church to explicate Jesus' relationship to God was still in the process of formation, and one should therefore not read later meanings back into earlier usage. Leaving this aside, we may pursue at least one issue that is germane to our discussion—namely, the possibilities that these early Spirit-christologies raise for contemporary christological interpretation.

The difference between the interpretations of Kelly and Pernveden are significant in highlighting the various directions along which a Spirit-christology might proceed. Spirit-christology may connote a dogmatic construction in which "Spirit" accounts for the *vere Deus* in the traditional Chalcedonian definition, with all the attendant problems—and this cannot be ignored—of adoptionism and modalism. Spirit-christology may also allow for the subject of divinity of Christ to be identified on other grounds—e.g., Logos or Word. This may still leave room for an intrinsic pneumatological dimension in christology, but would leave intact traditional trinitarian and christological formulations. Therefore, the revisionary impulse in dogmatic construction is greater in the former than in the latter.

The progress of Spirit-christology in the ancient church was short-lived. True, there are traces in Tertullian (*On The Flesh of Christ*, chs. 18–19;[91] *The Prescription Against Heretics*, ch. 13),[92] Hippolytus (*Against the Heresy of One Noetus*, chs. 4, 17),[93] and Cyprian (*That Idols Are Not Gods*, ch. 11), with the latter being the closest to the Spirit-christology of Hermas.[94] However, the dominance of Logos-christologies (both Antiochene *Logos-anthropos* and Alexandrine *Logos-sarx*) was soon unquestioned, even if pneumatology was by no means absent as in the more developed pneumatologies of the Cappadocians, who argued explicitly for the divinity and unique hypostatic identity of the Holy Spirit. For the moment, we simply note that these early developments can result in a variety of pneumatological modalities. In summary, different dogmatic options presented by the various pneumatic christologies of the pre-conciliar church could include: 1) Jesus as the bearer of the prophetic spirit of revelation—a christology of pneumatic inspiration; 2) the Spirit as the subject of divinity in the manifestation of the Son of God in the flesh—a christology of pneumatic incarnation; and 3) the Spirit as the medium for incarnation and salvation—a christology of pneumatic communication. In light of these perspectives, I shall now turn to the contemporary situation.

A Modern Post-Chalcedonian Spirit-christology

Each of the three types of pneumatic christologies have appeared in one form or the other in the works of contemporary christologists. Some are explicitly revisionary; others work within the categories of orthodox christology as do the models that emerge out of the neo-scholastic tradition, even if they stretch the limits of interpretation or seek alternative roots of construction without negating the basic conciliar norms. A programmatic example of the former is the work of Anglican theologian Geoffrey Lampe, the late Regius Professor of Divinity at the University of Cambridge. Both his article "The Holy Spirit and the Person of Christ"[95] and his book *God as Spirit*[96] address the variety of issues raised by Spirit-christologies. To that extent, a summary accounting and identification of those issues along with Lampe's recommendations are relevant for our purposes and can serve as a comparative model by which to evaluate Dunn's summation of the New Testament relationship between the Holy Spirit and the divinity of the incarnate Christ.[97]

Lampe's work is an example of a cogent proposal to reconsider traditional christology from a thoroughgoing pneumatological perspective. It involves, therefore, both a critique of Logos incarnation christology and a recovery of Spirit-christology, with the latter answering problems left unresolved by the former. He states these problems as follows. First, Logos-christology has a tendency to attenuate the two terms of Chalcedon, *vere Deus, vere homo*. On the one hand, Lampe claims that the construct of Logos-Son implies an inevitable subordinationism in which Christ does not mediate God in direct relation to humanity but is a distinct being who acts as God's agent. On the other hand, since the Logos-Son is the subject of Christ's actions, one must question whether the human nature assumed in the hypostatic union is indeed a full human personality.[98] The converse of this for Lampe is that the revelation of God in Jesus Christ requires a recognition of the direct presence of God in the human life of Jesus without the displacement of his humanity by an existent divine mediator. In other words, according to Lampe's evaluation of Logos-christology, the hypostatization of the Logos-Son as mediator detracts from both the divine revelation in Christ and the full humanity of Jesus.

Lampe is not unsympathetic to the efforts of the Fathers to ensure orthodoxy. However, the developments in orthodox christology in his view did involve a reductionism relative to the two christological terms. Lampe traces this to the transfer of the image of "Son of God" from the historical figure of Jesus to the construct, Logos-Son—i.e., "the pre-existent Logos as the Second Person of the Godhead." This tendency toward hypostatization, a move considerably beyond the flexibility of usage in pre-conciliar christology (as noted above), was due in part to three concerns of orthodox christology in response to pre-conciliar and heterodox christologies. First, orthodox christology tried to preserve the difference between Jesus and other humans; Jesus could not be considered a "mere man" (the psilanthropist danger). Second, the orthodox fear of patripassianism led to the necessity of positing the Logos as an existent mediator. Third, the earlier Spirit-christology could not maintain the difference between God-in-Christ and God-in-Christ's-people (or the presence of divine grace in the church).[99] However, the consequences in countering these concerns were equally negative.

The position of christological uniqueness—i.e., that there is a difference in kind, not just in degree, between Jesus and other humans—is counterproductive for soteriology. Lampe considers such uniqueness incompatible with the divine calling for all men and women to be conformed to the image of God revealed in Christ if, in fact, Christ is ontologically dissimilar from us. Further, the concern to avoid patripassianism entailed a restrictive limitation in the divine nature. Lampe argues that the Logos-Son as an existent mediator that distinguishes "God-in-himself" from "God-in-Christ" implicitly means that the divine self cannot be directly involved in creation, redemption, and human history. Finally, the necessary distinction between the predication of divinity in Christ and the Christian experience of the *Christus praesens* as divine Spirit led to speculative abstractions, which always attend any absolute affirmation of hypostatic distinctions in the Godhead, an abstractionism that Lampe contends is far removed from biblical theology.[100]

If the *bête noire* for Lampe is hypostatization, which he interprets as a concession to the cosmological Hellenization of early christological titles, then the solution is to return to the original intent of pre-Chalcedonian christological formulation. Lampe proffers a descriptive metaphor for the flexible usage of such titles as "Word," "Wisdom," and "Spirit" in early christologies. Commenting on their usage in the Old Testament and inter-testamental literature, he describes them as "bridge terms." Their utilization is "quasi-poetical" in nature rather than speculative and metaphysical. They are "expressive of God's relationship to men," and relate the "experience of encounter with God."[101] "Spirit," Lampe then argues, should be the least subject to hypostatization and the consequent tendency to devalue a relational ontology in favor of a static metaphysics of substance. As a christological subject it neither describes the structure of deity nor denotes a hypostatically existent mediator between God and world.[102] Understood only as a relational and functional term, Spirit avoids the excesses of Logos-christology—namely, the minimization of assumed humanity in the hypostatic union (the danger of Alexandrine *Logos-sarx* christology) and the radical distinction between the divine Word and human person of Jesus (the danger of Antiochene *Logos-anthropos* christology).[103]

Lampe's own proposal is constructed around the following affirmation:

> . . . a full recognition that Jesus was genuinely a man, and an equally full acknowledgement that his deeds and words were done and said divinely: that his Person mediates true God to man.[104]

The subject of christological formulation is not a divine hypostasis of Word, Wisdom, or Spirit but the human Jesus who is God adverbially: adverbial in contrast to substantive (as in orthodox christology) and adjectival (as in deism or unitarianism— e.g., Jesus acts in a God-*like* way) formulations of divinity in Christ. Adverbial predication recognizes that by "the mutual interaction of the Spirit's influence and the free response of the human spirit" there is a unity of will and operation between Jesus and God so that he can be said to speak and act "divinely." Lampe claims that this understanding of unity still holds to the Chalcedon's "without separation and without confusion," especially through utilization of the Cyrilline notion of "one theandric energy" operating in Jesus.[105]

Lampe describes this Spirit-christology as a christology of inspiration, indwelling, and possession. Rather than the incarnation of an existent divine mediator, it is the personal union of the human Jesus with God as Spirit—i.e., God in personal and active outreach to the world. In fact, through the Spirit indwelling, inspiring, and possessing Jesus, there is a more genuine incarnation of God in Jesus where God is truly God and the human Jesus is authentically human. He also avoids the danger of adoptionism, for the Spirit does not pertain to a certain point in Jesus' life—e.g., at his baptism—and is not dependent on his moral or spiritual perfection. Rather, the Spirit pervades the whole of his life, excludes human merit, and is the efficacious reality of God's prevenient grace.[106] It obviates, in Lampe's view, orthodox christology's "two-way projection of the Jesus of the Gospels onto a pre-existent Logos-Son, and of the pre-existent Jesus-Logos-Son onto the historical figure of the New Testament records."[107] It also enhances the notion of Christ as the "fount of grace," for the Spirit present in him is now present to believers in their experience of salvation through the Christ-Spirit.

Even though Lampe claims that Spirit-christology still maintains the uniqueness of Christ and does not lead to christological supersessionism—i.e., that another Christ will come who will surpass Jesus—his program is avowedly revisionary on at least three important issues. First, he completely dispenses with hypostatic distinctions within the triunity of God. There are no hypostases (or persons) distinct from the Father who function as divine mediators. God as Spirit present in Jesus and now to believers as the Christ-Spirit is an exercise in monopersonal theism.[108] Although there is a triadic dimension still present, his own confession is not trinitarian in the traditional sense, as the following illustrates:

> I believe in the Divinity of our Lord and Saviour Jesus Christ, in the sense that the same one God, the Creator and Saviour Spirit, revealed himself and acted decisively for us in Jesus. I believe in the Divinity of the Holy Ghost, in the sense that the same one God, the Creator and Savior Spirit, is here and now not far from every one of us; for in him we live and move, in him we have our being, in us, if we consent to know and trust him, he will create the Christlike harvest: love, joy, peace, patience, kindness, goodness, fidelity, gentleness, and self-control.[109]

Second, although he posits a Spirit-christology, Lampe is insistent that he does not mean Spirit as a third hypostatic identity in the Godhead. Spirit is representative of God active and involved in creation and redemption. Therefore, there is no distinction between the *Christus praesens* and the Holy Spirit. They are both expressive of the same experience; thus his choice of the term Christ-Spirit. It is not the agency of the risen Jesus that constitutes the *Chrisus praesens*, but rather the Spirit who was present decisively in Jesus and is now present to the faith and hope of believers.

Finally, Lampe has engaged in a thorough demythologization of all the christological loci. The pre-existent Christ, the post-existent Christ, the incarnation, resurrection, ascension, session, and parousia all express not an ontological affirmation of the person of the God-human in either heaven or on earth, but the activity of God as Spirit who will bring human creation to its completion in the endless progress and unceasing ascent of a transfigured human community.[110] Incidentally, a liturgical consequence of this revision is that prayer should be directed not "to Christ" but to God "through Christ."[111]

Three questions may be addressed to Lampe, especially in reference to his christology's being a systematic expression of Dunn's point that the divinity of Christ is a function of the Holy Spirit. First, is his negation of hypostatic distinction warranted? Even he admits that the New Testament does distinguish between the risen Christ and the Holy Spirit, and that this, combined with the move toward hypostatization, contributed toward trinitarian speculation.[112] Second, is his interpretation of Spirit as God immanent an adequate accounting of the biblical notion of Spirit? Although Lampe is willing to posit a triadic structure to the divine revelation—e.g., he states, "God in his transcendence (or the being of God) being distinguished from God 'reaching out towards' and addressing (or God's Word) and from God operating immanently, inspiring and possessing (or God's Spirit)"— he more often opts for the distinction "between God as transcendent Spirit and God as immanent Spirit."[113] This basic contrast between transcendence and immanence or between "God beyond and in relation to the world," to use Cyril C. Richardson's terminology,[114] must be examined as to whether it is adequate for a trinitarian (or binitarian?) doctrine of God. Finally, the question of whether Christ or the Christ-event is or is not confined to Jesus, and the resolution of this question by Spirit-christology, is both an old and a new christological issue and a favorite for revisionists for a number of reasons, not the least of which is the concern for inter-religious dialogue.[115]

For the moment we can simply note how this contemporary Spirit-christology takes up the different dimensions of pneumatic christology present in the ancient church. Pneumatic inspiration, incarnation, and communication all inform what we can designate as Lampe's post-Chalcedonian christology. In contrast to ancient Spirit-christologies, Lampe is on this side of the conciliar dogmatic norms. Thus, his return to the fluidity of Spirit-christology without hypostatization is based on the following two critical judgments on his part. First, although sympathetic to the developments in orthodox christology, he believes that their formulations are internally incoherent and speculatively unwarranted. Second, he maintains that theologically they lead to a diminution of the conciliar confessions—e.g., whether in fact the *vere Deus* and *vere homo* are upheld with integrity. These are both serious questions that neatly set the frame of dogmatic inquiry for this section.

Evaluation and Critique

The review of ancient and modern Spirit-christologies demonstrates alternative dogmatic constructions for this particular christological model. The key issue resolved by the christological and trinitarian debates of the ancient church, and now the subject of revision by Geoffrey Lampe, concerns the hypostatic identities of the Son and the Spirit. Whether or not hypostatization of the Son and Spirit is still a necessary hermeneutical development of the triadic testimony of the New Testament is called into question by Lampe precisely on the grounds that its maintenance obscures the intent of the Nicene and Chalcedonian conciliar definitions. Here the disagreement with Coffey is obvious. It focuses on the legitimacy of the move from functional to ontological predication of divinity in Christ and the Spirit. As reviewed in the previous chapter, Coffey upholds this change as the basis for his theory of doctrinal development. How does one adjudicate between these two approaches, and what is its bearing on the viability of Spirit-christology?

Our first comment is simply an observation with respect to Lampe's revision. By a return to functional predication in the Christ-event, Lampe effectively removes any reason to maintain a distinction between Logos and Spirit. Both are "bridge terms" that bespeak God's active relation to creation. Whichever term is utilized, the important thing is that Jesus' relationship to God as son is understood in reference to the presence of God incarnate in Jesus, with presence conceptualized not as an existent person—e.g., the divine Son—but as God's reaching out to the world. Considering that the power and presence of God have traditionally been associated with the Holy Spirit, Spirit-christology is a more suggestive model for this interpretation than the heavily weighted Logos-christology. If there is a reason to maintain a distinction between Son and Spirit, it is only to distinguish the man Jesus who prays to God as "Abba" and the active presence of God in him. In agreement with Dunn, Lampe could say that the adverbial predication of divinity in Jesus ("Jesus acts divinely") is a function of the Holy Spirit in him. The question, then, in response to this revision, with a view to Coffey's position and that of more traditional christology, is the following: What is gained by preferring a more ontological predication of divinity, with its trinitarian correlate that the Son and the Spirit are distinct subsisting relations or hypostases?

To answer this question, we begin with an examination of Spirit-christology as a theological and dogmatic construct. As a christological model, it attempts to include within its scope of reflection on the person of Jesus Christ direct reference to the constructive import of pneumatology. This is the case with the models proffered by both Lampe and Coffey. The inclusion of the Holy Spirit does not mean for either model that at the level of the divine economy the Holy Spirit is another name for Jesus Christ. On the contrary, without even proceeding to the question of the legitimacy of hypostatization relative to the subjects of the divine missions—i.e., the Son and the Spirit—it is the Holy Spirit precisely as distinct from Jesus Christ who is considered according to the model. This may or may not include reference to the Son. Therefore, initially we are still dealing with a distinction that at the very least is pertinent to the realm of the divine economy. Jesus Christ is who he is because of his relation to the Spirit, not his identity with it.

A Spirit-christology such as the one suggested by Geoffrey Lampe proceeds from the theological certainty that the man Jesus reveals God through the power of the Spirit. The Christian's experience of grace has as its subject the Christ-Spirit (to use Lampe's terminology), meaning that the divine presence is in the modality of Spirit and has about it a Christ-character pointing to the present formation of Christlikeness within the believer and to the memory of the Christ-event in the past. Both the contemporaneousness of "Christ in us" and the kerygmatic memory of "Christ for us" are mediated by the reality of Jesus' revelation of God—and to this extent the Spirit is distinct from Jesus—but it need not presume that the historical Jesus is now corporeally risen and is present to believers in a manner distinct from the Spirit. All that Jesus was in terms of his character and his unique relationship to God is now present in the Spirit who was present in him.

There are two issues that this explication of Lampe's position raises. First, are the *Christus praesens* and the *Spiritus praesens* identical? That issue will be the subject of our inquiry in the next section. Second, since the Spirit is the link between the memory of Jesus and the contemporary efficacy of grace, is a non-hypostatic pneumatology the proper formulation for christology and the confession of Christ's divinity? It should be noted that Lampe accords a similar non-hypostatic status to the "Son" and "Logos" as well, although he prefers spirit language for christological conceptualization. It is this preference that underlies the distinction that does exist between the Spirit and Jesus, although not between the "Spirit in us" and "Christ in us." By way of contrast, we are reminded that this is not the case with Coffey's more traditional model of Spirit-christology. In his explication of the model, the preservation of hypostatic differentiation in the Godhead does mean that the Spirit is distinct from Christ without implying the same for the Son, since the latter is the hypostatic subject of the incarnation.

The key issue is to inquire into the meaning of hypostatization, and in accord with the methodology utilized in the previous section, to evaluate whether its maintenance in trinitarian formulation enhances theology's understanding of the mystery of God in Christ. Lampe's complaint is that hypostatization objectifies and reifies "the human experience of being touched and moved by God"[116] in favor of the metaphysical passion to analytically describe "the structure of deity itself" or to posit "existent mediators between God and the world."[117] In both cases, he argues, the Christian witness to the revelation and presence of God made known in Jesus and now experienced in the Spirit is compromised. However, is this necessarily the case when it comes to the process of so-called "hypostatization"?

In neo-scholastic theology and in the broader church tradition hypostasis is a relational distinction in the divine being whether that relation is predicated on opposition (the Latin tradition) or on origin (the Greek tradition). When we transfer this notion to the divine economy and especially to an orientation that evokes the construct of salvation-history (as Vatican II did for Catholicism), there would have to exist a correlation between the three divine hypostases and three distinct agents of God's salvific work. For example, in the ministry of Jesus beginning with the baptismal narrative the Father sends Jesus by both a speech-act ("You are my beloved Son . . . ," Mk. 1:11) and a pneumatic anointing ("the Spirit descending on him like a dove," Mk. 1:10). Here the triadic testimony can be explicated by reference to three distinct agents—i.e., the Father who sends, Jesus who obeys ("to fulfill all righteousness," Matt. 3:15), and the Spirit who leads and empowers (Lk. 4:1, 14). The question before us is whether this filial relation of the human Jesus to God also bespeaks a similar relation in the divine being itself (the only legitimate means in the Latin tradition to distinguish the persons) that is distinct from Jesus' relation to the Spirit with whom he is anointed.

If we apply the test as to whether hypostatization increases understanding of the divine and salvific mysteries, as contrasted to decreasing it, the context for our answer should lie here in the evangelical narrative that witnesses to the divine economy. The speech-act of the Father is certainly associated with, and would even seem to be the basis for, the descent of the Spirit upon Jesus. However, the relationship expressed in the act, while pneumatologically confirmed, is not confined to pneumatology. This is not to say that any of the evangelists mean what the later church meant when it employed filial language to define the relationship between Jesus and God. There must be ample room for doctrinal development, as Coffey himself argues. We can assert, nevertheless, that the filiological relation is distinct from the pneumatological one, even at this stage of non-hypostasized (Lampe's language) or functional (Coffey's language) predication of divinity in Christ. At the very least, this sharply reduces the explanatory regime of pneumatology within Lampe's version of Spirit-christology. While there is a relationship between the Spirit and Jesus' status as the "beloved Son," the latter is not predicated on the pneumatic anointing but on the direct communication of the Father to the Son he anoints. What, then, do we make of Dunn's observation that in the New Testament the divinity of the incarnate Christ is a function of the Holy Spirit?

At the stage of New Testament theology concerning which Dunn remarks, we agree with all parties—i.e., Dunn, Lampe, and Coffey—that the relationship of Jesus to God is understood in a functional or salvation-historical perspective. The issue for dogmatic christology is whether a constructive model that may be developed out of this perspective is limited to the same form of predication. Thus, for example, Dunn's statement may lead down either of the roads that Lampe or Coffey pursues. There is an exclusively functional relationship between Jesus' divinity and the Spirit in Lampe's model, and an at least functional relationship in Coffey's—e.g., the Spirit creates, sanctifies, and unites Jesus' humanity to the divine Son. In the development that Coffey requires and Lampe prohibits, this functional relationship is explicated further to posit hypostatic relations in God as the subjects of this redemptive schema. To justify this development, one must be able to answer cautions expressed by Lampe—namely, the tendency of hypostatization to obscure the humanity of Jesus and the intervention of existent mediators between God and creation.

The traditional response by all the Catholic theologians we have reviewed, from traditional neo-scholastics to Coffey, would have no problem answering Lampe's query. First, the notion of "existent mediator" does not make any sense for traditional Latin trinitarianism, because the divine persons as subsisting relations in God are not something between God and the world but the divine being itself revealed and communicated in revelation. Lampe's position that the *vere Deus* or the *vere homo* is compromised by speech about Christ's pre- or post-existence limits the notion of the incarnation—now reinterpreted as pneumatic inspiration—to a Christ-ideal that has been pneumatized as impersonal Spirit. Both comments deserve explanation.

It may be objected that the traditional Latin model of trinitarian relations as a product of the process of hypostasization must be examined in light of the doctrinal development reviewed by Lampe and that led in his mind to the attentuation of the pneumatological dimension of the faith. I do not propose to examine the course of doctrinal development. However, the dogmatic implications of both positions—i.e., Lampe's and Coffey's—require assessment. It is my argument in favor of Coffey's position that this issue cannot be separated from the second problem suggested by Lampe. The issue of christological integrity, which entails even for Lampe an affirmation of Chalcedon's fourfold negation—"without confusion, without mixture, without separation, without division"—is the basis for the process of so-called hypostatization, which also returns us to our initial inquiry in this section. We now phrase it thus: Is there a filiological as well as a distinct pneumatological relation between Jesus and the God to whom he prayed?

Our affirmative answer to the above question is based on the insights of Spirit-christology, only partially assimilated by Lampe. By way of contrast, Coffey argues that the giving of the Holy Spirit by the Father constitutes the basis of both Jesus' mission in the world and his relation to the Father. Instead of substituting for the filiological relation of Jesus to the Father, pneumatology enhances that relation, especially with a view toward including in that relation all who are recipients of grace. The challenge posed to Lampe is whether the integrity of the pneumatological dimension of christology—i.e., that Jesus is bearer of the Spirit—is undermined if his filiological relation is strictly psilanthropic. Our positive answer to this issue rests strictly on christological grounds. In other words, the filiological dimension of Jesus' relation to God can be justified only from the perspective of christology and not vice versa. Before we proceed, however, an explanation of terms is warranted.

By the introduction of the term "filiological" I intend a descriptive reference to Christ as Son. Within the broad spectrum of doctrinal development this includes New Testament references to Jesus both as "Son" and "Son of God," which only later was identified by the church to be the consubstantial Son of the Father in the trinity. I have already referred to Coffey's sketch of this development from a systematic perspective. By contrasting the terms "filiological" and "christological," I simply intend to bring out in strong relief the possibility that exists in Spirit-christology to conceive Jesus' relation to God in terms that are exclusively pneumatological, so that reference to Jesus as "Son" is entirely abandoned or revised to the extent that it no longer implicates a Nicene understanding. On the other hand, continuing with this distinction between the terms also affords opportunity to distinguish Jesus' relation to God as Son (filiology) and that relation through the Spirit (when "pneumatological" or "Spirit" is used as a qualifier for christology.) Needless to say, because we are attempting to understand this new christological model from the perspective of God's work in the world, all filiological affirmations concerning Jesus can only proceed from a prior christological one—i.e, that Jesus is the anointed of God.

To return to the issue at hand, we may conclude with the following proposal, sketching in outline the basis for development of both the filiological and pneumatological aspects of Spirit-christology. Jesus anointed with the Spirit for mission also calls upon God as "Abba." Both of these elements appear in the oldest strata of the synoptic christologies. Only by development of each of these dimensions of Jesus' relation to God—i.e., his "Abba" relation and his Spirit-anointing, without confusion or separation—can we speak of Jesus' relation to God as Son in the Spirit. By invoking Chalcedonian terminology normally used in reference to the so-called divine and human natures of Christ (without separation, without confusion), I mean to suggest that Jesus' filial relation to God and his pneumatically inspired and empowered mission are directly related without implying identity. The human Jesus who calls upon Israel's God as "Abba" is also anointed with the Spirit to proclaim the approaching kingdom. The pneumatological dimension initially directs Jesus outward in mission, which mission then intensifies the "Abba" relation from Jordan to Gesthsemane to Golgotha. With a christology beginning from the perspective of

Jesus' ministry and eventual death, it is precisely the pneumatological dimension of his ministry that focuses the particularity and uniqueness of his "Abba" relation. Rather than being identical or one being displaced by the other, both relations are required for a christological confession. Jesus is Son because his Spirit-anointed mission culminates in the depths of encounter in doing the Father's will to the point of God-forsakenness on the cross. Gethsemane and Golgotha are no less Spirit-led than the Jordan event, leaving again to the Spirit of God Jesus' final vindication in the resurrection, which is also the declaration of his Sonship (Rom. 1:4).

Only from the above positions are we able to fully appreciate the Pauline insight into the pneumatological and christological dimensions of the believer's sonship (and daughterhood): "The proof that you are sons is the fact that God has sent forth into our hearts the spirit of his Son, which cries out 'Abba' ('Father')"—Gal. 4:6. Because the Spirit is the Spirit of God's Son, Christians enter into a filial relation to God. We are sons and daughters in the Son (*filii in Filio*). The Holy Spirit is the Spirit of the Son because it is as bearer of the Spirit that Jesus' own filial relation is actualized. In this respect, the Lukan development of the Spirit's role relative to the mission of Jesus to include the infancy narrative ("The Holy Spirit will come upon you . . . "—Lk. 1:35) is legitimate and quite insightful. Therefore, the inclusion of pneumatology does not substitute for the filiological dimension of christology but intensifies it to the point that the church recognized that it was the divine being itself that is revealed in Jesus' sonship. Rather than the imposition of an "existent mediator" between God and humanity, the process of hypostatization, which cannot be separated from the struggle over the *homoousios*, affirms the revelation of God in (and not behind) the humanity of Jesus. Adverbial predication of divinity in Christ ("Jesus acts divinely") or Dunn's statement that the divinity of the incarnate Christ is a function of the Holy Spirit can be affirmed only if they are not limited by a psilanthropic christology. It is neither an ideal nor an impersonal force that constitutes the reality of communion between the divine and the human, but the in-personed relations of filiation and the self-giving of divine love. To posit distinct hypostatic identities in God on the basis of the Christ-event is to speculatively extrapolate from Jesus' filial relation and Spirit-anointing a theological truth about God that is consistent with the Christian experience of describing grace as the reception of the Spirit of God's Son.

Modalist Identification of Christ and the Holy Spirit

In this section our inquiry will focus on the third of Dunn's exegetical conclusions relative to Spirit-christology. He states that the risen humanity of Jesus is a function of the Spirit. Again, the dogmatic task is how best to develop this insight in formal christology. At least two options present themselves. Following directly from our statement at the end of the preceding section, one might consider this issue in reference to the reception of grace as the mediation of the divine presence predicated on the preaching of the gospel. If the risen Jesus, who is the immediate subject of the Christian confession, is in his presence the function of the Holy Spirit, is it proper to distinguish between the *Christus praesens* and the *Spiritus praesens*? Can the relationship between the risen Jesus and the Holy Spirit be interpreted in a modalistic sense whereby the distinction between the two is purely functional, or must we affirm here that the hypostatic identities of the Son and the Spirit are an essential theological premise for a viable Spirit-christology? If in the previous section our focus was the hypostatic identity of the Son; here we query the hypostatic identity of the Spirit. To do this we will explore several dogmatic christologies that may be described as christologies of presence, which because of their focus on the *Christus praesens*— i.e., the risen humanity of Jesus—raise the specifically trinitarian issue about which we are concerned.

Exposition

Dietrich Ritschl, in the tradition of Karl Barth and Dietrich Bonhoeffer, plots a christology based upon the *Christus praesens* and argues for "*the ongoing function and work of the Risen Christ* "[118] as the fulcrum for ecclesial life and Christian witness. His *Memory and Hope: An Inquiry Concerning the Presence of Christ* is a constructive effort toward a christology of presence, although with minimal reference to the third article. He in fact criticizes the entire history of the Western theological tradition on the grounds that the notion and reality of the *Christus praesens* has been ignored. This makes for a rather interesting contrast between what he labels as the "historical-resurrected Christ" and the *Christus praesens*, a peculiar variation on the usual distinction between the historical Jesus and the Christ of faith. In any case, his main point is to argue against conceiving the relationship between Jesus and the church as an effort by faith either to interpret, represent, reenact or prolong a past event rather than to respond to a present reality.

For Ritschl, the reverse should be the case: "The situation, past, present or future, is to be made relevant to him [Christ] ."[119] This can be enacted only on the grounds that it is the *Christus praesens* who constitutes the church as that locus of corporate intentionality that interprets the past in light of the future vis-à-vis its perception and discernment of God's work in the present. Ritschl therefore proposes that the church envisage its christological confession not as the reenactment of a past event but as a response to "Christ's self-presentation in the present."[120] As the community that is "*being dealt with* by him,"[121] this relationship "opens for the Church the dimensions of the past and present in such fashion that history becomes transparent for the work and Lordship of Christ."[122] The church, then, is enabled to speak about God "as he has come and will come in Jesus Christ," because it also speaks to God in the present[123] and is that community with which Jesus Christ shares his history and presence.[124]

All of this is presented under the topic of christology with minimal reference to pneumatology. In his view a separate doctrine of the Holy Spirit would compromise the freedom of the Spirit as well as the necessary affirmation that "the material content of a doctrine of the Spirit of God is at the same time his cognitive access."[125] If the *Christus praesens* is in fact God's identity in the church, so too the Holy Spirit does not just "make relevant" the historical-resurrected Christ but "*is* the *Christus praesens*."[126] Ritschl does not deny a trinitarian theology (in fact, he implies quite the opposite), but he does call into question the traditional distinction between the second and third persons.[127]

... a modalism regarding the relation between "the first and the second person of the Trinity," i.e. regarding the coming of Christ, would lead to docetism, as it did in the third century. But would a modalistic view in respect to the so-called second and third persons of the Trinity not be a very adequate means of expression? Is the differentiation between the *Christus praesens* and the Holy Spirit more than a speculative prolongation of that which is historically known into the trans-empirical? The difficulties which the Western Church has had concerning the presence of Christ when speaking of the presence of the Spirit indicates at least that there is an unsolved problem.[128]

This tendency toward a modalism of the second and third persons is also present in other Protestant theologians. For example, the Dutch Reformed theologian Hendrikus Berkhof forcefully states this position in *The Doctrine of the Holy Spirit*. Berkhof identifies the Spirit as the action of the exalted Christ.[129] By this Berkhof neither denies the element of personality to the Holy Spirit nor reduces the Spirit to an instrumental entity of the risen Christ.[130] Rather, he opts for the replacement of the notion of person by an alternative one—namely, "mode of being," thus seeking to interpret Spirit as the dynamic movement of the one God revealed in Jesus Christ.[131] The Spirit is not exclusively confined to the action of the risen Christ (e.g., the Spirit in creation, in ancient Israel, in the life and ministry of Jesus); nevertheless, as the risen and exalted one, Christ is the life-giving Spirit (1 Cor. 15:45). Or, as Walter Künneth states in *The Theology of the Resurrection* (from the christological side), *"The presence of Christ is the present reality of the Holy Spirit."*[132]

A slightly different relationship between the *Christus praesens* and the Holy Spirit is suggested by Peter Hodgson. Returning to the tradition of Friedrich Schleiermacher and Wilhelm Herrmann, and more recently Gerhard Ebeling, he builds on the notion of "presence" as a fundamental ontological category. Hodgson employs the concept of "presence" to ground the soteriological efficacy of both the historical Jesus and the church's contemporary faith in the risen Christ. Therefore, presence encompasses "reconciliation, atonement and salvation."[133] Modifying the late Heidegger, Hodgson argues that word or language is the means of presence:

"... personal presence occurs when recognition is evoked by means of word, including also verbal action or enacted word."[134]

In the case of the historical Jesus, the word of his proclamation was a word that called into presence. This is an actualization of presence that involves at least three dimensions, which he enumerates as presence to oneself (or temporal presence), presence to the world (or spatial presence), and presence to God (or the transcendent power of presence). Additionally, these become productive for a new language, a new mode of existence, and a new praxis; in other words, the *novum* of the gospel receives articulation in this hermeneutics of presence.[135] Hodgson therefore affirms that identity is a constituent of presence. However, he also equally emphasizes the importance of agency with regard to presence. "Presencing" is actualized through the word, and this is true with respect to both the historical Jesus and the present, risen Christ. The historical Jesus was the word of God, meaning the co-presence of God and humanity in the word of faith that characterized his life, ministry, and death. When Hodgson states that "Jesus was Presence," he means that by faithfully speaking (and enacting) the word of God, both authentic humanity and true divinity were redemptively revealed.

Analogically, even as the being of God was present to Jesus, so, too, the being of the risen Jesus is present to believers.[136] In the tradition of Schleiermacher and Herrmann, the risen Jesus is "God's living agent" who "requires human response and practice, including both a coming-to-faith (where the personal-individual aspect is prominent) and a being-sent-to-mission (where the social-communal aspect is prominent)."[137] Concerning the resurrection of Jesus, one should separate neither its objective-transcendent dimension—i.e., Christ's living agency—from its subjective existential dimension—i.e., the practice of believers. Nor should one too severely divide its past, present, or future temporality. So, for example, in its present modality—viz., Christ's living agency—the resurrection is also a past historical occurrence (the "raising up of Jesus") and a future eschatological promise ("new life in the presence of God, by which death is overcome").[138] The risen Jesus is the word of faith, which creates and sustains the church, and enacts the threefold newness of presence today (a new language, a new mode of existence, a new praxis) as that was so enacted in the life of Jesus himself. Through correspondence or homology between the word of God and human words, the one who was presence—i.e., the historical Jesus—is now present to the church as an agent of reconciliation.[139] Therefore, the *Christus praesens* is constituted by both identity (as the warrant for the critical-historical dimension of relating the present Christ to the historical Jesus) and by agency (as the warrant for the practical-responsive dimension of relating the historical Jesus to the present risen Christ).[140] The relation between the two is expressed by Hodgson as follows:

> We exist *extra nos* in our faithful speech, in a peculiar relationship to Jesus, just as he existed *extra se* in his being as faith, in a peculiar relationship to God. Hence, just as God himself was present in Jesus' being-as-the-word-of-faith, so also Jesus himself is present —personally present—in our faithful speech and act.[141]

As in the case of Ritschl, this dynamic if revisionary christology of presence does not formally take up pneumatology. It is mentioned in a long footnote, that seems to have Barthian traces even though Hodgson's theological mentors are in a quite different tradition. Worth quoting in full, the note makes it apparent that the Spirit's identity and work are thoroughly christological in content, although an important distinction is maintained between the two, one that touches directly on the issue at hand:

> My conception of the agency of the risen Christ raises a question about the distinction between the work of Christ and that of the Holy Spirit. For orthodoxy, this distinction was no problem, since Christ was believed to be removed to heaven, where he rules at the right hand of the Father, while the Spirit carries on the work of redemption on earth. But if we conceive the risen Christ as the one who comes to stand *in* the world as agent, then we face the difficulty of distinguishing between the agency of Christ and the agency of the Spirit. This distinction, if it can be drawn at all, must be understood as a dialectical one. *Opera trinitatis ad extra indivisa sunt.* Bultmann points out that for Paul "in Christ" can interchange with "in the Spirit" (Rom. 8:9; 14:17; *ThNT*, Vol. I, p. 311). In so far as a distinction

can be made, we may say that the agency of Christ is objective and present (historical), whereas that of the Spirit is subjective and eschatological. In I Cor. 12,14, Paul understands the Holy Spirit as the subjective agency by which Christ constitutes his dominion in the world. I suggested earlier that God as word exists triunely in three modes of subsistence and in a twofold structure of self-communication. He is the uncreated one ("Father") who communicates himself in faith ("Son") and in love ("Spirit"). Faith is an historical virtue (marking the mode of present participation in the kingdom of God), whereas love is an eschatological virtue (descriptive of the final kingdom of presence). Man hears the word of God in faith as one who is under way in history through discipleship to Christ; he responds to the word in love as one who is completed by the return to God through the inner witness of the Spirit. Here the subjective and eschatological dimensions of the Spirit's agency are conjoined, in contrast to the objective and historical agency of Christ. Nevertheless, these distinctions remain relative, for history and eschatology, faith and love, objective and subjective agency are but different aspects of God's *one* self-communication *ad extra* .[142]

The distinction in agency between Christ and the Spirit is important on two counts. First, it offers the possibility for separate but coterminous missions of the Son and the Spirit, each with a particular characteristic. Whether the difference between objective and subjective is sufficient to bear this out, however, I think must be questioned. Second, it reconstructs the distinction in contrast to the orthodox version. Even though Hodgson's model has difficulty in distinguishing between the agency of Christ and that of the Spirit, it also raises the question whether orthodoxy has sufficiently conceived the distinctive mission of the Holy Spirit if it is simply just a matter of the latter being the immanent presence of the exalted Lord. These questions have been repeatedly addressed in this study.

As we have seen, James Dunn likewise identifies with these positions. In his examination of the various strata of New Testament pneumatologies, especially the Pauline and Johannine, Dunn states that the risen Jesus and the Spirit are for the believer experientially equated.[143] Therefore, he concludes that while there is a trinitarian structure to Christian experience—Christians experience a dual relationship to God and the risen Jesus vis-à-vis the Spirit—one would be hard-pressed to discover the dogma of the trinity in the New Testament. In fact, to return to his reading of Paul, pneumatology is identical to an immanent christology, with no real distinction between Christ and the Spirit in the experience of the believer. Although Dunn does not conclude to an absolute identity, he does leave the theologian with the following important observation: "A theology which reckons seriously with the [*egeneto*] of John 1:14 must reckon just as seriously with the [*egeneto*] implied in 1 Cor. 15:45b."[144]

All of the above positions—i.e., those held by Ritschl, Hodgson, and Dunn—call into question the traditional distinction of persons or hypostases in the doctrine of the trinity. At the most, such distinctions are confined to a second order of reflection, a specifically speculative one that does not seem to resonate with the more immediate need for christological or pneumatological formulation enacted on the basis of the *Christus praesens*, who is identical with the Spirit. While it is true that none would say the Spirit died and rose again, neither could they say that the Spirit is other than the presence of the risen Christ. On this level there is virtually no distinction between the *Christus praesens* and the *Spiritus praesens*.

This presents us with a description of the Christian experience of grace that includes coterminous reference to both Christ and the Spirit without at the same time providing an adequate theological construct that is sufficiently able to distinguish the two. This is not unusual; the divine subject for soteriological efficacy in the mediation of grace and the constitution of ecclesial existence has traditionally involved reference to both the presence of Christ and the presence of the Spirit—e.g., Ignatius of Antioch's "where Jesus Christ is, there is the Catholic Church" (*Smyrn.* 8:2)[145] and Irenaeus's "For where the Church is, there is the Spirit of God; and where the Spirit of God is, there is the Church, and every kind of grace," (*Against Heresies* 3, 24, I).[146] However, it also presents both a difficulty and an opportunity. On the one hand, the co-presence of Christ and the Spirit seems to complicate the theological warrant for the traditional hypostatic distinction between the two. This could in fact lead to binitarianism and to a modalism of the second and third persons, a tendency not entirely avoided by the theologians just reviewed. On the other hand, it can also result in innovative strategies for constructive christology and contribute to a more developed pneumatology. The most accessible option for such strategies that doctrinely develops the latter possibility are the proposals we have reviewed for Spirit-christology. However, we must now directly address the issue as to what advantage is gained by acknowledging the hypostatic distinction between the risen Christ and the Holy Spirit in light of the insights provided by these christologies of presence.

Evaluation and Critique

Is the risen humanity of Christ a function of the Holy Spirit? The christologies of presence that we have examined seemingly reverse the question. Is the Holy Spirit a function of the risen Christ? In either case the possibility of a modalist Spirit-christology presents itself, this time by subsuming the Spirit under the broader confession of Christ from the perspective of the *Christus praesens*. How to distinguish Christ and the Spirit in any of the aspects of presence—e.g., agency or identity—is problematic especially if we hold to the unity of the divine operation *ad extra*. Is the distinction between the *Christus praesens* and the *Spiritus praesens* anything beyond a nominal predication on the part of the theologian? If not, can we seriously hold to the hypostatic differentiation of the trinitarian persons in the realm of Christian practice, or simply consign such distinctions to an unrelated speculative theological enterprise?

To answer these questions, I propose to examine the constituent elements of the notion of presence and refer them separately to the risen Christ and the Spirit. Those elements of presence—namely, the notions of identity and agency—were to some extent examined in the exposition above. To this I will add memory, or more specifically, kerygmatic memory. If, as I hope to demonstrate, such references do not absolutely coincide, then we will be in a good position to elaborate further that the identity of the Spirit cannot simply be collapsed into that of the *Christus praesens*. This will be basis enough for the hypostatic differentiation of the Spirit from the Son.

A definition of the *Christus praesens* may be rendered as follows: the self-presentation of Jesus to the faith, hope, and love of the church. By "self-presentation" we ascribe the initiative within the divine self-communication to the risen Christ.

Faith, hope, and love are the responses of human agency to the divine initiative. The latter is actualized in christological and pneumatological modalities. Whether this involves a distinct *Spiritus praesens* remains to be resolved. For the moment, faith, hope, and love may be correlated with the constituent dimensions of presence. Faith is the actualization in human community of the memory of Jesus made present through a proclamation that is contemporaneous. Hope is the actualization in human community of the identity of Jesus made present through an advent that is still outstanding. Love is the actualization in human community of the agency of Jesus made present through a giving that is self-focused and relational. Each of these requires further elaboration.

We begin by first positing that the divine presence in the form of the *Christus praesens* is neither identical to nor separate from the *ecclesia*. The church is the locus of the *Christus praesens*, even while at the same time the *Christus praesens* is creative of the *ecclesia*. The church is that human community that owing to the *Christus praesens*, believes because it remembers and knows Jesus in the act of proclamation. It hopes because it confesses Jesus who is to come, and it loves because it acts in the self-giving of Jesus whose invitation extends to all.

By church I mean an ecclesial community—that is, a community of word and sacrament—and emphasize that this is a tangible community not an invisible one. I am not addressing the question of the divine presence outside of this community except to say that such presence would be manifest in either of two forms or *Gestalts* (or patterns). Here I mean the divine presence as a communicative presence, not the divine presence as immensity, which is a property of the divine being relative to all created reality. As communicative presence God is revealed in the *Christus praesens* with an orientation to the *ecclesia* (first pattern), or God is manifest strictly as the *Spiritus praesens* where christological implications are present as vestiges and traces (second pattern). The latter does not require a more definitive explication, since this introduces the concerns of interreligious dialogue (to be dealt with in the next chapter) where from the Christian side any further affirmations of the divine presence must necessarily remain open-ended.[147] However, it does require in our explication of the notion of the divine presence an examination of the precise distinctions between the *Christus praesens* and the *Spiritus praesens*. Here we shall proceed by inquiring whether such a distinction is coherent in the context of ecclesial faith, hope, and love.

Ecclesial faith is the actualization of the memory of Jesus through proclamation that is contemporaneous. Here the *Christus praesens* refers to the church's remembering and to its knowing. Both acts are related, although distinct. As Australian Anglican archbishop Peter Carnley has argued, remembering and knowing are not necessarily sequential; memory does not always precede knowledge.[148] Rather, the relationship between the two is reciprocal.

> Moreover, the two kinds of experience [remembering and knowing] are so inextricably mingled that they *are not without effect upon each other.* The memory cannot be explained as a mere projection backwards of the Church's later experience, but our present knowledge of the Spirit of Jesus is decisively affected by our memory of him; and it is probably just as true that our memory of him has to some extent been shaped by our knowledge of his present reality. Thus, there is a sense in which the Spirit is informed by the memory; the memory, by the Spirit.[149]

Carnley's introduction of the Spirit into the relationship between the memory and knowledge of Christ points to the necessary relation between the *Christus praesens* and the *Spiritus praesens*.

In the church's kerygma the memory of Jesus functions as an essential although not exclusive dimension of the *Christus praesens*. There is also a "knowing" of the risen Christ whose self-presentation to faith incorporates this ecclesial memory of Jesus, but within the wider horizon of contemporary proclamation and praxis. The relationship between these two aspects of the *Christus praesens* is mediated by the Holy Spirit. As the one who brings to mind the words of Jesus (Jn. 14:26) and in whom the risen Lord exists (1 Cor. 15:45; 2 Cor. 3:17) the Spirit is the modality by which the *Christus praesens* is the basis for ecclesial life. Is there, then, a distinction between the *Christus praesens* and the *Spiritus praesens*?

An affirmative answer to the above question is dependent on the following three factors: the corporeality of the risen Christ, the anonymity of the Holy Spirit, and the anamnetic and epicletic dimensions of Christian worship. The first refers to the somatic dimension of the *Christus praesens* that was already hinted at in the statement that the presence of Christ cannot be separated from ecclesial faith. The church is the body of Christ, a term that points to both a metaphorical and a sacramental reality. Focused in worship by both word and sacrament, especially in the Eucharist, the *Christus praesens* is actualized through sacramental sign and symbol as well as in the faith and praxis of believers. Although mediated by the Spirit, the corporeality of the glorified Christ is only properly his. Sacramentally present and eschatologically yet to be consummated, this somatic dimension is not a property of the Spirit. The church in the New Testament is described as a temple of the Spirit (1 Cor. 3:16; Eph. 2:21–22), but never the body of the Spirit. This is sufficient ground to discourage those who seek to recover the pneumatological basis of ecclesial life by substituting an image of the church as an incarnation of the Holy Spirit for the church as an extension of the incarnation of Christ. Incarnational language only should be predicated of the Holy Spirit in an indirect and qualified sense. This relates to our next point, the anonymity of the Holy Spirit.[150]

By the anonymity of the Holy Spirit I mean that the attribution of personality to the Holy Spirit is a more difficult task than is the case with the Father and the Son. Unlike the other trinitarian names, "Spirit" does not evoke the notion of a person-in-relation as do "Father" and "Son." Neither does it necessarily imply distinction. Clearly, in both ordinary and biblical language "Spirit" can connote an extension of something—e.g., the Spirit from God who falls upon someone—without requiring hypostatic or personal distinction. The New Testament employs both impersonal and personal language in description of the Spirit's activity. Wind, fire, water, and dove are used in addition to such verbs as to convict, to speak, to call to remembrance, to hinder, and to lead, the latter group all implying a personal agent. More important, the Spirit's work is always in reference to another, never to the Spirit itself. The Johannine "Paraclete sayings" depict the Spirit as directing the world and the disciples to God and to Christ, and similarly, in the eighth chapter of Paul's Epistle to the Romans the strong pneumatological flavor of that chapter is oriented to being in Christ as the basis for Christian existence. Therefore, when Heribert Mühlen refers to the Spirit as "We-act in person" he is only building on a basic anonymity concerning the Spirit's identity.

The implications that follow from this characterization of the Holy Spirit do not minimize the necessity for a mature pneumatology. In fact, quite the opposite is the case. All the more it suggests to the theologian that pneumatology ought not to collapse into christology. This certainly is not the intention of Spirit-christology as a new christological model. What the anonymity of the Spirit does suggest is that the Spirit's manner of being person—and this we must maintain if we are to give credibility to the personal attributes that do appear in the New Testament—is different from that of the Father and the Son. We may argue that this principle applies to all three persons of the trinity. So, for example, only the Son assumes a human nature and the Father cannot be sent into the world. At the very least, it also implies that with respect to the notion of presence, the *Christus praesens* and the *Spiritus praesens* cannot be simply identical. The anonymity of the *Spiritus praesens*, a presence that directs one to another, provides the possibility for the *Christus praesens* to be actualized without at the same time implying that the former assumes the latter's corporeality or identity.

The Christian liturgy is a form of praxis that has always been determinative for Christian reflection and belief—*lex orandi, lex credendi*. The eucharist as the central act of Christian worship explicitly confirms the distinction we have been drawing. As a particular and special mode of the *Christus praesens*, the eucharist as a prayer of thanksgiving and sacrifice to the Father consists of distinct moments of anamnesis and epiclesis referring, respectively, to Christ and the Spirit. Jesus Christ is the object of the church's memory even as he is proclaimed in the present, while the Spirit is not remembered but invoked. Here the *Christus praesens* and the *Spiritus praesens* converge while still remaining distinct. Only through the presence of the Spirit is it possible for the presence of Christ in the Eucharist to be actualized. This is true for all theologies of the "real presence," barring only those understandings of the Lord's Supper that are exclusively memorialist in orientation. The latter in effect limits the *Christus praesens* to a spiritual modality in which the distinction between the *Christus praesens* and the *Spiritus praesens* ceases to exist. The spiritualization of the *Christus praesens* restricts its somatic dimension to metaphorical attribution and the advent of the parousia. These different ecclesiological perspectives cannot be ignored in relation to christology and pneumatology.

The above distinctions also figure in the remaining two dimensions of the *Christus praesens*. I identified hope as the actualization in human community of the identity of Jesus made present through an advent that is still outstanding. Here the church confesses the eschatological future that belongs to Jesus Christ and that is its hope. The identity of Jesus that is central for the actualization of his presence is never wholly complete for the church. The church awaits *in visio* Christ as he is, this being also the reality *in actu* of its own transformation (1 Jn. 3:2). The incompleteness of the church's awareness of the *Christus praesens* points to its ever-new encounter with its *Kyrios* as it journeys through history in light of the divine promise of eschatological redemption. Messianic expectation is not negated by the *Christus praesens*, but rather intensified under the sign of the crucified Jesus who has yet to turn over the kingdom to the Father that God might be all in all (1 Cor. 1:23; 15:27–28).

If Christ is yet to be fully known, the Spirit is yet to be fully experienced. The

Holy Spirit is the pledge, or first payment (*arrabon*), of the divine inheritance (2 Cor. 2:22; Eph. 1:14). Here the relationship between the personal and impersonal descriptions of the Spirit takes on a new variation. On the one hand, the Holy Spirit is given to the believer and dwells in him or her (Rom. 5:5, 8:9). In this respect, the Spirit comes as gift and person to the Christian. On the other hand, the Spirit is known by measure or by portion. Jesus has the Spirit without measure (Jn. 3:34) whereas Christians receive particular gifts and manifestations of the Spirit (1 Cor. 12:3) and are sharers of the Spirit as a foretaste of the powers of the age to come (Heb. 6:4–5). If the identity of Jesus is still outstanding so that he will not be fully known until the parousia, so too the Spirit as firstfruits (Rom. 8:23) is a sign of the fullness of redemption manifested in the resurrection of the body (2. Cor. 5:1–5). The knowledge of Christ mediated by the *Christus praesens* is paralleled by the increasing manifestation of the *Spiritus praesens* who is the agent of our resurrection (Rom. 8:11). Here, again, the *Christus praesens* and the *Spiritus praesens* are inseparably related but not identical.

The final constituent dimension of the *Christus praesens* is ecclesial love as the actualization in human community of the agency of Jesus made present through a giving that is self-focused and relational.[151] The agency of the risen Jesus is known in the church as the self-giving of Christ, who is the salvation of God. The earthly ministry of Jesus culminated in his self-giving to the Father in the paschal mystery; now this self-giving is directed to the church by virtue of the pentecostal gift of the Holy Spirit sent by the glorified Christ. The human praxis that is evidence of this self-giving between Jesus and God, and Christ and the church, is love. The agency involved in this self-giving love is thoroughly pneumatological, so much so that Paul can speak of it as "the love of God shed abroad in our hearts through the Holy Spirit given to us" (Rom. 5:5).

By self-focused and relational I mean that the *Christus praesens* who is known in this complex event of giving—from Jesus through the Spirit to the Father and then from the Father through the risen Jesus to the church by the sending of the Spirit—achieves his identity through the agency of mutual giving that is essentially relational. As Hans Frei comments, the identity of Jesus is established in the passion and resurrection narratives by the relation between Jesus and God in which the divine agency passes from one to the other.

> In his passion and death the initiative of Jesus disappears more and more into that of God; but in the resurrection, where the initiative of God is finally and decisively climaxed and he alone is and can be active, the sole identity to mark the presence of that activity is Jesus. God remains hidden, and even reference to him is almost altogether lacking. Jesus of Nazareth, he and none other, marks the presence of the action of God.[152]

This relationality is also simultaneously multi-directional. The term is awkward but I mean it to convey its pluralistic or, better yet, trinitarian nature. Jesus' relation to the Father is the source of his relation to the church as its risen Lord. Likewise, the Holy Spirit in the church creates the possibility of its relation to the risen Jesus and through him to the Father. From the perspective of the church, the Holy Spirit is the agent who effects its awareness of the agency of Jesus as self-giving love in its own service of love, or as Hodgson states, in its new language, new mode of existence, and new praxis. The *Christus praesens* is actualized in the agency of the church through the modality of the agency of the *Spiritus praesens*, the two hands of the divine presence being neither separable nor identical.

By distinguishing between the *Christus praesens* and the *Spiritus praesens* we can return to our original inquiry—namely, is the risen humanity of Christ a function of the Holy Spirit? An affirmative answer to this question at the functional level does not exclude on the ontological level a predication of the relationality of the divine presence in hypostatic terms. When considered under the rubric of presence, the distinction between Christ and the Spirit is best understood as a distinction between subsisting relations who face each other by virtue of their different roles in the actualization of the divine presence in humanity, a presence that constitutes the basis of the church of God. At each level of the actualization of the *Christus praesens* in ecclesial faith, hope, and love the *Spiritus praesens* is the active modality—i.e., the agent—by which the former is realized without ever collapsing into it or vice versa. The *Christus praesens* is realized because the Holy Spirit is the agent by which the memory of Jesus is contemporaneous with the proclamation of the risen *Kyrios*. The *Christus praesens* awakens the church to his future because the gift of the Holy Spirit is a foretaste of eschatological transformation. The *Christus praesens* realizes in the church the love of God and neighbor, because the Spirit pours out such love in the hearts of those who believe, signifying the all-inclusive love (inviting all who are thirsty) between Father and Son that identifies each in relation to the other—e.g., God who is confessed in the Spirit to be the Father of our Lord Jesus Christ. The hypostatic being of each of the persons, and in this case especially the hypostatic being of the Spirit distinct from that of the risen Christ, is substantiated because only in the transcendent mystery of God, where the hypostases face each other in relation, is it possible to discover ground for the possibility of the same relations being realized in the two hands of the divine presence that constitute the economy of God.[153] The coherence of the two missions in the divine economy, inseparable but not identical, is possible only because of their immanent relational presence in the transcendent mystery that we name and worship as God.

Conclusion

We may now take inventory of Spirit-christology as a dogmatic construction and its implications for trinitarian doctrine. I will focus first on the development of Spirit-christology outside of the Catholic scholastic tradition, specifically the models proposed by Schoonenberg, Lampe, and the christologies of presence. I will then turn to the dogmatic issues that were addressed in the comparison of these developments with the construction proposed by David Coffey.

We have seen that the Spirit as medium for conceptualizing the reality of Jesus Christ can take a variety of forms. In antiquity we note what may be termed a minimalist and maximalist utilization of Spirit depending upon the outcome of intended christological formulation. When that outcome was restricted to a strictly human bearer of revelation (the Ebionite view), the Spirit was the medium of inspiration. When the outcome included the predication of divinity, the Spirit could be identified as that divinity (usually in contrast with *sarx*). I have already labeled these, respectively, christologies of pneumatic inspiration and pneumatic incarnation. With the consignment of the former to heterodoxy and the latter to displacement by Logos-christologies and the subsequent dogmatic affirmation of the Spirit as the third hypostasis in the trinity, there remains a christology of pneumatic communication that is perhaps the most accurate representation of the Spirit-christologies that have been examined in this study thus far. However, in turning to contemporary non-scholastic Spirit-christologies these categories are only partially applicable. The reasons are several.

Contemporary Spirit-christology as represented here by Lampe and Schoonenberg, aside from being on this side of the conciliar tradition, is responding to a series of critical questions directed at orthodox christology, some of which are motivated by a number of fundamental dispositions informing modern conciousness and sensibility. Primary among these is the methodological turn in philosophy from metaphysics to an ontology of the human subject. Translated theologically, this means an unqualified acceptance of the humanity of Christ, even proposing it as the starting point for christology. Also, biblical scholarship has illuminated the pluralism within New Testament christologies—e.g., as in Dunn's investigation—as well as the pre-conciliar understanding of theological terms such as Word and Spirit. These have led Lampe and Schoonenberg to investigate biblical patterns and pre-conciliar theologies. In addition, the perceived limitation of traditional metaphysics, accused of being static and ahistorical especially with regard to the understanding of "nature" in the Chalcedonian definition, has led both to pursue more dynamic conceptions of God and of divine agency in the world. So, for example, Spirit-christology seems to be particularly appropriate to this renewed sense of dynamism, especially considering the flexibility of Spirit as a "bridge term" or as "the extension of the divine person" in pre-conciliar christologies.

More to the point, however, is the stance taken toward traditional Logos incarnational theology. Lampe and Schoonenberg differ here in their choices for Spirit-christology: displacement by the former and complementation by the latter. Therefore, while each can appropriate aspects of pneumatic christological models of inspiration, incarnation, and communication, these models do not mean the same things that they mean in historical theological description relative to ancient christologies, and they perform a different constructive function vis-à-vis the stance taken toward the inherited tradition. One example can suffice.

I employed pneumatic inspiration as a descriptive term for Ebionite Spirit-christology with its psilanthropic restriction. However, pneumatic inspiration can inform a more orthodox construction of Spirit-christology; or, as in the case of Lampe whose project is revisionary, it can be the major component in his redefinition of the traditional christological *vere Deus*, a christological formulation that the Ebionites did not make. The same can be applied to pneumatic incarnation, which never (even in antiquity—witness the Kelly/Pernveden debate above) quite means the same thing as Logos incarnation, and to pneumatic communication, which any orthodoxy will still affirm. Therefore, it is better to draw only one conclusion from the interaction of ancient and modern Spirit-christologies and then proceed to map the differences of the contemporary debate on their own terms. That conclusion has already been noted. Namely, the flexibility of the term "Spirit," before the hypostasization of both Word and Spirit in conciliar orthodoxy, proffers Spirit-christology as a likely candidate for new avenues in christological formulation. The same is true for some contemporary Wisdom/Sophia or Sophia-oriented christologies.[154]

In addition, the Spirit-christologies of Lampe and Schoonenberg also offer with respect to trinitarian theology two distinct alternatives to the scholastic tradition that we explored. Specifically, the turn to pneumatology as a resource for christological construction may entail either a reconsideration of the ascription of "personhood" to the Holy Spirit or its continued affirmation, although revised—e.g., Schoonenberg's post-incarnational trinitarianism. The former position limits the identity of the Spirit to a formal description of God's activity. The latter clearly maintains the "personal" identity of the Holy Spirit as hypostatically distinct from the Father and the Son, but within the framework of the divine economy alone. These alternatives are substantially different and raised the question whether pneumatic christology adds to the richness of trinitarian theology or finally results in unipersonal theology with a christological component.

When we turned to the christologies of presence, based upon the concept of the *Christus praesens*, we inquired whether pneumatology is presupposed or even possibly absorbed in christology proper. All the theologians reviewed in that section proffered either anti-metaphysical or revised theological ontologies to offer alternatives to classical orthodoxy, especially with regard to hypostatic or personal distinctions in the trinity. Thus, it is possible for the relationship between Christ and the Spirit to be construed in a manner that considerably exceeds the boundaries of classical trinitarian dogma.

In the Roman Catholic tradition even in the early nineteenth century before the triumph of neo-scholasticism, theology did not and could not proceed in such a manner. This generally holds true even after Vatican II. Aside from questions of magisterial authority and the orthodoxy of theological schemas, important as they were and are, Catholic theology must make sense of the ecclesial and sacramental implications for any theologizing. It is my contention that this perspective requires the more positive accounting of hypostatic distinctions in the trinity especially with regard to the third person, whether it be by way of classical orthodox affirmation or alternative revisionary theological construction even as Schoonenberg attempts it.

The methodological shifts in fundamental and dogmatic theological inquiry undertaken by Roman Catholic theologians since the Second Vatican Council have been profound. The popular view that with the coming of the Council the dominance of neo-scholasticism and its "manual tradition" gave way to a plethora of theological approaches is certainly not entirely accurate, although there is some truth to the observation. So, for example, no longer can it be said that the "school" tradition is the dominant one in Catholic theology or that anything approaching the recommendation of Leo XIII in *Aeterni Patris* (1879) for the teaching and study of one of the Church's Doctors (for Leo XIII, this was St. Thomas Aquinas) is presently the case in Catholic Universities and theological faculties. There has been an opening up of inquiry since the Council, and this is reflected across the board in each of the theological disciplines. This is the case in systematic theology in particular, and one need refer to any number of well-published Catholic theologians to verify the fact.

The question therefore arises for the dogmatic theologian as to whether or not significant doctrinal interpretations have likewise shifted with the adoption of new methodologies. An important example in the field of christology is whether the turn to so-called christologies "from below" have significantly altered the Christian understanding of the person of Jesus Christ. Does it change the traditional Christian confession of the divinity of Christ? Answers to this question vary with the number of approaches that attempt in whole or in part to utilize this perspective. The situation is even more complicated with an area of Christian doctrine that is undeveloped and new with respect to constructive proposals. This is certainly true for that intersection between christology and pneumatology, resulting in the new christological model known as Spirit-christology. We have already seen that Spirit-christologies range from the thoroughly orthodox to critically revisionist ones. They therefore bear a peculiar burden for the dogmatic theologian. A summary accounting of those issues is worth repeating.

First, contemporary proposals for Spirit-christologies involve a resurrection of sorts. By this I mean (as illustrated above) one is restoring or constructing anew a christological model with roots in pre-Chalcedonian (and even pre-Nicene) christology in a theological milieu that is post-Chalcedonian. Where the final product ends up along the spectrum from orthodox to revisionist depends in part on an explicit or implicit evaluation of the Chalcedonian definition. Therefore, a typically important question for Spirit-christologies is whether they propose to replace or complement the traditional Logos-christology. And what type of christological formulation is involved with the introduction of "Spirit" into the equation? Is it Spirit qua the divine nature of Christ, or Spirit qua the divine action present in the human Jesus? The complexities involved in the introduction of this new model can be manifold.

Second, Spirit-christologies raise the issue of christology's relationship to pneumatology and vice versa. This is a problematic area, for it is the consensus among theologians in the Western Church that pneumatology has been a neglected area of Christian doctrine (especially in comparison to its prominence in the Eastern Church—see the Chapter 1). Here the question arises about the status of pneumatology relative to the new christological model. Are we seeing a development of pneumatology that has always been neglected, or is pneumatology being collapsed into christology (the latter being the perennial temptation for those whose pneumatology is informed by the *filioque*)? Inevitably the new model forces the dogmatic theologian into the broader area of trinitarian theology. How does one negotiate, for example, the traditional trinitarian terminology of "person" and "hypostasis" in relation to Spirit-christology?

Finally, in addition to the introduction of a new (yet old) christological model, its relationship to an oftentimes undeveloped pneumatology, and the combined implications for a theology of the trinity, we return to our initial observation. With these specific doctrinal questions in mind, one needs to analyze the significant import of differing theological methodologies. Especially in Roman Catholic theology the change from a classical metaphysics of Aristotelian-Thomistic vintage to more diverse methods of attaining a theological ontology has immense implications for answering the doctrinal questions just reviewed.

This is why I chose in this chapter to focus our reflections on the dogmatic differences between the non-scholastic models and scholastically based models of Spirit-christology. This required that we view Spirit-christology from a perspective beginning within salvation-history. If David Coffey's Spirit-christology arrived at this position, it was only after the developments we traced in Chapters 2 and 3 within the speculative ethos of neo-scholasticism. In other words, where Coffey ends coincides with the revisionary departures in the Spirit-christologies of Schoonenberg, Lampe, and the christologies of presence. The latter, with the qualified exception of Schoonenberg, eschew the speculative issues with which Coffey wrestles. The reasons, it should be noted, directly concern their devaluation of speculative theology for explicating the soteriological value of christology and pneumatology. Taking their criticism seriously, I have sought to test and eventually defend the integrity of Coffey's proposal. The issues all revolved around the coherence of trinitarian doctrine in relation to Spirit-christology. We may now summarize the results.

The results of New Testament theology as seen in the work of James Dunn highlight Spirit-christology as a nascent dogmatic construction. In fact, the pneumatological dimension of Jesus' relation to God and of the primitive church's perception of the kerygmatic Christ link together for the modern exegete and theologian the basic continuity between the Jesus of history and the Christ of faith. At the same time it suggests that Spirit-christology need not develop beyond the point of testimony to the risen Jesus in the power and modality of the Spirit. A rudimentary triadic witness may be acknowledged in the New Testament, but it certainly is not developed further into anything approaching the classic formulation of the doctrine of the trinity. By exploring doctrinal expositions that for all intents and purposes limit themselves to the scope of the biblical perspective, we were then able to test the classic doctrine that still sets the parameters for Coffey's proposal.

Schoonenberg raised the issue as to whether the differentiation between Christ and the Spirit in the divine economy merits the same distinction in hypostatic terms in the immanent trinity. By approaching this question from a starting point in salvation-history, I argued that the distinction between the christological and pneumatological missions, along with their convergence in Spirit-christology, not only justifies the speculative step toward reflection on the immanent trinity but enriches perception of these two dimensions within the divine economy.[155] Doing so demonstrates that Spirit-christology is revelatory of the being of God who communicates the divine self in these two missions. This underscores that the relation of the divine persons to one another in the divine being is the basis for communion with the other—i.e., the creature—that is actualized in the incarnation of the Son and the sending of the Spirit.

Lampe posed the question as to whether or not the divinity of Jesus may be interpreted in pneumatologically functional terms, thus ruling out the necessity for positing distinct hypostatic identities in God. By exploring the filiological and pneumatological dimensions of christology, I sought to demonstrate that Spirit-christology that neglects the former dimension limits the pneumatological dimension of christology as well. The pneumatological relation of Jesus to God intensifies rather than substitutes for Jesus' filial relation even as the Spirit's presence in believers makes them daughters and sons in the Son. The inseparable but non-identical relations of the Son and Spirit to Christ reinforce the notion that the believer's status by adoption proceeds from the same Spirit who forged the identity of Jesus over the course of his life, ministry, and death. In accordance with the insights gleaned from the previous section, this also rescues the Christian doctrine of God from a dipolar focus on the relationship between divine transcendence and divine immanence. Rather, all three trinitarian persons share in both these dimensions of our relationship to the divine, for neither Jesus nor the Spirit is reduced to a functional predication of the transcendent God's saving activity.

Finally, the christologies of presence forced the issue of binitarianism vs. trinitiarianism or the question of modalism regarding the christological and pneumatological missions. To be consistent with our starting point in salvation-history, it was important to confirm that the relationship between the *Christus praesens* and the *Spiritus praesens* is likewise inseparable but non-identical. By examining the constituent dimensions of the notion of the divine presence the distinctions became clear, while at the same time linking this truth to the real life of the church as the Body of Christ. Here I identified the relationality discerned in the differentiation between the *Christus praesens* and the *Spiritus praesens* as the basis for such relationality in the immanent trinity. Again, this is further evidence that relationality in God is the basis for the possibility of divine self-communication in creation and redemption.

Having concluded that a dogmatic Spirit-christology may be developed from New Testament sources in a manner that maintains and affirms hypostatic differentiation in God, it now remains to evaluate and critically assess the model as a whole. To this we now turn in the concluding chapter.

NOTES

1. See his *The Life of Jesus Critically Examined*, tr. George Eliot (Philadelphia: Fortress, 1972) and *The Christ of Faith and the Jesus of History: A Critique of Schleiermacher's "The Life of Jesus,"* tr. Leander E. Keck (Philadelphia: Fortress, 1977).

2. Hermann Gunkel, *The Influence of the Holy Spirit: The Popular View of the Apostolic Age and the Teaching of the Apostle Paul.* (Philadelphia: Fortress, 1979, original German edition, 1888), p. 2.

3. Leonhard Goppelt identifies this break with the nineteenth-century understanding of spirit as an effect of the work of the History of Religions school, of which Gunkel was a part: "Just as A. Schweitzer opposed the Kantian kingdom of God of liberal theology with the apocalyptic kingdom of God of the 1st century, so H. Gunkel opposed the 19th-century concept of the spirit with that of the Hellenistic world." *Theology of the New Testament*, Vol. 2: *The Variety and Unity of the Apostolic Witness to Christ* (Grand Rapids: Eerdmans, 1982), p. 119.

4. Even a cursory review of sections on the Spirit will confirm this. See Rudolph Bultmann, *Theology of the New Testament*, vol. I (New York: Scribners, 1951), pp. 330–339; Hans Conzelmann, *An Outline of the Theology of the New Testament* (New York: Harper & Row, 1969), pp. 38–41; Werner Georg Kümmel, *The Theology of the New Testament* (Nashville: Abingdon, 1973), pp. 123–125, 217–220, 312–318. Edward Schweizer's *The Holy Spirit*

(Philadelphia: Fortress, 1980) is a more concentrated work and fills out in greater detail much of the ground covered by Gunkel. Even more relevant is his article "Spirit of God" in Gerhard Kittel's *Theologisches Wörterbuch Zum Neuen Testament*. See *Bible Key Words, volume III,* translated and edited by Dorothee M. Barton et. al. (New York: Harper & Row, 1960). Schweizer provides more nuance than does Gunkel for the distinctive New Testament pneumatologies within the canon and to their relationship to contemporary Jewish and Hellenistic conceptions of spirit.

5. Ibid., p. 115. n. 82. Gunkel adds, "This in contrast to frequent modernizations." Gunkel also considers Paul's christology an expression of his pneumatology. To support this he notes that "the formula *in Christo* seems to be shaped after the analogy of the *in pneumati*." (pp. 115-116). For a similar reading, see Bultmann: "The phrase 'in Christ' has no exact analogies in the history of religions and was evidently coined by Paul himself after the broader analogy of 'in the Spirit' (*in pneumati*). For that very reason, 'in the Spirit' must be interpreted in accordance with 'in Christ' and not *vice versa*." "Church and Teaching in the New Testament," *Faith and Understanding* I. (New York: Harper & Row, 1969), p. 203.

6. Ibid., p. 115.

7. Adolf Diessmann, *Paul: A Study in Social and Religious History* (London: Hodder and Stoughton, 1926), p. 140. Also, "Christ is Spirit; therefore He can live in Paul and Paul in Him."

8. Albert Schweitzer, *The Mysticism of Paul the Apostle* (New York: Henry Holt, 1931), p. 392. One cannot truly appreciate Schweitzer's famous conclusion of *The Quest of the Historical Jesus* (New York: Macmillan, 1968)—"But the truth is, it is not Jesus as historically known, but Jesus as spiritually arisen within men, who is significant for our time and can help it. Not the historical Jesus, but the spirit which goes forth from Him and in the spirits of men strives for new influence and rule, is that which overcomes the world." (p. 401)—without examining this monumental work on Paul. Also see his *Out of My Life and Thought* (New York: Mentor, 1953), pp. 50-51.

9. Wilhelm Bousset, *Kyrios Christos: A History of the Belief in Christ from the Beginnings of Christianity to Irenaeus* (Nashville: Abingdon, 1970), p. 162.

10. See especially Bultmann's essay "The Christology of the New Testament" in *Faith And Understanding I*, pp. 262-285. For a systematic version of this identification, see Walter Künneth's *The Theology of the Resurrection.* (St. Louis: Concordia, 1965), pp. 189-194. For a more contemporary New Testament theological perspective, see John Frederick Jansen's *The Resurrection of Jesus Christ in New Testament Theology.* (Philadelphia: Westminster, 1980), pp. 104-113, and Edward Schillebeeckx, *The Christ: The Experience of Jesus as Lord* (New York: Seabury, 1980), pp. 534-538. For exegetical and theological criticisms of this position, see respectively Arthur W. Wainwright, *The Trinity in the New Testament.* (London: SPCK, 1962), pp. 199-223, and Lewis B. Smedes, *All Things Made New: A Theology of Man's Union with Christ* (Grand Rapids: Eerdmans, 1970), pp. 43-77. An interesting turn on this issue is the identification of Christ with Sophia/Spirit in the work of Elisabeth Schüssler Fiorenza, with consequent systematic implications. *In Memory of Her: A Feminist Theological Reconstruction of Christian Origins* (New York: Crossroad, 1983), pp. 184-199, 343-351. For the feminist systematic version of "Spirit-christology," see Rosemary Radford Ruether, *Sexism and God-Talk: Toward a Feminist Theology* (Boston: Beacon, 1983), pp. 127-138.

11. Dunn's work in this area has been quite extensive: *Baptism in the Holy Spirit: A Re-examination of the New Testament Teaching on the Gift of the Spirit in Relation to Pentecostalism Today* (Philadelphia: Westminster, 1970); *Christology in the Making: A New Testament Inquiry Into the Origins of the Doctrine of the Incarnation* (Philadelphia: Westminster, 1980); *Jesus and the Spirit: A Study of the Religious and Charismatic Experience of Jesus and the First Christians as Reflected in the New Testament* (Philadelphia: Westminster, 1975);

Unity and Diversity in the New Testament: An Inquiry Into the Character of Earliest Christianity (Philadelphia: Westminster, 1977).

12. James Dunn, *Unity and Diversity in the New Testament*, p. 216. All italics in Dunn's quotes are his.

13. Ibid., p. 226.

14. Ibid., pp. 209-216.

15. Ibid., p. 208. Also, "The same basic point can be put in more general terms: Jesus so proclaimed God that his hearers knew Jesus himself to be the one through whom God comes to expression."

16. Ibid., p. 216.

17. Ibid., p. 229.

18. Ibid.

19. Dunn, *Jesus and the Spirit*, p. 2. Also, "Is Jesus simply the first Christian or somehow the source of post-Easter Christian experience?"

20. Ibid., p. 13. This also functions as the basis of his critique of the old liberal tradition: "*Jesus' consciousness of Spirit is the eschatological dimension to Jesus' ministry which Liberalism missed.*" p. 90.

21. Ibid., p. 43, 90.

22. Ibid., p. 92.

23. See Gunkel, *The Influence of the Holy Spirit*, pp. 9-13. For Gunkel's evaluation of non-Pauline pneumatology in the New Testament, see p. 74. Dunn's own preference for Pauline pneumatology over Luke-Acts is revealed in the following passage: "Above all, the distinctive essence of Christian experience lies in the relation between Jesus and the Spirit . . . Jesus' relationship with God which we see coming to expression here and there in the gospels therefore becomes determinative for later Christian experience—not in the sense that Jesus appears as the first Christian, but rather as the one whose relation with the Spirit as God's son continued and developed through death to resurrection life. Through that unique event Jesus attained the life-giving power of the Spirit and the Spirit became recognizably the life-giving power of the crucified and risen Jesus. Henceforth the Spirit reflects the character of this Christ, of the whole Christ; so that experience of charisma is quintessentially experience of the grace of God as manifested in Christ, and experience of eschatological tension is characteristically experience of the Christ Crucified as well as Risen, of power in weakness, of life out of death." Ibid., pp. 358-359.

24. Ibid., p. 180.

25. Ibid., p. 298.

26. Ibid., p. 322.

27. Ibid.

28. Ibid.

29. Ibid., p. 323.

30. Ibid.

31. Ibid., p. 324.

32. Ibid. This distinguishes Paul especially from Luke-Acts. It should also be stated that what is characteristic of the Spirit emerges in the experience of Christ's suffering—i.e., the cruciform nature of Christian experience. "To experience the exalted Christ therefore is to experience not merely new life but new life which is life through death, life out of death, and which always retains that character." (p. 331).

33. Ibid., p. 325.

34. Ibid., p. 326.

35. Ibid., p. 351. Also, the Spirit as Jesus' alter ego in which the Spirit's work is by definition that of Christ-determined revelation. (p. 353).

36. Similar conclusions are provided Gary M. Burge in his study of the Johannine tradition: "It is *Christus praesens* that speaks through the Paraclete and directs his revealing activity. When one encountered the Spirit Paraclete in the Johanhine community, one encountered the risen Christ. *Therefore we can conclude that the single most important feature of the Johannine Paraclete is its christological concentration. Christ is the template within the Fourth Evangelist's thinking that has given shape and meaning to the Spirit in the Farewell Discourses.*" *The Anointed Community: The Holy Spirit in the Johannine Tradition* (Grand Rapids: Eerdmans, 1987), p. 41.

37. Ibid., p. 323.

38. James D. G. Dunn, "1 Corinthians 15:45—Last Adam, Life-giving Spirit," in *Christ and the Spirit in the New Testament*, edited by Barnabas Lindars and Stephen S. Smalley (Cambridge: Cambridge University Press, 1973), p. 139. Dunn frames this observation relative to the believer's experience, not in relation to Paul's doctrine.

39. Ibid., pp. 139-140. This last point agrees with Gunkel's observation but with more nuance between the significations of Christ and the Spirit. See n. 5.

40. Ibid., p. 141. See also his exegetical articles for similar conclusions: "2 Corinthians 3:17—'The Lord is the Spirit'" *Journal of Theological Studies*, n.s. xxi (1970), pp. 309-320; "Jesus—Flesh and Spirit: An Exposition of Romans 1:3-4," *Journal of Theological Studies*, n.s. xxiv (1973), pp. 40-68.

41. James D. G. Dunn, "Rediscovering the Spirit," *The Expository Times* 84 (1972), p. 12.

42. F. X. Durrwell, C.S.S.R., *Holy Spirit of God.* (London: Geoffrey Chapman, 1986), p. 42. See also his *The Resurrection* (London: Sheed and Ward, 1960).

43. Edmund J. Dobbin, O.S.A., "Towards a Theology of the Holy Spirit," *Heythrop Journal* 17 (1976), pp. 5-19, 129-149. Sabbas J. Killian, O.F.M., "The Holy Spirit in Christ and Christians," *The American Benedictine Review* 20 (1969), pp. 99-121. Edward J. Kilmartin, S.J., "The Active Role of Christ and the Holy Spirit in the Sanctification of the Eucharistic Elements," *Theological Studies* 45 (1984), pp. 225-253. Kilian McDonnell, O.S.B., "The Determinative Doctrine of the Holy Spirit," *Theology Today* 39 (1982), pp. 142-159; "A Trinitarian Theology of the Holy Spirit?" *Theological Studies* 46 (1985), pp. 191-227. John O'Donnell, S.J., "In Him and Over Him: The Holy Spirit in the Life of Jesus," *Gregorianum* 70,1 (1989), pp. 25-45. Philip J. Rosato, S.J. "Spirit Christology: Ambiguity and Promise," *Theological Studies* 38 (1977), pp. 423-449.

44. McDonnell, "The Determinative Doctrine of the Holy Spirit," pp. 151-153.

45. O'Donnell, "In Him and Over Him: The Holy Spirit in the Life of Jesus," p. 26. See also his *The Mystery of the Triune God* (New York: Paulist, 1989), pp. 40-56, 75-99.

46. Rosato, "Spirit Christology: Ambiguity and Promise," p. 435.

47. See the following by James Mackey: *The Christian Experience of God as Trinity*, pp. 241-251; *Jesus the Man and the Myth: A Contemporary Christology*; *Modern Theology: A Sense of Direction*, pp. 63-95, 128-130; *New Testament Theology in Dialogue: Christology and Ministry*, pp. 81-102.

48. Mackey, *The Christian Experience of God as Trinity*, pp. 245-246. "The 'Binity' would then consist of Jesus and his Father, and Spirit would name that one and the same divine being or essence, at once transcendent and immanent, the fatherly *hypostasis* or objectification of which is encountered definitively in the *hypostasis* of the Spirit of sonship objectified in the life of Jesus and his continual real presence amongst us. One divine *ousia*, two *hypostaseis*." (p. 246).

49. Roger Haight, S.J., "The Case for Spirit Christology," *Theological Studies* 53 (1992). p. 257. Haight draws on the work of Geoffrey Lampe and Paul W. Newman. The latter's work—*A Spirit Christology: Recovering the Biblical Paradigm*, (Lanham, Maryland: Univer-

sity Press of America, 1987) contrasts "intrapersonal" and "interpersonal" models of Spirit-christology, respectively representing classical and revisionary approaches to christology. See especially pp. 171–186. For a similar approach within the context of Jewish-Christian dialogue see Michael E. Lodahl's *Shekhinah/Spirit: Divine Presence in Jewish and Christian Religion,* (New York: Paulist, 1992), pp. 151–192. Since both are influenced by Lampe I will only consider his proposal in the course of this chapter.

50. Ibid., p. 286.

51. One should also note that the revisionary direction taken by Haight should be corre-lated with his treatment of the doctrine of the trinity. In his article "The Point of Trinitarian Theology," *Toronto Journal of Theology* 4 (1988), pp. 191–204, he argues that one should restrict positing "distinct differentiations within God," since this move would go beyond the *point* of trinitarian theology that is strictly soteriological and hence determined by the divine economy. Speculation on the divine persons within the immanent trinity is "purely specula-tive" and does not sit well with the affirmation of the "absolute mystery and incomprehensi-bility of God." Therefore, one might surmise that the more recent article on Spirit-christology carries foward this approach by offering the new model as a better alternative than Logos-christology without necessarily dealing with the distinction between the Son and the Spirit in the trinitarian life of God. The recent major contribution in trinitarian theology, which likewise reenvisages the nature of the speculative moment in trinitarian theology concerning the intra-trinitarian relations, is represented by Catherine Mowry LaCugna in *God for Us: The Trinity and Christian Life* (San Francisco: Harper, 1991).

52. Piet Schoonenberg, S.J., *The Christ: A Study of the God-Man Relationship in the Whole of Creation and in Jesus Christ* (New York: Herder & Herder, 1971). See also Mark Schoof, "Dutch Catholic Theology: A New Approach to Christology," *Cross Currents* 22 (1973), pp. 415–427.

53. Piet Schoonenberg, "Trinity—The Consummated Covenant: Theses on the Doctrine of the Trinitarian God," *Studies in Religion* 5 (1975–1976), pp. 111–116; and "Spirit Christo-logy And Logos Christology," *Bijdragen* 38 (1977), pp. 350–375.

54. "Spirit Christology and Logos Christology," p. 360.

55. Ibid., p. 361.

56. Ibid., p. 363.

57. Ibid., p. 361. Also see: *The Christ*, pp. 13–49.

58. This is a development over his argument in *The Christ*, where he simply inverted the traditional understanding of the enhypostasis. Beginning with the assumption that one must affirm the human person of Jesus, he then argued that the position of Leontius of Byzantium, the most important representative of neo-Chalcedonism, who argued that the human nature of Christ existed enhypostatically—that is, "it exists *in* the divine hypostasis of the Word" (p. 58)—was inadequate. The other side of this position is whether or not the human nature of Christ is also *an*hypostatic, without its own hypostasis—i.e., if it exists within the divine hypostasis of the Logos, does that mean it does not possess its own human hypostasis? If this is the case, argued Schoonenberg, then in effect we are denying full humanity to Jesus, since personhood—i.e., "a human, created act of being" (p. 73)—is essential to what it means to be human, to be truly consubstantial with us. Schoonenberg reversed this: "The concept developed here regarding Christ's being-person is a reversal of the Chalcedonian pattern insofar as it is influenced by neo-Chalcedonism, which has become our current christology. Now not the human but the divine nature in Christ is anhypostatic, with the proviso, moreover, that this is valid inasmuch as we do not know the person of the Word outside the man Jesus. However, it is primarily not the human nature that is enhypostatic in the divine person, but the divine nature in the human person" (p. 87). Under criticism from Walter Kasper, Schoonenberg in his later article continues to affirm his original position but now comple-

mented by the traditional understanding, thus rendering a reciprocal enhypostasis of both divine Word and human Jesus, each relative to the other. "Spirit Christology and Logos Christology," pp. 362–365.

59. Ibid., p. 365. As we shall see, this point is in direct criticism of Geoffrey Lampe, whose proposal we shall examine in the next section.

60. Ibid., p. 366.

61. Ibid.

62. References to this article will be cited in the text viz., the thesis numbers Schoonenberg employs.

63. Ibid., p. 367.

64. St. Basil the Great *On the Holy Spirit*, trans. David Anderson (Crestwood, NY: St. Vladimir's Seminary Press, 1980), p. 71.

65. Schoonenberg, "Spirit Christology and Logos Christology," p. 367.

66. Ibid. Here, Schoonenberg is dependent on Aubrey R. Johnson, *The One and the Many in the Israelite Conception of God* (Cardiff: University of Wales Press, 1961). Very similar to Lampe with his conception of "bridge terms" (to be exposited in the next section), Schoonenberg utilizes Johnson's understanding of Yahweh's activity as "extensions of the person" to interpret Logos and Spirit. Johnson's argument resides in the difficulty of applying such terms as monotheism or polytheism to the Israelite conception of God and revelation. By examining "prophetic psychology" and the Israelite notion of personality, Johnson argues that the prophet, Messenger, Angel, or Spirit of Yahweh are extensions of Yahweh's personality—i.e., Yahweh "in Person" (p. 33). In light of this, Johnson concludes: "It may also be argued that along this line we gain a new approach to the New Testament extension of Jewish Monotheism in the direction of the later Trinitarianism" (p. 37). Schoonenberg has taken him up on this suggestion.

67. Here Schoonenberg's reciprocal enhypostasis is evident: "The Logos, becoming flesh in the human person Jesus, becoming the divine *hypostasis* of that human person, personalizes itself over against the Father and becomes the divine Son. Or, to repeat the terminology used above, making the human person of Jesus enhypostatic in its own divine reality, the Logos itself becomes enhypostatic in the man Jesus, albeit in quite a different way. Whereas the enhypostasis of Jesus in the Logos is totally received, that of the Logos is (*sic*) [in] Jesus in (*sic*) [is] totally active. The human person Jesus is grounded in the hypostasis of the Logos but the Logos becomes hypostasis, indeed second person, by actively sustaining the personal being of Jesus." "Spirit Christology and Logos Christology," p. 368.

68. Ibid., p. 369.

69. Ibid., p. 370.

70. Ibid., pp. 370–371.

71. Ibid., pp. 371–374.

72. Ibid., p. 375.

73. Coffey, *Grace: The Gift of the Holy Spirit*, p. 65.

74. Schoonenberg, "Trinity—The Consummated Covenant: Theses on the Doctrine of the Trinitarian God," theses 7–8.

75. Ibid., theses 15, 22, 29.

76. Ibid., theses 34–35.

77. Coffey, "The Holy Spirit as the Mutual Love of the Father and the Son," p. 221. It will also be recalled that it is Coffey's contention that only the "bestowal" or "mutual love" model renders a meaning for the procession of the Holy Spirit in the immanent trinity. The "procession" model provides no unitive aspect to the procession—i.e., the Holy Spirit proceeds outward without any necessary intra-trinitarian reason except according to the psychological variant of that model where the Holy Spirit proceeds as the love inherent in the Father's

intellective act. However, here Coffey argues that this dimension of the Spirit's procession is better understood in terms of the bestowal model.

78. Schoonenberg, "Trinity—The Consummated Covenant: Theses on the Doctrine of the Trinitarian God," thesis 14.

79. Ibid., thesis 15.

80. Jean Daniélou, *The Theology of Jewish Christianity* (London: Darton, Longman & Todd, 1964), pp. 7–11.

81. Hans-Joachim Schoeps, *Jewish Christianity: Factional Disputes in the Early Church* (Philadelphia: Fortress, 1969), pp. 59–73.

82. Ibid., pp. 74–117.

83. Ibid., pp. 68–73. One should also emphasize that Ebionite halakah was in contrast not only to non-halakhic Christianity but also to Pharisaic and Rabbinic interpretation and halakah. Jesus not only confirmed the Mosaic law but reformed it!.

84. Daniélou, *The Theology of Jewish Christianity*, pp. 117–146.

85. Specifically, the need arises to discern pneumatic utterances in relationship to a true witness to Christ.

86. These and following quotes (notes 87 and 88) are taken from *Early Christian Fathers*, ed. Cyril C. Richardson (New York: Collier, 1970). "For our God, Jesus the Christ, was conceived by Mary, in God's plan being sprung both from the seed of David and from the Holy Spirit." pp. 92–93.

87. "The Spirit and the Power from God cannot rightly be thought of as anything else than the Word, who is also the First-born of God, as Moses the above-mentioned prophet testified. So this [Spirit], coming upon the Virgin and overshadowing her, made her pregnant—not by intercourse, but by [divine] power." (p. 263).

88. "If Christ the Lord who saved us was made flesh though he was at first spirit, and called us in this way, in the same way we too in this very flesh will receive our reward." (p. 196).

89. *Early Christian Doctrines* (San Francisco: Harper & Row, 1960, 1978), p. 143.

90. *The Concept of the Church in the Shepherd of Hermas* (Lund: CWK Gleerup, 1966), p. 49.

91. "He [the Son of God] is thus man with God, in short, since He is man's flesh with God's Spirit—*flesh* (I say) without seed from man, *Spirit* with seed from God." Also, "And very properly, because Christ is the Word of God, and with the Word the Spirit of God, and by the Spirit the Power of God, and whatsoever else pertains to God." *Latin Christianity: Its Founder, Tertullian*, The Ante-Nicene Fathers, Vol. III, ed. A. Cleveland Coxe D.D.(Grand Rapids: Eerdmans, 1951), pp. 537–538.

92. ". . . that this Word is called His Son . . . at last brought down by the Spirit and Power of the Father into the Virgin Mary, was made flesh in her womb, and, being born of her, went forth as Jesus Christ . . ." Ibid., p. 249.

93. "This, therefore, was signified, brethren, that in reality the mystery of the economy by the Holy Ghost and the Virgin was this Word, constituting yet one Son to God." Also, "And even as He [God the Word] was preached then, in the same manner also did He come and manifest Himself, being by the Virgin and the Holy Spirit made a new man . . ." *Fathers of the Third Century: Hippolytus, Cyprian, Caius, Novatian, Appendix*. The Ante-Nicene Fathers, Vol. V, ed. A. Cleveland Coxe, D.D. (Grand Rapids: Eerdmans, 1951), pp. 225, 230.

94. "He is the power of God, He is the reason, he is His wisdom and glory; He enters into a virgin; being the Holy Spirit, He is endued with flesh; God is mingled with man. This is our God, this is Christ, who, as the mediator of the two, puts on man that He may lead them to the Father. What man is, Christ was willing to be, that man also may be what Christ

is." *Saint Cyprian: Treatises*, tr. and ed. Roy J. Deferrari, The Fathers of the Church: A New Translation, Vol. 38 (New York: Fathers of the Church Inc., 1958), pp. 357–358.

95. In *Christ Faith And History*, eds. S. W. Sykes and J. P. Clayton (Cambridge: At the University Press, 1972), pp. 111–130.

96. London: SCM, 1977. Also his paper: "The Holy Spirit," *Fairacres Publication No. 41*. (Fairacres, Oxford: SLG Press, Convent of the Incarnation, 1974).

97. I am correlating the work of Dunn and Lampe in a manner that at least at one point Dunn would resist. He criticizes Lampe for employing only one "christology of God as Christ-Spirit,'" rather than maintaining a diversity of christological formulations. See his *Christology in the Making*, pp. 266–267.

98. Lampe, *God as Spirit*, pp. 13, 132, 140.

99. Lampe, "The Holy Spirit and the Person of Christ," pp. 120–123.

100. Ibid.

101. Lampe, *God as Spirit*, pp. 36–37.

102. Ibid., p. 37.

103. Lampe, "The Holy Spirit and the Person of Christ," p. 123.

104. Ibid.

105. Ibid., p. 124. It should be noted that Lampe's christological proposal also requires a revision of soteriology, one that is processive, immanent, and continuous with creation. God as Spirit is already present within human history and evolution; therefore, salvation cannot be an irruption from without but arises from within the creative process. See *God as Spirit*, pp. 14–16. It also means there is an analogy between the Christian experience of salvation and the adverbial predication of divinity in Christ. For example, "Salvation essentially consists in the attainment of communion with God, or, rather, the reception, as a gift from God, of a Christlike relationship to himself, constituted by divine love and grace and human faith and hope." Ibid., p. 16.

106. Lampe, "The Holy Spirit and the Person of Christ," p. 125: "There is no inherent improbability (quite the reverse) in the idea of a human soul growing to maturity in God, a soul of which God had taken possession from the first beginning of consciousness."

107. Lampe, *God as Spirit*, p. 141.

108. Lampe, "The Holy Spirit and the Person of Christ," p. 123.

109. Lampe, *God as Spirit*, p. 228.

110. Ibid., pp. 168–175.

111. Ibid., pp. 162–165.

112. Ibid., pp. 116–117.

113. Lampe. "The Holy Spirit and the Person of Christ," p. 129.

114. Cyril C. Richardson, *The Doctrine of the Trinity* (Nashville: Abingdon, 1958), p. 106.

115. To mention just a few examples, one need only think of the works of the great nineteenth-century revisionists: D. F. Strauss, F. C. Baur and G. F. Hegel. More recently, John B. Cobb, Jr., and Tom F. Driver present very different versions of this basic thesis. See, respectively, *Christ in a Pluralistic Age* (Philadelphia: Westminster, 1975), and *Christ in a Changing World: Toward an Ethical Christology* (New York: Crossroad, 1981); also, John Hick, "An Inspiration Christology for a Religiously Plural World," *Encountering Jesus: A Debate on Christology*, ed. Stephen T. Davis (Atlanta: John Knox, 1988), pp. 5–38.

116. Lampe, *God as Spirit*, p. 38.

117. Ibid., p. 37.

118. Dietrich Ritschl, *Memory and Hope: An Inquiry Concerning the Presence of Christ* (New York: Macmillan, 1967), pp. xii, 10.

119. Ibid., p. 64.

120. Ibid., p. 203.

121. Ibid., p. 220.

122. Ibid., p. 63.

123. Ibid. p. 168.

124. Ibid., p. 221: "He too [the present, risen Christ] , not just the Church, must have his mode of "intentionality" toward the Church, his "desire to be present," if this transposition of doxological language in propositional statements is permitted for a moment. With the resurrection he became what he was not before. He has a history. If his mode of existence were merely that of being the abstract summary of the Church's self-understanding and faith, he could not *share* his history and presence. He would be dissolved into the community of believers."

125. Dietrich Ritschl, *The Logic of Theology: A Brief Account of the Relationship Between Basic Concepts in Theology* (Philadelphia: Fortress, 1987), p. 158.

126. Idem, *Memory and Hope*, p. 224.

127. Although Ritschl admits the following is an exaggerated statement it nevertheless characterizes his revised if non-classical trinitarianism: "The Church is 'trinitarian' in regard to her memory, 'binitarian' at the present and 'unitarian' in hope." Ibid., n. 17.

128. Ibid.

129. Hendrikus Berkhof, *The Doctrine of the Holy Spirit* (Atlanta: John Knox, 1976), p. 21f.

130. Ibid., pp. 27, 115–121. "The Spirit is Person because he is God acting as Person." (p. 116).

131. "The triune God does not embrace three Persons; he himself is Person, meeting us in the Son and in his Spirit. Jesus Christ is not a Person beside the Person of God; in him the Person of God becomes the shape of a human person. And the Spirit is not a Person beside the Persons of God and Christ. In creation he is the acting Person of God, in re-creation he is the acting Person of Christ, who is none other than the acting Person of God." p. 116.

132. Walter Künneth, *The Theology of the Resurrection*, p. 189.

133. Peter Hodgson, *Jesus-Word and Presence: An Essay in Christology* (Philadelphia: Fortress, 1971), p. 220.

134. Ibid., p. 267. Also, *"God is the one who has word absolutely and in this sense is the primordial word-event, the event of being."* p. 116.

135. Ibid., p. 152.

136. He also utilizes "presence" or "presencing" as the link between the doctrines of the person and work of Christ: "The doctrine of the person of Christ, I argued, directs its attention to the historical Jesus, the one who was presence in virtue of God's self-presentation in word. The doctrine of the work of Christ is properly concerned with the one who is present, the one who is risen from the dead and 'comes to stand' in the world as the agent of reconciliation. 'Resurrection' means the contemporary practice of presence, which is reconciliation, atonement, salvation." (p. 220). This quote also highlights the revisionary nature of Hodgson's christology.

137. Ibid., p. 242.

138. Thus, Hodgson understands the resurrection of Jesus as a present event inclusive of both a past and a future. Ibid., p. 223.

139. Homology is clearly the key fundamental theological concept for Hodgson. It is a relationship between God and humanity of "correspondence rather than of proportionality." It also does not involve any concession to supernaturalism: "But the point is that this correspondence does not involve a 'supernaturalizing' of word but rather a restoration of human speech to its own most proper function. This point is essential for a proper understanding of the relation between the word of God and the word of man. When the latter is brought to authenticity by the former, i.e., when it becomes word of faith, then it exists in a relation of homology to the word of God, serving as the appropriate instrument or means for the coming

of speech of God's creative, redemptive, and unconcealing word. Rather than referring to the *analogia fidei*, as Karl Barth does (thus suggesting the suprahistorical character of the word of God), we may refer to the *homologia fidei*. Faith means precisely homologous speaking." Ibid., pp. 101-102. This also has consequences for his doctrine of God: "Thus to define God as 'presence' is not to think of him as timeless eternity in the traditional sense, but as the most 'primordial and infinite temporality.'" (p. 121).

140. Ibid., p. 40.

141. Ibid., p. 273. This also reveals the revisionary nature of Hodgson's project. The *vere Deus* and *vere homo* is affirmed on the basis of this homologous co-presence of God and humanity in Christ, not on the basis of the hypostatization of Word vis-à-vis the second person of the trinity, which Hodgson views as a substitute for the human agency of Jesus. See pp. 115-116.

142. Ibid., p. 244, n. 41.

143. We have already noted—for example, in Dunn's *Jesus and the Spirit*—that his characterization of Paul's pneumatology includes the following: *"Paul equates the risen Jesus with the Spirit who makes him alive"* (p. 322); *". . . the Spirit has himself taken on the character of Christ"* (p. 322) and *"If Christ is now experienced as Spirit, Spirit is now experienced as Christ."* (p. 323). The same hold true for the Johannine perspective: "the personality of Jesus has become the personality of the Spirit" (p. 326).

144. James D. G. Dunn, "1 Corinthians 15:45—Last Adam, Life-giving Spirit," p. 139. See again his exegetical articles for similar conclusions: "2 Corinthians 3:17—'The Lord is the Spirit,'" *Journal of Theological Studies*, n.s. xxi (1970), pp. 309-320; "Jesus—Flesh and Spirit: An Exposition of Romans 1:3-4," *Journal of Theological Studies*, n.s. xxiv (1973), pp. 40-68.

145. *Early Christian Fathers*, ed. Cyril C. Richardson, p. 115.

146. *The Apostolic Fathers with Justin Martyr and Irenaeus*. The Ante-Nicene Fathers, Vol. I, ed. A. Cleveland Coxe, D.D. (Grand Rapids: Eerdmans, 1981), p. 458.

147. Although this subject will be broached in the next chapter, a brief explanation is in order. By open-ended I mean that the Christian enters such dialogue with both conceptions of the divine presence in mind. On the one hand, the Christian knows no other confession except that of Christ. To presume a non-christocentric identity for the Christian is to misrepresent the faith. Christians can approach dialogue only evangelically in light of the church's confession. On the other hand, Christian identity is also pneumatocentric and indeed the Spirit blows where it wills (Jn. 3:8). Here dialogue ought to be approached in openness to the *Spiritus praesens* known both in other religious traditions and in the encounter between religions. At such a stage the nature of dialogue demands that the christological dimension of the faith both informs and is informed by the dialogue conducted with the *Spiritus praesens* in view. How the faith has two centers—i.e., Christ and the Spirit, or more accurately, two dimensions of one divine center—is I think at the very heart of the trinitarian theology that will be elaborated in the remainder of this study.

148. Peter Carnley, *The Structure of Resurrection Belief* (Oxford: Clarendon Press, 1987), pp. 297-326.

149. Ibid., p. 326.

150. Both William Hill *The Three-Personed God*, pp. 302-303) and Kilian McDonnell ("A Trinitarian Theology of the Holy Spirit," Theological Studies 46 (1985) pp. 191-227) have been very suggestive on this point.

151. Carnley develops the notion of the self-giving of Jesus in his final chapter, titled "Easter Faith and the Self-Giving of Jesus." *The Structure of Resurrection of Jesus* pp. 327-368.

152. Hans Frei, *The Identity of Jesus Christ: The Hermeneutical Bases of Dogmatic Theology* (Philadelphia: Fortress, 1975), p. 121.

153. Here I follow Walter Kasper, who in his critique of Rahner's trinitarian axiom on the identity of the immanent and economic trinity rephrases it thus: "In the economic self-communication the intra-trinitarian self-communication is present in the world in a new way, namely, under the veil of historical words, signs and actions, and ultimately in the figure of the man Jesus of Nazareth." Kasper's main concern is to emphasize both the gracious and kenotic character of the divine economy. *The God of Jesus Christ* (New York: Crossroad, 1984), p. 276. Similar concerns inform Yves Congar's qualifications of the axiom. See *I Believe in the Holy Spirit*, Vol. III, p. 15.

154. For example, Elisabeth Schüssler Fiorenza, *In Memory of Her: A Feminist Theological Reconstruction of Christian Origins*; and more recently, building on Fiorenza, Frederick Herzog, *God-Walk: Liberation Shaping Dogmatics* (Maryknoll: Orbis, 1988).

155. This is not to affirm that the immanent trinity is simply a deduction or "kind of extrapolation from the economic Trinity." Again with Kasper, I would maintain that "the immanent Trinity is and remains a *mysterium stricte dictum* in (not behind!) the economic Trinity." *The God of Jesus Christ*, p. 276. Recently, Catherine Mowry LaCugna deals with similar issues in *God for Us: The Trinity and the Christian Life*. (San Francisco: Harper, 1991), with slightly different results in which speculative trinitarian theology (regarding the immanent trinity) is strictly disciplined by both the divine economy and a relational ontology, not too dissimilar from Schoonenberg's thesis "The question of whether God is trinitarian apart from his self-communication in salvation history could be answered if the relationship between God's immutability and his free self-determination were accessible to us. Because this is not the case, the question remains unanswered and unanswerable. It is thereby eliminated from theology as a meaningless question" (thesis #8 in "Trinity—The Consummated Covenant: Theses on the Doctrine of the Trinitarian God"). Coffey's contribution is to suggest a dialectic between complementary models of the trinity (procession and bestowal models) through inclusion of a dynamic pneumatology gleaned from the biblical testimony.

6

Spirit-christology:
Evaluation and Assessment

In the course of this study we have charted a very specific path in our investigation of Spirit-christology as a contemporary dogmatic christological model. By beginning with a critique of the Latin trinitarian tradition exercised by Eastern Orthodox theology, there immediately surfaced a number of dogmatic problems that the Western model was required to address if its own pneumatology was to develop in comparison with that of the East. This led to an examination of the developments within Roman Catholic neo-scholasticism that resolved these issues as a necessary step in order from within that tradition to construct a viable Spirit-christology. As we have seen, this entailed theological argument in favor of a proper mission of the Holy Spirit, a theology of grace that gave priority to uncreated grace as a prerequisite to a real relation between the divine persons and created reality, and a theology of anointing that situated the role and function of the Holy Spirit in christology in relation to that of the divine Son. Each of these steps ensured that Spirit-christology would maintain and even deepen the integrity of the Christian trinitarian confession.

Indeed, to accomplish the above I have argued in favor of the proposals advanced by David Coffey in particular, which demonstrated the need for advancing a new model of intra-trinitarian relations that is consistent with Spirit-christology. This translated into an appeal to a dogmatic perspective, which was gleaned from the ascending christologies of the New Testament. Even though I, along with Coffey, maintain that a speculative effort is required to proceed to the intra-trinitarian relations of the immanent trinity for the purpose of distinguishing the persons, this turn to salvation history as the starting point for dogmatic reflection cannot be overestimated. Only on the basis of such a turn is Coffey able to legitimate his new christological and trinitarian models.

In the previous chapter we stepped outside of the neo-scholastic perspective to test the mature Spirit-christology of David Coffey. We had already witnessed how Coffey transcended the strictures of the traditional paradigm as he sought to integrate the insights of personalist and transcendental theology into his own more scholastically oriented proposal. His abandonment in his later work of the scholastic idiom provides further testimony that his new dogmatic models do not require the maintenance of the scholastic enterprise as long as the intent of the latter's doctrinal distinctions is maintained. The dialogue with contemporary non-scholastic Spirit-christologies focused on three dogmatic issues that implicated major points in trinitarian theology with which an orthodox Spirit-christology must be integrated even outside of scholasticism.

First, the methodological starting point of non-scholastic theology in salvation-history directs one to an understanding of the intra-trinitarian relations that sheds further light on the distinction of persons that to some extent are already perceived within the economic trinity. The differentiation of the christological and pneumatological missions, and their relationship to each other in the divine economy, reveals the mutual self-giving within the divine being that is the basis for the *ad extra* acts of creation and redemption. Second, in contemplating the divinity of the incarnate Christ it is important to distinguish its filiological and pneumatological dimensions to underscore the relationship between sonship and anointing in the ministry and passion of Jesus. Here the humanity of Jesus, which is both mediatorial and exemplary for the church, reveals the mystagogical (viz., Jesus' "Abba" relation) and apostolic (viz., Jesus' anointing with the Holy Spirit) dimensions of the divine election of humanity in Christ. Third, in the ecclesial witness to the divine agency and presence the distinction between the *Christus praesens* and the *Spiritus praesens* is preserved by recognition of the corporeal and anamnetic dimensions of the former and the anonymous and epicletic dimensions of the latter. "Inseparable but non-identical" was the formula I utilized to describe the relationship between these aspects of the divine presence that was intended to preserve the integrity of the hypostatic distinctions in God and, therefore, the uniqueness of each of the temporal missions.

If the second issue addressed excludes a psilanthropic christology, the third one prevents a modalist collapse of the second and third persons into one another. This latter possibility can take either a christological or pneumatological form. On the one hand, it could lead to a docetic christology wherein the Christ-figure is only a cipher for human soteriological aspiration, this in the absence of kerygmatic memory as the criterion for the identity of the *Christus praesens*. On the other hand, it could lead to an instrumentalist pneumatology wherein the Holy Spirit is reduced to the subjective consciousness of a basic anthropological state (the tendency in religious liberalism) or an existential grasping for the authenticity of an extrinsic doctrine (the tendency in heteronomous orthodoxy), these in the absence of the free invocation of the Spirit as the agent of the divine presence. In both of the above cases the distinctive contributions of christology and pneumatology to the Christian knowledge of God are attenuated to some degree.

Having investigated these three dogmatic issues, which emerge out of an examination of the relationship between Spirit-christology and a trinitarian understanding of God, it now remains for us to assess the model as a whole. We propose to accomplish this by exploring the model for its productivity in advancing the theological grasp of three major issues on the agenda of contemporary theology. They are 1) contextual issues of culture and human experience, 2) emancipatory concerns of social praxis and a just society, and 3) religious pluralism and the quest for dialogue. Each will be examined in the light of Spirit-christology, particularly as the church's witness to Christ and the Spirit is the foundation for its own mission and evangelization. Since our interest is a particular christological model and how it works, we will not focus on an analysis of the issues themselves but on the dogmatic structure of the christological model in relation to them. The relevant aspects of the problem will emerge in the first section; therefore, that will be the most involved (and lengthy). The next two sections will follow in a derivative fashion for the purpose of illustrating the cogency and versatility of the model.

Contextual Issues of Culture and Human Experience

Ever since the publication of Friedrich Schleiermacher's *On Religion: Speeches to Its Cultured Despisers* (1799), the relationship between faith and culture has been on the agenda of modern theological investigation. The tradition that he engendered of theology's engagement with culture has been a distinguished one. Theologians within the modern period such as Albrect Ritschl, Paul Tillich, Rudolph Bultmann, H. Richard and Reinhold Niebuhr, and even Karl Barth (although from an entirely different perspective) reflect the influence of Schleiermacher and his theological investigation of the relationship between religion and culture.

A contemporary statement of this issue is even more complicated than originally envisioned by Schleiermacher. Cultural diversity and the various readings of culture—e.g., post-modernism, deconstructionism, feminism—considerably intensify the sense of fragmentation in society and culture and also make nearly impossible a consensual understanding of what is meant by the human experience upon which cultural analysis and criticism is based.[1] Our interest in these issues is strictly a dogmatic one—namely, how does this challenge to theological reflection relate to the task of doctrinal construction that we have examined in this study? Or, more specifically, is Spirit-christology as a model of dogmatic interpretation of the central mysteries of the Christian faith accessible to this type of theological engagement?

To answer these questions, it behooves us to consider the relationship between pneumatology in particular and this form of theological inquiry. It is the work of the Spirit that has been traditionally associated with human experience and the creativity that is the origin of cultural formation and production. We shall briefly mention three examples in which the relationship between Spirit and human experience have received theological articulation. We will begin with Schleiermacher and his theology based on religious consciousness or affections. We will then turn to the theology of Paul Tillich, and finally to Tom Driver. In all of these we shall note the difficulty in distinguishing between a notion of human experience or religious subjectivity and the Holy Spirit.

Schleiermacher has been widely criticized for his marginal treatment of both the trinity and the Holy Spirit. His deferral of discussion of the trinity in *The Christian Faith* to a conclusion of the final section of the *Glaubenslehre* and his description of the Holy Spirit as "the common Spirit of the new corporate life founded by Christ"[2] evoked this sarcastic evaluation by Karl Barth: "As if pneumatology were anthropology!"[3] This is the crux of the matter. Does an anthropological starting point, beginning with human religious self-consciousness, endanger the integrity of pneumatology as a theology of the Holy Spirit? To quote Barth again:

> Is the spirit which moves feeling, speaking, and thinking persons, when things come about properly, an *absolutely* particular and specific Spirit, which not only distinguishes itself again and again from all other spirits, but which is seriously to be called "holy"?[4]

Yet, how else except from the notion of spirit (Holy or otherwise) is one to engage the issue of human experience and culture? Indeed, Schleiermacher offers a model that despite the criticisms of Barth is a cogent one on its own terms.

Schleiermacher's pneumatology is summed up in the following theorem (#123 in *The Christian Faith*):

> The Holy Spirit is the union of the Divine Essence with human nature in the form of the common Spirit animating the life in common of believers.[5]

The proposition allows for what he later defines as the "ever self-identical attitude to Christ and the Spirit" of the ecclesial community, while it is simultaneously related to the world in a manner that is "subject to change and variation."[6] Herein lies the possibility for a thoroughly contextualized theology.

The manifestation of Spirit is always for Schleiermacher a common spirit, known, experienced and communicated in community. His dogmatics is itself an accounting of the experience or consciousness of the Christian community—i.e., "accounts of the Christian religious affections set forth in speech"[7] (specifically, those of the Evangelical Church and confession). These affections are the modification of the affective self-consciousness that is intrinsic to human being, now expressed in the symbolic speech of a particular community. To the extent that this faith community is of a particular time and place—what Schleiermacher calls "the characteristic form taken by human nature in a nation"[8]—the possibility is certainly available to include within theological reflection the specificities raised by context.

Of course, any contemporary analysis would exceed the suggestions enjoined by Schleiermacher regarding the particularity of culture, "nation," or symbolic confession. The important point is the dogmatic structure that enables this. In this regard, Schleiermacher evokes both pneumatology and christology. If, on the one hand, he states that the "presence of the Spirit rather is the condition of anyone sharing in the common life," he can also state that "this common spirit is . . . derived from one and the same source, namely, Christ."[9] Therefore, while Christian self-consciousness is a common consciousness derived from participation in the Spirit and entails a union of the divine with the human nature in believers, it is dependent on the the person-forming union between divine and human nature that exists in Christ[10] (described as "the potency of His God-consciousness, which was a veritable existence of God in Him"[11]). Christ supplies the unifying principle for this common consciousness that is pneumatically mediated through the spontaneous activity of the members of the community—hence, diversity is preserved in the context of unity.[12]

The model thus suggested by Schleiermacher approximates aspects of Spirit-christology. Specifically, what is present in Jesus—i.e., his God-consciousness—is communicated to believers, this being analogous to the notion within Spirit-christology that the bearer of the Spirit is also the sender of the Spirit. Schleiermacher's contribution is to situate the reality of the Spirit's communication within the common life of the community, with all its variations and changes. Access to the Spirit is only possible through the human reality of a common or shared consciousness.

As already stated, Schleiermacher's construct is coherent in its own right. The critical issue is whether or not it can endure Barth's criticism. Is pneumatology eventually reduced to anthropology and, if so, is there an alternative construct that is as accessible to cultural context while simultaneously being grounded in the missions of Christ and the Spirit?

Since I am not proposing a dogmatic investigation into the dialogue between Barth and Schleiermacher, I will limit this query to the subject at hand by extracting the following challenge posed to Spirit-christology. Does the inclusion of the variations and changes within human culture and experience into theological reflection vis-à-vis the pneumatological dimension of God's saving action in Christ uphold the integrity of the agency and freedom of the *Spiritus praesens* without being reduced to its human acceptation? If for no other reason than that Schleiermacher prefers to identify the Holy Spirit as the common spirit of the Christian community that danger does exist, whether or not in fact Schleiermacher himself succumbed to it, as Barth judges that he did. However, even with this caution one cannot simply dismiss Schleiermacher's insight that the work of the Spirit is known only in a particular culture and ecclesial setting. To further explore this issue we turn now to Paul Tillich, who happened also to be an advocate of a version of Spirit-christology.

Paul Tillich's theology of culture is well known and a mark of his profound theological engagement of the relationship between religion and culture. His formula—"culture is the form of religion and religion the substance of culture"[13]—so contextualizes the theological question that no theological answer may be given without a prior cultural question (his "method of correlation"[14]). For our purposes, his theological answer to the cultural question relates directly to the question of whether Spirit-christology is a productive model for this issue. For the sake of brevity, I will focus specifically on those elements of his christological and pneumatological constructions that relate to the issue at hand.

Tillich prefers to designate the Holy Spirit as the "Spiritual Presence," because it more closely relates to an understanding of "spirit as a dimension of life [which] unites the power of being with the meaning of being."[15] Without an appreciation of the latter—i.e., lowercase spirit—it is impossible to speak of the divine Spirit (uppercase). In fact, the fading of the symbol "Holy Spirit" from the living consciousness of Christianity is due in Tillich's view to the disappearance of the word "spirit" from the doctrine of the human.[16] Therefore, Tillich seeks to recover the latter notion so as to fully restore the revelatory experience of the presence of God.[17]

The result is an impressive accounting of how the actualization of life even amid its ambiguities can be integrated with the divine presence. So, for example, the dimensions of spirit may be categorized as the self-integration of life in morality, the self-creativity of life in culture, and the self-transcendence of life in religion.[18] The ambiguities of life inherent in each of these dimensions answer to the Spiritual Presence (the Holy Spirit), which provides an unambiguous although fragmentary experience of the New Being in Christ that restores the integrity and relatedness of all these dimensions of human existence.[19] The possibility for this resides in Spirit-christology.

Tillich understands Spirit-christology to be based on the relationship between the Spiritual Presence and the New Being in Jesus as the Christ. The New Being is his soteriological term for the salvation that is revealed in Christ; in his language of existential ontology, it is "essential being under the conditions of existence, conquering the gap between essence and existence."[20] From the perspective of Spirit-christology it may be posited that it is the undistorted presence of the divine Spirit in Jesus as the Christ, his human spirit being entirely grasped by the Spiritual Presence, which makes him "the decisive embodiment of the New Being for historical mankind."[21]

Three implications are drawn by Tillich from Spirit-christology. First, it makes the "faith of the Christ" understandable in that because he was always upheld by the Spiritual Presence—"The Spirit never leaves him"—the power of unambiguous life was present in the fragmentary character of his faith, including the elements of struggle, exhaustion, and despair. Second, it is the divine Spirit, not his human spirit, that makes Jesus the Christ, excluding thereby a Jesus-theology instead of a proper christology. Third, Jesus as the Christ is in the words of Tillich the "the keystone in the arch of Spiritual manifestations in history." The Christ is organically linked to both the past and the future. The Spiritual Presence in history both before and after Christ—understood theologically (not chronologically) as "an existential encounter with the New Being in him"—is "essentially the same as the Spiritual Presence in Jesus as the Christ."[22]

Tillich's Spirit-christology taken in the context of his soteriological understanding of the New Being provides a dogmatic construct that answers the concerns of the contextual challenge to theological understanding. Here I am not necessarily defending Tillich's analysis of culture (which may in fact require revision), but rather the relationship between the Spirit and Christ that is inclusive of the possibility of bringing various human concerns into the realm of encounter with God's saving reality. The essential point is that the Spirit that was present in Jesus and made him the Christ is the same Spirit that draws all our human concerns into the realm of salvation or the New Being.

Tillich therefore demonstrates the productivity of Spirit-christology in relation to this issue. Regarding the concern expressed over the possibility in Schleiermacher's theology that pneumatology might collapse into anthropology, Tillich both distinguishes the divine Spirit from the human spirit and posits a mutual immanence between the two.[23] Additionally, like Schleiermacher he also acknowledges that the functions of the human spirit are "conditioned by social context," a point essential for the subject at hand.[24] Tillich also maintains a Christocentric focus that leads us to a critical alternative to his position essayed in the work of Tom F. Driver.

Driver is critical of Tillich for a number of reasons, not the least of which is the ontological texture of his theology.[25] Here I will focus, however, more on Driver's christology and his "radical trinitarianism," in which he reconstructs the relations between God, Christ, and Spirit. His proposal centers on the notion of a present-future christology, one that also militates against any form of Christocentricity, specifically the presentation of "Christ past" as the center, model, and norm of all things.[26] If Jesus of Nazareth is that individual in whom we discover God's infinite commitment to finitude, as Driver proposes, we then cannot limit that to a "once for all" act that has solidified itself in the Nazarene. Christology "requires freedom from the past in order to generate a freedom in the present for the sake of the future."[27] Since God changes, so too, does Christ who "is the changing pattern of our relation to a living God."[28] The risen present Christ or the present-future Christ is "a figure momentarily representative of all creation . . . [in the] . . . mutual recognition and mutual transaction between God and world."[29] These entail specific acts of God-human encounter emerging out of the indeterminacy of Spirit, who is the "the infinite contextual ground of life."[30] As was the case with the teaching of Jesus of Nazareth, nothing is final in the expectation of the kingdom or "world" of God in present-future time; rather, christology or "christic relatedness" is relative to our conscience in its own analogous expectations.[31]

Against this background, Driver is clear that the church must reevaluate the formative role in christology of the "scriptural Jesus" (the Jesus of the Gospels) and the "historical Jesus" (the Jesus uncovered by historical-critical research). Since christology is not constructed from some record in the past but from the discernment of the present-future actions of God, from discernment of "what the resurrected Christ is doing today," the life, death, and resurrection of Jesus can only be considered a "prologue to the present act." Consistent with this is the programmatic guidance that christological statements are primarily affirmations concerning God (as subject and not just object) and secondarily concerning Christ, which affirmations are the subject of re-envisionment by the community of faith open to the ever new and creative power of God.[32]

Because for Driver the identity of the present-future Christ is always changing, the question of agency is resolved through the mutual and reciprocal interaction of both God and humans. The creative and changing God and the relativities of human conscience in present-future time are productive for new envisionments of Christ, the one with a thousand faces.[33] Clearly this christological model is directed to the plurality and diversity in human culture and experience. Distinct from Tillich, it is not necessary to posit Jesus as the Christ as the center of God's salvation-history or of the New Being. Rather, because God is infinitely committed to finitude in Jesus[34] in a pattern that points to a similar continuing commitment whenever humans confess the Christ, Driver prefers to reorder the structural priority of the trinitarian persons in favor of Spirit, God, and Christ (as contrasted with a hierarchically ordered Father, Son, and Holy Spirit). Here pneumatology figures prominently. The Spirit "is that meaningful power of God's life which is infinite and which resists figuration because its function is to provide meaning and power *to* the figures we encounter."[35] Since both God and humans are of Spirit, "Spirit is the 'more' of any relation" that exists in the divine/human context, including that between Jesus and God as well as contemporaneous manifestations of the Christ. This priority of Spirit no longer requires that the unity of Christ Jesus with God at the center of time be "forever decisive." This would put a frame around the divine/human context and set limits to the Spirit.[36]

Driver's "radical trinitarianism," a dogmatic concept that embodies his religious principle that "transcendence is radical immanence,"[37] poses an alternative model for conceiving the contemporaneity of culture and ethics in theological reflection. However, as with Schleiermacher and Tillich, it is the relationship between Christ and the Spirit that allows for this engagement. How do they relate to the model of Spirit-christology that we have examined in this study? Are all of these proposals paradigmatic for the possibilities of Spirit-christology, or do the differences between them and Coffey's model limit the productivity of the latter in relation to this issue?

The key dogmatic issues may be stated as follows: 1) How does one distinguish between the agency of the Spirit and the human acceptation of Spirit relative to human concerns and experience within the work of God? Is this the substitution of anthropology for pneumatology and theology (Barth's concern) or the inclusion of the human into the transfiguring work of the trinitarian economy? 2) Is the human moment in the divine work, specifically the christological one, determinative for the continuing work of God as Spirit or simply repesentative of the divine/human encounter that is ever new and changing on the basis of the mutuality of that relation (Driver's concern)? Or, more dogmatically, is Spirit-christology (which Tillich affirms) descriptive of this relation or should we prefer a Christic pneumatology in which the manifestation of Christ changes according to the indeterminacy of Spirit as the context for all divine/human encounter (Driver's proposal)? (3) How is the inclusion of context conceived in its soteriological dimension? In other words, who are the agents of transformation—Christ, the Spirit, the human? I will take up these questions from within the perspective of Spirit-christology as a way of determining more definitively the value of this christological model.

All of these issues require examination of how the human is the object of the christological and pneumatological missions. According to the model of Spirit-christology developed from within the Catholic scholastic tradition, the human is the formal object of these missions as either a human nature or a human person. The human nature of Jesus is assumed by the divine Son in the incarnation, and human persons, members of the church, receive the gift of the Holy Spirit through the divine inhabitation. Formally speaking, all that is human is included in these temporal missions of the Son and the Spirit. Also, as we have seen, the two missions are not identical but neither are they separated. The Holy Spirit creates, sanctifies, and unites the human nature of Jesus to the divine Son, while the risen Lord is present through the modality of the Holy Spirit who is the mutual love of the Father and the Son and who now in the divine economy extends that love to include all those who are sons and daughters in the Son. However, this delineation of the model does not extend to a material explanation of the manner in which the various concerns, actions, and dimensions of the human are the object of the missions. This would come under the rubric of a more practical exposition of the theology of grace and the Christian life.

The previous chapter's examination of the hypostatic integrity of each person within the context of Spirit-christology underscored the necessity to maintain that integrity but should not be taken to discount the concerns of the other theologians examined. By way of review, they were: a primary focus on the presence and identity of the persons in the divine economy (Schoonenberg), the direct dynamic presence of the Spirit as the manifestation of divinity in both Christ and his church (Lampe), the reality of the *Christus praesens* as the focus for the identity and agency of Jesus Christ (D. Ritschl, P. Hodgson, and the christologies of presence). Each of these points is important and is not negated by maintaining the hypostatic identity and differentiation of the persons of the trinity. Here, too, the proposals of Schleiermacher, Tillich, and Driver do not proceed to the level of hypostatization. However, they do map the possibilities of contextualization in reference to christology and pneumatology. To that extent they provide a more accessible model for this concern than that proposed by David Coffey. On the other hand, an accounting of these same concerns in reference to hypostatic identity and differentiation in the context of Spirit-christology enables us to address the three major issues that are our present focus. A preliminary word is in order before we proceed to the specific issues.

Throughout this study I have argued in favor of those positions that maintain the non-identity and inseparability of the trinitarian persons. It is this position in the theology of the trinity that is the basis for Spirit-christology and that finds its fullest expression in the divine economy through the utilization of this model. However, it is also clear that this particular development in doctrine is precisely that, a development, which while taking nothing away from its truth is only justified at a secondary level of theological discourse. By secondary level, I mean a correlation of existing theological affirmations that, while constructed at a secondary level, expresses the Christian knowledge of God evident not only at the primary level of theological discourse—e.g., that Jesus' filial relation is revealed in his "Abba" experience and that his mission proceeds from his being anointed with the Spirit—but also at the even more primary level of Christian worship (doxology) and confession (homology)—e.g., that "in the Spirit" Christians confess Jesus as *Kyrios*. The contribution of much modern theology to dogmatics has been the exploration of the primary level of theological discourse in reference to the primary level of Christian experience. This has often resulted in the complete eschewal of the speculative enterprise so dear to the scholastics. It is also the refusal of any extrinsicism in doctrinal affirmation, sometimes to the extent of assuming a completely anti-dogmatic posture. Our concern in examining alternative doctrinal formulations (which are by no means anti-dogmatic) and correlating them with Catholic scholastic orthodoxy is to bring into focus the interaction between the different levels of theological discourse and dogmatic construction. In this regard, Schleiermacher is quite right when he remarks that the doctrine of the trinity "is not an immediate utterance concerning the Christian self-consciousness, but only a combination of several such utterances."[38] However, Barth is also correct when he argues that the content of the doctrine of the trinity is "decisive and controlling for the whole of dogmatics."[39] Granted, we now are speaking of two nearly diametrically opposed views of theological methodology. Yet, it is true that from the perspective of Christian consciousness or the experience of salvation the doctrine of the trinity is not an immediate datum (as Dunn illustrated from his exegetical investigations—see Chapter 5) but a dogmatic conclusion (which even Coffey acknowledges). Barth says as much when he declares that the root of the doctrine lies in the biblical revelation of God as Lord.[40] It is also true, however, that what the doctrine expresses about God is the ground of Christian worship and identity.[41] All of this is simply to highlight that there is a dialectical relationship between the formative dimensions of trinitarian faith and the developed doctrine that itself profoundly reveals what is distinctive about Christianity. In this section I am proposing that awareness of this relationship will help direct our efforts to integrate the insights of the different models of Spirit-christology (or approximations of Spirit-christology) that we are examining.

To return to our first concern—namely, how the anthropological issues of culture and context are related to the trinitarian missions in a more than formal manner—we may proceed along the following lines. Here I am indebted to the works of Walter Kasper[42] and Frans Jozef van Beeck, S.J., especially his *Christ Proclaimed: Christo-logy as Rhetoric.*[43] We may define the relationship between anthropological concerns and the christological and pneumatological missions in terms of the integrity of each of the missions. In our efforts to highlight the convergence of these missions in Spirit-christology, we have consistently sought to distinguish them as well. Only in this manner are we able to articulate a Spirit-christology in trinitarian perspective.[44]

Walter Kasper makes the argument that "theological anthropology must begin theologically, not anthropologically."[45] I certainly agree; in fact, this would directly meet the Barthian concern, as Kasper observes. However, Kasper also criticizes "Barth's narrowly concentrated christological approach" to this issue.[46] Rather, Cath-olic theology as a whole, both scholastic and non-scholastic, presupposes anthropol-ogy while seeking to surpass and perfect it in the light of Jesus Christ (*gratia supponit naturam et perficit eam*—grace presupposes and perfects nature).

Kasper suggests a threefold relation between christology and anthropology by utilizing the doctrine of analogy. Christology stands to anthropology (for it is the human being as it appears in Jesus Christ that is the subject of theological anthro-pology) as the *via positionis*, the *via negationis*, and the *via eminentiae*.[47] Respec-tively, Jesus Christ is the truth about human being in its creatureliness (*via positionis*), its judgment *coram Deo* (*via negationis*), and in its divinization (*via eminentiae*). This relationship may be systematized (although not the only system-atization) relative to Christ's three offices as Prophet, Priest, and Pastor.[48] Kasper thus coordinates in terms of a material theological content the relationship between anthropology and christology. Various aspects of the human are related to Christ according to truth (prophet), life (priest), and community (pastor). This suffices for the integrity of the christological moment in reference to the inclusion of human concerns by way of their transfiguration in Christ rather than any reduction of the theological to the anthropological. What now remains is an accounting of the same in reference to the pneumatological mission.

Kasper's christological hermeneutic of the human is meant to affirm the modern turn to the human subject and its notion of autonomy (*via positionis*), exercise a prophetic critique of the human situation (*via negationis*), and "outbid" anthropology by defining the meaning and purpose of humanization in the light of divinization (*via eminentiae*).[49] This threefold relation of the anthropological to the christological may also be interpreted vis-à-vis the rhetoric of inclusion, obedience, and hope, terms employed by van Beeck in his christology.[50] For van Beeck a rhetorical hermeneutic of christology requires that attention be given to the constructive moments of chris-tological doctrinal formulation, which is really an accounting of the pneumatological acceptation of the risen Kyrios in worship. Since his proposal provides the frame-work for our own critical conclusions in regard to Spirit-christology, I shall briefly summarize his position.

Van Beeck integrates pneumatology with christology by demonstrating, in a fashion similar to Kasper's but with a different focus, how the process of conversion contributes to christological doctrinal formulation. The threefold rhetoric of inclusion, obedience and hope marks how the Christian proceeds in the thematization of faith. The process begins with a series of partial discernments of the risen Christ (inclusion), moves to the conversion of those discernments to his presidency (obedience), and finally culminates in a christological confession of Jesus in ultimate terms and in reference to the totality of meaning (hope). Relevant to our subject is that all things human, including every cultural concern, may present a possibility for the naming of Jesus. In other words, through the process of conversion (embodied in the rhetoric of obedience) and the surpassability of grace beyond the potential of the actually sinful (this being the source of hope), the thematization of Christian faith may be thoroughly contextualized in any particular christological confession. Doctrinal formulations must be measured by this process of rhetorical interpretation that highlights the pneumatological dimension of worship and witness, the latter being the privileged setting for the origin of christological statements. In sum, the Christian is one who in confessing Jesus Christ "speaks in the Spirit," thus testifying to the basic conversion that is hospitable to all things human and calls them to eschatological fulfillment in Christ.

By appropriating van Beeck's proposal, we may now more clearly delineate the pneumatological aspect of Spirit-christology's accessibility to cultural context. The strictly christological mission opens the possibility for the inclusion of human and cultural concerns into the divine/human relation of which the incarnation is the basis. The Holy Spirit is the agent of that inclusion, first in the life and ministry of Jesus and now through the agency of the risen Christ who with the Father is the sender of the Spirit. Van Beeck's accounting of being "inspirited" in worship and witness is focused on the process by which human concerns are accepted, converted, and transfigured by the eschatological gift of the Spirit. This process distinguishes each of the agents: Christ, the Spirit, and believers (our third query).

Jesus Christ, crucified and risen, is the human ground in God for the ultimate transfiguration of created reality. Directed to God in the paschal mystery and to the whole of creation in the sending of the Spirit, the agency of the risen Lord is all-embracing and fundamental, so that humanity may be fully pervaded by the mystery of God and humanity may fully commune with God. The Holy Spirit is the agent of inclusion, conversion, and transfiguration. The various discrete concerns of the human, inculturated and historically specific, are the fertile ground for the work of the Spirit who unites the human with Christ through the divine inhabitation. Human agency is also part of this complex, in an obvious sense as the object of divine salvation, but also as those who are anointed with the Spirit even as Jesus was so anointed. As bearers of the Spirit they enter into this process of inclusion, conversion, and transfiguration, in a fundamental sense through their identification with Christ in baptism (justification/regeneration) and in a processive and discrete sense through their immersion into and life in the Spirit (sanctification/mission). In answer, then, to our first query, we can respond that pneumatology does not collapse into anthropology, but rather through the insights of Spirit-christology the *humanum* is the locus for the temporal (and eschatological!) missions of the Son and the Spirit.

Our second query posed the question of whether a Christic-pneumatology or a

Spirit-christology is best able to answer to the implications of a changing and pluralistic context for dogmatic reflection. The difference between the two positions is whether the christological dimension is either determinative (Spirit-christology) or simply descriptive (Christic-pneumatology) of the interaction between the changing human context and the divine. Two responses can be made in answer to this question.

On the formal level the query poses a false dilemma. In trinitarian perspective, the formal theoretical setting for Spirit-christology, there is no christology without pneumatology, nor pneumatology without christology.[51] Therefore, the answer must focus more particularly on the material content of christology and pneumatology. Here the question may be posed as follows: Is the Christ simply the manifestation of mutual encounter between divine Spirit and human being, or is the humanity of the Christ—namely, Jesus crucified and risen—the bearer and sender of the Spirit and the one to whom the Spirit bears witness?

To answer the above question, we may draw on a distinction maintained throughout the neo-scholastic development of Spirit-christology. There it was important to uphold the integrity of each of the trinitarian missions and in doing so to distinguish between the relation of each mission to human reality—the christological mission to a human nature and the pneumatological mission to human persons. This formal distinction may also be translated into the material identity of each. For example, the term of the christological mission in the crucified and risen Jesus enfleshes that mission in the particularity of the evangelical narrative that is indispensable to the Christian proclamation. Because of that particularity, which the church confesses is of saving significance, the inclusion of the particular within the divine economy is ensured. The proper pneumatological mission to many persons proceeds from both God and the risen humanity of Jesus. The dual dangers of docetism, wherein christology collapses into pneumatology, and of the reduction of soteriology to anthropological aspiration are here avoided. The latter should not be underestimated, as Hans Frei once remarked in reference to anthropologically centered notions of the divine presence:

> What is grasped is empty space—the shadow of our own craving for full and perpetual presence.[52]

We conclude, then, that it is Jesus Christ, whose identity is still eschatologically outstanding and therefore does not entirely foreclose the meaning of that identity in continued Christian confession, who is both of the Spirit (the basis of Spirit-christology) and the sender of the Spirit. He it is who now invites and seals the many with the diversity of all their concerns in the return of all things to God who will be all in all (1 Cor. 15:34).

Emancipatory Concerns of Social Praxis and a Just Society

In this section I propose to examine the productivity of Spirit-christology for the emancipatory concerns of the church's social praxis in the interests of constructing a just society. As raised by many liberation theologians, the key dogmatic issue is the relationship between salvation from God and liberation in history. Does Spirit-christology provide an accessible dogmatic model to address this issue? I do not propose here to directly debate the theological meaning of freedom, liberation, or emancipation.[53] My intent is only to probe our model to see if it may shed light on the specific issue mentioned.

This query again focuses attention on the relationship in the trinitarian missions between the agency of the divine persons and that of the church. Who is active in the praxis and agency of human beings for liberation and freedom? The question might be posed slightly differently. Whose history unfolds in the liberating agency of human beings: that of Christ, the Spirit, or the church as distinct from both Christ and the Spirit? Jürgen Moltmann, for instance, refers to the trinitarian history of God and the histories of both Christ and the Spirit.[54] Kilian McDonnell describes the Holy Spirit as the "point of contact" between God and humankind so that one may consider the mission of the Spirit in history and in the church.[55] Walter Kasper attests to the "universal historical activity of the Spirit" that reaches its goal in Jesus Christ.[56] Both William Hill and David Coffey make similar statements, although they distingush between the transhistorical work of the Spirit and the historical work of the Son.[57] Coffey makes the following distinction: The divine Son has a history in the incarnate Jesus, but the Spirit who is affected by history and works in history does not have a history. The only proper history is that of the church which the Spirit inhabits; only the "specifically human dimension" may have a history.[58] What is the significance of these fine distinctions and how do they relate to our query in the light of Spirit-christology?

The issue has been posed as the relationship between salvation from God and liberation in history. Let us consider these in reference to the trinitarian missions and their convergence (without identity) in Spirit-christology. Indeed we may speak of the work of the Holy Spirit in history, and Kasper is certainly correct to point to its culmination in Jesus Christ. Both the christological mission and the pneumatological mission are described as temporal missions by Thomas Aquinas (a term we have continued to employ). What constitutes the temporality of these missions, and do each of the persons "inhabit" that temporality in the same manner? Only after answering these questions can we address the relationship between salvation and liberation, upon which turns the church's understanding of its emancipatory engagement in social praxis toward a just society.

The temporality of each of the missions may be defined in the dual dimensions of history and eschatology. Temporality in the biblical sense is not simply a polar contrast to eternity, but rather the reality of the contingent in time and space under the divine promise that proceeds from its fulfillment in the eschaton. Therefore, while we have argued for the necessary relationship between the temporal missions and the eternal processions, this should not obscure the modality of temporality into which the Son and the Spirit are missioned. Both the Son and the Spirit actualize their missions historically in the power of eschatological fulfillment. The manifestation of each particular mission appears specifically historic depending on the relative point of salvation-history. For example, especially with regard to the Son, the manifestation of his mission emerges throughout the course of the evangelical narrative from life to ministry, passion, death, and resurrection, bearing its own eschatological tension between the proclamation of Jesus and his destiny (as the coming Son of Man on the clouds of heaven and the suffering Son of Man on the cross). In the resurrection, history takes a turn, so to speak, surpassing history in eschatological fulfillment, although even here there exists a temporal/historical tension between the risen Christ and the parousial Christ, at least in the ecclesial witness to Christ with its implications for sanctification (1 Jn. 3:2). Christ still has a future, one that is inseparable from his Body, the church, and from the eschatological renewal of all creation.

When we turn to the Spirit we must examine how the third person inhabits the same modality of temporality in the tension between history and eschatology. With Hill and Coffey, we agree that incarnation and inhabitation differ. The Spirit is never incarnated in the same manner that the Son is in the man Jesus.[59] This excludes the same historical modality that is properly the Son's, although it does not exclude the tension between history and eschatology in the Spirit's actualization of a temporal mission. It is to this particular actualization that we must now turn before we examine the convergence of the missions in Spirit-christology.

The Holy Spirit active as subject is "the glorifying God" and "the unifying God."[60] In the history of God's economy the Spirit is subject even in the christological mission, creating, sanctifying, and uniting Jesus' humanity to the divine Son and enabling his ministry and paschal mystery. In this respect, the Spirit is the agent of the *transitio* of Jesus from history (indeed, a cruciform history) to eschatological glory. In its own proper mission beginning at Pentecost, the Spirit as gift and ecstatic love of God (Rom. 5:5) intensifies the tension between the eschatological already and the historical not yet (the reversal is intentional). As downpayment and firstfruits of what is to come, the Holy Spirit inhabits its temporal mission in a manner different from that of the Son. The Spirit is not the direct subject of historical experience as is Jesus and the church. To this extent, Hill and Coffey are correct to distinguish the christological and pneumatological missions relative to their persons as historical and transhistorical. However, as the agent of the church's life, worship, and mission, the Holy Spirit manifests through its guidance, strengthening, and gifts a taste of the powers of the age to come in the historical specificity of Christian praxis. Any attribution of history to the Holy Spirit is an indirect one but one that makes possible the real history of the church. This history is a history of Christian witness and mission in the Spirit, precisely the history of the church as the manifestation or sacrament of the trinitarian missions of the divine economy. Without the eschatological gift of the Spirit, no such history is possible.

Before proceeding to the import of this for the church's social praxis, one dogmatic issue requires attention. It surfaced in previous chapters in the debate between the different schools of neo-scholasticism over the nature of the trinitarian missions *ad extra*, whether union with the divine persons is measured within the structure of grace itself or in the elevated intentionality of knowledge and love. The concern of the traditional school, which advocated the latter position, was to preserve the transcendence of God relative to the created order. Even the school of de la Taille, Rahner and others who advocated the former position were careful to qualify their presentation of the issue in a manner that recognized the validity of this concern; hence the notion of *quasi*-formal causality in reference to uncreated grace. In this discussion, where our focus is the relationship of history to eschatology in the trinitarian missions, we may answer that same concern by pointing out how the presence of the Son and the Spirit in history, and the issue of whether as persons they possess a history, directly proceeds from the eschatological fullness that the persons bring to bear in the contingency of the church's historical existence. The unifying action of the Spirit, which in the neo-scholastic tradition caused both schools to identify the union with the divine persons relative to their *ad intra* relations (so that God does not so much change in history but that humans are transfigured in God) may now be translated as the transformation of the historical by the fullness of the eschatological. The divine promise is fulfilled in the eschatological return of the Son and the Spirit to the Father inclusive of a transfigured creation.

The convergence of the two missions in Spirit-christology provides the following texture to the explication of the issue under discussion. In Jesus Christ the relationship between history and eschatology includes both a filiological and a pneumatological dimension. As explicated above, Jesus as the divine Son incarnate embodies the reality of sonship (and by theological relevance, daughterhood) in the conditions of history with a view toward the eschaton. In fact, sonship and daughterhood is that relation to God in which the eschatological—i.e., the undiminished relation to God—appears under the conditions of history (the reason liturgically why the baptism of Jesus is the mark of his epiphany in the Eastern tradition, now also acknowledged in the West). The decisive eschatological declaration of Jesus' sonship was his resurrection (Rom. 1:4). In both cases, in history and in the *transitio* into the eschaton, the pneumatological dimension is also important.

As we have seen, the Holy Spirit is the Spirit of sonship and daughterhood. The filial relation of Jesus Christ to the God he proclaimed becomes through the adoption of grace the filial relation of all whom God elects. The Holy Spirit is therefore the agent of this filial relation for both Christ and the church. In that respect Jesus and all who are in Christ bear in their historical activity, their social praxis, the signs of the Spirit's presence. The Spirit, who does not possess its own history and yet has a definitive role as agent in salvation-history, is manifested in the words and deeds of the church in mission. As a historical reality the praxis of the church is a manifestation of the Spirit's guidance, strengthening, and energies that is the modality of the risen Lord's liberative action in the world.

Recalling our discussion of the relationship between the *Christus praesens* and the *Spiritus praesens* in the previous chapter, we can add to it and now make the argument that the salvific action of the risen Christ can be characterized by a threefold discreteness in agency. First is the "once for all" *transitio* of Jesus' pasch to the Father (Rom. 6:10, Heb. 9:28). Here the primordial filial relation between the first and second persons of the trinity is historicized in the flesh of Jesus, which signifies the cross as the mark of history. Second, there is the sending of the Holy Spirit by the risen Christ (in Johannine terms, the Father sends the Spirit at the request of Jesus [Jn. 14:16]; in Lukan terms, Jesus himself sends the Spirit who is the promise of the Father [Lk. 24:49]), a sending that is both "once for all" as in the symbol of Pentecost and continual as embodied in the epicletic character of Christian liturgy. Third is the agency of Christ manifested in his Body, the church. Here, historical agency and the eschatological energies of the Spirit combine. This distinguishes the church as *ekklesia*, a called-out assembly by and in the missions of Christ and his Spirit.

Spirit-christology, therefore, functions as a dogmatic model in which the convergence of the christological and pneumatological missions points to the connection between the divine economy and the social praxis of the church. The witness and deeds of the church in mission are human actions that participate in the agency of the risen Christ through the energizing power of the Holy Spirit. They are historically specific but full of the eschatological life of the Spirit. The relationship between salvation from God and liberation in history is indirect but profound. It entails the mediation of divine agency—specifically, the "two hands of God" through the human agency of the People of God. Such agency means that human emancipatory action in history may be a sign of God's salvation, the parabolic manifestation of the Holy Spirit who is the liberating grace of God—"For the law of the spirit, the Spirit of life in Christ Jesus, has freed you from the law of sin and death" (Rom. 8:2).

Religious Pluralism and the Quest for Dialogue

This third and final issue raises a pneumatological question that is also present in the previous two issues, although we did not address it. It concerns the presence of the Spirit outside of the church, in other religions but also in culture generally or in various social and political movements. We will examine this question in reference to a theology of interreligious dialogue, although insights here may also be extracted and applied to the other categories as well. Again, the options in Spirit-christology can be quite diverse. I shall mention one alternative model before suggesting my own reading.

First, John Hick in the interest of advancing a pluralist model for interreligious dialogue proposes that an inspiration christology is the only cogent model for such an enterprise. His is a Spirit-christology similar to that of Geoffrey Lampe's (explicated in the previous chapter), except that Hick posits only a relative manifestation of divinity in Christ.[61] In other words, he argues that the human life of Jesus is an instance of divine immanence through the inspiration of God as Spirit but not an absolute or exclusive instance. The logic of the latter he contends stems not from the model of Spirit-christology but is misapplied to the model from incarnation christology, which he disavows.[62] It is his view that such a christology, which is experiential and theocentric, allows for dialogue with other religions, for it affirms the religious meaning of Jesus without making it final or supremely unique.

The response to Hick's proposal would be much the same as that directed toward Lampe, so I do not propose to repeat it here. Suffice it to say that if Hick is to be refuted, then the hypostatic predication of the Son and the Spirit within the framework of Spirit-christology should be able to enrich the possibilities for interreligious dialogue rather than attentuate it, as he would argue. My tack will be, then, to exploit the model of Spirit-christology arrived at in this study in the direction of a theology of interreligious dialogue. As in the previous two sections, I will focus only on those dogmatic points relevant to the model that facilitate such a possibility.

I begin with a paradigm of interreligious dialogue suggested by Aloysius Pieris,

S.J.[63] He describes his model as a core-to-core dialogue through a *communicatio in sacris* (communion in ritual).[64] It is a model that seeks to enter into the "primordial *experience*" of a given religion while at the same time negotiating its "collective *memory*" of that experience and its philosophical, theological, and exegetical inter- petations.[65] Our adaptation of that model will seek to correlate it with a Spirit-christo- logy that upholds the hypostatic integrity of trinitarian theology.

As has been alluded to in the previous two sections, the reality of the divine self-communication (in the sense meant by Rahner and Coffey—i.e., the Father who communicates in his Son and Spirit; the latter two persons do not communicate but are communicated—see Chapter 4) is possessed of three distinct moments—namely, the christological, the pneumatological, and the ecclesial. These may be correlated with the three dimensions of Pieris's core-to-core dialogue in the following fashion:

primordial experience > pneumatological
collective memory > christological
interpretation > ecclesial

These three levels of dialogue along with these three distinct dimensions of the divine self-communication enable the Christian to enter the conversation at any one of the levels but without exclusion of the other two. Each level now requires explication in light of the relevant dogmatic issue proffered by Spirit-christology. I will begin in reverse sequence.

Interpretation of religious experience takes place at the level of ecclesial location (with "ecclesial" for the moment understood in a generic sense relative to other non-Christian religious communities). As an ongoing enterprise it develops the traditions of the community with respect to cultural and intellectual changes. It is also the moment of reception vis-à-vis the interpretive act that defines the community and underscores the role of human agency. Theologically, such reception is depen- dent on the other moments of experience and memory, or in the language of Christian dogmatics, the ecclesial event is dependent on the christological and pneumatological missions. In a Christian theology of interreligious dialogue, the ecclesial dimension ensures that the dialogue is between communities of faith and that the communal acceptation of religious event is a constituent dimension of the human experience of the transcendent through which God is made known in the world. That the Christian church is an instance of this is interpreted theologically not within the confines of that ecclesial locus as if it was formed of itself, but with respect to the christological and pneumatological missions that actualize the divine election within the human community. In interreligious dialogue, the same respect is accorded to the other communities relative to their instantiation of religious event and its forma- tive and therefore self-critical transcendental influences.

The collective memory of religious experience evokes in the Christian context its proclamation, witness, and confession of Jesus Christ. It is the mediating moment between religious event and religious community. It demands anamnesis and epicle- sis (the christological can never be totally separated from the pneumatological). The christological moment is formative of the ecclesial community for its passage through history as it seeks to "remember the future" (pointing to its eschatological location between the ages—2 Cor. 5:16–17) of the risen Christ.[66] In interreligious dialogue, christology as the Christian representation of collective memory responds to the memory of other religious traditions by seeking out not only possible christological analogues but more profoundly the central motifs that structure the practices and beliefs of the other religious tradition. By the former the Christian seeks points of similarity; by the latter the Christian interlocutor enters into a christological kenosis—what Pieris calls a "self-effacing baptismal entry" into another religion[67]— in an effort to understand it and to be open before the divine mystery. It is the path of conversion in dialogue whose goal is neither proselytism nor eclecticism but communion and mutual witness.

The primordial experience of the Christian life is the reception of the Holy Spirit. As most of the advocates of Spirit-christology stated, the Holy Spirit is the contact person in whom the Christian is united with God. Therefore, the pneumatological mission is the Christian theological context for entry into the *communicatio in sacris*, the core-to-core dialogue. Two dogmatic issues are raised in this regard. First is the relation of the pneumatological mission to the christological one. Second is the theological explication of this mission in interreligious dialogue. We begin with the former.

The relationship between the two trinitarian missions has been the subject of our inquiry throughout this study. Does the challenge of interreligious dialogue contribute any insights? The dialogue simply highlights the possibility that the Holy Spirit may be considered in its own right in distinction from Jesus Christ. Can there be distinct theologies of *Spiritus Creator* and *Spiritus Redemptor*, as Philip Rosato suggests in criticism of Karl Barth's Christocentric pneumatology?[68] Indeed, we are required to speak of the Spirit's cosmic role in creation both protologically (Gen. 1:2) and eschatologically (Rom. 8:22–23; Rev. 22:17). In addition, the ecclesial locus of the Spirit's work does not exclude a secular focus as well (especially in relation to the previous two queries). Whether we need to speak of two distinct theologies of the Spirit requires further examination, although I think not. By preserving the integrity of the hypostatic distinction between the Son and the Spirit (including its explication vis-à-vis identity, agency, and presence—see Chapter 5), we may speak of the work of the Spirit in other than christological terms. This does not betray the instincts of Spirit-christology, where we have sought the convergence without identity of the two missions. Rather, it enables us to theologize about the Spirit in either of two directions. Because Christ is the bearer and sender of the Spirit, we speak of the Spirit in relation to Christ and his work. However, because Christ is of the Spirit (*conceptus de Spiritu Sancto*) we can also speak of the Spirit's work in creation, Israel, the secular order, and in other religions even as we still confess the unique work in Jesus Christ. Both Christ and the Spirit each bear their own agency toward the other. There is no subordinationism. Rosato has eloquently stated both sides of the Spirit's work:

> Nor does a Pneuma-Sarx Christology confuse the unmatched presence of the Spirit in Jesus with His pervasive indwelling in the rest of creation. . . . Thus Jesus surpasses the universal work of the Spirit while at the same time He furthers and condenses the Spirit's ongoing cosmic action.[69]

To return now to the specific issue of interreligious dialogue, we can venture the following. The pneumatological mission, like the christological mission, undergoes its own kenosis through its cosmic action and the divine inhabitation. So, too, in reference to the primordial experience of the diverse religious traditions, the Spirit leads the Christian interlocutor into the depths of the *communicatio in sacris* by her or his participation in the poverty and riches of the pneumatic self-giving of God. Since the Holy Spirit is personally the love and gift of God as well as life-giver ("I believe in the Holy Spirit, the Lord and *Giver of Life*"), the Christian witness in dialogue seeks such life at the first level of religious experience, a level Pieris in the wisdom of the Spirit describes as "ineffable and incommunicable but realizable."[70]

Therefore, in all three stages of the dialogue there is a relationship between the meaning the theological rubric bears in Christianity and the possiblity it extends toward dialogue. Here Spirit-christology functions more on the level of its discrete distinctions rather than the convergence of its constituent elements. This displays the versatility of the model. In Christian faith it is the convergence of the elements—e.g., Christ, Spirit, faith—that is significant; in dialogue with other religions, this convergence allows its own elements to be focused at the point of inquiry where the dialogue will be most fruitful.

Conclusion

This chapter has examined the productivity of Spirit-christology in relation to three areas of contemporary theological concern and investigation. We employed the particular model of orthodox Spirit-christology developed out of the neo-scholastic tradition in Roman Catholic theology. This model is marked by its accessibility to the convergence of the christological and pneumatological missions without collapsing one into the other. This required the development of trinitarian models that allowed for this possibility through their ability to maintain the hypostatic integrity of the trinitarian distinctions along with the relations of the missions to one another in the divine economy.

Previously we tested the maturely developed model of David Coffey against alternative models of Spirit-christology to both examine the precise dogmatic issues that concerned the relationship between the second and third persons in Spirit-christology and to translate the truth of these orthodox distinctions into a different theological idiom. This final chapter explored the utilization of Spirit-christology in a non-scholastic idiom in relation to the issues under discussion. In all three cases Spirit-christology deepens trinitarian faith and enables theological investigation at a number of complex but related levels.

In conclusion, Spirit-christology as the theological focus for this investigation and for the theologians who were examined, leads us to consciously identify the sources of renewal for Christian reflection on the triune God as Christ and his Spirit who as the "two hands of God" are the mystagogical entry into a renewed ecclesial life for the sake of the gospel in the world. Many consider this to be the true promise of the Second Vatican Council, foreseen especially in the invocation by Pope John XXIII to the Holy Spirit for renewal "as by a New Pentecost."[71]

Notes

1. This is due in part to the challenge posed to the dominant culture by previously marginalized groups—e.g., African Americans, other people of color, and women.

2. Friedrich Schleiermacher, *The Christian Faith* (English translation of the second German edition), ed. H. R. Mackintosh and J. S. Stewart (Philadelphia: Fortress, 1928), p. 560, Proposition 121.

3. "Concluding Unscientific Postscript on Schleiermacher," *Karl Barth: The Theology of Schleiermacher* ed. Dietrich Ritschl, tr. Geoffrey W. Bromiley (Grand Rapids: Eerdmans, 1982), p. 279. Of course, Barth's well-known criticism of Schleiermacher proceeds out of the greatest respect. Barth comments: "The first place in a history of the most recent times belongs and will always belong to Schleiermacher, and he has no rival."—From Barth's *Protestant Theology in the Nineteenth Century* (Valley Forge: Judson Press, 1973), p. 425. An excellent acount of Barth's own pneumatology is provided by Philip J. Roasato, S. J., *The Spirit as Lord: The Pneumatology of Karl Barth* (Edinburgh: T & T Clark, 1981). Included in partial critique of Barth is his final chapter, "Christology in a Pneumatic Framework," pp. 157–180, which addresses many of the important issues in Spirit-christology, including the "Ontic Validity of the Spirit's Mission."

4. Idem., "Concluding Unscientific Postscript," p. 276.

5. Idem., *The Christian Faith*, p. 569.

6. Ibid., p. 582, Proposition 126.

7. Ibid., p. 76, Proposition 15.

8. Ibid., p. 563.

9. Ibid.

10. Ibid., pp. 400–402, 563.

11. Ibid., p. 385, Proposition 94.

12. Ibid., pp. 562, 568.

13. Paul Tillich, *Systematic Theology,* Volume III: *Life and the Spirit, History and the Kingdom of God* [henceforth, *ST* III] (Chicago: University of Chicago Press, 1963), p. 158.

14. Idem, *Systematic Theology, Volume I:* Reason and Revelation, Being and God [henceforth, *ST* I] (Chicago: University of Chicago Press, 1951), pp. 59–66.

15. Tillich, *ST* III. p. 111.

16. Ibid., p. 22.

17. Ibid., p. 111

18. Ibid., pp. 30–110.

19. The distinction between fragmentation and ambiguity is an important one for Tillich. The Spiritual Presence and the New Being are the source of unambiguous life; however, it is still fragmentary in its manifestation in space and time. *ST* III, p. 140.

20. Paul Tillich, *Systematic Theology,* Volume II: *Existence and The Christ* [henceforth, *ST* II] (Chicago: University of Chicago Press, 1957), pp. 118–119.

21. Tillich, *ST* III, p. 144.

22. Ibid., pp. 146–147.

23. Ibid., p. 114.

24. Ibid., p. 139.

25. For this criticism see especially Tom F. Driver, *Patterns of Grace: Human Experience as the Word of God* (San Francisco: Harper & Row, 1977), pp. 29–49.

26. Tom F. Driver, *Christ in a Changing World: Toward an Ethical Christology* (New York: Crossroad, 1981), p. 45.

27. Ibid., p. 24.

28. Ibid., p. 75.

29. Ibid., p. 109.

30. Ibid., p. 108.

31. Ibid., pp., 18, 76.

32. Ibid., pp. 28-31.

33. Ibid., p. 168.

34. In one of his most eloquent passages, Driver describes this as follows: "In Jesus, the gospels suggest, God's interest in humanity and a human interest in God (both personified in Jesus) took a leap across the sparking gap and made lightning." Ibid., p. 110.

35. Ibid., p. 108.

36. Ibid., pp. 111-112.

37. Ibid., pp. 76, 111.

38. Schleiermacher, *The Christian Faith*, p. 738, Proposition 170. It should also be noted that Tillich follows Schleiermacher in placing the doctrine of the trinity toward the end of his systematic theology—specifically, at the end of Part IV (Life and the Spirit) of vol. III.

39. Karl Barth, *Church Dogmatics I,1* (The Doctrine of the Word of God: Prologomena to Church Dogmatics), tr. G. W. Bromiley (Edinburgh: T & T Clark, 1975), p. 303.

40. Ibid., 307.

41. Barth states it thus: "The doctrine of the Trinity is what basically distinguishes the Christian doctrine of God as Christian, and therefore what already distinguishes the Christian concept of revelation as Christian, in contrast to all other possible doctrines of God or concepts of revelation." Ibid., p. 301.

42. *Theology and Church* (New York: Crossroad, 1989), especially pp. 73-108.

43. New York: Paulist, 1979. Also his more recent *God Encountered: A Contemporary Catholic Systematic Theology,* Vol. I: *Understanding the Christian Faith* (San Francisco: Harper & Row, 1989).

44. Kasper uses similar language. In his chapter on christology titled "One of the Trinity . . ." he subtitles it "Re-establishing a Spiritual Christology in the Perspective of Trinitarian Theology." Ibid., p. 94. It should be noted that Kasper, whose own theological heritage is the "Catholic Tübingen School," represents a distinctly non-scholastic approach to theology as a whole and the issues that we have investigated. His own preference for Spirit-christology is essayed in his *Jesus the Christ* (New York: Paulist, 1976): ". . . the mediation between God and man in Jesus Christ can be understood theologically only as an event 'in the Holy Spirit.' This leads us to a pneumatologically-orientated theology." (p. 249). His book *The God of Jesus Christ* (New York: Crossroad, 1984) thoroughly examines the theology of the trinity.

45. Kasper, *Theology and Church*, p. 82.

46. Ibid.

47. Ibid., p. 83.

48. Ibid., pp. 84-91.

49. Ibid., p. 92.

50. Kasper himself is an advocate of Spirit-christology, or what he terms a "Christology in a pneumatological perspective." *Jesus the Christ*, p. 267. There, he also states what is in effect a Spirit-christology in language close to the neo-scholastic tradition: "In the language of the dogmatic tradition, the Spirit as the *gratia unionis* is not only his private endowment of grace, but is at the same time *gratia capitis*, which overflows from Christ the head into his body the Church and is transmitted by the Church to the world." (p. 253). This could be a summary of our arguments in Chapters 2-5.

51. This is the basic thesis of Yves Congar, O.P., in his work on the relationship between Christ and the Spirit. See his *The Word and the Spirit* (San Francisco: Harper & Row, 1986).

52. Hans Frei, *The Identity of Jesus Christ: The Hermeneutical Bases of Dogmatic Theology* (Philadelphia: Fortress, 1975), p. 34.

53. Aside from the numerous works of liberation theologians, the issue has also been joined by other theologians—e.g., Walter Kasper, *Theology and Church*, pp. 54–72; *The Christian Understanding of Freedom and the History of Freedom in the Modern Era: The Meeting and Confrontation Between Christianity and the Modern Era in the Postmodern Situation* (Milwaukee: Marquette University Press, 1988)—as well as by the Roman Curia: see "Instruction on Christian Freedom and Liberation," promulgated in 1986 by the Congregation for the Doctrine of the Faith.

54. Jürgen Moltmann, *The Church in the Power of the Spirit* (San Francisco: Harper & Row, 1977), pp. 50–65.

55. Kilian McDonnell, O.S.B., "A Trinitarian Theology of the Holy Spirit?" *Theological Studies* 46 (1985), p. 208.

56. Walter Kasper, *Jesus the Christ*, pp. 266–267.

57. William Hill, *The Three-Personed God*, p. 290.

58. David Coffey, "A Proper Mission of the Holy Spirit," p. 243.

59. This despite the recent suggestion by Leonardo Boff that the Holy Spirit so "pneumatized" Mary that it took human form in her even as the Son did the same in Jesus. He advances this only as a theologoumenon and leaves many questions open—e.g., whether the union with Mary is a hypostatic union and whether the Holy Spirit takes on her human nature or her person. See his *Trinity and Society* (Maryknoll: Orbis, 1988), pp. 210–212.

60. Jürgen Moltmann, *The Trinity and the Kingdom: The Doctrine of God* (San Francisco: Harper & Row, 1981), p. 126.

61. See his essay with responses, "An Inspiration Christology for a Religiously Plural World," in *Encountering Jesus*, ed. Stephen T. Davis, ((Atlanta: John Knox, 1988), pp. 5–38.

62. Ibid., pp. 20–21. See also his essay, "Jesus and the World Religions," in the book of his editing, *The Myth of God Incarnate* (Philadelphia: Westminster, 1977), pp. 167–185.

63. See his *Love Meets Wisdom: A Christian Experience of Buddhism* (Maryknoll: Orbis, 1988).

64. Ibid. pp. 110, 119–123.

65. Ibid., pp. 120–121.

66. See J. Louis Martyn, "Epistemology at the Turn of the Ages: 2 Corinthians 5.16," in *Christian History and Interpretation: Studies Presented to John Knox*, ed. W. R. Farmer et al. (Cambridge: Cambridge University Press, 1967), pp. 269–287.

67. Pieris, *Loves Meets Wisdom*, p. 123.

68. Rosato, *The Spirit as Lord*, pp. 179–180. For a theology of the *Spiritus Creator*, see Jürgen Moltmann, *God in Creation: A New Theology of Creation and the Spirit of God* (San Francisco: Harper & Row, 1985). It also should be noted that although too late for consideration in this work, Moltmann's two recent books on christology and pneumatology each propose a Spirit-christology within the context of a comprehensive trinitarian theology. He advances the discussion considerably (and entirely within a non-scholastic context). See especially: *The Way of Jesus Christ: Christology in Messianic Dimensions*, (San Francisco: Harper, 1990), pp. 73–94; *The Spirit of Life: A Universal Affirmation*, Minneapolis: Fortress, 1992), pp. 58–77. In the latter work Moltmann critically interacts with the Encylical Letter of John Paul II (*Dominum et Vivificantem*— "On the Holy Spirit in the Life of the Church and the World," 1986) who to some extent develops his own Spirit-christology. See especially I, 1–7; II, 4–5.

69. Ibid., p. 176.

70. Pieris, *Love Meets Wisdom*, p. 120.

71. "Prayer of Pope John XXIII to the Holy Spirit for the Success of the Ecumenical Council," in *The Documents of Vatican II*, ed. Walter M. Abbott, S.J. (New York: Guild Press, 1966), p. 792.

APPENDIX

The Christologies of
Piet Schoonenberg, S.J.
and Frans Jozef van Beeck, S.J.

"After Chalcedon": The Revisionary
Christology of Piet Schoonenberg, S.J.

Schoonenberg's book *The Christ* was an attempt to construct a new christology on the basis of a reconception of God's relationship to the world.[1] He begins with criticism of the notion that there is some sort of conflict between divine and human causality.[2] Because creation's dependence on God's total causality is continuous, this is a false dilemma.[3] Divine and worldly causality concur through God's transcendent initiative, which "does not stand beside a worldy cause, and is immanent in all cause and in all reality."[4] Schoonenberg is clear that this is an exercise in metaphysical theology, but one that the biblical concepts of creation and covenant demand. The traditional Catholic distinction between nature and grace is elaborated by reference to God's covenant in the very act of creation. One can distinguish nature and grace only in theory; in actuality, God's covenantal grace is active in creation through the mediation of creatures one to another eliciting their own vocation and mission.[5] Against the background of this theology of creation, Schoonenberg proceeds to revise Chalcedon.

His revision of Chalcedon is somewhat indirect in that his real target is neo-Chalcedonism, which he basically turns on its head. It was Leontius of Byzantium, the most important representative of this trend, who argued that the human nature of Christ existed enhypostatically—that is, "it exists *in* the divine hypostasis of the Word."[6] The other side of this position is whether or not the human nature of Christ is also *an*-hyposatic, without its own hypostasis—that is, if it exists within the divine hypostasis of the Logos, does that mean it does not possess its own human hypostasis? If the anhypostasis of Christ's humanity is affirmed, argues Schoonenberg, then in effect we are denying full humanity to Jesus, since personhood—i.e., "a human, created act of being"—is essential to what it means to be human and therefore for Christ to be truly consubstantial with us.[7]

Schoonenberg accounts for the criticism of the two-nature pattern of Chalcedon as being due to the confusion engendered by the terms, nature, and person. One can

217

recall Friedrich Schleiermacher's objection to Chalcedon on the same grounds. In that instance, Schleiermacher argued that "nature" could not be used for both God and humanity since nature and God are opposing realities. Whereas nature is divided and conditioned, God is unconditioned and absolutely simple, the real issue being that one cannot indifferently bring together the divine and human under one and the same universal. In addition, one could not logically combine a dual use of nature with a single use of person. Either one nature will be subsumed by the other or both will combine to form a third.[8] In either case, the intent of Chalcedon is subverted, especially if the unity of the person is to be maintained—i.e., "a constant unity of life . . . an Ego which is the same in all the consecutive moments of existence."[9] Schoonenberg, on the other hand, does note that "nature" (*phusis*) as used in patristic times "simply expressed the reality of a determined being" and could thus be taken as a synonym for the Nicene *ousia*. However, he admits that misunderstandings arose in interpretations of Chalcedon that, because they held the divine and human elements in equal relation, by necessity needed to subsume one to the other as seen, for instance, in the anhypostasia of Christ's humanity in neo-Chalcedonism—a development, by the way, that is affirmed by Coffey.[10] His solution is to begin christological reflection on the basis of the unity of Christ's person, purportedly "a christology without dualism."[11]

Although Schoonenberg proposes a christology that exceeds the scope of Chalcedon, it is only in reference to Chalcedon that his christology is constructive. If Chalcedon is to be interpreted on the basis of its own distinction between "nature" and "person"—i.e., "everything pertaining respectively to the divine and the human, by which Jesus Christ is one in being respectively with the Father and with us"—then one must revise interpretations of Chalcedon that compromise the unity of Jesus Christ as a human person.[12] This holds true for past christologies—e.g., neo-Chalcedonism—as well as for modern christologies that impose their definitions on the various ancient terms of the christological equation. Therefore, before proposing a positive christology under the title *"The Human Transcendence of Jesus Christ as a Man,"* Schoonenberg posits a rather distinctive and critical reversal.[13]

> The concept developed here regarding Christ's being-person is a reversal of the Chalcedonian pattern insofar as it is influenced by neo-Chalcedonism, which has become our current christology. Now not the human but the divine nature in Christ is anhypostatic, with the proviso, moreover, that this is valid inasmuch as we do not know the person of the Word outside the man Jesus. However, it is primarily not the human nature which is enhypostatic in the divine person, but the divine nature in the human person.[14]

The reasons for this reversal in Schoonenberg's mind are threefold. First, the integrity of Christ's human personhood and his human personality require it. Second, the ontological probability of this proposal is greater than its opposite, because the perfection of personhood is also a limitation insofar as what exists-in-itself in consciousness and freedom is also an individuality. One must deny this limitation and transcend human conceptuality—in this case arising as it does out of the experience of human personhood—to speak of personhood in God. Such a limitation—i.e., the ontological reality of what it is to be a person—can be applied to God only insofar as God identifies the divine self with a creature—namely, the incarnation in the history of salvation (for example, the economic trinity). For Schoonenberg, this is more on-tologically probable than the nullification of human personhood in Jesus through his enhypostatization in a pre-existent divine Word. Third, it removes the dualities in traditional christologies—e.g., two wills, two energies, adoptive vs. natural sonship, etc—therefore avoiding the possibility of heretical excess resulting from the constant struggle between Antiochine and Alexandrine christologies—e.g., Nestorianism in the case of the former and Apollinarianism and Monophysitism for the latter.[15]

In sum, Schoonenberg's project is to replace a christology of a divine person in Christ—i.e., a diphysite christology—with that of God's total presence in Christ—one that he believes is more in conformity with the New Testament.[16] Hence, when he turns to the Gospels to fill out the various dimensions of his christology, he is able to utilize biblical criticism in presenting a Jesus whose self-consciousness is strictly human and historically particular and contextualized. Two movements then take place in Schoonenberg's christology. First, he revises dogmatic christology according to the pattern just elucidated and that elsewhere he describes as the inclusion of an adoption christology within an incarnation christology.[17] Second, he correlates this dogmatic shift with elements of New Testament christologies. This entails a progressive revision of aspects of the traditional topics in the christological tractate—e.g., Jesus' earthly knowledge, his volition, sinlessness, temptations, faith, etc. Finally, he also extends this christology of God's presence to the reality of the glorified Christ.

In affirming "the personal reality and presence of the glorified Christ," Schoonenberg primarily attests to God's offer of salvation in its fullness. It is present in Jesus, who "evokes our faith, that he himself lives and makes himself present to us."[18] It possesses its own corporeality through the extension of Christ's glorified body in the church (although Christ does not coincide with the church) and awaits its future in the parousia.[19] Schoonenberg introduces pneumatology as an essential dimension of this confession. The *"Heavenly Completion"* of Jesus's life is the occasion for the Spirit's sending and presence, and although Schoonenberg understands this as the fullness of God's triune essence, he has difficulty in the positing of a "third person." Similar to his economic trinitarian interpretation of the enhypostasis of the Word in Jesus Christ, so, too, the Holy Spirit appears as an individual third person only over against the community of the glorified Jesus—i.e., in the salvific history of God's self-communication in the risen Lord. But how the Spirit "stands as a person over against God and Christ remains in question."[20] This problem, especially as it appears as a modalism of the second and third persons of the trinity, was taken up by him in subsequent articles in which his position on enhypostatic christology also slightly shifted. These articles were the subject of our inquiry in Chapter 5.

"Speaking in the Spirit": The Rhetorical Christology of Frans Jozef van Beeck, S.J.

Van Beeck's delineation of the "Rhetoric of Christology" begins with a non-cognitive moment—namely, a response to Jesus Christ, that precedes reflective christology. He describes this moment as the "christological situation." In it the personal response to Jesus is irreducible to cognition, and out of it the cognitive structuring of that response evolves from within the initial metaphorical designations utilized to handle this new reality.[21] For example, the early christological titles are evidence of this process in the primitive community. The high degree of conceptualization that characterized later christology was a reflective process that in response to new situations operated within the field opened by these titles, exploiting some, dropping others, to further structure the understanding of the reality encountered in Jesus Christ. However, even at this level, it cannot be denied that in the christological situation—e.g., worship—metaphor still functions as the irreducible given in response to the person of Jesus Christ; and on this basis it always represents a greater reality than can be encompassed by knowledge of Christ through either titles or reflective doctrine.

> Personal response to Christ is the setting of all cognitive christological statements. This personal response is conveyed by the rhetorical elements in christology.[22]

> All christological statments, while having clear cognitive functions are embedded in this act—an act of worship and witness—of surrender to Jesus Christ.[23]

On a theological level van Beeck describes this situation in pneumatological terms. To engage in the rhetoric of christology is to speak in the Spirit— *"Christ-talk is talk in the Spirit."*[24] The christological situation is a situation created by the presence of the Holy Spirit who is the inner motive force of the Christian and who stands outside the Christian—i.e., the Spirit is pure gift and pure faith not subject to any causality except God's freedom and love.[25] On the level of human consciousness and action, this entails three dimensions: (1) the commitment to Jesus Christ is as original a "given" as the awareness of the Spirit, (2) that this commitment is not one among others but the source, medium, and goal of all concerns and commitments, and (3) that the articulation of this commitment is shaped by particular concerns brought into this act of total commitment and all-embracing concern.[26] It is the presence of the Spirit that evokes this commitment or act of surrender to Jesus Christ. Confession of Christ, then, is a "Spirited" act; it is expressive of a response to Christ alive in the Spirit. It is in this setting, the christological situation identical with the situation of the Spirit, that christological statements are made in acknowledgment of Jesus Christ. Such statements reflect the power or *dynameis* of the situation and are particular to the extent that they express pneumatological discernments of the original or fundamental commitment.

Starting from the premise that "total surrender to Jesus Christ in the Spirit is the all-encompassing 'christological situation,'" van Beeck distinguishes among its partial apprehensions vis-á-vis terms, discernments, and concerns.[27] The first has been the traditional norm for christology, although both discernments and concerns were important factors. Therefore, the Chalcedonian statement, in which terminological language dominates, was a response to a particular threat that evoked a doctrinal definition as an act of faith (or discernment) in recognition of *"relevant cultural concerns,"* thereby motivating specific *"culturally significant terms."*[28] Van Beeck's strategy is to return to the example of New Testament language wherein the priority in cognitive structuring is given to words and not terms, the advantage being that there is a much closer relationship between words and their referents than between terms and their meaning. Terms are stable only for those who know how to use them and are aware of the cultural shifts that take place behind the terms. Words, on the other hand, preserve the dynamic connection between rhetoric and cognitive structuring—i.e., between "names and words, evocation and articulation."[29]

In practice, van Beeck envisions this process as evolving within the christological situation already described. Through surrender to Christ in worship and witness, a setting of discernments is created. Human concerns are brought to Christ, who presides over them. The discernments, partial as they are relative to the fundamental commitment to Christ,[30] initiate the cognitive structuring of christology within the situation and not prior to it. They are concerns related to our being in the world, which bond is necessary for any metaphorical outlook on Christ to attain its full meaning.[31] Van Beeck explores the relationship between these concerns and Christ's presidency over them by examination of the existential stances of inclusion and obedience.

The presentation of human concerns in the christological situation produces a rhetoric of inclusion. All human concerns are embraced and accepted—*"every human concern is capable of becoming a name of Jesus."*[32] The variety of christological titles used in the New Testament testifies to this, even as the historical Jesus eludes categorization. The risen Christ is the focus of these concerns—that is, only after the resurrection does this naming become thematized and expressed, the dynamics of which can be observed in the rhetorical structure of the New Testament witness. Van Beeck elucidates four ways in which the style of New Testament rhetoric embraces, assays, and puts into perspective these human concerns.[33] First, it radically transforms them. One striking example is the "transformation of familiar Jewish titles into related abstract nouns that function as personal titles."[34] In other words, the salvific function of Jesus Christ becomes absolutized through the identification of Jesus' person and cause in the bold metonymic Christian response to Christ—e.g., Paul's *parrhesia* (confidence) in 2 Cor. 3:12. Second, this leads to the naming of Christ by way of excellence—i.e., how believers handle the reality of encounter with the *Christus praesens*. Third, this is accomplished by the use of key-titles—e.g., vine, door, shepherd, etc.—and headship images—e.g., head, key-stone. Finally, the act of articulate surrender to Christ that such rhetoric expresses also entails the dynamic of Jesus's presidency over the particular concerns brought to him. This effects a metaphoric self-correction over the act of naming during this initial stage of cognitive christological structuring.[35]

It is clear that one cannot separate the rhetoric of inclusion from the rhetoric of obedience or, as we shall soon see, from the rhetoric of hope. However, the constructive possibilities of each type of christological rhetoric are distinct as well as related. For example, the classical locus for the rhetoric of inclusion is the consubstantiality of Jesus Christ with us according to humanity, the Chalcedonian *homoousios hemin.*[36] Van Beeck argues that the original function of this consubstantiality was "to express Jesus' *universal relatedness.*"[37] In his language this means that the Christian finds all human concerns appropriated by Christ in the surrender of faith. However, through speculation, this original christological rhetoric of inclusion became abstracted in the terminological concentration on the "human nature" of Christ and "its place in the hypostatic union of the God-Man *taken as an individ-*

ual."[38] The consequences of this move are twofold. First, the tendency in neo-Chalcedonian anhypostatic christology leaned toward monophysitism. Second is, the mistaken notion that attention to the instrumentality of such language was an adequate expression of christological thought. This criticism becomes more clear when we turn to the rhetoric of obedience.

If it is the case that all human concerns are embraced by the risen Christ, it is also the case that Christ exercises presidency over them.

> They find themselves tested and assayed, humbled and purified. They are called to obedience and converted to the way of Jesus. No human concern will be the same once it has become a name of Jesus.[39]

In terms of the rhetorical structure of christological naming, this ensures a process of self-correction vis-à-vis the metaphoric self-designations of the Christian community. For example, the designations "Son" and "Vine" are applied not to Christians but to Christ, with the former now named as "adoptive children" and "branches." This correction is a result of the original inclusion of human concerns expressed relationally, but now corrected and judged through surrender to Christ. It is a judgment or correction, however, realized within the horizon of total acceptance, within the grace of Christ's presence in the Holy Spirit.

Christ's presidency over human concerns is exercised not from above—i.e., lording it over them—but from below—i.e., serving them. Van Beeck argues that this particular rhetoric has its foundation in the poverty of Jesus and the freedom that comes from poverty as the basis for obedience. The *humanum* embraced in christology, because it is justified in Christ, is able to be converted from self-assertiveness and the use of force. Concerns are stripped of their inherent power only after being embraced by Christ, thus establishing Christian self-denial as the fruit of freedom. The rhetoric of obedience, as much as the rhetoric of inclusion, is an act of worship and witness in which "*every human concern is corrected and converted from self-assertiveness, surrenders to Christ's presidency, and thus becomes the stuff of obedience.*"[40]

Van Beeck returns to Chalcedon and evaluates the impact of the rhetoric of obedience on the formula. In the first instance he argues that the formula is not based on the rhetoric of obedience as it was on the rhetoric of inclusion. The abstractness of the "human nature" in the two-nature definition does not signify the obedient posture of Jesus' humanity. This concern was more explicit in the Third Council of Constantinople (680–681), which condemned monothelitism.

> We also proclaim two natural willings or wills in him and two natural operations, without separation, without change, without confusion, according to the teaching of the holy Fathers—and two natural wills not contrary [to each other] . . . but his human will following, and not resisting or opposing, but rather subject to his divine and all-powerful will. For it was proper for the will of the flesh to be moved [naturally], yet to be subject to the divine will.[41]

However, this definition along with Chalcedon still leaves unresolved the issue of Jesus' personalness. In both councils, the term "person" was reserved only for the result of the hypostatic union and not for Christ's human nature in particular—a necessarily anti-nestorian stance. The problem for modern christology and for the rhetoric of obedience concerns the necessarily "personal" nature of obedience. To resolve the issue, van Beeck considers and evaluates Schoonenberg's proposal.

In his christology Schoonenberg engages the neo-Chalcedonian tradition of anhypostatic christology through a reversal of its terminological intent. The Word is enhypostatic (in-personal) in the human person of Jesus, rather than the human nature being enhypostatic in the divine person of the Word—the bottom line being the one human personhood of Jesus Christ, with "person" being understood in its modern sense as an individual center of consciousness and freedom. Van Beeck does not deny the cogent speculative argument of anhypostatic christology against the background of neo-Chalcedonianism. However, in the modern discussion, the denial of Jesus' human personhood is problematic. Therefore, he agrees with Schoonenberg that a "good christology . . . [must] attribute full human personalness to Jesus Christ, without any limitation or diminishment, and this is certainly not effectually done by saying that Jesus Christ is not a human person."[42] And, more to the point, the *"rhetoric of inclusion* demands that a 'fully human person' become a name of Jesus."[43]

Van Beeck also considers the human personhood of Christ in light of the rhetoric of obedience. Before consideration of the speculative coherence of the concept of "person" when applied to Christ, one must first examine this term vis-á-vis the existential and practical posture of conversion. Jesus' human personhood is totally dependent on the the will of God—i.e., his basic "Abba" experience—and not in self-possession, self-maintenance, and self-actualization. The same is true of the Christian who surrenders to Christ. Even as Jesus gave himself willingly on the cross, revealing his self as gift and surrender in total openness and vulnerability—e.g., the traditional identification of Christ as both priest and victim—so, too, the Christian discovers self-actualization not as self-justification but as gift through that poverty in the Spirit which is faith.[44] Because the denial of human personhood in Jesus Christ would obviate the foundation necessary for the christological rhetoric of obedience, it is an act of Christian conversion to relativize the anhypostatic construct in favor of discourse that affirms the full personalness of Jesus on the basis of his transformation of the reality of power. Van Beeck does return to a more constructive rendering of this problematic, one that accounts for the divine hypostatic identity of the Logos as openness to the world in the modality of paschal service.[45] For the moment the terminological confusion between neo-Chalcedonian speculative effort and modern cultural sensibility on the value of human personhood must be resolved on the primary level of christological naming made explicit in a rhetoric of conversion.

The final foundational rhetoric for christological construction is that of hope. In addition to the possibility of universal inclusiveness and the call to total obedience, the grace of God in the risen Christ offers an absolute hope.[46] Each existential stance, each particular discernment, represents a concrete instantiation of a total commitment against a horizon of ultimate meaning. I have already mentioned the tension between "the partiality of the discernments in christology and the totality of the commitment involved in the surrender to Jesus Christ."[47] Van Beeck evaluates the transition in the surrender from partiality to totality as a *"qualitative leap* . . . , [that] which is involved in the Christian's announcement that Jesus Christ is vindicated, risen from the dead, exalted in virtue of his self-emptying unto death."[48] In this confession and proclamation the Christian speaks out of proportion to any particular discernment, warranted only by the presence of Christ in the Spirit.

The qualitative leap ensconced within the rhetoric of hope is not simply a delineation of subjective religious feeling—that is, a pious mythologoumenon. Nor is it a response only to the cause of Jesus that carries on in the lives of believers. It is the result of an encounter with the person of Jesus Christ present in the Spirit, the compelling experience of Christ in power.[49] Van Beeck situates this confessional leap within the context of surrender to Christ, even as it necessarily surpasses it by virtue of its own structure.

> What 'happened to Jesus' is adequately conveyed, not by the partiality of concerns, but only by the totality of the surrender.[50]

> The surrender to Jesus Christ is an *act of response* to his presence in the Spirit. That means: *in the act of surrender to Christ the human concerns drawn into it are revealed as having a capacity for response-in-total-surrender to Jesus Christ.*[51]

Thus, van Beeck rounds out the foundation for positive christological construction. The ground of hope is the third dynamic involved in christological rhetoric, in addition to inclusion and the call to obedience. It animates the Christian life with confidence and courage—i.e., the Pauline *parrhesia*—in a fourfold way. First, it unveils that "*reality itself* participates in the ultimate perspective." Second, it provides the inspiration for historical commitments. Third, it fosters relationships of service and openness to others. Fourth, it keeps all human concerns responsive to "the *receding* standard of excellence which is the presence of Christ in the Spirit as the ultimate fulfillment of all things."[52]

In sum, van Beeck proposes a christological project that attempts a christology "from below" founded upon the response of Christians to the presence and power of Christ in the Spirit. This response is initially structured as rhetoric rather than as speculation over the meaning of terms. It is a "speaking in the Spirit," for it arises out of conversion grounded in the experience of grace with at least a threefold dimension. In the first instance, one is "struck by the encountering presence of Christ in the Spirit" in which all human concerns are accepted (the rhetoric of inclusion) and who in this encounter "gains personal identity by being responsive" (the rhetoric of obedience). Finally, "the rhetoric of hope clinches the rhetoric of inclusion and the rhetoric of obedience on the strength of the ecstatic encounter with Jesus Christ in the Spirit, in his risen life Christ invites and draws the Christian into the total surrender in and through and beyond all his actual potentials."[53]

Notes

1. Note the subtitle: Piet Schoonenberg, S.J., *The Christ: A Study of the God-Man Relationship in the Whole of Creation and in Jesus Christ* (New York: Herder & Herder, 1971).

2. This was reflected, for example, in the seventeenth-century debates between Domini-

cans and Jesuits over free will and grace (the Catholic version of the Calvinist-Arminian debates). Ibid., pp. 13-18.

3. Ibid., pp. 20-21.

4. Ibid., p. 27.

5. Ibid., p. 44.

6. Ibid., p. 58.

7. Ibid., p. 73.

8. Friedrich Schleiermacher, *The Christian Faith* (Philadelphia: Fortress, 1928), pp. 391-394.

9. Ibid., p. 393.

10. Schoonenberg, *The Christ*, pp. 62-63.

11. Ibid., p. 91.

12. Ibid., p. 62.

13. Ibid., p. 91.

14. Ibid., p. 87.

15. Ibid., pp. 87-89.

16. Ibid., p. 123. This is also the substance of his article "From A Two-Nature Christology to a Christology of Presence," *Theological Folia of Villanova University, Speculative Studies, Vol. II.* (Villanova: The Villanova University Press, 1975), pp. 219-243.

17. Ibid., pp. 114-116, 146.

18. Ibid., p. 166.

19. Ibid., pp. 166-175.

20. Ibid., p. 182.

21. Frans Jozef Van Beeck, *Christ Proclaimed: Christology as Rhetoric*, (New York: Paulist, 1979), pp. 108-114.

22. Ibid., p. 115.

23. Ibid., p. 120.

24. Ibid., p. 119.

25. Ibid., p. 118.

26. Ibid.

27. Ibid., pp. 128-129.

28. Ibid., p. 133.

29. Ibid., p. 131. Also, p. 133.

30. Ibid., p. 141: ". . . no discernment may ever belie or curtail the total commitment, nor may any discernment ever lay claim to being the sole bearer of the commitment."

31. Ibid., pp. 137-143.

32. Ibid., p. 154.

33. Ibid., pp. 146-150.

34. Ibid., p. 150.

35. Ibid., pp. 150-153.

36. Ibid., p. 156.

37. Ibid. With respect to this he quotes liberally from the Fathers—e.g., Maxentius, Gregory of Nyssa, Anastasius, John Damascene—see p. 158, n. 44.

38. Ibid., p. 158.

39. Ibid., pp. 162—63.

40. Ibid., p. 165.

41. "The Statement of Faith of the Third Council of Constantinople," in *Creeds of the Churches: A Reader in Christian Doctrine from the Bible to the Present*, 3rd ed., ed. by John H. Leith (Atlanta: John Knox, 1982), pp. 51-52.

42. Van Beeck, *Christ Proclaimed*, p. 173.

43. Ibid.

44. Ibid., pp. 175–177.

45. Ibid., pp. 455–463.

46. Ibid., p. 185.

47. Ibid., p. 190.

48. Ibid., p. 191.

49. Van Beeck also contrasts this notion of objectivity with that of an historicist perspective: "To insist, therefore, on the objectivity of the Resurrection is not to suppose a factuality accessible, in principle, to historical verification or to defend a quality of Christ that is strictly for himself and not for us, but to convey the overriding, compelling presence of Christ both as the power that releases the believer's speech and as the fulfillment of what he has to say." Ibid., p. 197.

50. Ibid., p. 195.

51. Ibid., p. 200.

52. Ibid., pp. 224–225.

53. Ibid., p. 226.

Bibliography

Abbott, S.J., Walter M., ed. *The Documents of Vatican II*. New York: Guild Press, 1966.

Adam, Karl. *The Christ of Faith: The Christology of the Church*. Translated by Joyce Crick. New York: Mentor Omega, 1957.

Anselm. Monologium, in *St. Anselm: Basic Writings*. Translated by S. N. Dean. La Salle, IL: Open Court, 1962.

Aquinas, Thomas. *Summa Theologica*. 5 vols. Translated by Fathers of the English Dominican Province. Westminster: Christian Classics, 1948.

Barth, Karl. *Church Dogmatics* I/1. Translated by G. W. Bromiley Edinburgh: T & T Clark, 1975.

_____. *Church Dogmatics IV/1*. Translated by G. W. Bromiley. Edinburgh: T & T Clark, 1956.

_____. *Protestant Theology in the Nineteenth Century: Its Background and History*. Valley Forge: Judson Press, 1973.

_____. *The Theology of Schleiermacher*. Translated by Geoffrey W. Bromiley and Edited by Dietrich Ritschl. Grand Rapids: Eerdmans, 1982.

_____. *The Word of God and the Word of Man*. Translated with a new Foreword by Douglas Horton. Gloucester, Mass: Peter Smith, 1978.

Basil the Great. *On the Holy Spirit*. Translated by David Anderson. Crestwood, NY: St. Vladimir's Seminary Press, 1980.

Berkhof, Hendrikus. *The Doctrine of the Holy Spirit*. Atlanta: John Knox, 1976.

Bonhoeffer, Dietrich. *Christ the Center*. Introduced by Edwin H. Robertson and translated by John Bowden. New York: Harper & Row, 1966.

Bourassa, Francois. "Adoptive Sonship: Our Union with the Divine Persons," *Theological Studies* 13 (1952), pp. 309-335.

Wilhelm Bousset. *Kyrios Christos: A History of the Belief in Christ from the Beginnings of Christianity to Irenaeus*. Translated by John E. Steely, with an Introduction by Rudolf Bultmann. Nashville: Abingdon, 1970.

Bultmann, Rudolf. "Church and Teaching in the New Testament," *Faith and Understanding I*. Translated by Louise Pettibone Smith, Edited and with an Introduction by Robert W. Funk. New York: Harper & Row, 1969.

_____. *Theology of the New Testament*, vol. I, Translated by Kendrick Grobel. New York: Scribners, 1951.

Burge, Gary M. *The Anointed Community: The Holy Spirit in the Johannine Tradition*. Grand Rapids: Eerdmans, 1987.

Carnley, Peter. *The Structure of Resurrection Belief.* Oxford: Clarendon Press, 1987.

Chirico, S.S., Petro F. *The Divine Indwelling and Distinct Relations to the Indwelling Persons in Modern Theological Discussion.* Rome: Pontificia Universitas Gregoriana, 1960.

Cobb, Jr., John B. *Christ in a Pluralistic Age.* Philadelphia: Westminster, 1975.

Coffey, David. *Believer, Christian, Catholic: Three Essays in Fundamental Theology.* Manly, N.S.W., Australia: Catholic Institute of Sydney, 1986.

_____. "The Gift of the Holy Spirit," *The Irish Theological Quarterly* 38 (1971), pp. 202–223.

_____. *Grace: The Gift of the Holy Spirit.* Manly, N. S. W., Australia: Catholic Institute of Sydney, 1979.

_____. "The Holy Spirit as the Mutual Love of the Father and the Son," *Theological Studies* 51 (1990), pp. 193–229.

_____. "The Incarnation: Fact Not Myth," Faith and Culture, vol. 1. Sydney: The Catholic Institute of Sydney, 1978, pp. 466–480.

_____. "The 'Incarnation' of the Holy Spirit in Christ," Theological Studies. 45 (1984), 466–480.

_____. "The Palamite Doctrine of God: A New Perspective," *St. Vladimir's Theological Quarterly.* 32 (1988), 329–358.

_____. "The Pre-existent and Incarnate Word," Faith and Culture: Contemporary Questions. Sydney: *Faith and Culture,* 1983, pp. 62–76.

_____. "A Proper Mission of the Holy Spirit," *Theological Studies* 47 (1986), 227–250.

Congar, Yves. *The Mystery of the Church.* Translated by A. V. Littledale. Baltimore: Helicon, 1960.

_____. *I Believe in the Holy Spirit, Volume I: The Experience of the Spirit.* Translated by David Smith. New York: Seabury, 1983.

_____. *I Believe in the Holy Spirit, Volume II: Lord and Giver of Life.* Translated by David Smith. New York: Seabury, 1983.

_____. *I Believe in the Holy Spirit, Volume III: The River of Life Flows in the East and the West.* Translated by David Smith. New York: Seabury, 1983.

_____. *Jesus Christ.* Translated by Luke O'Neill. New York: Herder & Herder, 1966.

_____. *The Word and the Spirit.* Translated by David Smith. San Francisco: Harper & Row, 1986.

Conzelmann, Hans. *An Outline of the Theology of the New Testament.* Translated by John Bowden. New York: Harper & Row, 1969.

Coxe, A. Cleveland., ed. *The Apostolic Fathers with Justin Martyr and Irenaeus.* The Ante-Nicene Fathers, Vol. I. Grand Rapids: Eerdmans, 1981.

_____. *Fathers of the Third Century: Hippolytus, Cyprian, Caius, Novatian, Appendix.* The Ante-Nicene Fathers, Vol. V. Grand Rapids: Eerdmans, 1951.

_____. *Latin Christianity: Its Founder, Tertullian.* The Ante-Nicene Fathers, Vol. III. Grand Rapids: Eerdmans, 1951.

Daniélou, Jean. *The Theology of Jewish Christianity.* Translated and Edited by John A. Baker. London: Darton, Longman & Todd, 1964.

Deferrari, Roy J., trans. and ed. *Saint Cyprian: Treatises.* The Fathers of the Church: A New Translation, Vol. 38. New York: Fathers of the Church, Inc., 1958.

Deissmann, Adolf. *Paul: A Study in Social and Religious History.* Translated by William E. Wilson. London: Hodder and Stoughton, 1926.

De la Potterie, S.J., Ignace. "The Anointing of Christ," *Word and Mystery: Biblical Essays on the Person and Mission of Christ*, ed. Leo J. O'Donovan. S.J. New York: Newman, 1968, pp. 155–184.

De la Taille, S.J., M. *Hypostatic Union and Created Actuation By Uncreated Act.* Translated by C. Lattey, S.J. and Cyril Vollert, S.J., West Baden Springs, IN: West Baden College, 1952.

De Letter, S.J., P. "Created Actuation by the Uncreated Act: Difficulties And Answers," *Theological Studies* 18 (1957), pp. 60–92.

_____. "Grace, Incorporation, Inhabitation," *Theological Studies* 19 (1958), pp. 1–31.

_____. "Sanctifying Grace and our Union with the Holy Trinity," *Theological Studies* 13 (1952), pp. 38–58.

_____. "Sanctifying Grace and the Divine Indwelling," *Theological Studies* 14 (1953), pp. 242–272.

_____. "Sanctifying Grace and Divine Indwelling: Fr. de la Taille and St. Thomas," *Gregorianum* 41 (1960), pp. 63–69.

_____. "The Theology of God's Self-Gift," *Theological Studies* 24 (1963), pp. 402–422.

De Margerie, S.J., Betrand. *The Christian Trinity in History.* Translated by Edmund J. Fortman, S.J. Still River, MA: St. Bede's Publications, 1982.

Dobbin, O.S.A., Edmund J. "Towards a Theology of the Holy Spirit," *Heythrop Journal* 17 (1976), pp. 5–19, 129–149.

Donnelly, S.J., Malachi. "The Indwelling of the Holy Spirit According to M. J. Scheeben," *Theological Studies* 7 (1946), pp. 244–280.

_____. "The Inhabitation of the Holy Spirit," *Proceedings of the Catholic Theological Society of America* 3 (1949), pp. 39–77.

_____. "The Inhabitation of the Holy Spirit: A Solution according to de la Taille," *Theological Studies* 8 (1949), pp. 445–470.

_____. "Sanctifying Grace and our Union With the Holy Trinity: A Reply," *Theological Studies* 13 (1952), pp. 190–204.

_____. "The Theory of R. P. Maurice de la Taille, S.J., on the Hypostatic Union," *Theological Studies* 2 (1941), pp. 510–526.

Driver, Tom F. *Christ in a Changing World: Toward an Ethical Christology.* New York: Crossroad, 1981.

_____. *Patterns of Grace: Human Experience as Word of God.* San Francisco: Harper & Row, 1977.

Dulles, S.J., Avery. *Models of the Church.* Garden City: Doubleday, 1978.

Dunn, James D. G. *Baptism in the Holy Spirit: A Re-examination of the New Testament Teaching on the Gift of the Spirit in Relation to Pentecostalism Today.* Philadelphia: Westminster, 1970.

_____. *Christology in the Making: A New Testament Inquiry Into the Origins of the Doctrine of the Incarnation.* Philadelphia: Westminster, 1980.

_____. *Jesus and the Spirit: A Study of the Religious and Charismatic Experience of Jesans as Reflected in the New Testament.* Philadelphia: Westminster, 1975.

_____. "Jesus—Flesh and Spirit: An Exposition of Romans 1:3-4," *Journal of Theological Studies*, n.s. xxiv (1973), pp. 40–68.

_____. "1 Corinthians 15:45—Last Adam, Life-giving Spirit," in *Christ and the Spirit in the New Testament.* Edited by Barnabas Lindars and Stephen S. Smalley. Cambridge: Cambridge University Press, 1973, pp. 127–141.

_____. "2 Corinthians 3:17—"The Lord is the Spirit,'" *Journal of Theological Studies*, n.s. xxi (1970), pp. 309-320.

_____. "Rediscovering the Spirit," *The Expository Times* 84 (1972), pp. 7-12, 40-44.

_____. *Unity and Diversity in the New Testament: An Inquiry Into the Character of Earliest Christianity*. Philadelphia: Westminster, 1977.

Durrwell, C.S.S.R., F.X. *Holy Spirit of God: An Essay in Biblical Theology*. Translated by Sister Benedict Davies OSU. London: Geoffrey Chapman, 1986.

_____. *The Resurrection*. Translated by Rosemary Sheed with an Introduction by Charles Davis. London: Sheed and Ward, 1960.

Faricy, S.J., Robert L. "The Trinitarian Indwelling," *The Thomist* 35 (1971), pp. 369-404.

Florensky, Pavel Aleksandrovich. "On the Holy Spirit," *Ultimate Questions: An Anthology of Modern Russian Religious Thought*. ed. Alexander Schmemann. Translated by Asheleigh E. Moorhouse. New York: Holt, Rinehart and Winston, 1965, pp. 135-172.

Foyas, Methodios. *Orthodoxy, Roman Catholicism, and Anglicanism*. Brookline, MA: Holy Cross Orthodox Press, 1984.

Fransen, Peter (Piet). *The New Life of Grace*. Translated by Georges Dupont, S.J. with Foreword by John Macquarrie. Tournai: Desclee, 1969.

Frei, Hans. *The Identity of Jesus Christ: The Hermeneutical Bases of Dogmatic Theology*. Philadelphia: Fortress, 1975.

Gillet, L. ("A Monk of the Eastern Church") *Orthodox Spirituality: An Outline of the Orthodox Ascetical and Mystical Tradition*. Crestwood, NY: St. Vladimir's Seminary Press, 1978.

Goppelt, Leonhard. *Theology of the New Testament, Volume 2—The Variety and Unity of the Apostolic Witness to Christ*. Translated by John Alsup. Grand Rapids: Eerdmans, 1982.

Gunkel, Hermann. *The Influence of the Holy Spirit: The Popular View of the Apostolic Age and the Teaching of the Apostle Paul*. Translated by Roy A. Harrisville and Philip A. Quanbeck II. Philadelphia: Fortress, 1979.

Haight, S.J., Roger. "The Case for Spirit Christology," *Theological Studies* 53 (1992), pp. 257-287.

_____. "The Point of Trinitarian Theology," *Toronto Journal of Theology* 4 (1988), pp. 191-204.

Herzog, Frederick. *God-Walk: Liberation Shaping Dogmatics*. Maryknoll: Orbis, 1988.

Hick, John. "An Inspiration Christology for a Religiously Plural World," *Encountering Jesus: A Debate on Christology*. ed. Stephen T. Davis. Atlanta: John Knox, 1988, pp. 5-38.

_____ ed. "Jesus and the World Religions," *The Myth of God Incarnate*. Philadelphia: Westminster, 1977, pp. 167-185.

Hill, William J. *Proper Relations to the Indwelling Divine Persons*. Washington, D.C.: Thomist Press, 1955.

_____. *The Three-Personed God: The Trinity as a Mystery of Salvation*. Washington D.C.: The Catholic University of America Press, 1982.

_____. "Uncreated Grace—A Critique of Karl Rahner," *The Thomist* 26 (1963), pp. 333-56.

Hodgson, Peter. *Jesus-Word and Presence: An Essay in Christology*. Philadelphia: Fortress, 1971.

Irenaeus. *Against Heresies*, *The Ante-Nicene Fathers* vol. I. ed. A. Cleveland Coxe. Grand Rapids: Eerdmanns, 1981.

Jansen, John Frederick. *The Resurrection of Jesus Christ in New Testament Theology*. Philadelphia: Westminster, 1980.

Johnson, Aubrey R. *The One and the Many in the Israelite Conception of God.* Cardiff: University of Wales Press, 1961.

Kasper, Walter. *The Christian Understanding of Freedom and the History of Freedom in the Modern Era: The Meeting and Confrontation Between Christianity and the Modern Era in the Postmodern Situation.* Milwaukee: Marquette University Press, 1988.

_____. *Jesus the Christ.* Translated by V. Green. New York: Paulist, 1976.

_____. *The God of Jesus Christ.* Translated by Matthew J. O'Connell. New York: Crossroad, 1989.

_____. *Theology and Church.* Translated by Margaret Kohl. New York: Crossroad, 1989.

Kelly, J.N.D. *Early Christian Doctrines.* San Francisco: Harper & Row, 1978.

Killian, O.F.M., Sabbas J. "The Holy Spirit in Christ and Christians," *The American Benedictine Review* 20 (1969), pp. 99–121.

Kilmartin, S.J., Edward J. "The Active Role of Christ and the Holy Spirit in the Sanctification of the Eucharistic Elements," *Theological Studies* 45 (1984), pp. 225–253.

_____. *Christian Liturgy: Theology and Practice, I. Systematic Theology of Liturgy.* Kansas City: Sheed & Ward, 1988.

Küng, Hans. *Theology for the Third Millenium: An Ecumenical View.* Translated by Peter Heinegg. New York: Doubleday, 1988.

Kümmel, Werner Georg. *The Theology of the New Testament: According to Its Major Witnesses Jesus-Paul-John.* Translated by John E. Steely. Nashville: Abingdon, 1973.

Künneth, Walter. *The Theology of the Resurrection.* Translated by James W. Leitch. St. Louis: Concordia, 1965.

LaCugna, Catherine Mowry. *God for Us: The Trinity and Christian Life.* San Francisco: Harper, 1991.

Lampe, Geoffrey. *God as Spirit.* London: SCM Press, 1977.

_____. "The Holy Spirit," *Fairacres Publication No. 41.* Fairacres, Oxford: SLG Press, Convent of the Incarnation, 1974.

_____. "The Holy Spirit and the Person of Christ," in *Christ Faith And History.* eds. S. W. Sykes and J. P. Clayton. Cambridge: At The University Press, 1972, pp. 111–130.

Leith, John H., ed. *Creeds of the Churches: A Reader in Christian Doctrine from the Bible to the Present.* 3rd. ed. Atlanta: John Knox, 1982.

Lodahl, Michael E. *Shekhinah/Spirit: Divine Presence in Jewish and Christian Religion.* New York: Paulist, 1992.

Lossky, Vladimir. *In the Image and Likeness of God.* eds. John H. Erickson and Thomas E. Bird with Introduction by John Meyendorff. Crestwood, N.Y: St. Vladimir's Seminary Press, 1974.

_____. *The Mystical Theology of the Eastern Church.* Translated by members of the Fellowship of St. Alban and St. Sergius. Crestwood, NY: St. Vladimir's Seminary Press, 1976.

_____. *The Vision of God.* Translated by Asheleigh Moorhouse with Preface by John Meyendorff. Crestwood, NY: St. Vladimir's Seminary Press, 1973.

Mackey, James. *The Christian Experience of God as Trinity.* London: SCM, 1983.

_____. *Jesus the Man and the Myth: A Contemporary Christology.* New York: Paulist, 1979.

_____. *Modern Theology: A Sense of Direction.* New York: Oxford, 1987.

_____. *New Testament Theology in Dialogue: Christology and Ministry.* with James D. G. Dunn. Philadelphia: Westminster, 1987.

Martyn, J. Louis. "Epistemology at the Turn of the Ages: 2 Corinthians 5.16" in *Christian*

History and Interpretation: Studies Presented to John Knox. ed. W. R. Farmer et al. Cambridge: Cambridge University Press, 1967, pp. 269-287.

McCool, Gerald. *Catholic Theology in the Nineteenth Century: The Quest for a Unitary Method.* New York: Seabury, 1977.

McDonnell, O.S.B., Kilian. "The Determinative Doctrine of the Holy Spirit," *Theology Today* 39 (1982), pp. 142-159.

_____. "A Trinitarian Theology of the Holy Spirit?" *Theological Studies* 46 (1985), pp. 191-227.

Mersch, S.J., Emile. *The Theology of the Mystical Body.* Translated by Cyril Vollert, S.J. St. Louis: Herder, 1951.

_____. *The Whole Christ.* Translated by John R. Kelly, S.J. Milwaukee: Bruce, 1938.

Moltmann, Jürgen. *The Church in the Power of the Spirit: A Contribution to Messianic Ecclesiology.* Translated by Margaret Kohl. San Francisco: Harper & Row, 1977.

_____. *The Crucified God: The Cross of Christ as the Foundation and Criticism of Christian Theology.* Translated by R. A. Wilson and John Bowden. San Francisco: Harper & Row, 1974.

_____. *God in Creation: A New Theology of Creation and the Spirit of God.* Translated by Margaret Kohl. San Francisco: Harper & Row, 1985.

_____. *The Spirit of Life: A Universal Affirmation.* Translated by Margaret Kohl. Minneapolis: Fortress, 1992.

_____. *The Trinity and the Kingdom: The Doctrine of God.* Translated by Margaret Kohl. San Francisco: Harper & Row, 1981.

_____. *The Way of Jesus Christ: Christology in Messianic Dimensions.* Translated by Margaret Kohl. San Francisco, 1990.

Mühlen, Heribert. *Der Heilige Geist als Person.* Münster Westfalen: Aschendorffsche Verlagsbuchhandlung, 1963.

_____. *Una Mystica Persona.* Paderborn: Verlag Ferdinand Schöningh, 1968.

Mullaney, Thomas U. "The Incarnation: de la Taille vs. Thomist Tradition," *The Thomist* 17 (1954), pp. 1-42.

Newman, Paul W. *A Spirit Christology: Recovering the Biblical Paradigm.* Lanham, Maryland: University Press of America, 1987.

Nissiotis, Nikos A. "The Main Ecclesiological Problem of the Second Vatican Council: And the Position of the Non-Roman Churches Facing It," *Journal of Ecumenical Studies.* 2 (1965).

_____. "Pneumatological Christology as a Presupposition of Ecclesiology," *Oecumenica 1967.* eds. Friedrich Wilhelm Kantzenbach and Vilmos Vajta, (Minneapolis: Augsburg, 1967), pp. 235-252.

O'Connor, William R. "Discussion of *The Inhabitation of the Holy Spirit*," *Proceedings of the Catholic Theological Society of America* 3 (1949) pp. 39-89.

_____. "The Theory of the Supernatural: A Critique of P. de la Taille," *Theological Studies* 3 (1943), pp. 403-412.

O'Donnell, S.J., John. "In Him and Over Him: The Holy Spirit in the Life of Jesus," *Gregorianum* 70,1 (1989), pp. 25-45.

_____. *The Mystery of the Triune God.* New York: Paulist, 1989.

Ott, Ludwig. *Fundamentals of Catholic Dogma.* Ed. by James Canon Bastible and Translated by Patrick Lynch. St. Louis: B. Herder Book Company, 1958.

Pannenberg, Wolfhart. *Jesus-God and Man*. 2nd. Edition. Translated by Lewis L. Wilkins and Duane A. Priebe. Philadelphia: Westminster, 1977.

Pernveden, Lage. *The Concept of the Church in the Shepherd of Hermas*. Lund: CWK Gleerup, 1966.

Pieris, S.J., Aloysius. *Love Meets Wisdom: A Christian Experience of Buddhism*. Maryknoll: Orbis, 1988.

Pokorny, Petr. *The Genesis of Christology: Foundations for a Theology of the New Testament*. Translated by Marcus Lefébure. Edinburg: T & T Clark, 1987.

Rahner, Karl. "Current Problems in Christology," *Theological Investigations* I. Translated by Cornelius Ernst, O.P. New York: Crossroad, 1982, pp. 149–200.

_____. "Dogmatic Reflections on the Knowledge and Self-Consciousness of Christ," *Theological Investigations*, Vol. V. Translated by Karl-H. Kruger. New York: Crossroad, 1983, pp. 193–215.

_____. *Foundations of Christian Faith: An Introduction to the Idea of Christianity*. Translated by William V. Dych. New York: Seabury, 1978.

_____. "Some Implications of the Scholastic Concept of Uncreated Grace," *Theological Investigations I*. Translated by Cornelius Ernst, O.P. New York: Crossroad, 1982, pp. 319–346.

_____. *The Trinity*. Translated by Joseph Donceel. New York: Herder & Herder, 1970.

_____. "The Two Basic Types of Christology," *Theological Investigations*, vol. XIII. Translated by David Bourke. New York: Crossroad, 1983, pp. 213–223.

Richardson, Cyril C., ed. *Early Christian Fathers*. New York: Collier, 1970.

_____. *The Doctrine of the Trinity*. Nashville: Abingdon, 1958.

Ritschl, Dietrich. *The Logic of Theology: A Brief Account of the Relationship Between Basic Concepts in Theology*. Translation by John Bowden. Philadelphia: Fortress, 1987.

_____. *Memory and Hope: An Inquiry Concerning the Presence of Christ*. New York: Macmillan, 1967.

Rosato, S.J., Philip J. *The Spirit as Lord: The Pneumatology of Karl Barth*. Edinburgh: T & T Clark, 1981.

_____. "Spirit Christology: Ambiguity and Promise," *Theological Studies* 38 (1977), pp. 423–449.

Ruether, Rosemary Radford. *Sexism and God-Talk: Toward a Feminist Theology*. Boston: Beacon, 1983.

Scheeben, Matthias. *The Mysteries of Christianity*. Translated by Cyril Vollert, S.J. New York: Herder, 1947.

Schillebeeckx, Edward. *Christ the Sacrament of Encounter with God*. New York: Sheed & Ward, 1963.

_____. *The Christ: The Experience of Jesus as Lord*. Translated by John Bowden. New York: Seabury, 1980.

_____. *Jesus: An Experiment in Christology*. Translated by Hubert Hoskins. New York: Seabury, 1979.

Schleiermacher, Friedrich. *The Christian Faith*. eds. H. R. Mackintosh and J. S. Stewart. Philadelphia: Fortress, 1928.

Schoeps, Hans-Joachim. *Jewish Christianity: Factional Disputes in the Early Church*. Translated by Douglas R. A. Hare. Philadelphia: Fortress, 1969.

Schoof, Mark. "Dutch Catholic Theology: A New Approach To Christology," *Cross Currents* 22 (1973), pp. 415–427.

Schoonenberg, S.J., Piet. *The Christ: A Study of the God-Man Relationship in the Whole of Creation and in Jesus Christ.* Translated by Della Couling. New York: Herder & Herder, 1971.

_____. "From a Two-Nature Christology to a Christology of Presence," *Theological Folia of Villanova University,* Speculative Studies, vol. II. Villanova, PA: The Villanova University Press, 1975, pp. 219-243.

_____. "Spirit Christology and Logos Christology," *Bijdragen* 38 (1977), pp. 350-375.

_____. "Trinity—The Consummated Covenant: Theses on the Doctrine of the Trinitarian God," *Studies In Religion* 5 (1975-1976), Translated by Robert C. Ware. pp. 111-116.

Schüssler Fiorenza, Elisabeth. *In Memory of Her: A Feminist Theological Reconstruction of Christian Origins.* New York: Crossroad, 1983.

Schweitzer, Albert. *The Mysticism of Paul the Apostle.* Translated by William Montgomery with a Prefatory Note by F. C. Burkitt. New York: Henry Holt, 1931.

_____. *Out of My Life and Thought.* Translated by C. T. Campion with Postscript by Everett Skillings. New York: Mentor, 1953.

_____. *The Quest of the Historical Jesus: A Critical Study of Its Progress from Reimarus to Wrede.* Translated by W. Montgomery with an Introduction by James M. Robinson. New York: Macmillan, 1968.

Schweizer, Edward. *The Holy Spirit.* Translated by Reginald H. and Ilse Fuller. Philadelphia: Fortress, 1980.

_____. "The Spirit of God," in *Bible Key Words, Volume III.* Translated and Edited by A. E. Harvey. New York: Harper & Row, 1960.

Smedes, Lewis B. *All Things Made New: A Theology of Man's Union with Christ.* Grand Rapids: Eerdmans, 1970.

Sölle, Dorothee. *Christ the Representative: An Essay in Theology After the "Death of God."* Translated by David Lewis. Philadelphia: Fortress, 1967.

Strauss, David Friedrich. *The Christ of Faith and the Jesus of History: A Critique of Schleiermacher's "The Life of Jesus."* Translation and Introduction by Leander E. Keck, Philadelphia: Fortress, 1977.

_____. *The Life of Jesus Critically Examined.* Translated by George Eliot and edited by Peter C. Hodgson with Introduction. Philadelphia: Fortress, 1972.

Tillich, Paul. *Systematic Theology, Volume I: Reason and Revelation, Being and God.* Chicago: University of Chicago Press, 1951.

_____. *Systematic Theology, Volume II: Existence and The Christ.* Chicago: University of Chicago Press, 1957.

_____. *Systematic Theology, Volume III: Life and the Spirit, History and the Kingdom of God.* Chicago: University of Chicago Press, 1963.

Tracy, David. *The Analogical Imagination: Christian Theology and the Culture of Pluralism.* New York: Crossroad, 1981.

_____. *Blessed Rage for Order: The New Pluralism in Theology.* New York: Seabury, 1975.

_____. *Plurality and Ambiguity: Hermeneutics, Religion, Hope.* San Francisco: Harper & Row, 1987.

Van Beeck, S.J., Frans Jozef. *Christ Proclaimed: Christology as Rhetoric.* New York: Paulist, 1979.

_____. *God Encountered: A Contemporary Catholic Systematic Theology, Vol. I : Understanding the Christian Faith.* San Francisco: Harper & Row, 1989.

Wainwright, Arthur W. *The Trinity in the New Testament.* London: SPCK, 1962.

Wainwright, Geoffrey. *Doxology: The Praise of God in Worship, Doctrine and Life.* London: Epworth, 1980.

Wallington, Amanda G., ed. *Official Catholic Teachings: Christ Our Lord.* Wilmington: McGrath Publishing Co., 1978.

Wilhelm, Joseph and Scannell, Thomas B. *A Manual of Catholic Theology: Based on Scheeben's "Dogmatik".* Preface by Cardinal Manning. New York: Benzinger, 1899.

Wong, Joseph H. P. *Logos-Symbol in the Christology of Karl Rahner.* Foward by Karl Rahner, S.J. Rome: Las, 1984.

Zizioulas, John D. *Being as Communion: Studies in Personhood and the Church.* Foreword by John Meyendorff. Crestwood, NY: St. Vladimir's Seminary Press, 1985.

Index

DATE DUE